Classics and Translation

Contents

Acknowledgments

FOR PERMISSION TO REPRINT ARTICLES, I AM GRATEFUL TO BETH AND Nancy Arrowsmith (part of chap. 10), Boston University (chap. 1 and chap. 12), Farrar, Straus, and Giroux (chap. 3 and part of chap. 4), Loraine Fletcher (for the translation by Ian Fletcher that appears in chap. 13), the *New York Review of Books* (part of chap. 4 and part of chap. 6), Penguin Books (chap. 14), Nora Shattuck (part of chap. 10), Sidney Shiff (chap. 11), the University of Texas, Graduate School (part of chap. 4, chap. 5, part of chap. 6, chap. 7, chap. 8, part of chap. 10, and chap. 13), and, for all the essays, to Teresa Iverson. Full bibliographical information is given at the foot of each chapter. It is a pleasure to acknowledge the advice, enthusiasm, and support I have received; in addition to Teresa Iverson, I would like to thank Greg Baker, Adam Gitner, Greg Mellen, Christopher Ricks, Matthew Spencer, and Rosanna Warren.

Classics and Translation

Introduction

Kenneth Haynes

In my opinion, D. S. Carne-Ross was the finest critic of classical literature in English translation after Arnold.[1] Most readers today encounter the classics through the medium of translation, and one reason for collecting these essays is to provide a guide to that medium, a critical account of the ways it distorts and clarifies. Effective close criticism—joining text and context, theory and practice—does not otherwise exist for most of the English versions discussed here and is not plentiful in any case. Around the mid-twentieth century, New Criticism mostly left translations alone; after that, translation studies (as the field is now known) was largely occupied with the essential work of recovering historical contexts, understanding cultural assumptions, and investigating linguistic and theoretical problems of translating. It is not common for the two to be brought together.

For Carne-Ross, the translated work is not only a medium to be judged against the Greek and Latin but also a means to judge the original; translation and original both serve as agent and as object of criticism. The main difficulty for the critic is to describe the large number of relations this involves: you have to make arguments about what is valuable and not valuable in both the original and the English work—and then about the relationship between the two. All this requires knowledge, of languages and literatures and whatever else, but this is a necessary, not a sufficient, condition. The relevance of such knowledge must not be prejudged; what is an error in one context may be an inspired re-creation in another.

Translating, after all, refers to a number of possible activities, and in some cases it will be a legitimate question whether a work should even be called a translation. One source of the variability is the unit chosen as a basis on which to translate; it might range from the word, sentence, or even phoneme to more general aspects of the plot, setting, or genre. Another is the difference in basic method or approach—for example, whether the translator is seeking English equivalents or prefers to introduce traces of the foreign original, and in what proportions (a pessimist could describe the choice as between domesticating the foreign and so being misunderstood or exoticizing it and so not being understood at all); or again whether the translator chooses verse or prose, opts to preserve an ancient form or adapt an existing English one, and so on. Another factor is the particular audience for a translation, who may or may not know the original, who have varied motives and various competences. Much debate, sometimes very heated, has surrounded these choices.

These debates are pragmatic ones for Carne-Ross, which is not to imply that they shouldn't be heated, but that they are not going to be resolved by appeal to theoretical considerations. One translation does not cancel out another. The crib and the imitation can both succeed, potentially, depending on whether the translator writes well and knows enough. The original is as likely to be travestied by foreignizing strategies as by domesticating ones. The trot used in the classroom has its legitimate purpose, and so does an aggressively un-idiomatic version intended to assert cultural difference, and likewise the imitation intent on finding cultural parallels. Translators can try what they like. Elaborating the implications may be useful for a particular effort or to suggest a new possibility when one sort of translation is lacking, but this does not show us how we ought to proceed in general.

A basic fact of translation is that it is ontologically incomplete.[2] It does not replace the original, and it is truncated and provincialized when taken to be an autonomous work in its own language. It cannot, that is, be reduced either to native or foreign, otherness or sameness, identity or nonidentity; instead, it insists on the relationship between the two (though it may also reveal these categories to be impoverished or otherwise inadequate). The bilingual format, whether Locke's interlinear classics or Pope's imitations of Horace, best reveals the nature of translation, which not only brings a nexus of relations into being, as do other works influenced by classical texts, but insists on this nexus as a condition of its being a translation at all. "The interest of the operation," Carne-Ross writes, "is in the essentially critical comparison which is thereby set up between the two objects" (p. 152), or, in ambitious cases like Hölderlin's, Pope's, or Pound's, between the two languages, cultures, forms of perception.

Whatever the relation is between a work and its translated version, it cannot be one of identity. Yet translation is "often saddled with an improper obligation: it is supposed to 'give you the original.'" The problem is that "it doesn't and can't and shouldn't try to." The only place to get Homer's *Iliad* is in the Greek text (which "is going to take you anything up to three months" to learn to read; see p. 152). Since an English version does not give you the original, we need to ask what it does give. The answer is not known in advance, and the question must be put to each version; this is the reason why translation is an essentially critical act. The tendency persists, however, to bypass the criticism, and instead to see a translated work as a necessarily failed attempt at equivalence, as an approximation of the original or an approximation of an English work. As a result, translation (like illustration) still meets with a double condescension.

In some of the essays translation is discussed more prominently than in others; they are all, however, concerned with the criticism and valuation of texts. Chapters 3 and 9 offer readings of the *Odyssey* and the *Oresteia*, respectively; other essays focus on significant and influential translators of those works (chapters 4, 5, and 10). Two long essays give extended accounts of two of the most widely read twentieth-century translators of Greek and Latin, Robert Fitzgerald and Richmond Lattimore (chapters 4 and 5); there are also incisive studies of translations by H. D., Robert Fagles, David Ferry, Christopher Logue, and others (chapters 2, 6, 7, and 10). Some essays focus on a particular work, author, or genre in translation—for example, Pindar's Pythian 12, Horace, Greek tragedy, and Greek epigram (chapters 8, 14, 10, and 13). Chapters 7 and 13 range more widely than their titles suggest. The essay on Paul the Silentiary treats not just ekphrasis but also the question of innovation in the poetry of late antiquity, while the one on Bacchylides deals not only with the distinctive features of his odes and with Fagles's version, but also with general problems of translating Greek poetry into English.

The first and the final chapters use translation as a point of departure in order to investigate questions about transfers between ancient and modern literatures. In these essays translated works are considered in their relation to Greek or Roman literature and also as contributions to English literature, as a source of innovation for it, or as a way of laying bare connections between past and present moments. Conversely, flawed or inadequate versions suggest the absence of connection; if a convincing contemporary translation does not exist, it is likely, Carne-Ross has argued, that we are missing something essential when we try to read the original.

Carne-Ross was once praised, along with Bentley, for raising cruelty to translators from a "recognized blood sport" to an art,[3] but this is a little misleading. In the first place, he has praised some versions very highly, including Davenport's Archilochus, Logue's *Patrocleia*, Fitzgerald's *Odyssey*, and Ferry's Horace. Secondly, he finds that some translations fail honorably, responding to some of the excitement of the originals even if not being able to realize their own ambitions (he

might include H. D.'s *Ion* or MacNeice's *Agamemnon* in this category).
Thirdly, he acknowledges that a verse rendering may be decently
mediocre, and in some instances such versions are the best we have,
or a past age had, of the works of a poet (Thomson's *Oresteia*, Romagnoli's Pindar). It is also true that he has found some verse translations bad and others contemptible, including some that were nearly
universally praised in their time. However, as John Gibson Lockhart
pointed out in 1833, poetical translation is "of all other kinds of composition that in which the *possible* praise bears the smallest proportion
to its inherent difficulty and labour."[4] What good does bad verse do
anyone? Carne-Ross believes it does harm, particularly in the classroom "where monoglot students must be conned into believing" that
what they are studying "is 'really' by Dante or Sophocles or whoever,
a practice that plants a lie in their souls and is calculated to deaden
whatever native sense of poetry, of language, they may possess."[5] Is it
such a trivial thing, he asks, the first encounter with Greek or Latin
that might make you want to learn the original language?

Carne-Ross consistently speaks of the value of good prose translation, including some that he finds outstanding, such as Yourcenar's selection from Cavafy and Davenport's version of Ausonius's "Mosella."[6]
The need for prose versions is perhaps greater than that for verse,
and they are more likely to succeed at something. In a review essay
on Leopardi in translation, he advises that the "translator of the *Canti*
who suspects that his powers are not of this order"—the order of
Sophocles or Milton in *Samson Agonistes*—"would do well to stick to
plain prose and allow us, with its aid, to find our own way to the original."[7] He does not, however, pretend that "plain prose" is easy; he is
highly critical of Rieu's Homer, for example, and he has noted several cases where so-called close versions do not have the accuracy for
which they are praised. Moreover, his close studies of English versions
of European fiction (notably Stendhal)[8] document the many demands
that prose places on a translator.

In the 1950s Carne-Ross began his literary career, not as an academic
but as a man of letters, reviewing for the *Times Literary Supplement*, ed-
iting and contributing to the literary magazine *Nine*, and producing
talks for the BBC Third Programme. In each of these venues he discussed subjects that he would explore throughout his career: translation, classical literature, Italian literature, and contemporary poetry.
The experience in radio was formative; it permitted Carne-Ross to
imagine an ideal auditor (the Third Programme was not under an
obligation to find actual listeners), someone well-read, critically demanding, and intelligent who was free from the *déformation profession-
nelle* of the academy, who had not internalized its implicit expectations.

In 1961 he joined the faculty of the University of Texas, Austin; there he became an editor of and active contributor to *Arion*, which ran for nine volumes. The journal carried literary criticism by William Arrowsmith, Norman Austin, Guy Davenport, Bernard Knox, H. A. Mason, and J. P. Sullivan; it included articles on classics and contemporary culture by writers as different as Paul de Man and H. A. Mason; and, true to its insistence on translation as a mode of critical engagement, it printed versions of poems by Davenport, Fagles, Fitzgerald, Ted Hughes, Lattimore, Logue, Edwin Morgan, Peter Whigham, and others. Few journals in its time could rival it for the serious criticism of the classics.

Carne-Ross, with other members of the Texas faculty, moved to Boston University in the early seventies. A second series of *Arion* was launched for a few years (1973–76) from the new location. In 1979, he published *Instaurations*, a collection of essays "from Pindar to Pound." The book contains essential essays on Góngora and Pound, a dissentient view of Dante, a close and ardent reading of Leopardi, as well as pieces on Pindar and Sophocles. In all his writings, literary criticism maintains some relation to cultural criticism; it is never aesthetic in a narrow sense. At this point in his career, however, he became committed to cultural criticism of a Heideggerian sort. *Instaurations* develops in its first and last chapters the view that the problems of late capitalism and mass industrial society can be traced back to Western attitudes that had emerged decisively in classical Greece and, consequently, he insists that an effort to recover archaic Greece can provide a necessary critical distance in the present. The belief is consistent with High Modernism, with its "renaissance of the archaic," the conviction that preclassical Greece has a special claim on our own time; his critique reflects as well the heightened temper of the American university in the seventies.[9]

He subsequently abandoned this position. His book on Pindar, published by Yale in 1985, is fully aware that it is addressing an incurious world. It is also one of the best works on Pindar. Scholars had identified the conventions within which the Pindaric ode operated, and the time was right for a literary critic to show how the poet actively shaped and used the conventions for his purposes. In his review of the book, Bernard Knox points to the reasons for Carne-Ross's success: a wide knowledge of literature, including modern literature, in several languages; a scope of vision that is not limited to the university or the profession; and the ability to write well.[10] After this book came long and deeply considered essays, on English literature in its relation to Greek and Latin, on the *Odyssey*, on Horace, and on Ariosto.

More than four decades of Carne-Ross's writings are included here, with an emphasis on the essays about translation from the first *Arion* and the long articles written toward the end of his career. With the exception of the first and last chapters, the essays have been arranged chronologically by subject. Full consistency among them is not to be expected. An antithesis or set of terms useful at one moment will not necessarily be preserved at later times, and some reconsiderations and changes of mind are inevitable. I have revised the essays mainly in order to eliminate repetitions, make the format consistent, and remove dated references. Two of the essays, chapter 4 on Robert Fitzgerald's translations of Homer and Virgil and chapter 10 on English versions of Greek tragedy, were subject to more extensive alterations because they combine pieces that were published separately.

1
Jocasta's Divine Head:
English with a Foreign Accent

Ian Fletcher: 1920–1988

IN THE EPILOGUE TO HIS 1567 TRANSLATION OF OVID'S *HEROIDES*,
George Turberville wrote:

> it is a worke of prayse to cause
> A Romaine borne to speake with English jawse.

That is, to bring over the foreign work into English in such a way that
it reads as though it had originally been written in English. This is the
dominant mode of translation, what most good translators do and
no doubt what they ought to be doing. Here is Dryden, a great translator who handled the dominant mode as confidently as anyone has
ever done, providing Roman Juvenal with a pair of splendidly English
jaws:

> In *Saturn's* Reign, at Nature's Early Birth,
> There was that Thing call'd Chastity on Earth . . .
> Those first unpolisht Matrons, Big and Bold,
> Gave Suck to Infants of Gygantick Mold;
> Rough as their Savage Lords who Rang'd the Wood,
> And Fat with Acorns Belcht their windy Food.
> (Satyr 6, lines 1–15 [6.1–10])

This keeps sufficiently close to the original, for an age when every educated person knew Latin, but, or perhaps I should say "and," there
is no trace of a foreign accent. This is English, the massive, truculent
English of John Dryden.

Translation of this sort serves so many cultural and pedagogic purposes, binding up the wounds of Babel so valiantly that it is almost

"Jocasta's Divine Head: English with a Foreign Accent," *Arion* 3rd ser. 1, no. 1 (Winter 1990): 106–141.

beyond the reach of criticism. Almost, but not quite, for is there not in this ethnocentric mode, as the French are calling it, a certain provincial arrogance? It sets over the door of the house of translation a sign announcing, "English only spoken. No foreign tricks allowed here." It preserves the native grain of English (let "English" stand for the receiving language) but does not add to it, does not cross-fertilize English with foreign forms of expression or fresh syntactical possibilities, and where it introduces unfamiliar kinds of thought or feeling it lends them a familiar cast and hue.[1] More seriously, one may argue that it misrepresents its original not only in the obvious sense of turning it into something different, which translation must always do, but by misrepresenting the directest experience one can have of a foreign work, that of someone possessing the original language and reading the work in that language. When we read Sophocles in Greek, we know that we are abroad. Ethnocentric translation naturalizes Sophocles, leaving us with the false comfort of feeling *chez nous.*

Just enough can then be said against the dominant mode to make it worth considering another, an alternative mode in which the translator makes no secret of the fact that he is taking us abroad. He accepts the foreignness of the original and lets it color his diction and syntax. What he writes will not and should not sound quite "natural." I may seem to be speaking of the literal word-for-worder, translationese, but even if the alternative mode will often be, though it need not be, literal, its literalism will be bolder than that of its plodding congener below the salt.[2] To put it in Turberville's terms: instead of causing a Roman born to speak with English jaws, it will seek to cause or allow a Roman born to speak English with jaws still partly Roman.

The line that divides translation from original composition is a thin one and easily transgressed. Pope's *Iliad* is a free translation. With Horace, Pope employs that still freer, rogue form of the species which allows the writer to "run division on the groundwork as he pleases."[3] Imitation, Dryden called it. "Sapphics" is a poem of Swinburne, a poem that conveys so much of Sappho's manner and matter that it can be claimed as yet another still freer form of the species. Seen in this light, translation provides a convenient means of introducing the real subject of this paper, which is not translation (though I shall periodically be reverting to it), but original composition in which the writer, like the alternative translator, "takes us abroad" and submits his language to the transforming pressure of foreign idioms, constructions, and rhythms. Poets have always drawn on this resource.

Chaucer's "And smale foweles maken melodye" (*General Prologue*, line 9) brings to English the liquid vowelling of Italian. Synge's "Draw a little back with the squabbling of fools when I am eaten up with misery" (*Deirdre of the Sorrows*, act 3) is very beautiful, and very alien; Irish (one assumes) has insinuated its way into English. When Horatio says that the elder Hamlet "smot the sledded Pollax on the Ice" (act 1, scene 1) the sense is not that he smote them when they were sitting on sleds but that sledding was their habitual mode of travel. "Sledded" functions in the manner of a Greek formular epithet like "swift-footed," which can be used of Achilles when he is standing still.[4] In Othello's heroic line "It was a Sword of Spaine, the Ice brookes temper" (act 5, scene 2) the appositional phrase is Greco-Roman rather than English. With Shakespeare, the command of our language is so sovereign that whatever he writes can sound native, even "the Priest in Surples white, / That defunctive Musicke can" ("The Phoenix and the Turtle," lines 13–14)—no English we have ever heard but English as our first parents might have used it in Eden. The effect is quite different in "Lycidas" when Milton writes "the fable of *Bellerus* old." The genitive, a Greek genitive like "the might of Heracles" for "mighty Heracles," is meant to sound foreign, part of Milton's poem-long assertion that pastoral is not simply an English but also a common European genre. The foreign accent that is so prominent in his later writing is already heard here.

It is this, English with a foreign accent, that I want to pursue, and also the appropriation of foreign metrical forms. My purpose is not simply to chronicle what has been done but to consider what could have been done and what could still be done, rather in the spirit of Pound when he asked why English poets, having taken over the sonnet from Italy, were not enterprising enough to go on and borrow or adapt the more challenging Italian canzone. (His prejudices prevented him from seeing that Milton had done so in "Lycidas.") First, though, I need to stay briefly with translation, using two examples of this dominant mode in order to contrast them with the alternative. Take these lines near the start of the sixth *Aeneid*:

> at pius Aeneas arces quibus altus Apollo
> praesidet horrendaeque procul secreta Sibyllae,
> antrum immane, petit.

Here is Dryden's 1699 version, composed in the dominant, Englishing mode:

> The Pious Prince ascends the sacred Hill
> Where Phoebus is ador'd; and seeks the Shade,

> Which hides from sight his venerable Maid.
> Deep in a Cave the Sibyl makes abode.

Writing in a Latin-nourished age when epic was regarded as the
supreme, still living literary form (*Paradise Lost* had appeared only
thirty years before), Dryden uses the high style of the day, confidently
offering his *Aeneid* as part of contemporary literature, much as one
might do today with a new version of *Madame Bovary*. He can be quite
matter-of-fact about the action: an epic hero is consulting the oracle.
Not of course something one did in the England of William and Mary,
but the sort of thing that happens in the familiar world of classical
epic. There is no sense here that an old and culturally distant work is
being brought into the present. This is Virgil our contemporary.

The culture for which Robert Fitzgerald composed his 1983 version of the poem is altogether different. Most of those who read Latin
at all do so with a certain difficulty, and the conventions of epic are
likely to be no more than a classroom memory. Fitzgerald responds
to this new situation by trying to bring off what is, in an entirely honorable sense, a kind of confidence trick. Although his verse is more
consciously dignified than is usual today, it is still the language of today, and yet his translation asks our acceptance of something wholly
outside the experience of today, an epic hero consulting the oracle
of Apollo:

> Aeneas,
> In duty bound, went inland to the heights
> Where overshadowing Apollo dwells
> And nearby, in a place apart—a dark
> Enormous cave—the Sybil feared by men.

(Note "in duty bound." Dryden can assume that his reader knows what
pius means.)

What I mean by "confidence trick" should be clear if we look next
at the French translation by Pierre Klossowski, published in 1964. At
first and even second sight it is scarcely comprehensible, following
as it does the word order of the Latin, and recalls the Oxbridge joke
about those Loeb versions where one must look across to the Greek
or Latin to find out what the English means. Taking full face the shock
of the foreign, Klossowski confronts us with the alternative mode at
its most uncompromising:

> Mais le pieux Énée les sommets auxquels le haut Apollon
> préside et de l'horrifiante au loin les solitudes de la Sibylle,
> l'antre immense, gagne.

This does not simply admit the foreignness of the original; the translator gets right down into his language, into word order and syntax, forcing into it elements of the source language that significantly contribute to the tone and total effect. Drawing on the violent dislocations of French usage and linguistic expectation practiced by avant-garde French writers from Mallarmé on, Klossowski presents us with a modern *Aeneid*, as Dryden's was in its day and as Fitzgerald's is not. Here, three centuries later, is Virgil our contemporary again, of necessity a strange and difficult Virgil. (The literary question, which does not directly concern me, is whether Klossowski writes well enough to achieve his purpose. I judge that on the whole he does not, despite some notably resourceful coups like the phrase describing Dido's pack of hunting dogs, "la flairante meute," as energetically odd as I take Virgil's *odora canum vis* at 4.132 to be.)

The lines I quoted do not show his approach to advantage, and it is hard to distinguish them from the crudest interlinear trot. He does better in book 8 with the famous scene where Venus makes love to Mars, which prompted a notable essay of Montaigne:

> Elle avait dit et, neigeux d'éclat, par-ci, la divine, par-là, de ces bras,
> l'hésitant d'une étreinte souple échauffe.

> dixerat et niveis hinc atque hinc diva lacertis
> cunctantem amplexu molli fovet.
>
> (8.387–88)

Klossowski's French enacts the situation it describes. Just as Venus's arms encircle Mars, the adjectival phrase *neigeux d'éclat,* and its noun, *bras,* encircle the intervening words. Although Virgil's Latin does the same thing, the French claims more attention, for whereas hyperbaton of this sort is familiar in Latin, and made immediately comprehensible by the case endings, the dislocated word order is more striking in French and makes us struggle our way to the meaning. One could argue that Klossowski has minimally improved his original. Where Virgil writes *hinc atque hinc diva,* Klossowski inserts *la divine* between the two phrases describing the goddess's movements, thus defining them more exactly. While following Virgil almost word for word, he has transformed a passage of classical poetry into modern poetry. In aspiration at least, this is translation of the school of Pierre Menard.[5]

In a contemporary writer, Latinism serves to distance and estrange. In earlier centuries, when Latin was close enough to the everyday business of life to constitute virtually a living language, almost an alternative English, Latinism served different purposes and was used in different ways. The two languages might be set side by side ("The multitudinous Seas incarnadine / Making the greene one, red" (*Macbeth*, act 2, scene 2); "wit enough to keep it sweet . . . vitality enough to preserve it from putrefaction," Boswell's *Life of Johnson*, June 1784), or Latin might underlie English as a kind of grid. This alternative English is found not so much in translation as in original writing, for obvious enough reasons. Since the originals were in everyone's hands, there was no need for two-ply translation with the Latin showing through like a strange, alien presence, hence representative Tudor translations—Golding's *Metamorphoses*, for instance, or Marlowe's *Amores*—were written in "ordinary" English. The alternative, Latinate language was reserved for other purposes. When Jonson translates Catullus, he uses the lyric idiom of his day ("Kisse me sweet: the warie lover / Can your favours keepe, and cover"). When he writes a poem in praise of the antiquary William Camden, his tutor at Westminster, he turns to the alternative language and puts on the decent Roman toga that hung in every educated man's wardrobe:[6]

> Camden, most reverend head, to whom I owe
>   All that I am in arts, all that I know,
> (How nothing's that?) to whom my countrey owes
>   The great renowne, and name wherewith shee goes.
> Than thee the age sees not that thing more grave,
>   More high, more holy, that shee would more crave.
> What name, what skill, what faith hast thou in things!
>   What sight in searching the most antique springs!
> What weight, and what authoritie in thy speech!
>   Man scarse can make that doubt, but thou canst teach.
> Pardon free truth, and let thy modestie,
>   Which conquers all, be once over-come by thee.
> Many of thine this better could, then I,
>   But for their powers, accept my pietie.

Decorum requires that so notable a man be praised in the high Roman fashion. Although neither Latinate syntax or diction are intrusive, the slow, weighted movement and the concision of the language ("Man scarse can make that doubt, but thou canst teach," Pliny's *nihil est quod discere velis quod ille docere non possit*) bespeak their grave Roman provenance. As the notes to the useful Penguin edition show, Jonson has Latin warrant for every other sentence. The thrust of the whole poem is behind its final words, "accept my piety": Roman *pietas*, the debt a man must pay to parents and benefactors.

Most striking, though readers seem not to have found it so, is the opening address to Camden's *head*. This idiom is marginally Latin but essentially Greek and quite foreign to English. Swinburne uses it in *Atalanta in Calydon*, "O holy head of Oeneus" (line 2182), but where everything is so Greek the expression does not much stand out. Shelley uses it in his great elegy for Keats, "O weep for Adonais! though our tears / Thaw not the frost which binds so dear a head" (lines 2–3). He eases the alien idiom into English by treating the frost as a garland round the head of the dead poet, and his source here is not Greek but Latin, Horace's poem for the death of a friend in which he asks what measure there can be in our grief *tam cari capitis* (*Odes* 1.24). The common Latin use of genitival *caput* in legal and political usage referring to a charge endangering one's civic rights or life probably allowed a Roman reader to take the expression in his stride. I do not believe that we should take in our stride the opening line of *Antigone*, literally "O joint self-sister head of Ismene" (Ὦ κοινὸν αὐτάδελφον Ἰσμήνης κάρα). Hölderlin certainly did not, and came up with the astonishing line *Gemeinsamschwesterliches! O Ismenes Haupt!* which George Steiner has explored with much imaginative energy.[7] A great Sophoclean scholar, Jebb no less, tells us that its "pathetic emphasis . . . gives the key-note of the drama,"[8] yet most translators have been content to let it go with "Oh my dear Ismene" or the like.

There is another Sophoclean head, in *Oedipus Rex*, that seems to me no less imposing, though again most translators have let it go. Announcing the death of Jocasta, the messenger declares: τέθνηκε θεῖον Ἰοκάστης κάρα, "The divine head of Jocasta is dead" (line 1235). Hölderlin writes:

> Es ist das schnellste Wort, zu sagen und
> Zu hören, tot ist es, Jokastas göttlich Haupt.

His success in making what I take to be convincing poetic speech from a literal rendering of the Greek no doubt reflects the German language's ability to absorb foreign linguistic usage.[9] And yet in French too, notoriously impervious for most of its history to foreign turns of speech, the literal rendering can be powerful, as anyone will testify who heard Jean Cocteau deliver the running commentary to Stravinsky's *Oedipus Rex*: "La tête divine de Jocaste est morte" (*divum Iocastae caput mortuum* in the libretto). And in English? "Our royal lady Jocasta is dead," Jebb wrote. Yeats was briefer; "Jocasta, our Queen, is dead." Briefer still, Fitts and Fitzgerald, and Fagles: "The Queen is dead." But this Greek head strikes at the English like an African mask at a tea party.[10] Must Sophocles' words be so reduced?

Wait, though, what we have here may be no more than a *façon de parler*, so that a literal rendering would be as misleading as representing French *mon vieux* by "my old." Yet as E. R. Dodds once remarked, even a *façon de parler* must have an origin,[11] and a poet's job is to keep origins alive. We should at this point try to determine what force κάρα, "head," has in Greek, and here we must seek counsel of an expert. Used *pars pro toto* of a person, we are told, the word κάρα "has strong emotional colouring; the emotion is normally affection . . . or respect" (W.S. Barrett on Euripides *Hippolytus* 651). In Greek, that is, not necessarily in English, but since Jonson was able to make it powerful, there is no reason why a poet translator could not do so today. What of "divine," θεῖος? Plato, using a noun of the same meaning, speaks of the divine head of a friend supposedly in a state of Dionysiac exaltation (*Phaedrus* 234d). No doubt the context mocks the stately expression, yet it is stately, even in prose, and likely to be more so in verse. So "divine" had better be kept too—in the hope that some trace of the numinous still sticks to the word even in our profane world. One wonders next about the coupling of *divine* and *dead*: how can the divine die? Perhaps we may suppose that Jocasta, having taken on the dread solemnity of death and hence freed from mortality, is now in some sense a divine being. Is there, preserved in the words of this poet (whose imagination reached back to the archaic dark that bred those sweet children, the Furies) at this point of this play, some memory of the divine kingship of the older Mediterranean world? We must not cut Sophocles down to our measure.

Risk it, then, why not? Let English take the shock of the foreign and go all out with Hölderlin: *tot ist es, Jokastas göttlich Haupt.* The English translator still has the awkward "head"/"dead" rhyme to deal with, but this need not be too troubling if the rhyming words can be kept apart: "The queen is dead, Jocasta, that divine head gone." I can't do it, but a poet should be able to.[12]

Perhaps I have dwelt too long on a single expression—without convincing the reader that it carries the weight I have claimed for it. And yet this single expression may serve to open the way to a question of larger scope, one that ought to matter to those who continue to value Greek poetry. Have we made ourselves too much at home in the remote world from which it addresses us? Do we, by our usual ways of translating, and understanding, filter out much that is strange and disturbing, even frightening, there? Take, almost at random, these words near the start of *Odyssey* 13: τοῖσι δὲ βοῦν ἱέρευσ᾽ ἱερὸν μένος Ἀλκινόοιο / Ζηνὶ κελαινεφέϊ Κρονίδῃ (lines 24–25). Fitzgerald translates: "As the god's anointed, / Alkinoos made offering on their behalf—an ox / to Zeus beyond the stormcloud." This does not ruffle our composure. Leconte de Lisle, who sought to give the French a ruder, more Homeric Homer than they had had before, offered a different reading: "Au milieux d'eux la Force sacrée d'Alkinoos égorgea un bœuf pour Zeus Kronide qui amasse les nuées." Most people would say that to render ἱερὸν μένος in this literal fashion grossly overtranslates an expression that in the original hardly makes itself felt. (It is used of Alkinoos six times in the *Odyssey*, once with another proper name occupying the same position in the line.) Milman Parry would certainly have said so. The novice, he tells us, finds much poetic excitement and meaning in the formulaic elements of Homeric diction to which the practiced reader learns to become indifferent. He "passes over them, scarcely heeding their meaning."[13] If so, heaven help the practiced reader, and heaven help the rest of us who put our trust in him.

Milton created a new language, Samuel Johnson claimed. "Through all his greater works there prevails an uniform peculiarity of *Diction*, a mode and cast of expression which bears little resemblance to that of any former writer." A new or third language poised confidently between English and Latin. Call it Miltonic. "He was master of his language in its full extent," Johnson added.[14] Milton speaks Miltonic like a native.

We see him practicing this language in the more Latinate sonnets, "essays . . . in the 'magnificent' style," F. T. Prince calls them.[15] Sometimes, it is true, the Latinisms sound clumsy. "Lawrence of vertuous Father vertuous Son" might be a schoolboy's construe. The clumsiness here is, I think, deliberate, a polemical announcement that he is writing not in the lax Elizabethan but in the severe Italian manner created a century before by poets like Pietro Bembo and Giovanni della Casa, who treated the sonnet as the high vernacular equivalent of the Horatian epistle or ode.[16] The announcement once made, all trace of clumsiness vanishes. The language of the sestet is poised, urbane, on civil terms with English and yet keeping its fastidious distance. This is not the friendly cohabitation of Pope's "easy Ciceronian Style / So Latin, yet so English all the while" ("Epilogue to the Satires"). The movement, the fingering, are subtly foreign:

> What neat repast shall feast us, light and choice,
>   Of Attick tast, with Wine, whence we may rise
>   To hear the Lute well toucht, or artfull voice
> Warble immortal Notes and Tuskan Ayre?

> He who of those delights can judge, and spare
> To interpose them oft, is not unwise.

The Latinisms of *Paradise Lost* are too pervasive, and too familiar a theme, to allow or need discussion here. It is, though, perhaps worth remarking, since Latinate diction is often thought of as contributing primarily severity or elevation, how well it serves for the stylized social comedy of book 9 as "domestick" Adam (line 318) tries to warn Eve of the danger of going off alone. She of course will have none of it:

> To whom the Virgin Majestie of Eve,
> As one who loves, and some unkindness meets,
> With sweet austeer composure thus reply'd.
>
> (9.270–72)

It is a stroke of exquisite wit to use the grand Homeric periphrasis "the Virgin Majestie of Eve" (compare, e.g., "the sacred force of Telemachus") to introduce a family dispute. Eve, in the manner of any clever woman who is not going to be put down, turns Adam's case against him, arguing that his flattering concern for her safety in fact reveals his doubts about her ability to deal with Satan ("His fraud is then thy fear, which plain inferrs / Thy equal fear that my firm Faith and Love / Can by his fraud be shak'n or seduc't," 9.285–87). She ends with a stately, defiant flourish, the word order delicately intricated:

> Thoughts, which how found they harbour in thy brest,
> Adam, missthought of her to thee so dear?
>
> (9.288–89)

She goes on her way, and as she sets out to the fatal encounter with Satan, Milton changes his notes to tragic.

It is hard to imagine at what other level of style or diction this scene could have been presented if it were not to be altogether out of place in its heroic setting. Shakespeare in a comedy could have done it directly, in "English," a novelist more directly still in prose. Mozart does it in *Figaro*, but there the music of itself creates the necessary distance from the workaday world. This is a husband and wife quarreling in Eden: Eden just before but still before the fall. Miltonic provides the right medium, distancing the action while showing itself fully capable of striking the note of high comedy.

Up to this point it is the relation of English to Latin that has occupied us, the relation to Greek, far less known and culturally more remote, only marginally. Knowledge of the language increased steadily in England from the mid-seventeenth century on and was widespread in the eighteenth—how deep it went is another matter.[17] Yet clear evidence of Greek influence is hard to pin down; the language is too quicksilvery and inconstant. "There is a want of salient points to seize . . . which makes imitation impossible" (to use Arnold's words of Homer),[18] except in the case of direct adoption of a Greek poetic usage like Milton's "flowry-kirtl'd Naiades" in *Comus* (line 254), which beautifully re-creates the decorative Greek compound epithet, or his use now and then of a Greek construction. When Eve plucked the forbidden fruit, she "knew not eating Death" (9.792), where "eating" is a Greek participle (she did not know that she was eating death) and an English adjective (she did not know the devouring power of death).

As one might expect, it is in *Samson Agonistes* that Greek influence makes itself most fully felt in the language. An indication of its presence there is noted by one of Milton's most acute verbal critics, Christopher Ricks, unwittingly, since he takes it to be the *absence* of something which he believes ought to be there, namely, the use of metaphorical, figurative language that is so abundant in Shakespeare. On the assumption that when he turned to drama Milton tried to adopt "the Shakespearian type of metaphor," Ricks finds that he fails, fails by introducing a metaphor and then, instead of developing it in the Shakespearian manner, either lets it drop or, worse, combines it with another metaphor with which it doesn't mesh.[19] Look, with Ricks, at a passage like this (189ff.):

> How counterfeit a coin they are who friends
> Bear in their Superscription (of the most
> I would be understood) in prosperous days
> They swarm, but in adverse withdraw their head.

Friends are *counterfeit*, like bad coins, and they *swarm*, like flies presumably, then *withdraw their head*, which flies, so far as we know, don't do and coins can't do. Shakespeare would not have written like this. But is Milton trying to write like Shakespeare? He describes his play as "coming forth after the antient manner, much different from what among us passes for best . . . In the modelling . . . of this Poem, with good reason, the Antients and *Italians* are rather follow'd, as of much more authority and fame." His model is Greek; he has his eye not on Shakespeare but on Greek tragedy, primarily I believe on Sophocles, and of Sophocles a classical scholar remarks that when he "employs metaphors in dialogue—as of course he often does—he rarely works them for all they are worth. They do not interest him so much that he feels impelled to draw them out for their own sake. Their purpose served, he readily lets them go."[20] Some lines from *Oedipus Rex*, describing the state of Thebes devastated by the plague, illustrate the critic's point:

πόλις γάρ, ὥσπερ καὐτὸς εἰσορᾷς, ἄγαν
ἤδη σαλεύει κἀνακουφίσαι κάρα
βυθῶν ἔτ᾽ οὐχ οἵα τε φοινίου σάλου,
φθίνουσα μὲν κάλυξιν ἐγκάρποις χθονός,
φθίνουσα δ᾽ ἀγέλαις βουνόμοις τόκοισί τε
ἀγόνοις γυναικῶν.

(*Oedipus Rex* 22–27)

Fagle's translation of the first three lines renders the Greek quite closely, except that where Sophocles speaks simply of the city, he first writes "our city," then shifts to "our ship":

> Our city—
> look around you, see with your own eyes—
> our ship pitches wildly, cannot lift her head
> from the depths.

Jebb, always sensitive to Sophocles' style, evidently judging that the ship-of-state metaphor is hardly felt, translates "is sorely vexed" rather than "pitches wildly," although he keeps the Greek "lift her head." Does "head" stand for prow, one may wonder, or is J. C. Kamerbeek right in supposing that "the image shifts from a sinking ship to a drowning man"?[21] However this may be, Sophocles now abandons his figure and turns to what may seem figurative to us but in Greek is almost direct statement, given the archaic sense of the unity of being that binds the life of man and nature within an enfolding whole. The city is "dying in the buds and fruits of the earth, dying in the herds at pasture and in the barren pangs of women."

Any competent reader of Greek verse would I think agree that this is powerful dramatic speech. Ricks, were he to subject it to the Shakespearian standard he applies to *Samson*, would have to censure the way Sophocles briefly introduces the jaded ship-of-state metaphor (possibly blending it with another figure) and lets it go when it has served its limited purpose. This is Milton's practice in this play, and it is illicit to fault it by comparing it with a different practice. There is no rule about how long a metaphor should be sustained, and to create one from Shakespeare's highly individual style is provincial.

The critic's task here is descriptive, not prescriptive: let him for our instruction observe that Shakespeare almost always, Aeschylus often, keeps a figure going, whereas Sophocles usually does not, nor does Milton—in *Samson*, that is. In *Paradise Lost*, as Ricks himself brilliantly demonstrates, Milton can sustain and develop a figure with the best of them.

The language of this play is not, like that of *Paradise Lost*, a new or third language; in no sense is it a "Babylonish dialect" formed "by a perverse and pedantic principle."[22] This is English, often as sinewy an English as one could wish ("God, when he gave me strength, to show withal / How slight the gift was, hung it in my Hair," lines 58–59). Here, in his final work, Milton gives us something we have all too little of, great English poetry that is quite uninfluenced by Shakespeare and sparing in its use of metaphor:

> Nothing is here for tears, nothing to wail
> Or knock the breast, no weakness, no contempt,
> Dispraise, or blame, nothing but well and fair,
> And what may quiet us in a death so noble.
>
> (lines 1721–24)

Beside these unadorned words, the last line and a half above all, the gorgeous flourishes that mark the Shakespearian hero's closure can sound a little gaudy.

It is in the nineteenth century that Greece really comes into its own, penetrating deeply into English life. "We are all Greeks," Shelley said; "we are now pensioners upon the Greeks only," Ruskin said; and John Stuart Mill could claim that the battle of Marathon, "even as an event in English history, is more important than the battle of Hastings."[23] All the major poets except Keats knew Greek, most of them very well. It is at this period, then, that we would expect Greek influence to be most richly present. In one sense, it is; the poets draw abundantly on Greek myth and heroic saga—think only of *Prometheus Unbound*, *Endymion*, Tennyson's idylls, *Atalanta in Calydon*. Yet in the sense that concerns us here, the Greek language actively at work in the diction and texture of English verse—in anything like the degree to which it is found in the later Hölderlin:[24] this we do not find. Arnold comes closest in *Sohrab and Rustum*, a fine poem in its way and his most successful attempt to disguise his troubled mid-Victorian self in robes borrowed from Greek antiquity. Inevitably, he wears them too self-consciously, dutifully imitating Homeric parataxis, for instance, in the series of lines beginning with "and" in Rustum's speech to his dying son, in the too-frequent Homeric allusions, and the often rather pointless epic similes. All this makes the poem not so much Homeric as a pupil's exercise in the manner of his master, like the unrhymed "terza rima" sequence in *Little Gidding*. It takes a mightier hand than Uncle Matthew's to purloin the club of Heracles.

And there is Browning's version of *Agamemnon*, written "in as Greek a fashion as English will bear."[25] Indeed there is. Many hard words have been said of this work, most of them deserved, though Steiner's attentive reading discovers occasional virtues that others have missed.[26] Browning tried, he tells us, "for the very turn of each Greek phrase," but in so doing he violates English while only occasionally managing to sound Greek. For Aeschylus's compendiary expression describing the storm that wrecked the Greek fleet, δυσκύμαντα . . . κακά (line 653), he writes "bad-wave-outbreak evils." "Bad," particularly feeble with "evils," misses the idea of something unlucky or ill-omened that the prefix δυσ- probably suggests here. To render κυμ- by "wave" unpacks Aeschylus's Greek too quickly. A κῦμα is indeed a wave, but literally and first of all it is anything swelling or swollen, so that these δυσκύμαντα κακά are both like waves, swelling in a way that bodes disaster, and are waves. "Outbreak," energetically gathering the verb ("arose") into the phrase, would be one strike for Browning if he had not already provided the sentence with a verb ("began"). He does no better with Aeschylus's syntax. The poet describes Agamemnon and Menelaus, hearing the seer Calchas hint at the terrible sacrifice required to still the waves that stop them sailing for Troy, as, literally, the "earth-with-their-staffs-striking Atreidai" (χθόνα βάκτροις | ἐπικρού-σαντας Ἀτρείδας, lines 202–3). Hopkins, possibly with these very words in mind, writes "his riding / Of the rólling level úndernéath him steady áir" ("The Windhover") showing that it is possible to reproduce loaded word-groups of this kind in strange but powerful English. All Browning can come up with is

So that the Atreidai striking staffs on earth.

In the fragmented, appalled vision of Agamemnon, just back from the war, murdered by Clytemnestra as she bathes him, Cassandra sees or seems to see a cow tangling a bull in cloths and striking it/him down with her horns, or is it a two-bladed axe? To find adequate words for this inversion of every known norm and usage, Aeschylus (to the distress of grammarians) disruptively forces the participial phrase into the main clause:

ἐν πέπλοισιν
μελαγκέρῳ λαβοῦσα μηχανήματι
τύπτει.

(lines 1126–28)

Browning writes

> In the vesture she catching him, strikes him now
> With the black-horned trick.

Useless. What is needed is a poet willing to take this sort of risk, and bring it off:

> In the cloths
> with a blackhorned CAUGHT HIM thing she
> strikes!

Poetic form. English is so different from Greek and Latin that exact formal imitations are seldom possible, but I know from experience how stimulating a study their forms can be in suggesting forms which might suit English, but which one would not have thought of had one not studied Greek and Latin prosody.
—W.H. Auden[27]

If one is looking at the ways whereby a foreign born can be brought to speak English with foreign jaws, at the ways in which our native speech may be taught to move to strange, new musics, then meter can hardly be left out of account. It may be not so much in diction or syntax as in meter that the influence of Greek in nineteenth-century poetry can best be studied. The endeavor by poets of this period to accommodate classical meters to English—that is, usually, by employing what John Hollander calls the stress-analogue principle, replacing classical quantity with English stress accent: this has received less attention than the sixteenth-century experiments in classical form, which from a literary point of view are less rewarding. Unskillful attempts to impose quantity on English too often led good poets to write less well than they otherwise would. Sidney's poems in native measures are notably superior to those in classical meters, and of these even the best, like "O sweet woods the delight of solitarines," are most attractive when they evade the alien encasement he sought to impose upon them. The movement yielded work of the first quality only in Campion, "the seraphic doctor of English prosody," C. S. Lewis calls him,[28] who opened up a range of formal possibilities, few of which were to be developed. With his *Observations in the Art of English Poesie* of 1602, and Daniel's reply, or rebuttal as it is commonly taken to be, *A Defence of Ryme*, the following year, the struggle was largely abandoned (I am omitting the odes of *Samson Agonistes*, which are far too complex for a passing reference) and not taken up until the nineteenth century when poets began experimenting again.

They were helped by advances in metrical scholarship, and they knew a great deal more Greek, so that now we can speak not simply of classical but often of specifically Greek meters, though inevitably the distinction cannot always be pressed. Tennyson experimented with the Greek form of the Alcaic stanza in his "Milton" ("O mighty-mouthed inventor of harmonies"), yet a few years before he had devised a stanza "representing in some measure the grandest of meters, the *Horatian* Alcaic" (my emphasis), and employed it in two fine original poems, "The Daisy" and "To the Rev. F. D. Maurice." A good solid structure that feels homebred, only the dactylic ripple of the last line reveals its classical origin:

> For groves of pine on either hand,
> To break the blast of winter, stand;
>   And further on, the hoary Channel
> Tumbles a billow on chalk and sand.
>   ("To the Rev. F. D. Maurice," lines 21–24)

Tennyson's quatrain belongs to a distinguished company of English stanzaic forms, not specifically Alcaic but simply Horatian, that date back to the seventeenth century and takes its place beside the stanza of Marvell's Ode, Milton's Pyrrha, and Collins's unrhymed, beautifully voweled "Ode to Evening."

In "Boädicea" he tried to acclimatize a more exotic, far more recalcitrant meter, the galliambic, originally Greek but apart from a two-line excerpt quoted by an ancient metrist surviving only in Catullus's great poem "Attis" (*super alta vectus Attis celeri rate maria,* ˇˇ–ˇ –ˇ–– ˇˇ–ˇ ˇˇˇˇ). With its riot of short syllables, this meter, exceptionally difficult in Latin, is almost impossible to reproduce in English. (Pound's remarkable line in *Homage*, "The twisted rhombs ceased their clamour of accompaniment," in fact comes somewhere near it. By my scansion: ˇ/ˇ / /ˇ/ˇ/ˇˇˇˇˇˇ/ [?]). To make the meter a little less unmanageable, Tennyson refashions the first half of the classical line, turning it into a trochaic dimeter ("While about the shore of Mona"), a sensible compromise giving the ear something to hold on to. Then in the second half, taking advantage of the Brittonic proper names whose pronunciation is anyone's guess, he lets go with a slither of short or unstressed syllables ("hear it, Spirit of Cássivĕlaún"). "Let it be read straight like prose and it will come all right," he said, although later he wondered who could read the poem except himself.

Three years after Tennyson's poem appeared, Meredith, not gifted with so fine an ear, tried in his "Phaéthôn" to hew a little more closely to the classical pattern, although too frequently he treats the first half of the line as trochaic. In the second he sometimes produces something rhythmically intelligible and sufficiently galliambic, if hardly attractive ("the insanity pitiless," ˘˘/˘˘˘˘˘; cf. Catullus's *tua, mater, initia,* ˘˘‒˘ ˘˘˘˘, 63.9), but too often he gives us a hemistich as uncouth as "therewithal that thine origin." A brave attempt, perhaps just worth trying—once, but the poem as a whole gives one metrical earache and fails to perform the function that justifies such experiments, that of providing English poetry with new metrical forms, which Campion claimed with some justice to have done.

In "Love in the Valley," a poem, not an exercise, Meredith is more successful. The meter can fairly be described as his own invention, although it has been argued that it ultimately derives from the classical trochaic tetrameter catalectic (‒˘‒˘̆ ‒˘‒˘̆ ‒˘‒˘̆ ‒˘‒), which goes readily into English accentual verse and was used "correctly" by Tennyson in "Locksley Hall" and by Browning in "A Toccata of Galuppi's."[29] If Meredith did have the classical line in mind, he took very great liberties with it. Here are the opening verses of his poem:

> Under yonder beech-tree single on the green-sward,
>   Couched with her arms behind her golden head,
> Knees and tresses folded to slip and ripple idly,
>   Lies my young love sleeping in the shade.

In the first and third lines, the medial caesura often turns the second hemistich iambic, as in the third line here, and the even-numbered lines show still greater variation—if we are to speak of variation at all. In the quatrain just quoted, we find the trochaic, falling rhythm of the first line modulating to the iambic step of the second hemistich in line 2 via the four-syllable unit "couched with her arms" (/˘˘/), trochee plus iamb. Sometimes there is no caesura ('Fleeter she seems in her stay than in her flight"), sometimes the line continues the trochaic movement of its predecessor ("Nodding! O the girdle slack about the waist"). To continue in this vein and attempt any general metrical analysis of the poem would be laboriously unprofitable, and it is best to say simply that we have here a new, ingenious prosodic invention, this or that effect suggested no doubt by Meredith's classical reading, but no more than that. The lilting, rather singsong rhythm is charming, sometimes beautiful ("Lovely are the curves of the white owl sweeping / Wavy in the dusk lit by one large star"), but it easily grows monotonous even though it is checked, not often enough, by syncopation, the suppression of short syllables: "Large and smoky red the sun's cold disk drops," a shorter trochaic hemistich, /˘/˘/ followed by ˘////, then once again in the following line trochaic and iambic units are combined. "Love in the Valley," it seems to me, is the kind of poem that a poetry workshop might usefully study, taking it to pieces and seeing how its metrical components could be reassembled and improved.[30]

A classical model has been claimed for Meredith's poem, unsuccessfully, one may think. For my next exhibit, Shelley's "Hymn of Pan," no such provenance has to my knowledge ever been proposed, yet I hope to show that it is directly patterned on a classical, Greek, form. The third stanza best illustrates my point:

> I sang of the dancing stars,
>   I sang of the daedal Earth,
> And of Heaven—and the giant wars,
>   And Love, and Death, and Birth,—
>   And then I changed my pipings,—
> Singing how down the vale of Maenalus
>   I pursued a maiden and clasped a reed:
> Gods and men, we are all deluded thus!
>   It breaks in our bosom and then we bleed:
> All wept, as I think both ye now would,
>   If envy or age had not frozen your blood
>   At the sorrow of my sweet pipings.

Rather than scan these verses, I note simply the way the stanza falls into a number of metrically distinct units, with much variation of rhythm and pace: a rhyming quatrain composed of seven- or eight-syllable lines, a single line, another rhyming quatrain composed of ten-syllable lines, a rhyming couplet, the first line fast-moving, staccato, to my ear, then a single line ending with the same word as line 5. This way of articulating a stanza is, in a more sharply defined form, found in the odes of Greek choral poetry, which often combine lines of passages composed in different, clearly distinguishable meters. (Readers not at home in this territory may want to turn to the appendix.) The possibility that Shelley patterned his stanza after the Greek model is strengthened when we notice that he starts off with three lines that can be analyzed in terms of Greek lyric meter. Lines 1 and 2 are accentual telesilleans (/ /˘˘/˘/, = quantitative –˘˘–˘–˘–), line 3 is a Lesbian form of the glyconic (˘˘/˘˘/˘/, = quantitative ˘˘–˘˘–˘–), and several other lines suggest classical analogues. Shelley's interest in the Greek choric ode is shown elsewhere in his writing, in the "Ode to Naples," for instance, with its strophes, antistrophes, and epodes, or the odes of his translation of the *Cyclops*. The claim I wish to make, then, is that in this seemingly modest form we have an English equivalent of the jewel of Greece's metrical crown, the choric ode of Attic tragedy.

The fact that so little of this sort has been attempted in English is no proof that it cannot be done. It shows rather that our poets, so bold in other respects, have been relatively unadventurous in extending the formal, metrical range of our poetry. English has many resources that remain to be explored. In its primarily accentual way, our speech can pattern sound almost as well as Greek, but whereas Greek poets developed the rhythmical potentialities offered by their language very fully, English poets have done so far less. Take Swinburne's line from the famous ode in *Atalanta*, "Fleeter of foot than the fleet-foot kid" (/⌣⌣/⌣⌣///). If "fleet-foot" can pass as a spondee, the sound pattern is identical to that of Aeschylus's κριμναμεναν νεφελαν ὀρθοῖ (–⌣⌣–⌣⌣–––, *Seven against Thebes* 229). The difference is not that one line is accentual, the other quantitative, but rather that Swinburne's is a one-timer, something he came up with on a particular occasion and did not, so far as I have been able to notice, use again, whereas in Greece when the line was popularized by the sixth-century lyric poet Ibycus (metrists called it an ibycean), it became a common poetic property for other poets to employ. Hence it was that when, in the fifth century, the Athenian dramatists drew on the metrical inventions bequeathed them by the earlier lyricists, and proceeded to combine them in ways that had never been done before, they created that poetic marvel, the choric ode. We look on their achievement, rightly, with wonder and delight, and say, quite wrongly, that alas nothing of the sort can be done in English. In point of fact, it *has* been done, very occasionally. There is, incomparably as always, Milton, with the odes of *Samson*. There is Campion, of whose poem "Author of Light" C. S. Lewis remarks that it "really has to be learned as we learn a strophe and antistrophe of Pindar" (not of course that Campion had Pindar in mind).[31] We have to compare "each metrical phrase with its fellow . . . before its full beauty is apparent." And there is Hopkins, who told Robert Bridges that the rhythm of the long lines in "The Leaden Echo and the Golden Echo" is "like . . . the rhythm of Greek tragic choruses or of Pindar."[32] Compared with the strident novelty of a poem like this, Shelley's "Hymn" seems a slight affair, and his intentions have not (I believe) been understood. It is nonetheless a pioneer attempt to bring to our poetry a beauty it possesses very little.

Much that could have been done has not been done. Perhaps the trouble lies with the disjunction, since the late sixteenth and early seventeenth centuries, of poetry and music. The Greek ode was set to music, and music can define and clarify the sound patterns of poetry in a way that words alone do only with great difficulty. (It was also danced; this was a poetry that moves to "the cadence of consenting feet," to borrow a curiously good expression noted by Herbert Read.)[33] Have we left it to music to satisfy our desire for musical, rhythmical delight, and allowed too much of our poetry to plod along in iambics?

(This is too brisk, of course, and leaves a lot out of account. One of the reasons why English has availed itself so seldom of the metrical resources offered by Greek is that it has had increasingly to meet a challenge that Greek poetry was spared. "During the eighteenth century," John Hollander writes, "all poetry save the sung lyric begins to have to confront the growth of prose as an authentic vehicle of imaginative expression."[34] Poetry was drawn into the sphere of prose, more and more into the recesses of the solitary mind, and away from music, in the process gaining new powers and losing old ones.)

We would expect to find Swinburne, the most passionate and, with Hopkins, most scholarly of nineteenth-century Hellenizing poets, and one of our finest metrists, developing the formal possibilities of Shelley's pioneering venture in his *Atalanta in Calydon*. The odes exhibit great rhythmical variety and inventiveness, but what we do not find in this flamboyantly Greek play is the specifically Greek structure or articulation of Shelley's "Hymn," a single stanza composed of rhythmically distinct units. Swinburne is nonetheless the poet who most successfully adopted Greek meters in English, and although he produced no theoretical account of his principles, in the introductory note to his magnificent translation of the anapestic parabasis from Aristophanes' *Birds*, he usefully distinguished the meters that English will accept from those it will not, as Campion had done in his *Observations*. "All variations and combinations of anapaestic, iambic, or trochaic metre," Swinburne wrote, "are as natural and pliable as all dactylic and spondaic forms of verse are unnatural and abhorrent."[35] (So much for Arnold's belief that the dactylic hexameter is the best medium into which to translate Homer.)

Nowhere is Swinburne's metrical skill shown more fully than in his choriambic poem very properly called "Choriambs," since that is what, indeed all, it is about. The four-syllable phrase $/ \smile \smile /$ that we may call a choriamb has long provided a rhythmical variant in otherwise iambic lines (Milton's "Into a Gulf shot under ground, till part," for example, *Paradise Lost* 9.72). Occasional use of the choriamb is one thing; using it as the basis of a whole poem is far more difficult. Both Sidney in his "O sweet woods the delight of solitarines" and Campion in his "Canto Secundo" tried their hand at the classic lesser asclepiad ($-\smile$ $-\smile\smile-$ $-\smile\smile-$ $\smile-$, Horace's *ergo Quintilium perpetuus sopor*, Ode 1.24). Of the two, Campion is intermittently the more successful. He manages one choriamb well enough ("What faire pompe have I spide of glittering Ladies"), now and then two ("On their yvorie browes, trackt to the daintie thies"), but the meter does not come readily to him, and the best course is to let the poem move to its own delicate, wayward music without bothering much about the classical model. Swinburne, with no apparent strain, handles the three central choriambs of the more difficult greater asclepiad, used by Sappho and by Horace (*O crudelis adhuc et Veneris muneribus potens*). To manage this line successfully, the poet must be able to counterpoint the natural speech phrases against the metrical pattern, as Sappho does:

> ἔσσετ' οὐδὲ πόθα εἰς ὕστερον· οὐ γὰρ πεδέχῃς βρόδων.
> [esset' oude pothaˉeis usteron; ou gar pedekhēis brodōn.][36]

Swinburne follows her. Having first established the pattern ("What sweet visions of sleep lured thee away, down from the light above"), he is then free to introduce lines like "Colder surely than past kisses that love poured for thy lips as wine," in which, if we let the words establish their natural rhythm, the pattern almost vanishes. The meter is, however, too difficult, and too artificial, to be of any general use in English verse, although perhaps an isolated Asclepiadic line could provide an interesting variant in otherwise metered verses. Technically, "Choriambs" is a triumph, but it is a virtuoso exercise rather than a poem, written after the fire in him had burnt out and he was consigned to the tutelage of Theodore Watts-Dunton at The Pines, 2 Putney Hill.

More than virtuosity went to the creation of "Sapphics," which belongs to the first series of "Poems and Ballads" written in Swinburne's heyday. This famous meter has for century after century been used by poets in every Western country for the widest variety of themes, from the Day of Judgment to the return of Benjamin Franklin to Philadelphia.[37] Most of those who practiced it, having no direct access to Sappho, took as their model not the Sapphic hendecasyllable but the Horatian, with its caesura after the fifth syllable (*Persicos odi / puer adparatus*), less often after the sixth. Sappho's line, which until recently has not been well understood,[38] is built around a choriamb

($-\smile\smile-$), preceded by $-\smile-\underset{\smile}{}$ and followed by $\smile-\underset{\smile}{}$. There may be a caesura in this or that place, but often the line moves along its eleven syllables at a single unbroken breath:

ποικιλόθρον᾽ ἀθανάτ᾽ Ἀφρόδιτα,

where the poet's cry is lifted up to the goddess by the thrust of the choriamb. Listen now to Swinburne:

> Saw the white implacable Aphrodite,
> Saw the hair unbound and the feet unsandalled
> Shine as fire of sunset on western waters;
>   Saw the reluctant
>
> Feet, the straining plumes of the doves that drew her.

One may fault the diction (the third line is rather picture-postcardy), yet here for once is a line that moves and feels like Sappho's, not simply because Swinburne has discarded the Horatian caesura, but much more because in his line almost as in her Greek line we hear the length of the syllables. This is *English quantitative verse*, composed in the way that is proper to English. Quantity (to use the familiar if strictly incorrect term)[39] has been consistently, indignantly denied largely because when it was first attempted by the classicizing poets and theorists of the later sixteenth century they went the wrong way about it, above all in the absurd pedantry of imposing on English the classical rule of length by position that led even a poet with so good an ear as Sidney's to scan a word like *violence* as quantitative $\smile\smile-$. Swinburne made no such elementary blunder. He *heard* Greek poetry, found what he heard most beautiful, and, without troubling to come up with a formal defense, set about creating a comparable beauty in English. He never makes an unstressed syllable stand in the place of a classical long syllable, and, as Campion had done before him, he usually lets stress and quantity coincide.[40] *Lets* is the key word here. In Greek and Latin verse, some syllables are long by established convention and (more clearly in Greek than in Latin?) by the nature of the language, hence quantity, the pattern of long and short, can serve as the basic metrical principle. This is not possible in English, since a great many syllables are common (contrast "and what's more" and "And, what is more": the first "and" is unstressed and could be treated as short, the second stressed, hence long), and very few syllables are necessarily long, irrespective of speech emphasis. (No one, though, could take Milton's *clomb* to be short: "So clomb this first grand Thief into Gods Fold," *Paradise Lost* 4.192.) Syllabic length is, however, a potential reality in English: *saw* usually takes longer to say than *sat*, *white* than *wit*. Let a poet deeply at home in classical verse take advantage of this phonetic fact; let him ensure that stress and length coincide and be careful to base quantity on accent, then you have something that can properly be called *English* quantitative verse.

There is of course no way of "proving" that quantity can play an occasional role in English verse, and convincing those who insist that "saw the white" is simply accentual / ˘ / . One can only say, with Pound, "LISTEN to the sound it makes,"[41] and appeal to the instructed ear of the classically trained reader who can *also* hear –˘– there. The appeal to this privileged organ need not be dismissed as special pleading by those who are familiar with the uninstructed ear of the average student and have heard a line of formal verse turned into flat prose.

Is it worth arguing the case for English quantity, given the vehemence with which it is usually denied? Yes. When a poet, without doing a mischief to our native speech rhythms, is able to let what an English reader hears as quantity play its part alongside stress accent, as Swinburne has done here, he has brought English verse an additional resource, a new beauty. A learned beauty, no doubt, but why should a poet not be *doctus*, learned in his art? "Sapphics" is learned poetry where learning, not pedantry, offers us the chance of hearing Greek-born Sappho speak with almost English jaws. To be driven by our prejudices to refuse the gift seems churlish.[42]

What of the present century? Have there been, are there going to be, experiments of the kind we have been looking at? Out of classical Latin, Milton created what almost amounts to a new language. Has Pound (who hated Milton and resembles him in so many ways) created something similar from classical Chinese? Will other languages, as they come within our widening ken, offer further possibilities of this sort? Our poets, with little if any Latin and no Greek, have been unable to follow (and have shown few signs of wanting to follow) the lead of their nineteenth-century predecessors and devise new metrical forms by experimenting with classical meters, even though they may admire the prosodic skill of Auden who would not have been the brilliant metrist he was had he not known Latin. Experiments of all kinds there have nonetheless been: that they are going to result in the creation of stable forms for poets to use is still far from certain. Those who believe that verse must always possess or suggest form, and that when it moves away from forms that seem exhausted it is to move toward fresh ones, must hope so.

Our century can, however, claim one quite new, fully fledged prosodic invention, although it has not been recognized. It is to be found in the last of the great modernists, David Jones, and emerges clearly in his major work *The Anathémata*. Jones's unit is not the line but the metrical phrase or colon, very deliberately accented, the movement sometimes almost that of prose:[43]

> Six centuries
> > and the second Spring
> and a new wonder under heaven:
> > man-limb stirs
> > > in the god-stones
> and the kouroi
> > are gay and stepping it
> but stanced solemn.

The metrical phrases are usually paired, half lines balanced against each other on the principle of parallelism. Jones's prosodic model, it has been convincingly argued, is the "antiphonal structure . . . of versicles and responses in the Catholic liturgy and the antiphonal singing of Psalms."[44]

There is a further formal development in his last book, *The Sleeping Lord*, notably in the magnificent final poem bearing the same title. We find the same combination of paired phrases or half lines mostly of two, three, or four stresses, with or without weak or unstressed syllables. (Jones learned from Hopkins, of course, but the movement of his verse is quite different.) Phrases with the same number of stresses are often very deliberately balanced against each other, giving effects as formal as

> Is the tump by Honddu
> > his lifted bolster?
> > does a gritstone outcrop
> incommode him?

Within this regularity there is, however, room for much variety, since falling rhythm can be balanced against rising, phrases very strongly accented may be combined with others whose movement is that of ordinary speech, and units as different as "they shóvelled asíde the shárds & bréccia" and "of wárm-félled greát faúna" are metrically equivalent.[45]

David Jones's verse carries too unmistakably his own very personal signature for there to be any question of other poets taking over his principle of verse composition. Yet they might surely learn from it, above all how to move toward forms that provide the recurring satisfaction of rhythmical expectation checked and kept pleasurably alert by perpetual slight variety. Hopkins's manner is often even more idiosyncratic than that of Jones, and yet his formal innovations have proved influential. The lessons offered by Jones might prove no less so, once he achieves the recognition that is unquestionably his due.

Is there something of the same sort in Pound? I once argued, too hastily, that, clearly revealed first in *Homage* and then with ever-increasing subtlety throughout the lyrical sections of *Cantos*, there is a principle of composition, distantly analogous to that of Greek choral lyric, in which we find recurrent, clearly defined rhythmical phrases linked by groups of syllables that are "free" and play no analyzable part in the metrical structure.[46] I still believe there is something to this, but to make it good would require demonstration of a kind clearly out of place at this late stage of an already lengthy paper. Instead, I propose to return to my point of origin, translation, to the alternative mode in which the translator makes no secret of the fact that he is taking us abroad, deliberately letting the foreignness of his original show through. Here is Pound, *le grant translateur*, at work on a passage from the Chinese *Book of Rites*:

> Know then:
>   Toward summer the sun is in Hyades
> Sovran is Lord of the Fire
>   to this month are birds,
> with bitter smell and with the odour of burning
> To the hearth god, lungs of the victim
>   The green frog lifts up his voice
>   and the white latex is in flower
> In red car with jewels incarnadine
>   to welcome the summer.

In these verses from Canto LII, Charles Tomlinson writes, "one hears English being drawn into a dialogue" with very ancient Chinese. Pound "gives us in magnificent processional rhythms something English and something irreducibly foreign and distant."[47] The last stanza of his version of one of the odes traditionally attributed to Confucius stands at a still greater distance. The lines deserve to be set beside Jonson's noble poem for Camden:[48]

High destiny's not borne without its weight
(equity lives not save by constant probe)
Be not thy crash as Yin's from skies, foreseen.
The working of Heaven hath neither sound nor smell,
Be thy cut form of justice as Wen's was, shall rise
ten thousand states, thine, and with candour in all.

The writing is no less masterly, there is a comparable weight and authority, a comparable and even greater concision in the diction ("Man
scarse can make that doubt, but thou canst teach," "Be thy cut form
of justice as Wen's was, shall rise"). The difference is no less striking.
In Jonson's poem, we feel the controlling presence, like a kind of grid
on which the English words are laid, of our classical Western language,
Latin. In Pound's stanza we feel or guess the controlling presence of
another classical language, Chinese, and what we take to be a Chinese cast of thought. Pound has done something astonishing here.
He writes from or within a tradition that does not exist and which he
himself has invented, a tradition to which Chinese has stood in the
same close family relation that Latin stood for so long in our real tradition. Tomlinson's belief that translation can provide English verse
with alternative rhetorics is here realized.[49]

And alternative, new, metrical forms? Yes, sometimes (Pound's early
Provençal translations, for instance, even if these are largely exercises); so too can original composition, particularly in a poem like
Swinburne's "Sapphics," which brings Sappho across to us in a way
that allows us to call it a translation of Sappho, perhaps the best we
have. I used this poem to advance my case for quantity as a possible
element in English verse. I would have hesitated so to oppose received opinion had I been trusting simply to my own ear. I was not;
my trust was in Pound's. "As to quantity," he wrote in 1913, "it is foolish to suppose that we are incapable of distinguishing a long vowel
from a short one." Four years later we find him writing: "I think the
desire for vers libre is due to the sense of quantity reasserting itself
after years of starvation." This applies to Pound's own vers libre but
not, I think, to anyone else's. Exactly what relation he saw between
vers libre and quantity he never explains. Whatever the explanation,
the effect in performance is that the lines move more slowly, the
stressed syllables weighted and prolonged in the way that we hear
from Pound's reading of his verse. Still on the same tack, he asks Mar-
ianne Moore: "I want to know . . . whether you are working in Greek
quantitative measures," presumably hearing or hoping that he heard
quantity in her syllabics.[50]

In Pound's own writing, quantity makes its first notable appearance in "The Return," which Eliot called "an important study in verse which is really quantitative."[51] He quoted the opening lines:

> See, they return; ah, see the tentative
> Movements, and the slow feet,
> The trouble in the pace and the uncertain
> Wavering!

The tentatively moving feet we are called on to see are those of the ancient gods, returning to us after their long absence. On the poem's secondary level we are invited to *hear* the feet of the ancient poems that celebrated their presence, the Greek poems composed in the quantitative measures now returning to assume new forms in the English verse. Donald Davie described this poem as "the etiolation of the Sapphic stanza."[52] What we have here, I submit, is rather its reconstitution, the reassembling of its component parts, tentatively at first, but with more confidence as the poem proceeds. "These were the 'Wing'd-with-Awe,'" a Poundian rhythm but not a metrical element of Sappho's stanza—one syllable too short. Three times he tries again:

> Gods of the wingèd shoe!
> With them the silver hounds,
>   sniffing the trace of air!

No, still not quite right. Then he gets it, a complete Sapphic hendecasyllable (if we lean a little on "harry"), even though set out as two lines:

> Haie! Haie!
>   These were the swift to harry.
>
> [Poīkĭlōthrŏn'
>   āthănăt' Āphrŏdītā.]

In the next line, "These the keen-scented," he has a shot at the adonean that concludes the Sapphic stanza (πότνια, θῦμον, scanned pōtnĭă, thūmōn). Again, not yet quite right, but the final line does it: "pallid the leash-men!"

A few years later, in *Homage*, quantity asserts its presence with full confidence:

> Flame burns, rain sinks into the cracks
> And they all go to rack ruin beneath the thud of the years.

Stands genius a deathless adornment,
a name not to be worn out with the years.

If we hear in these lines, as we do so often in the *Cantos,* English moving to a music not heard elsewhere in our poetry, it is because quantity is one (*one*—I am claiming no more) of the elements that have gone into their making.

What there might be for other poets to draw on in these Poundian bequests, the alternative rhetorics and metrical forms he has provided, is not for a critic to say. In the matter of translation, though, here perhaps the critic can put in a word. Whether or not this has been a great age of translation, as some have claimed, a great deal has certainly been published. The ecumenical spread of our interests has led us far afield, so that there is now the odd situation whereby students unfamiliar with many of the classics of their own language can write knowledgeably about the *Gilgamesh Epic*—read of course in translation. The forced public of the classroom consumes translation in large quantities, much of it inevitably journeyman stuff, and even the work of finer quality has been inhibited by the dogma that translation, from whatever period and whatever the stylistic level of the original, must speak the language of today—a leveling veto (no high talk allowed here!) that ought to be questioned. What room is there, in our diminished speech, for the larger utterance, the lexical daring, the ebullience and sheer outrageousness, of the major classics of the past? It is like trying to put a mad giant into a dwarf's straitjacket, as Christopher Middleton has brilliantly observed.

What should be done? No one wants to return to the methinkses and yea verilies of Victorian translationese. (The once admired authors of a late nineteenth-century version of the *Iliad,* having to describe Odysseus's treatment of that unfortunate prole Thersites, wrote "him he drave with his sceptre and chode him with loud words" [2.199].) There is another course, opened up once again by Pound, who dug down to older, still valid linguistic strata and came up with diction and syntax unfamiliar enough to sound startlingly new, confronting us with ancient texts that we know could only have been written in this century. The archaisms, the thees and thous and so forth, of his earlier writing often strike one as tiresomely affected, yet as the *Cantos* proceeded he was able to make them sound quite natural. The solemn couplet that brings the *Pisans* to a close ("If the hoar frost grip thy tent / Thou wilt give thanks when night is spent") could not without grave loss be rewritten with *your* and *you*.

Pound had to learn to write like this; it took time. Others, poet translators, should surely be able to do so too, and in so doing might not only liberate some of the great works of past ages from the drab it is forced to wear today—Greek tragedy, for instance (not, however, an area where Pound provides sure guidance). Who knows what splendors they might reveal? Jocasta might even recover her divine head. Faced with new formal challenges, poets might also devise responses, new alternative rhetorics and metrical resources, that would not otherwise have occurred to them—inappropriate, very likely, to their original work today, but which might serve them or their successors tomorrow. There is no such thing as progress in literature, but if there were, this is one of the forms it would take.

APPENDIX: A NOTE ON THE GREEK CHORIC STANZA

τίς ὄντιν᾽ ἁ θεσπιέπει-
α Δελφὶς εἶπε πέτρα
ἄρρητ᾽ ἀρρήτων τελέσαν-
τα φοινίαισι χερσίν;
ὥρα νιν ἀελλάδων
ἵππων σθεναρώτερον
φυγᾷ πόδα νωμᾶν.
ἔνοπλος γὰρ ἐπ᾽ αὐτὸν ἐπενθρῴσκει
πυρὶ καὶ στεροπαῖς ὁ Διὸς γενέτας,
δειναὶ δ᾽ ἅμ᾽ ἕπονται
Κῆρες ἀναπλάκητοι.

(Sophocles *Oedipus Rex* 463–72)

tis hontin' ha thespiepei-	⌣–⌣– –⌣⌣–
a Delphis eipe petra	⌣–⌣– ⌣–⌣
arrēt' arrētōn telesan-	–––– –⌣⌣–
ta phoiniaisi khersin?	⌣–⌣– ⌣––
hōra nin aelladōn	––⌣⌣–⌣–
hippōn sthenarōteron	––⌣⌣–⌣–
phugai poda nōman.	⌣–⌣⌣––
enoplos gar ep' auton epenthrōskei	⌣⌣– ⌣⌣– ⌣⌣– ––
puri kai steropais ho Dios genetas,	⌣⌣– ⌣⌣– ⌣⌣– ⌣⌣–
deinai d' ham' hepontai	––⌣⌣––
Kēres anaplakētoi.	–⌣⌣⌣⌣––

[Who is the man that Delphi's oracular rock said has performed horrors beyond all horror with murderous hands? It is time he set his foot to flight swifter than storm-footed horses. For armed with fire and lightning the son of Zeus leaps upon him, and close behind follow the death spirits who do not miss their mark.]

The strophe is composed of several clearly distinguishable metrical units. By following the pattern of long and short syllables, one quickly makes out the different steps to which they move. The first quatrain is built from two metrical phrases, the iambic metron ⌣—⌣— (lines 2 and 4 ending with the syncopated form ⌣—⌣) and the choriamb —⌣⌣— (another form of which is ————). Next, a three-line unit again employing the choriamb; lines 5 and 6 are the quantitative equivalent of the accentual couplet with which Shelley's "Hymn of Pan" starts. Lines 8 and 9 shift unexpectedly to a swift and in context menacing anapestic step (⌣⌣—). Line 10 returns to the meter of 7, and the strophe ends with a resolved trochaic phrase (the unresolved form would be —⌣—⌣——).

The various classes of meter out of which this strophe is composed are all familiar and readily perceptible to the ear: shaped phrases cut out of sound. What is new and unfamiliar here, as in every Greek choric ode, is the way the poet, who is both poet and musician, combines them and builds, by means in themselves simple, a poetic, musical structure often of considerable complexity and great formal beauty.

2

From the Baked Bricks:
The Poem of Gilgamesh

A GREAT WORK OF THE IMAGINATION IS *TOUJOURS EN ACTE,* OPEN TO new readings and modified to whatever extent by them. This is true in an unusually literal sense of the *Gilgamesh Epic*. Since it was first disinterred from the ruins of the royal library of Assurbanipal at Nineveh in the 1850s and the initial decipherings began, the poem has grown steadily. The provisional rendering of portions of the narrative which George Smith read to the Society of Biblical Archaeology in 1872 and published three years later in *The Chaldean Account of Genesis,* exciting though it was at the time, is a mere skeleton of the work represented in the 1955 version by E. A. Speiser, which served for decades for many of us as the standard text.[1] Since then, with a number of gaps filled in and advances in the understanding of the language, completer versions have appeared, and more than half a dozen have appeared since the mid-1980s.[2] *Toujours en acte* indeed! There has been nothing like it since the recovery of Greek and Latin texts in the earlier Renaissance.

Proceeding step by step with the discovery of the text has come a fuller comprehension of the elements out of which the poem was built, and the stages of its composition. The story begins sometime in the first half of the third millennium BC with a historical figure called Gilgamesh, ruler of the Sumerian city of Uruk in southern Mesopotamia. The fame of his actions passed into the folk imagination and inspired a number of heroic lays, which were not, it seems, brought together into a single poem until the center of power moved north into Babylonia. It is here that the decisive creative act took place and the great poem first assumed its form. Of this, the Old Babylonian poem, we have at present only about five hundred short lines, many incomplete, with some sizable holes in the narrative. The next and final step occurred several centuries later, probably in the last half or

"From the Baked Bricks: The Poem of Gilgamesh," *New Criterion* 11 (September 1992): 68–74.

quarter of the second millennium BC, and now we have a name, Sin-leqe-unninni, for the man we should perhaps call an editor but surely also a poet, whose work or something close to it eventually found its way to the palace library at Nineveh. From our perspective, we inevitably see this poem as a monumental beginning, the first great epic of the world, but it is in fact late. So far as a layman can judge, the palace version has shed or lost the ruder energies of its Old Babylonian predecessor and achieved the repose of classic status.

Hitherto the layman has had in a real sense to make the *Gilgamesh Epic* up for himself, guessing at the poetry lying somewhere behind the toneless words of the scholarly cribs. By now, however, scholarship has gone far enough in its labor of elucidation to allow a closer engagement, and this means that the Assyriologist has ceded some of his absolute rights to the poet, the poet capable of finding an English voice for Sin-leqe-unninni. David Ferry, seeing his opportunity, has stepped in and given us the finest translation of *Gilgamesh* that we are likely to have until the time, should it ever come, when the Near Eastern classic is revealed to us as fully as the classics of Greece and Rome.[3]

To carry out his difficult task, Ferry had to avoid two opposing errors. The kind of free version that is acceptable with a familiar Western masterpiece—the radical freedoms of Pope's *Iliad,* or the relative freedoms of Fitzgerald's *Odyssey*—would be unwelcome with a poem still so distant. Nor on the other hand do we want the pedissequous fidelity that makes much of Lattimore's *Iliad* such heavy going. With no access to the original, Ferry used all the scholarly versions he could lay his hands on and kept as close to the letter as he could if he was to make a poem of it. In the introduction, the Assyriologist professor William L. Moran writes that this "is David ferry's poem. It is not Sin-leqe-unninni's or anyone else's, any more than *The Vanity of Human Wishes* is Juvenal's and not Johnson's. He has given us, not a translation, not at least as that term is ordinarily understood, but a transformation" (p. xi). Unseemly though it is for a layman to question the words of an authority in this arcane field, surely Johnson, enjoying the broad license of an imitation, goes a great deal farther than Ferry in recasting his original. For Juvenal's account of how Sejanus fell from imperial grace, Johnson substitutes the fall of Cardinal Wolsey in the reign of Henry VIII, an apt enough historical parallel but differing widely in circumstance and detail. Ferry's innovations are by comparison inconsiderable and for the most part required of him to keep the story line going. He fills in some gaps in the narrative, rearranges it when it seems incoherent, condenses a little here, expands there, and where the ancient text repeats a series of lines over and over in the epic manner, he introduces variations of his own. His liberties are for the most part local, his interventions temperate, and all in all I think we should believe him when he says that he tried "to be as respectful of the professional scholarship as it is feasible to be."

What matters for the general reader, once he has satisfied himself that Ferry has played fair and not smuggled in a poem of his own under the guise of a translation, is, as I put it, that he has found a voice for the old poet, has given us today's words tuned to the gravity and simplicity of ancient speech:

> And may the stars, the watchmen of the night,
> watch over Gilgamesh and the companion.

(The prayer of Gilgamesh's mother as he and his friend Enkidu go out to fight the monster Huwawa.) Listen to this voice *tam nova et tam antiqua* directing us, at the start of the poem, to contemplate the great city built by Gilgamesh:

> He built Uruk. He built the keeping place
> of Anu and Ishtar. The outer wall
>
> shines in the sun like brightest copper; the inner
> wall is beyond the imaginings of kings.
>
> Study the brickwork, study the fortification;
> climb the great ancient staircase to the terrace;
>
> study how it is made; from the terrace see
> the planted and fallow fields, the ponds and orchards.
>
> This is Uruk, the city of Gilgamesh
> the Wild Ox, son of Lugalbanda, son
>
> of the Lady Wildcow Ninsun, Gilgamesh
> the vanguard and the rear guard of the army,
>
> Shadow of Darkness over the enemy field,
> the Web, the Flood that rises to wash away
>
> the walls of alien cities, Gilgamesh
> the strongest one of all, the perfect, the terror.

Plain, direct syntax, sentences in general fairly short, diction at the right remove from the quotidian yet not distracting us by its strangeness. "Keeping place," for instance, is nicely distanced. It sounds familiar (older American usage has "keeping room" in the sense of living room), but the compound is unfamiliar and we must, though not at a first reading, dredge up whatever we may know about Mesopotamian religion. The city belongs to the gods, it is their place of residence; and the fact that they are in place there keeps it a safe place for mortals. The line about the ancient staircase swaggers a bit and we catch an echo of Yeats; Ferry rarely draws on other poets. Having climbed the staircase, from the terrace we look, as we are bidden, at the landscape, not in any way alien and yet not one we have ever seen, for this is the landscape of an earlier world. Gilgamesh's mother belongs to no pantheon we know of, and poses a problem, the naming of august personages, that faces the translator of Homer (what to do about "ox-eyed Hera" and the like). The Lady Wildcow Ninsun is a convincing divinity and clearly the right mother for the Wild Ox Gilgamesh. The handsome line "Shadow of Darkness over the enemy field" is for once of Ferry's own making and, strictly, gratuitous, though it fits in so well that one would not know this without checking the various translations.

Ferry's task was to give us the freedom of a world very far from our own, respecting its distance and yet bringing it close enough to set our imagination working and allow us to respond to the poem's central core of humanity. There is no problem—except the problem of writing with complete simplicity—when Gilgamesh, grieving for the death of his friend, says, "Enkidu has died. / Must I die too? Must Gilgamesh be like that?" It is another matter when Enkidu describes his dream vision of the realm of the dead, for the Mesopotamian afterworld— not a hell where sinners are punished but the condition awaiting all mankind—is stranger than anything the Western imagination has conceived, and more terrible than Dante's carefully constructed torture house. Yet it must be made real if this death-haunted world is to work for us:

> On a dark plain
> I was alone. But there was one, a man,
>
> with a lion head, and the paws of a lion too,
> but the nails were talons, the talons of an eagle.
>
> The face was dark. He took hold of me and seized me.
> I fought with him, I hit at him, but he
>
> kept moving about in the dark, too quick for me,
> and then with a blow he capsized me like a raft . . .
>
> Then I was changed into something like a bird,
> with a bird's arms, as spindly as a bird's,

and feathered like a bird. He seized an arm
and led me to the dwelling of Irkalla,

the House of Darkness, the House of No Return.

The difficulty of bringing remote cultural experience home to modern readers is something that many translators have had to face in this century, for although our age is in many ways sealed off from the past, it has found itself strangely drawn to the antique. The paperbacks keep us well supplied with renderings from the ancient Chinese or Egyptian, from tribal societies, and so forth. Translators have regularly failed to find an appropriate language and mistakenly supposed that making an old work new means making it sound contemporary. Ferry fell into no such vulgar error, nor did he try to follow the great time-traveler Pound, who was able to draw on archaic but still vital strata of our language and, at farthest reach, in his late translations from the Chinese, invented an authoritative speech of unknown provenance ("The working of Heaven hath neither sound nor smell").[4]

Ferry keeps to the lingua franca, using it in a way that allows it to speak of and from quite another day. The nearest parallel I can think of is Kipling's practice in *Puck of Pook's Hill*. When he is dealing with England soon after the Norman Conquest, a distant period but not severed from us by any historical break, Kipling permits himself some archaisms ("he . . . threddled the long-ship through the sea. When it rose beyond measure he brake a pot of whale's oil upon the water, which wonderfully smoothed it, and in that anointed patch he turned her head to the wind"). This, however, would be out of place in the stories set in Roman Britain, for here a break has occurred. To indicate this, Kipling uses not an archaic language, which would suggest a particular historical time, but a current language that has been purged of whatever belongs specifically and only to our time and hence can sound timeless. As the centurion Pertinax describes his journey up country to Hadrian's Wall, the landscape grows wilder and the language is imperceptibly heightened until, just before the Wall itself comes into sight, we are ready for this sentence: "Red-hot in summer, freezing in winter, is that big, purple heather country of broken stone." There is no word here that could not be used today, yet the order of the words and the stately cadence tell us that the world we are seeing is not one known to today's eyes.

Ferry, when he needs to elevate the tone, employs roughly comparable means. Describing Gilgamesh's approach to the formidable barrier through which he must pass on his journey in quest of immortal life, he writes:

> Gilgamesh came to the mountain called Mashu,
> whose great twin heads look one way and the other:
>
> the one looks toward the setting of the sun;
> the other toward the rising of the sun.
>
> The great twin heads brush up against the Heavens;
> the great udders of the mountain hang down into
>
> the shadows of the Cavern of the Earth.
> Twin Dragon Scorpion Beings whose look is death
>
> are the guardians of the entrance into the mountain.
> The aura of the demon guardian Beings
>
> shimmers across the surface of the mountain.
> The shimmering of the light is death to look at.

Note "Scorpion Beings". Most translations have "scorpion-men," which brings them uncomfortably close to the bogies of interplanetary fiction. These are not scorpions but Scorpion *Beings*, oversized arachnids yet just close enough to humanity to be able to speak without sounding ridiculous. This kind of unobtrusive tact characterizes Ferry's translation throughout. The least showy of writers, he has brought this ancient poem across to today with such apparent ease that one may not recognize the magnitude of his achievement. He has added a great epic poem to world literature.

Inevitably one is drawn to make comparisons with our own epic tradition, above all with the *Iliad*. Although it is hard to point to clear traces of influence, similar impulses are at work in both poems. Both the Near Eastern and the Greek epic face the fragility of our tenure in a world that has no special care for us and may even be hostile to our presence. Both confront the absolute fact of death head on, but they do so in different ways. There is only one death in the Gilgamesh poem, countless ones in the *Iliad*, yet in a sense they are always the same death, the same phenomenon, the abrupt fall of an erect, flourishing creature. In the last third of the *Iliad* the sense of pervading mortality grows heavier with the momentous, the great deaths. First that of Sarpedon, who "dies raging" (16.491) at the hands of Achilles' beloved friend Patroclus, who later in the same sixteenth book is killed by Troy's champion, Hector, who will himself be killed by Achilles, the tragic event portending the fall of the whole city which will lead the poem to its close.

A work so full of suffering and death should, one might think, end in an abyss of sorrow. Instead, the *Iliad* leaves us with a sense almost of triumph, a great human triumph in the face of the worst that life can throw at us. How this is achieved will be understood when someone has explained why tragedy affects us as it does. The young Nietzsche pointed a way when he spoke of the "metaphysical solace" which all true tragedy brings, the strength that comes from the lived knowledge that "despite every phenomenal change, life is at bottom indestructibly joyful and powerful" (*The Birth of Tragedy*, section 7). Homer gives us the solace of this joy, above all by the unfailing, terrible joy of his language, and the lordly accent of his verse, admitting no defeat, grants the solace of this power. "Homer's princes bestride their world boldly," E. R. Dodds wrote.[5] Seldom again have we stood so high in our own eyes.

Ancient Mesopotamia thought less well of our kind. In the other most notable poem of the culture, the *Creation Epic*, it is accepted that man was created merely to serve the gods and allow them to live at ease. Certainly the *Gilgamesh Epic* quite lacks the Homeric confidence, and the latter part of the poem strikes a darker, disconsolate note. "Death is in my chamber when I sleep," Gilgamesh says, "and death is there wherever I set foot." Enkidu dies more grievously than Patroclus, not falling bravely in battle as a hero should, but wasting away of a fatal sickness on "the bed of terror" for twelve long days and nights, watched over by Gilgamesh, a *praeparatio mortis* grimmer than anything that Achilles has to bear. Appalled at the thought that he must face a like end, he sets out on a journey in search of the Babylonian Noah, Utnapishtim, "the only one of men by means of whom / he might find out how death could be avoided."

Utnapishtim won immortality through his piety, and was allowed to survive the flood in which the rest of the race perished. (It was the powerful description of the flood that so excited earlier students of the poem because of its resemblance to the account in Genesis.) After so many dangers Gilgamesh eventually reaches the patriarch, who tests his worthiness to win the privilege he seeks by requiring him to stay awake for six full days. Gilgamesh fails the test, but Utnapishtim's wife pleads that he be granted something in return for his long journey, so Utnaphistim tells him of a magical plant called How-the-Old-Man-Once-Again-Becomes-a-Young-Man. But here again Gilgamesh is unsuccessful, for having procured the plant it is stolen by a snake as he bathes in a pool. Accepting now that death cannot be evaded, Gilgamesh returns home and the poem ends, as it began, with the proud verses describing his city, Uruk. Though he himself, like all men, must die, the great city he built will endure and preserve his fame through the centuries.

In the *Iliad*, death is a familiar presence; there is no thought of escaping it. Man is the mortal one, βροτός, θνητός, death-directed from birth. In the Gilgamesh poem, death is experienced as an alien force that breaks unexpectedly into the fabric of human life. The shock to Gilgamesh of Enkidu's death is that it is something he never expected could happen, even though theoretically (a word hardly in place in this poem) he was already aware of mortality. "Only the gods / can live for ever. The life of man is short," he cried, holding out to Enkidu the consolation of the heroic code in order to persuade him to join in the expedition against the monster Huwawa. But this knowledge avails him nothing when faced with the actual fact of Enkidu's death, and he responds to it as though this were the first death in the world. "A demon has come and taken him away," he exclaims. "You are asleep. What has taken you into your sleep? / Your face is dark. How was your face made dark?"

In this respect, we may feel that there is something naïve, almost childlike, in the poet's vision. And yet the poem, so full of the gravity of the early world, strikes us as in no way immature, and perhaps we should rather say that it reaches further back than the *Iliad*, to an earlier stage in the human story. For it knows not only of the time when death first came, but offers an explanation of how it was that death came. So at least we may understand the opening episode, the account of Enkidu's life before he met Gilgamesh. We first see him as an *homme sauvage*, a mighty being still in the state of nature:

> the hairy-bodied wild man of the grasslands,
> powerful as Ninurta the god of war,
>
> the hair of his head like the grain fields of the goddess,
> naked as Sumuqan the god of cattle.
>
> He feeds upon the grasslands with gazelles;
> visits the watering places with the creatures
>
> whose hearts delight, as his delights, in water.

He is unlike Ted Hughes's wodwo, another reach into the mists of our origin, who is only dimly beginning to feel that he is no longer quite a part of the animal world ("What shall I be called am I the first / have I an owner what shape am I what / shape am I am I huge"). Enkidu is already poised on the verge of human status and needs only a push to pass over. It comes when the city wants someone to curb the oppressions of Gilgamesh's youthful surquidry. Hearing of Enkidu's great strength, the citizens send out a temple harlot called Shamhat to seduce him, and it is this, the experience of human sexuality, that brings about the change in him. (According to some accounts of Eden, it was only after the fall that Adam and Eve knew each other sexually.) His speed is no longer what it was, and the animals, with whom he had lived in amity, now run away from him. "But in the mind of the wild man / there was beginning a new understanding . . . [his] heart was beginning to show itself." To confirm his new status, Shamhat, a kindly girl, gives him cooked food and beer, "the food and drink / men eat and drink." They then go off to the city, Enkidu sees Gilgamesh, they wrestle mightily, and quickly become fast friends.

Had Enkidu remained in the wild living with the beasts, we may suppose that he would have enjoyed their species immortality. In becoming human, he becomes—though he does not yet know this—mortal. In Gilgamesh we see an inverse transformation. His mother was a goddess and he himself, we are told, is "two-thirds a god. The third part is mortal." As two-thirds divine, he presumably would have been immortal; there is a line in the Old Babylonian version tentatively translated "[Your mother] raised your head above death."[6] Bonded in heroic friendship with the mortal Enkidu, he becomes mortal himself. The pair of them, one moving from part god to all man, the other from part animal to all man, together constitute a full human being and provide an account of the development of our kind. We may take this not simply as an etiological myth, but rather as a poetic fable that throws light on the two aspects of our nature: a mind capable of transcending time and space tied to a vestigial animality that resists all attempts to overcome it.

The *Gilgamesh Epic*, fruit of three millennia of Mesopotamian meditation, "burdened, in its ancient way," as a classical scholar once wrote of Aeschylus, "with the mystery of all the unintelligible world,"[7] was read and admired throughout the Near East. Gradually its day passed —the latest datable cuneiform tablet belongs to the second or first century BC—and the poem finally sank into oblivion in the early years of the Christian era. Unknown for fifteen hundred years, it came to light again in the mid-nineteenth century, and thanks to the labors of an arduous, exacting philology, slowly began to assume its place as one of the great poems of the world. Hitherto, however, it has existed only *in posse*, waiting for a poet who could actualize it. David Ferry has performed this service, and given us a noble poem as close to the ancient original as we in our ignorance have any right to.

3

The Poem of Odysseus

THE *ODYSSEY* IS THE *ILIAD*'S WIFE, SAMUEL BUTLER OBSERVED IN HIS schooldays,[1] a quip that is quite to the point, for whether or not the same poet composed both poems (a question that is never likely to be settled), the poet of the *Odyssey* knew the *Iliad* very well. If we call the *Iliad* a war poem, or with Simone Weil the poem of force, the *Odyssey* is a postwar poem. Menelaos, who should be at ease in his great house, still grieves for the comrades he lost at Troy. We see Odysseus recovering from his long military service, putting himself together again, and learning the more difficult arts of peace, above all how to deal with women. In the *Iliad* women play a small though memorable part; in the *Odyssey* they are everywhere—even the man-eating sea devil Skylla is female. Odysseus has, when we first see him, to free himself from the amorous bondage of the goddess Kalypso, and earlier on in his story from the deadly-dangerous but alluring witch Kirke. More testing still at least to our romantic eyes is Nausikaa, the most attractive girl in classical literature. In the second half of the poem we find him, many rungs higher on the social scale, with his comrade-in-arms the great goddess Athena. "Two of a kind, we are," she says fondly (13.379 in Fitzgerald's translation, line 296 in Homer). And above all there is his wife, Penelope, whom he must wean from the cocoon of lonely grief that she has defensively spun around herself before he can reknit their marriage.

Hence it is that the *Odyssey* has often been called the first novel, for our own great narrative genre has much to say about the relations of the sexes, and is rich in the social nuances and psychological delicacies where Homer in his antique way is no less at ease. Readers have often wondered how a poem composed almost three millennia ago can offer so fine a register of moods and emotions and possess the "Jamesian precisions" that Pound saw in it.[2] At all events a very different poem from the *Iliad*, a huge tragic masterpiece that must be taken on its own terms before it will speak to ours, the *Odyssey* is an amenable poem open to all comers in search of delight, and from antiquity onwards has lent itself to a wide range of interpretation. And yet, strangely it must seem, we have had no really satisfactory translation, certainly nothing to stand beside Pope's *Iliad*, "that poetical wonder," as Johnson called it in his life of Pope. In 1961 Robert Fitzgerald's *Odyssey* appeared. Here at last was a translator who could "lift the great song again" (1.18 [cf. 10]), to borrow words from the prelude to his version, because he caught the music of Homer's Greek and heard the way his characters speak to each other. This is our classic version, effortlessly surpassing its several successors.

PRELUDE AND THE VOYAGES

We first hear of Odysseus in the opening scene of the poem as the gods gathered in council listen to Athena complain of the way they have neglected the great hero. The Trojan War ended years ago and he should have been back home; instead he has been detained by a minor goddess, Kalypso, on her island of Ogygia. Zeus, a Zeus more concerned with justice on earth than the somewhat pococurante supreme deity of the *Iliad*, assures her that he has Odysseus well in mind—the divine messenger Hermes is to go to the island and see to it that he is allowed to set out for home. We expect at this point to turn directly to the hero of the poem, but instead we follow Athena to Ithaka, where, disguised as a family friend called Mentes, she proposes to send Odysseus's son Telemakhos on a mission abroad to seek news of his father. The goddess is displeased by what she sees in Ithaka, a crowd of men living it up and behaving as though they owned the place. They "are here courting my mother," Telemakhos tells her, "and they use / our house as if it were a house to plunder" (1.293–94 [248]). Bad behavior, we agree, but the poet takes a graver view. He is in love with civilization, with the courtesies and seemly usages that could not play much part in wartime. He delights to be able to report that even in this disorderly ménage a few decent practices still prevail. As Telemakhos sits down with his guest, a maid

> brought them a silver finger bowl and filled it
> out of a beautiful spouting golden jug,
> then drew a polished table to their side.
> The larder mistress with her tray came by
> and served them generously. A carver lifted

> cuts of each roast meat to put on trenchers
> before the two.
>
> (1.170–76 [136–40])

These lines will be repeated a number of times in the poem. Even in Kirke's house in the woods the same civilities are observed (see 10.411–15 [368–72], with some variations). The ceremonies of civilization do not mean much to us today; we tend to see them as insincere, a gloss laid over the realities of human relations. To Homer they are very beautiful and their violation a more serious matter than we can imagine.

If there is a touch of Bronze Age Miss Manners about the poet of the *Odyssey*, and some justification for calling his poem the first novel, it must be said that it reaches well beyond the competence of that instructive lady and beyond the normal reach of the novel. There the natural world acts primarily as a background (in Jane Austen, bad weather means that a lady taking a walk may get the hem of her dress wet) against which the complexities of human relations can be explored. Being a poem, the *Odyssey* cannot but be open to the forces of nature and the fierce west wind can go shouting over the wine-dark sea. We feel that when a novelist lets nature speak out in this way he is poaching on the poet's preserve, as Hardy does in the pastoral episode at Talbothays Dairy in *Tess of the D'Urbervilles*, beginning chapter 16 with "On a thyme-scented, bird-hatching morning in May."

And there is another large region that the *Odyssey* claims as its own, one ignored by the poet of the *Iliad* and open only to the novelist if he first transforms it for his own sophisticated purposes: the region of faerie and folktale and fable—the world of myth. Myth the novel can hardly do without. In *The Europeans* Henry James re-creates an earlier America that is recognizably Eden, an Eden corrupted by the arrival of two Europeanized snakes, the Baroness Münster and her brother. In *Wuthering Heights*, Heathcliff is seen as a goblin, a demonic creature of the wild heath, but he must play his part in a household that was orderly before he came there. The mythical element is a pattern or design traced lightly beneath the realistic action. In Odysseus's adventures, however, where he has to deal with goddesses and ogres and a wind king who lives on a floating island, the mythical or folktale structure is dominant. Not that we are taken into the nursery to listen to these tales. It is not in the light that never was on sea or land that we meet these strange personages; they are set before us matter-of-factly, standing beneath what Kinglake called the strong vertical light of Homer's poetry.[3]

Enough for the present of the world of Odysseus; what of his poem's artful plotting and structure? A fine literary scholar of an earlier day, W. P. Ker, wrote soberly: "The labour and meditation of all the world has not discovered, for the purpose of narrative, any essential modification of the procedure of Homer."[4] And yet many scholars have taken "our seamless *Odyssey*," as Norman Austin called it, to be a conflation of shorter preexisting tales—no doubt to some extent it is: a great creator seldom creates ex nihilo—stitched together by a character known to German learning as the *Bearbeiter*, a redactor or editor who did the work skillfully, some have held, clumsily according to others, and left inconsistencies that careful analysis has revealed—inconsistencies, it must be said, that are bound to occur in any long work. These lines of inquiry are no longer so widely pursued, and the *Odyssey* is recovering its status as a finely unified poem. Yet there are still Homerists who would parcel it out to a number of hypothetical authors, an *A* poet who created an ur-*Odyssey*, a *T* poet who composed a poem about Telemakhos, and then *B* (the *Bearbeiter*) who fused the productions of poets *A* and *T*—and so forth.

Those who continue to find in Homer the virtues possessed by the great poets of later days, however, are more seriously challenged by the view, now generally held, that the author (or authors) of our poem belonged to a long tradition of oral poetry. From an oral poet composing at speed the refinements of pen-and-paper composition cannot be expected. A brilliant Scottish scholar, Douglas Young, proposed a different scenario, coming up with an unlettered eighteenth-century Gaelic bard called Duncan Macintyre capable of composing orally poems of up to five hundred lines as carefully considered as one could wish. Earning his keep as a game warden, Macintyre roamed the mountainous borders of Argyll and Perthshire meditating his poetry at leisure. Possessing a trained memory he was able to hold in his head what he had composed, going over and reshaping his verses until he had them the way he wanted.[5] Nothing prevents us from supposing that Homer worked in the same way as the wandering Gael.

The general reader will do well to leave these learned preoccupations to the learned and attend to the *Odyssey* as it has been handed down.[6] He will not go far wrong—indeed he will hardly go wrong at all—if he brings to Homer the same expectations that he brings to pen-poets like Virgil and Shakespeare. Immediately he comes on the evidence of design. Why, he may wonder, does the poem of Odysseus's homecoming leave him and turn to his son Telemakhos in Ithaka? In order that we may see through Athena's eyes the misrule in his house that he will eventually correct. The poem begins by pointing straight to its conclusion. Again, with a structural elegance that the reader can only admire, the poem at once sets in motion two parallel actions. On the orders of Zeus, Odysseus sets out on a journey that with one stop on the way will take him back to Ithaka. Telemakhos is sent by Athena to look for his father and when he has found him, we must suppose, bring him home.

Telemakhos's journey takes him first to Nestor, the veteran warrior of the *Iliad*, then to Menelaos, the husband of Helen, for whom the long war was fought. On neither visit does he learn much about his father except that he is still alive—Menelaos says that the sea-god Proteus saw him in Kalypso's island, held there against his will and unable to return home—but both visits tell the reader a good deal. The two men speak of their difficult voyages over seas that Odysseus sails on his far more difficult return, giving us a sense of the poem's geographical reach. And both houses serve to affirm the great theme of order and decorum. Telemakhos, accompanied by the disguised Athena, is received with a courtesy so lacking in Ithaka. The second visit is particularly rich—here is Homer the novelist showing us the fine manners of this great house and not at all overawed by the task of presenting a legendary beauty like Helen. She duly appears, a domestic figure but no doubt dressed in full rig and accompanied by two maidservants bringing her golden distaff and a silver basket holding her yarn. At once she guesses the young visitor's identity:

> ". . . This boy must be the son of Odysseus,
> Telémakhos, the child he left at home
> that year the Akhaian host made war on Troy—
> daring all for the wanton that I was."
>
> (4.154–57 [143–46])

She is still as full of herself as she was in the *Iliad* and freely admits, not without satisfaction, that her conduct has left much to be desired. Oh I was terribly wicked, I know, but how bravely they all fought for me! She recalls how when Odysseus came on a mission to Troy disguised as a beggar, she alone was clever enough to recognize him. Menelaos takes over and describes another of her performances: on the evening of the night when Troy was to be sacked she was out with a new boyfriend, and to amuse him as they strolled round the wooden horse in which the Akhaian commandos were crammed she imitated the voices of their wives. A writer like Flaubert would have seen this as a mark of the incurable *bêtise* of our species, and few writers would have cared to introduce this little scene at such a point, just before the tragic fall of the great city that was to reverberate through Western poetry. Homer takes it in his stride. He finds people too interesting to be shocked by the things they do.

A curious feature of the life in Menelaos's mansion is the note of sorrow that lies just below the surface. As the episode opens, the marriage of his son is being celebrated. His name is Megapenthes, Great Sorrow. Later, as the company sits drinking wine before dinner, Helen pours into their cups a few drops of a drug described as νηπενθής (4.221), which allays pain and makes men forget their sorrows. Why is it needed? It is natural that Menelaos should feel sad about the comrades he lost in the great war, yet this happened years ago and on the face of it he has much that should make him content. Enormously rich, he enjoys a princely style of life and is married to the most beautiful woman in the world, Helen, daughter of Zeus. True, she deserted him and ran off with a colorful playboy, Paris, but this too is past history and she is now a respectable married lady. Thanks to this alliance, moreover, he is strangely privileged. On his way home he spent some time in Egypt, where he was told by Proteus, Homer's Old Man of the Sea:

> ". . . you shall not die in the bluegrass land of Argos;
> rather the gods intend you for Elysion
> with golden Rhadamanthos at the world's end,
> where all existence is a dream of ease . . ."
>
> (4.598–601 [561–65])

No really satisfactory explanation is offered of the note of sorrow that is felt here, and to understand it we must turn—a deft transition linking the Telemachy to the Odyssey—to the next book, which at last lets us meet face-to-face the hero of the poem, much-enduring, resourceful Odysseus. He too is living with a beautiful companion, the goddess Kalypso, who can grant him a life that will not end in death. "I fed him, loved him, sang that he should not die," she says, "nor grow old, ever, in all the days to come" (5.142–43 [135–36]). Her island of Ogygia is as lovely and as easeful as the Elysion that awaits Menelaos, so beautiful that "Even a god who found this place / would gaze, and feel his heart beat with delight" (5.79–80 [73–74]). Yet there is something disquieting, even sinister, about it. Black poplars grow there, trees that, as we hear later, are also found in Persephone's grove in the world of the dead (10.565–66 [509–10]). Cypresses too, funerary trees in the Mediterranean.[7] Her name suggests that she is the Hider (καλύπτειν, to hide), fittingly so called, for she has hidden Odysseus, withdrawing him from the life of heroic action. He was happy there at first and we can understand why. After his trials at war and at sea, her island paradise must have come as a blessed relief, but her spell has worn off and she "had ceased to please," Homer says laconically (5.161 [153]).

We would like to know more of how he spent his earlier years with Kalypso, but only the bare outlines of the story are given and we are left to imagine our way into it as best we can. There may be something to learn from the name of her island, Ogygia. The adjective ὠγύγιος means in Greek "primeval." It is an ancient place belonging to another time zone where, we guess, human life was part of the circular life of nature that men left behind them when they set out on their restless linear course. What did they do, this odd pair, what did they talk about? Cautiously we may seek help from a modern writer with a sense of ancient things, Cesare Pavese. Scholarship provides the approved highway to our older literature, but there are unlicensed byways that may lead there too. In his *Dialogues with Leucò* Pavese gives us a snatch of their conversation. His Kalypso speaks of herself as one of the pre-Olympian gods forgotten by the world. Once, she tells her Greek friend, "I had terrible names . . . The earth and sea obeyed me. Then I grew tired. Time passed. I lost the will to move."[8] Odysseus too lost it and let himself be lulled into an endless life of slothful ease. But mere existence denied the outlet to action could not long satisfy Odysseus, and upon his arrival Hermes bid Kalypso send Odysseus on his way again. He recovered his will and with it the noble virtue which the Greeks called σωφροσύνη, not "moderation," the lackluster sense to which the word was reduced when poetry ceded its place as the *magister vitae* to prose and philosophy, but rather "man's pride," as Camus understood it, "fidelity to his limits, lucid love of his condition" ("Helen's Exile"). Had he stayed with Kalypso, he would have been not a god but godlike in his freedom from death. But Odysseus wanted to be a man, what Greek poetry calls a θνητός, a mortal being subject to death, θάνατος, as distinct from the gods, the ἀθάνατοι, whose differentia is that they do not die.

Here we need no help from a modern writer, for Homer gives us what we want in the conversation between Odysseus and Kalypso when she learns that he is resolved to leave her. She addresses him in full heroic style:

"Son of Laërtês, versatile Odysseus . . ."

Fifteen times in the poem he is addressed in this way. It is used here for the first time. She continues:

". . . after these years with me, you still desire
your old home? Even so, I wish you well.

If you could see it all, before you go—
all the adversity you face at sea—
you would stay here, and guard this house, and be
immortal—though you wanted her forever,
that bride for whom you pine each day.
Can I be less desirable than she is?
Less interesting? Less beautiful? Can mortals
compare with goddesses in grace and form?"

To this the strategist Odysseus answered . . .

(Literally, the Greek reads: "The resourceful Odysseus spoke in turn
and answered her." Fitzgerald regularly refashions lines of this sort to
suit the context.) This introductory verse will be used repeatedly; it
is used here for the first time and marks Odysseus's recovery of heroic
status. Homer's formulaic style, as it is called (an adjective better
suited to chemistry than to poetry), can be beautifully functional. He
replies:

. . . "My lady goddess, here is no cause for anger.
My quiet Penélopê—how well I know—
would seem a shade before your majesty,
death and old age being unknown to you,
while she must die. Yet, it is true, each day
I long for home, long for the sight of home.
If any god has marked me out again
for shipwreck, my tough heart can undergo it.
What hardship have I not long since endured
at sea, in battle! Let the trial come."

(5.212–33 [203–24])

Gracefully the goddess yields and provides him with the tools and
timber that he needs to build a boat. A man of parts if ever there was
one, he makes a very professional job of it, the first bit of real work
he has done for seven years. Where Menelaos surrendered and paid
the price of surrender by the sadness that underlies the account of
his splendid life with an easeful immortality to come granted him
through his wife, Odysseus recovers his will and rejects what Kalypso
offers him in favor of full human life with death at the end. He could
do nothing else and still be Odysseus. Keeping faith with our great
and in some ways disastrous tradition, he pursues his linear course
and sets out once more on the cruel sea.

It is an old story. The Elizabethan poet Samuel Daniel, with the
fervor of the Renaissance in his veins, gives it lyrical expression in his

poetic dialogue "Ulysses and the Syren." He might equally have called her Kalypso. She begins:

> Come worthy Greeke, Ulysses come
> Possesse these shores with me;
> The windes and Seas are troublesome,
> And here we may be free.
> Here may we sit, and view their toile
> That travaile in the deepe,
> And ioy the day in mirth the while,
> And spend the night in sleepe.

He replies:

> Faire Nimph, if fame or honor were
> To be attayned with ease
> Then would I come, and rest me there,
> And leave such toyles as these.
> But here it dwels, and here must I
> With danger seek it forth,
> To spend the time luxuriously
> Becomes not men of worth.

The temptress tells him that the dangers he pursues lead only to human misery and war. Her pleas have no effect on him:

> But yet the state of things require
> These motions of unrest,
> And these great Spirits of high desire
> Seeme borne to turne them best.

A run-of-the-mill narrator would probably have sent Odysseus straight home at this point, but to pass directly from Kalypso's enchanted realm to the everyday bread-and-butter world of Ithaka would have been jarringly abrupt, so—a beautifully pivotal transition—he is sent to the happy land of the Phaiakians, human beings but kinsmen of the gods, Zeus calls them, and free from the normal constraints of mankind. Remote enough not to be threatened by enemies, blest with a climate that allows trees to bear fruit twice a year, possessing uncannily clever ships that know where to go without the aid of a pilot, they indulge in the pleasant rivalry of athletics, and the upper crust listen to a minstrel singing songs of love and war while they sit feasting. Before reaching this haven, however, Odysseus has one more trial to endure. His voyage from Kalypso's island begins well and for seventeen days his little craft speeds on, driven by favoring breezes sent by the goddess until his old enemy Poseidon, still angry with him for putting out the eye of his son Polyphemos, wakes up to what is happening and launches a storm that sinks his boat, leaving him to swim for his life to shore. Worn out, naked, he covers himself with leaves and sinks into the long sleep of exhaustion.

His awaking could hardly be more pleasant. This ancient poem shrugs off its years and like nothing in classical and little in later poetry comes to us fresh as paint in the colors of morning. The narrative moves so easily that it seems to tell itself, bringing the goddess Athena to visit Nausikaa in a dream. You will soon be married, she says, and should see that your linen is freshly washed. So next morning the girl has a word with her father, King Alkinoos—πάππα φίλε she calls him, "my dear Papà," Fitzgerald translates (6.63 [57]) with a touch of the right formality, not the homespun "daddy dear" with Richmond Lattimore (1967) and Robert Fagles (1996)—and asks if she may have a wagon to take the family laundry to the shore to be washed. Alkinoos can deny her nothing and her mother is equally accommodating. For their luncheon she packed a hamper

> with picnic fare, and filled a skin of wine,
> and, when the princess had been handed up,
> gave her a golden bottle of olive oil
> for softening girls' bodies, after bathing.
> Nausikaa took the reins and raised her whip,
> lashing the mules. What jingling! What a clatter!
> (6.84–89 [76–82])

Nausikaa and the party of girlfriends who come with her get busy on the washing, take "a dip themselves," then play ball. At one point Nausikaa throws the ball too far and the girls' cries wake Odysseus up. He handles the situation with his usual aplomb. He is famished and badly needs help, but how to get it? Act as a suppliant and clasp her knees? No, that might offend her, so he stands a little distance away and

> let the soft words fall:
> "Mistress: please: are you divine, or mortal?"
> (6.160–61 [148–49])

He begins by comparing her beauty to that of the goddess Artemis, then hits on a trope that touches us more directly, one that by the happiest of chances was to occur to the first great poet of our language:

> "Never have I laid eyes on equal beauty
> in man or woman. I am hushed indeed.

So fair, one time, I thought a young palm tree
at Delos near the altar of Apollo—. . ."

(6.172–75 [160–63])

Chaucer says of the frisky young woman in "The Miller's Tale":

She was ful moore blisful on to see
Than is the newe pere-jonette tree.

Rather calculatingly Odysseus ends by putting into her head the idea
of marriage. It distinctly appeals to her—this stranger is a most interesting man, good-looking, too (Athena gives him a head of red-
golden hair with curls like petals of the wild hyacinth). Nausikaa has
enchanted many readers, but there is no indication that this young
beauty interested Odysseus. All in all he probably preferred his goddesses, more experienced ladies.

She tells him how to make his way to her father's grand house. He
will be in his great chair facing the fire: "there like a god he sits and
takes his wine." Odysseus is to go past him and make his appeal to
Queen Arete:

". . . cast yourself before my mother,
embrace her knees—and you may wake up soon
at home rejoicing, though your home be far.
On Mother's feeling much depends; if she
looks on you kindly, you shall see your friends
under your own roof in your father's country."

(6.328–334 [309–15])

Odysseus is probably coming to realize that were he to remain in Phaiakia he would find himself repeating his experience in Ogygia: living
very well but submitting to the will of women.

He is made welcome and moves freely among these fortunate
people, joining in their sports and revealing his heroic strength by
casting the discus farther than anyone else, and listening to their
minstrel making fine poetry of an episode during the Trojan war. Recalling his own sufferings there, he weeps, but to these people war is
merely matter of an evening's entertainment. Questioned by Alkinoos about his identity, he shows that he, too, possesses the minstrel's
art and relates the full story of his voyages, beginning by proudly naming himself, an essential step in his recovery:

". . . I am Laërtês' son, Odysseus.

                                          Men hold me

formidable for guile in peace and war:
this fame has gone abroad to the sky's rim.
My home is on the peaked sea-mark of Ithaka . . ."

(9.20–23 [19–21])

At this point Homer as it were hands the poem over to his hero, letting Odysseus himself tell the story of his voyages. They take him to
strange regions, to the world of folktale and fable. Odysseus, however,
belongs to a very different world and a very different genre, that of
heroic saga and epic poetry with its own characteristic diction and
meter. By letting Odysseus tell his story in first-person narrative,
Homer goes a long way towards solving the problem of inserting
into a heroic poem unheroic material that has no business there.
Odysseus says that he met these outlandish figures, and we are prepared to believe him. Once he gets back to Ithaka there is no reason
for him to continue to assume the role of narrator, for by this point
the action takes place on solid human ground even though here too
the theme belongs to folklore, the widely diffused tale of a man who
after many years returns home and finds that his wife has remained
faithful to him.

Before he begins his story, Odysseus singles out two of his experiences. After naming his homeland he says:

". . . I shall not see on earth a place more dear,
though I have been detained long by Kalypso,
loveliest among goddesses, who held me
in her smooth caves, to be her heart's delight,
as Kirkê of Aiaia, the enchantress,
desired me, and detained me in her hall . . ."

(9.31–36 [27–32])

The poetic freedom of Fitzgerald's translation misses something in
the Greek. Homer says that Kalypso detained him in her caves desiring to make him her husband, in the same way that Kirke detained
him in her dwelling desiring to make him her husband—the identical phrase is repeated. For whatever reason, he begins by naming the
two goddesses (Kirke is a goddess too) who both wanted the same
thing, to make a husband of the man who is already a husband, Penelope's. We don't make much of this at the time, but it comes to mind
later when we notice that a number of apparently unrelated episodes
are linked in some way with each other.[9]

The first adventure, the attack on the Kikones, presents no problem, for they are a historical people living to the north of Troy in
Thrace (modern Turkey) and are mentioned in Herodotus's history.

What Odysseus describes is the kind of buccaneering raid that the Akhaian heroes in the *Iliad* went in for when they were not fighting the Trojans, a foolish affair that nearly ends in disaster. The raiders collect some plunder, but the Kikones rally and attack, and Odysseus and his men are sent running back to their ships, suffering heavy casualties. They set sail across the Aegean intending to make for home, but winds drive them around Malea, the southeastern cape of the Peloponnese, and then way off course southward to a coast inhabited by people who live on the Lotos flower. They are now right off the map into fabulous territory, but the Greek genius is little given to romance fantasy, and although the Lotos Eaters have no historical reality they are recognizable enough, members of our own society indeed, aimless folk who drift away their minds and memories as they munch their honeyed plant. Some of the crew are tempted by the life these feckless dropouts lead—"they longed to stay forever, browsing on / that native bloom, forgetful of their homeland" (9.103–4 [95–97])—and have to be driven forcibly back to their ships. The temptation the Lotos Eaters present, to sit back and relax the will, specifically to lose the desire to return home, the magnetic attraction that keeps Odysseus on the go, is one that will be found in several of these stories. He himself is untouched by what they offer; the indignity of vegetable repose can get no purchase on his iron will.

"In the next land we found were Kyklopês," he continues; among them dwells one Polyphemos (generally referred to as the Kyklops), a giant man-eating ogre with only one eye. The story that follows is adapted from a folktale found in many parts of the world. Typically it begins like this version from Serbia:

> A priest and his scholar were once walking though a great mountainous region when night overtook them. Seeing a fire burning in a cave some way off, they made for it. On reaching the cave they found nobody in it except a giant with one eye in his forehead. They asked him if he would let them enter and he answered, "Yes." But the mouth of the cave was blocked with a huge stone, which a hundred men could not have stirred. The giant arose, lifted the stone, and let them in. Then he rolled back the stone into the mouth of the cave and lit a great fire. The travelers sat down beside it and warmed themselves. When they had done so, the giant felt their necks in order to know which was the fatter that he might kill and roast him.

And so forth.[10]

Odysseus tells his story in the manner of an anthropologist describing some primitive people, though he doesn't always sound sufficiently objective. He begins by calling them "giants, louts, without a law to bless them," but then gets down to the job and reports their soil to be so rich that

> ". . . In ignorance leaving the fruitage of the earth in mystery
> to the immortal gods,

[more literally "trusting in the immortal gods"]

> they neither plow
> nor sow by hand, nor till the ground, though grain—
> wild wheat and barley—grows untended, and
> wine-grapes, in clusters, ripen in heaven's rain . . ."
>   (9.113–19 [106–10])

That is, these loutish giants live as virtuous men did in the Golden Age. They hold no town meetings, Odysseus goes on professionally, nor do they have any common legal system, but each one deals out rough justice in his own home. They possess a good natural harbor, yet they make no use of it, knowing nothing of ships or seafaring. Clearly this is a place that should be developed—"seagoing folk would have annexed it" (9.141). These words, it must be said, are not in the Greek; Fitzgerald is making a justifiable guess at what is in Odysseus's mind. Greek colonialism was under way in the eighth century BC, the probable period of the poem's composition.

He and his men head for a cave that they have seen from shipboard. A prodigious man lives there alone, he says, a complete savage. Since they have only just arrived, we are bound to wonder how he knows this. They find the cave well provisioned with racks full of cheese and pens crowded with lambs and kids. Let's grab this loot and run for it, the men say, but Odysseus wants to stay and have a word with the proprietor. The Kyklops appears and sits down to milk the ewes, obviously a skilled dairyman, since he makes a practiced job of it. Hardly what one expects of an oversized cannibal. Odysseus asks that he give them good treatment, reminding them that "Zeus will avenge / the unoffending guest" (9.291–92 [270–71]). Since they have just been proposing to raid his stores, this is a piece of effrontery that the giant brushes aside. "We Kyklopês / care not a whistle for your thundering Zeus / or all the gods in bliss" (9.298–300 [275–76]). Yet Odysseus has just told us that they trust in the immortal gods. A slip of the tongue? He knows, however, how to deal with characters of this sort:

> ". . . A wineskin full
> I brought along, and victuals in a bag,

for in my bones I knew some towering brute
would be upon us soon—all outward power,
a wild man, ignorant of civility . . ."

(9.227–31 [212–15])

Hardly the obvious means of defense against a towering brute.

The Kyklops—or let him sometimes have his name, Polyphemos—
at once seizes a couple of the men and devours them raw. Appalled,
Odysseus is about to draw his sword and run him through when he
reflects that if he does so they will be unable to get out of the cave,
since Polyphemos has blocked the entrance with a boulder too big
for anyone but himself to shift. Never at a loss, Odysseus once again
knows how to deal with the difficulty. Next morning when the brute,
after having had a couple more men for breakfast, goes off to pasture
his flock (reblocking the entrance), Odysseus takes a great wooden
log—the Kyklops uses it as a cane, a cruel touch—and, cutting it down
to size, hews it to make a stake with a pointed end. Back comes Kyklops in the evening and Odysseus plies him with the wine he has
brought. Becoming more cordial in his cups, he asks the visitor's name.
"My name is Nohbdy" (9.398 [366]), Odysseus replies, an old joke
that will soon be put to good use.[11] In high good humor, the Kyklops
turns witty: Well, Nohbdy, he says, I've a gift for you—I'll eat you last!
and then falls heavily asleep. This gives Odysseus the chance to put
his plan into operation. He takes the log from the embers where he
has hidden it—we are not told that the weather is cold, so why is
there a fire in the cave, since the Kyklops doesn't cook his victims?
The story, however, needs a fire to heat the spiked log (Why? The log
will serve its purpose as it is) to drill out the brute's eye and allow
Odysseus and his men to escape undetected. The nasty business of
the blinding proceeds according to plan and the Kyklops yells in
agony. His fellows come to ask him what the matter is, and now for
the great joke:

"Why are you shouting? Has somebody hurt you?"
"Nohbdy has hurt me."
"If nobody's hurt you, why are you shouting?"

They make their escape next morning tied under the bellies of
the rams with Odysseus clinging for dear life to the woolliest ram—
another piece of Odyssean cunning. The flock leaves the cave, a handsome ram usually their leader in the rear. The Kyklops pats him and
says, showing an affectionate side to his nature that we had not expected, "Sweet cousin ram, why lag behind the rest? . . . Can you be

grieving / over your Master's eye?" (9.487–94 [447–53]). Blindly he follows the men as they rush to their ships and get away—only just, for Odysseus is rash enough to taunt him by describing the trick he has played and to identify himself—he who was Nobody is now Somebody, Odysseus! This nearly leads to disaster, for the Kyklops tears off the top of a hill big enough to sink them, then prays to his divine father Poseidon to punish the man who has injured him. The god hears his prayer and will cause Odysseus a lot of trouble on his later voyages.

This celebrated episode reads well but has some odd features. How does Odysseus know that a prodigious man lives in the cave? Why does he take wine rather than a long spear to defend himself? The explanation must be that this is first-person narrative not quite perfectly handled, with the archnarrator Homer making the fictional narrator Odysseus know things that he cannot possibly know, a fault that novelists were sometimes to be guilty of. It is Homer who knows about the inhabitant of the cave, adding this detail as a way of promising an exciting story to come. It is Homer, not Odysseus, who knows that the plot is going to require some wine.[12] Some faults are due to Homer's drawing on different versions of the story. "In the common folk-tale," Denys Page tells us, "the giant cooks his victim on a spit over the fire. When he is asleep the hero takes the spit, heats it in the fire, and plunges it into the giant's eye. The *Odyssey* [almost] alone among all versions of this folk-tale, substitutes a log of olive-wood for the spit."[13] It may also be Homer, whose all-embracing humanity can reach beyond the human realm to the animal, who gives the Kyklops a pet ram, an affecting trait quite inconsistent with the way that Odysseus depicts him.

Some anomalies may be due not to Homer but to the fictional narrator whose account of Kyklopean culture is designed to show him in a good light. If we look through this account we see a very different picture, a pretechnological people who do not welcome intruders with designs on their land. To eat them is admittedly a bit much, but the story requires a man-eater, so Polyphemos's cannibalism cannot be omitted. Perhaps the other Kyklopes do not have this bad habit. They enjoy a prelapsarian existence and trust in the immortal gods to grant them the fruits of the earth without labor. And yet Odysseus represents Polyphemos as saying that Kyklopes don't give a damn for the gods.

Faults in this story there undoubtedly are, but frankly they don't much matter. Most people never notice them. And before we blame Homer for being careless, we should bear in mind that this is only the second of the tales he puts in Odysseus's mouth, and he has not yet quite mastered the difficult art of first-person narrative. He becomes more skillful as he goes on.

On next to the floating island of Aiolos the wind king. Islands of this sort are said to be a common feature of seamen's yarns, but the picture that Homer presents (Odysseus hardly seems to be speaking here) suggests a more elevated source, certainly in Fitzgerald's translation, which gives the description of this little realm a fragile grace hardly present in the Greek, which is more matter-of-fact:

> Twelve children had old Aiolos at home—
> six daughters and six lusty sons—and he
> gave girls to boys to be their gentle brides;
> now those lords, in their parents' company,
> sup every day in hall—a royal feast
> with fumes of sacrifice and winds that pipe
> 'round hollow courts; and all the night they sleep
> on beds of filigree beside their ladies.
>
> (10.6–13 [5–12])

Nowhere does the poem move so far from everyday reality; this sweetly ceremonious household is half fairy-tale enchantment, half ancient Egypt where son married daughter to preserve the purity of the line. Odysseus is kindly welcomed and Aiolos gives him a bag of winds to waft him safely home. His men, alas, thinking that the bag contains gifts for Odysseus but none for them tear it open, the winds break loose, and a storm drives them back to Aiolos's island, where they are sent off in disgrace. They sail next to a land occupied by giant cannibals called Laistrygones, but having recently had a fine tale about a giant cannibal we are not very engaged and may be forgiven for thinking that Homer nods here. He includes this brief episode, it has been suggested, because the story was popular but had been associated with a different hero. The only positive contribution it makes to the narrative is that as Odysseus's little fleet is desperately pulling away from land the Laistrygones bombard them with boulders (just as the Kyklops had done), sinking every ship except his own.

But if Homer nods here, he is wide awake when he comes to the story of Kirke. Some scholars have complained that she is merely a variation of Kalypso. It is better to see her, with Stephen Scully, as an example of deliberate doubling. In no sense, however, is this story repetitious, for Kirke is a stranger, more sinister figure and this is a more complex story. Like other characters whom Odysseus meets, she belongs to folklore, a type of the witch who lures travelers to her home, transforms them into animals, and sometimes eats them. (Hansel and Gretel provide the children's version.) Yet if she is part witch, she is also a goddess, seemingly young and beautiful.

A day or so after arriving on her island, Odysseus climbs a hill to survey the territory and looks for signs of human habitation. Seeing smoke rise from a house in the woods, he sends a party of men to reconnoiter. Approaching the house, they come on lions and wolves ensorcelled, we are told, by Kirke. They are quite tame and fawn on the men. She welcomes them into her house where she gives them a drugged potion "to make them lose / desire or thought of [their] dear father land" (10.260–61 [236])—we seem to have heard of something like this before—then waves her magic wand and transforms them into pigs. The leader of the party, seeing no one come out, suspects mischief and goes back to report to Odysseus. He sets off to do what he can for his men and on the way meets Hermes disguised as a young man who gives him a plant called *molü* that has the power to render him immune to Kirke's witchery. Odysseus goes in and she gives him a drink, first adding a pinch of her drug. It has no effect on him, thanks to the *molü*, we assume, but we would expect to be told what he did with the plant—break off a piece perhaps and put it in his cup. But Homer (here again we seem to be listening to Homer rather than Odysseus) has no taste for magic and is content simply to mention the plant as a way of describing Odysseus's immunity. His interest is rather in Kirke's words when she sees that she has failed to bewitch him: "Hale must your heart be and your tempered will" (10.370 [329]). Fagles's rendering, "you have a mind in you no magic can enchant," is closer to the Greek, but Fitzgerald, whose translation is as usual interpretative rather than literal, rightly sees that what saves Odysseus is his will.

Having failed to transform him, Kirke now proposes to use another weapon in her arsenal: she invites him into her bed. He rejects her offer until he has made her swear a great oath that she will not harm him, fearing that once she has him stripped she will take his manhood. This is most readily understood as referring to castration, but that is not the threat she poses and the Greek should be taken to mean "make me other than a man"—like the lions and wolves outside her house, transformed, we are told, by her evil drug?[14] No, these must be victims of Kirke in her other aspect, not witch but goddess in search of human lovers whom she transforms once she tires of them, like the Babylonian Ishtar, who, Denys Page conjectures, "may well be the prototype of the Homeric Circe."[15] In the Near Eastern epic Ishtar seeks the love of Gilgamesh, who rejects her, reminding her of what happened to other mortals who succumbed to her advances:

Who were your lovers and bridegrooms? Tammuz the slain,
whose festival wailing is heard, year after year . . .

You broke the great wild horse and snaffled him:

he drinks the water his hobbled hooves have muddied.
The goatherd who brought you cakes and daily for you

slaughtered a kid, you turned him into a wolf . . .

You loved Ishullanu, your father's gardener,

who brought you figs and dates to adorn your table . . .

Some say the goddess turned him into a frog . . .

some say into a mole whose blind foot pushes

over and over again against the loam
in the dark of the tunnel, baffled and silent, forever.

And you would do with me as you did with them.[16]

Odysseus is content simply to negotiate his own safety and, having done
so, demands that she return his men to human form. She does so and
a strange scene follows:

Their eyes upon me, each one took my hands,
and wild regret and longing pierced them through,
so the room rang with sobs.

(10.441–43 [397–99])

That their restoration should be an emotional moment is understandable, but why the wild regret and longing? (More literally, "a
yearning sorrow," which amounts to much the same thing.) What is
it that they yearn for? Can it really be that they would sooner have
been left as they were to gruntle in their sty rather than be forced
back into human life with all its trials and dangers? A strange suggestion but one that the poem will support. There were those who were
willing to accept the groundling existence offered by the Lotos Eaters
and had to be driven back wailing to their ships. Odysseus himself
accepted the slothful ease that Kalypso offered, and he does the
same thing here, spending a year as Kirke's lover and getting under
way again only when his men reproach him: "Captain, shake off this

trance, and think of home" (10.521 [472]). Even his iron will can be softened[17]—as Menelaos's will was softened by Helen, who, like Kirke, adds to the wine she offers her guests a substance that allays sorrow, a milder form of Kirke's potion but working to the same end, a variation of the same theme.

They cannot make directly for home, Kirke tells them. They must first journey to the underworld. The famous episode that follows, Homer's book of the dead, which inspired Virgil and through Virgil Dante, has often been seen as occupying a pivotal place in the poem. It should, but does it? Aeneas's descent to the dead in book 6 of the *Aeneid* really is pivotal, preparing him for the role he is to play in the second half of the poem as founder of a new civilization on Italian soil. He is granted a vision of Roman heroes to come and learns of the nature of Rome's destined achievement as notable in the political sphere as that of Greece in the cultural. Nothing comparable is found in Homer's book of the dead. The ostensible purpose of Odysseus's visit is to consult the prophet Teiresias, who gives him only one useful piece of advice: not to lay hands on the cattle of the Sun god when he comes to his island of Thrinakia. The prophet also tells him of some rough sea passages he must still face, and that on reaching Ithaka he will find the lawless suitors of his wife, Penelope, in possession of his house. But he is not told how to deal with the situation there.

Not that Odysseus's descent is irrelevant. There is a moving encounter with the shade of his mother that reveals an aspect of his character we had not suspected. She says to him:

> ". . . only my loneliness for you, Odysseus,
> for your kind heart and counsel, gentle Odysseus,
> took my own life away."
>
> (11.225–27 [203–4])

And there is the vision he is granted (lines 267ff. [225ff.]) of what W. B. Stanford calls "a masque or pageant of beautiful women"[18] (the classical profession prefers to speak of a catalogue, a word best left to Sears, Roebuck). This is not essential, yet in his postscript Fitzgerald claims—and if anyone has a right to speak of the *Odyssey* he has—that "the honor roll of lovely dead ladies . . . is fully appropriate to this poem." Appropriate that a work so much concerned with women, young and beautiful or seemingly so like the goddesses, judicious like Queen Arete, wise like Penelope, should include this accolade, this pageant of storied beauties some of whom enjoyed the supreme privilege of marriage with a god, the gracious infusion of divine strength in mortal stock that antiquity called the Sacred Marriage (ἱερὸς γάμος), a stumbling block to some in later classical days and a scandal to Christian readers. Strangely, this ancient mystery has come to life again in the poetry of the twentieth century, in Yeats and Pound.

After this there is a break in the narrative and we return to Phaiakia, where Odysseus is telling his story:

> Down the shadowy hall
> the enchanted banqueters were still. Only
> the queen with ivory pale arms, Arêtê, spoke.
> (11.387–90 [333–35])

Here indeed is a man to honor! she tells them; we must load him with precious gifts when he leaves us.

The tone grows darker when he resumes his account. He speaks first of his meeting with some of his old companions-in-arms, a reminder, after so many folktale adventures, of the heroic breed to which he belongs. Agamemnon tells how on coming home he was killed by his wife, one of the poem's several contrasts between his return and that of Odysseus. Akhilleus tells of the wretched life of the dead—better to be the meanest serf on earth than a prince in the world below. Odysseus next sees some of the archetypal sinners, Tantalos and others, paying for their crimes. Only at the very end of the book are we made to feel that he is coming face-to-face with death itself, the terror of death. There is a commotion among the shades and he is afraid that Persephone "had brought from darker hell some saurian death's head" (11.754 [634–35]), Fitzgerald's powerful rendering of a strange line, rather more literally, "the grim spectral head of some dread monster" (Stanford), still more literally "the head of the Gorgon [which had the power to turn into stone whoever looked upon it], that dread monster." Elsewhere the splendor of the poetic imagination brings the shades so vividly to life that we have little sense of being in the world of the dead or that Odysseus, in going down there, has himself experienced a kind of death. Hence Homer's *descensus ad inferos* does not have the pivotal effect it might otherwise have possessed, with Odysseus's "death" serving as the prelude to the rebirth that awaits him when finally he sets foot on his native land.

Odysseus's little company now returns to Kirke, no longer a dangerous figure, who welcomes them warmly and tells of perils to come. First are the Sirens—or "Seirenes," as Fitzgerald calls them—who sing a man's mind away. He who hears their song, she tells him, "will not see his lady nor his children / in joy, crowding about him, home from sea" (12.51–52 [42–43])—like those who ate the Lotos plant and became "forgetful of their homeland"—another link or recall. Next comes the narrow sea-pass between the whirlpool Kharybdis and the man-eating monster Skylla before whom he must take flight; then the island of the Sun of which Teiresias spoke. It may not be clear why Odysseus's final adventures are predicted in this way, with the risk of weakening the force of the adventures when they come, but it serves to give his voyages a new sense of direction. Hitherto he made land on this coast or that largely by chance or impelled by some power beyond his control. However this may be, we can combine prediction and event.

As he draws near the island of the Sirens, they address him in a lilting line (12.184) that asks to be sung:

δεῦρ᾽ ἄγ᾽ ἰών, πολύαιν᾽ Ὀδυσεῦ, μέγα κῦδος Ἀχαιῶν.

Literally, "come hither, famous Odysseus, great glory of the Akhaians," but Fitzgerald hears the sweetly rhyming vowels—*iōn aiōn, lu du ku, ain ai*—and he turns Homer's hexameter into a lyric:

> *This way, oh turn your bows,*
>   *Akhaia's glory,*
> *As all the world allows —*
>   *Moor and be merry.*
>
>   (12.220–24)

What they go on to offer, however is not the South Seas beguilement we expect from these enchantresses but knowledge, knowledge of the Trojan War and of all that happens on the fruitful earth. (Fitzgerald's *"No life on earth can be / Hid from our dreaming,"* 12.244–45 (191), plays down the sense of the Greek.)

> *Sea rovers here take joy*
>   *Voyaging onward,*
> *As from our song of Troy*
> *Greybeard and rower-boy*
>   *Goeth more learnèd.*
>
> *All feats on that great field*
>   *In the long warfare,*
> *Dark days the bright gods willed,*
>   *Wounds you bore there.*
>
>   (12.232–40 [188–90])

Had he stayed to listen to their singing he would have been trapped in the memory of his past instead of going forward into the future where a more difficult victory is to be won. The temptation to stay on this deadly shore strewn with the bones of those who let themselves be enchanted is so powerful that he must be tied to the mast and have the sailors' ears plugged with wax to prevent them from hearing the siren call or hearing him when he begs to be set free.

This is the keenest test that Odysseus has had to face, but something worse and stranger is coming, the encounter with Skylla. Kirke told him:

> ". . . That nightmare cannot die, being eternal
> evil itself—horror, and pain, and chaos;
> there is no fighting her, no power can fight her,
> all that avails is flight. . ."
>
> (12.139–41 [118–20])

Readers who cannot directly consult the original are likely to wonder if they can trust the translation here. Surely "eternal evil" intensified by "itself" belongs to a religious thinking beyond Homer's ken? Other translators have thought so. Lattimore writes: "Scylla is no mortal thing but a mischief immortal"; Fagles has "Scylla's no mortal, she's an immortal devastation." Earlier translators fought shy of the Greek in the same way.[19] There is no nightmare or chaos in the Greek, it must be granted, but there is ἀθάνατον κακόν, for which "immortal evil" or "eternal evil" is a valid translation. Beyond the range of Homeric diction the expression is not, for in the *Iliad* we find the war god Ares described as a τυκτὸν κακόν (5.831), "a wrought evil," or however one should translate it. If, however, the expression does seem to be beyond the bounds of Greek thought, we should allow that great poets can on occasion reach past the limits of their culture: witness only *Antony and Cleopatra*, where, in Christian England, Shakespeare creates a world untouched by the religion. Can we be so sure of the Greek master's range that we deny him a comparable power?

We should not take the words ἀθάνατον κακόν out of their context, but neither should we underrate their presence there. If we let them mean what they say, they assume an importance out of all proportion to the brevity of the scene. This is the supreme challenge that Odysseus must face to prepare him to return home and set the great wrong right. His visit to the underworld might have presented such a challenge, but it is hard to believe that it does. Here he meets something worse than death, evil, not so much metaphysical evil but rather a power, a malevolence, in nature that threatens man's tenure in the world. He had known the cruelty of the sea, but here it is concentrated in the single figure of the devil hag waiting to grab and devour his men. To put heart in them, he compares this danger with a previous one which they survived, just as he paired his experiences with Kalypso and Kirke before he began the story of his travels. "Have we never been in danger before this?" he asks them. "More fearsome, is it now, than when the Kyklops / penned us in his cave?" (12.270–72 [208–10]). Forgetting Kirke's injunction not to try to fight Skylla, he arms himself and picks up his two spears, a foolish piece of Iliadic bravado. He fails the test, in a sense—perhaps it is too much for any man—but he and his men get away, all but six, whom Skylla seizes.

They next make landfall at Thrinakia, "the island of the world's delight, the Sun" (12.348 [261]), where the cattle he cherishes pasture, seven herds and flocks with fifty beasts in each (three hundred and fifty, approximately the days of the solar year). These cattle, Teiresias had warned, must not be touched, for they are sacred to the great deity who shines on the Mediterranean world with a splendor he has nowhere else. The men are mad enough to ignore the interdiction and, taking advantage of Odysseus's absence while he catches an hour or so of sleep, they seize the cattle, slaughter them, and devour them. The episode is not in itself among the most memorable, yet it is the last one that Odysseus narrates, and the poet obviously thought it important, for in the prelude to his poem he singles it out from all the others telling how Odysseus's men were destroyed by their own reckless folly:

> children and fools, they killed and feasted on
> the cattle of Lord Hêlios, the Sun,
> and he who moves all day through heaven
> took from their eyes the dawn of their return.
>
> (1.13–16 [8–9])

A little later, when the scene moves to Ithaka, Telemakhos complains to Athena that the suitors "eat their way through all we have" (1.297 [250–51]), an offense that will bring them to their deaths. The crime of transgressive eating is a theme that the great poets of our tradition have dwelt on with a curious insistence. We may understand why it has bulked so large if we reflect that one of our most beautiful human achievements has been to transform the ingestion of food, a simple biological necessity, into a cultural ceremony, from the homely family dinner to the high formality of the banquet. Greek piety attributed a special sanctity to the meal, which "knits the partakers together in a sacred community," and a poet can speak of "the great oath by table and salt."[20] The *Iliad* begins with an anger that makes men's bodies the food of wild beasts and reaches down to encompass the abomination of Akhilleus's threat to hack off the flesh of his enemy and devour it. The horror that sets the *Oresteia* in motion is the act of brother tricking brother into eating the flesh of his own children. *Paradise Lost* begins with Milton calling on the muse to sing of "the Fruit / Of that Forbidden Tree whose mortal tast / Brought death into the World and all our woe." This great theme is at the heart of the *Odyssey*.

The Sun, enraged by what the sailors have done, complains to Zeus, who, as soon as Odysseus's ship puts to sea again, shatters it with a thunderbolt. He alone survives—it takes more than a thunderbolt to do this man in—and, fastening together bits of timber, straddles his makeshift craft and is driven once again to the straits guarded by Skylla and Kharybdis. Keeping clear of the monster, he gets too close to Kharybdis and, to avoid being sucked down by the whirlpool, manages to jump onto an overhanging fig tree and waits till the dreadful gulf spews up his raft. Using his hands to paddle, he drifts for nine days in the open sea until on the tenth he is washed up on Kalypso's island, "naked Ulysses, clad in eternall Fiction," as Chapman saw him.[21] We are back where we started and the tale of his travels is over.

The Return

> Half yet remains unsung, but narrower bound.
> — *Paradise Lost* 7.21

When Odysseus has completed his story, Alkinoos tells him that a ship is ready to take him home and promises a swift and safe journey. He is as good as his word, and on the evening of the next day Odysseus is taken on board. He falls asleep as the vessel skims across the water:

> Slumber, soft and deep
> like the still sleep of death, weighed on his eyes
> as the ship hove seaward . . .
> Hour by hour
> she held her pace; not even a falcon wheeling
> downwind, swiftest bird, could stay abreast of her
> in that most arrowy flight through open water,
> with her great passenger—godlike in counsel,
> he that in twenty years had borne such blows
> in his deep heart, breaking through ranks in war
> and waves on the bitter sea.
> This night at last
> he slept serene, his long-tried mind at rest.
>
> (13.98–115 [79–92])

When he is carried ashore to Ithaka he cannot recognize the place: "The landscape then looked strange, unearthly strange / to the Lord Odysseus" (13.245–46 [194]). This magical voyage over the night sea is the first indication that the poem is changing gears. The voyage is a rebirth, bringing a new Odysseus to an old place that looks new. Nothing like this has happened before. The previous twelve books led us to queer places, to an ogre's cave, a witch's dwelling in the woods, a land where natives live on nothing but the Lotos plant. The person we took for an attractive young hostess waved a wand and turned her visitors into pigs. A very large man—he had only one eye in the middle of his forehead, as it happened—ate people who came to see him. Oh well, *autres pays, autres mœurs*. With Odysseus back in Ithaka, we spend most of our time in a human household and expect to feel relatively at home there even though the story is set in distant times. The central theme, the long train of hints and guesses, of revelation and occlusion, which at last brings husband and wife into each other's arms, is within our imaginative reach, for Homer is pioneering here in territory that novelists were later to make their own. Yet the atmosphere in Odysseus's house is stranger than anything we have met so far, for divinity is at work here in the person of Athena, and her presence creates a sense of psychic disquiet and even panic. Zeus himself periodically gives intimations of his purposes. Most readers probably take this sort of thing in their stride—odd Greek happenings, just part of the plot. The learned of course know all about this sort of thing and are unperturbed, since long habituation has made ancient ways of being in the world quite familiar. The religious, their bumper stickers bearing the message "Jesus loves you," are likely to be puzzled, for the divine acts here with no care for our comforts and pursues ends of its own.

Best perhaps not to pay too much attention to all this—not much attention has in fact been paid. The *Odyssey* is after all a poem, not a treatise on Homeric theology, and we are free to accept its invitation to sit back and enjoy the lively play of the action. All the same, it might be worth a good reader's while to look below the surface of the action to discover what is going on there.

As Odysseus is looking round for the gifts that the Phaiakians put on board the ship, Athena, disguised as a young man, turns up. She left him to prove himself until near the end of his voyages she came to his aid, providing him with means of getting away from Kalypso and smoothing his way in Phaiakia. Her guidance is now more urgently needed, for a greater task awaits Odysseus: the restoration of order in his house. She tells him that the strange land he has come to is

Ithaka. Ah yes, he says, "Far away in Krete I learned of Ithaka" (13.327 [256]), and spins an entirely fictitious story. This amuses Athena and she reveals herself, then dispels the mist that had prevented him from recognizing his own country. They sit down together, clever goddess by clever man, planning "to work the suitors death and woe" (13.466 [373]). Revenge, the first of the three themes that dominate this half of the poem. She transforms him into a wrinkled old man, the poet's oblique way of introducing the second theme, Recognition. To be recognized in his home, he must go there in disguise. She tells him to make his way to the faithful swineherd Eumaios while she goes to Sparta to bring Telemakhos back, preparing for the third main theme, Reunion.

The poet leaves Odysseus in the swineherd's steading for three whole books—14, 15, and 16. Why not send him to his troubled home at once? There are practical reasons for not doing so. Had he gone there in his own person, he would probably have been killed. Nonetheless, in comparison with the fast-moving action of the first part of the poem the second seems to take its time unduly, and one can't help wishing that Homer would get a move on. Great narrator that he is, he knows that he can afford to take his time here and that he needs the time to domesticate the voyager in strange seas and set him solidly on terra firma among ordinary people—like Eumaios, the first of the allies who will help him to settle his score with the suitors. A decent straightforward man, the swineherd is like no one we have met in the poem, and Homer describes his life in loving detail. "All wanderers / and beggars come from Zeus" (14.69–70 [57–58]), he says piously as he sets Odysseus down to a good plain meal of roast pork, explaining that the best pork has gone to feed the suitors, "cold-hearted men, who never spare a thought / for how they stand in the sight of Zeus" (14.100–101 [82]). He warms Odysseus's heart by speaking of his love for his old master, now dead and gone, he laments. Having fed his guest, he asks where he has come from, giving Odysseus his cue for another long slice of autobiographical fiction, not quite so fictional this time, since it includes an incident that resembles his own raid on the Kikones, and he claims that on one occasion he met Odysseus preparing to return home. You might have spared us that, Eumaios says; too many travelers on the make have been arriving with tales of this kind. The evening turning cold, Odysseus feels the need for some warm wear, but instead of asking this kindly host for something to put on, he comes out with a rather pointless story of how on an ambush in wartime he played a trick to get a comrade's cloak. Not to be outdone, Eumaios now tells the story of his life, presumably a true story. The poet needs to take his time, but does he really need quite so much time?

Athena has now set off for Sparta, where she finds Telemakhos still enjoying Menelaos's princely hospitality. She takes him to the steading, where father and son, reunited, fall into each other's arms, and together they too begin to plan for the day of revenge; the armor in the great hall of Odysseus's house must all be stored away to prevent the suitors from getting at it.

At last the time has come for Odysseus to return home, disguised by Athena as a beggar. She tells him to see what he may get from the suitors:

> ". . . You may collect a few more loaves, and learn
> who are the decent lads, and who are vicious—
> although not one can be excused from death!"
>
> (17.471–73 [362–63])

We understand that the goddess intends to help Odysseus to recover his estate and punish the intruders who have been paying court to his wife, the bad and not-so-bad alike, it seems. But why is she so malignant? And why in later scenes do we find her leading them on and making them behave worse than they usually do? The reader is likely to miss the ancient religious thinking that lies below the action. Athena is doing what churchgoers repeating the Lord's Prayer on Sunday morning ask God not to do: "lead us not into temptation."[22] This dark old fear is more fully expressed in later Greek poetry. Aeschylus grimly spells it out in some lines from the *Persians* where he speaks of "the crafty deception of Zeus" through whose agency "Delusion with kindly seeming leads men into her nets" (lines 95ff.). Heaven, working through involuntary mortal agents, is bringing about the restoration of order. Disorder in the home or state shakes the very sum of things and cannot be allowed to continue.

Intimations of the return of Odysseus, the conscious agent of heaven's will, are beginning to gather. Telemakhos, back from his trip abroad, tells Penelope what he heard from Menelaos, that his father is alive but unable to come home, detained on a remote island by Kalypso. Theoklymenos, a visionary whom Telemakhos met while on his travels and brought home with him, intervenes and sets the matter straight:

> ". . . O gentle lady,
> wife of Odysseus Laërtiadês . . ."

This is the first time that she has been addressed in this way: she is the wife, not the widow, of Odysseus. He goes on:

> ". . . Zeus be my witness, and the table set
> for strangers and the hearth to which I've come—
> the lord Odysseus, I tell you,
> is present now, already, on this island!
> Quartered somewhere, or going about, he knows
> what evil is afoot. He has it in him
> to bring a black hour on the suitors . . ."
>
> (17.191–200 [152–59])

"If only this came true" (17.205 [163]), she says sadly; it will be some time before she recognizes as her husband the man who is coming to the house.

Odysseus is in fact already on his way there and arrives without being recognized by anyone except his old dog Argos, whom he sees lying neglected on a heap of dung. He had trained him as a hunter before sailing for Troy. Hearing his master's voice, the dog is just able to wag his tail but is too weak to get up. Odysseus says a few words about his bravery and skill,

> but death and darkness in that instant closed
> the eyes of Argos, who had seen his master,
> Odysseus, after twenty years.
>
> (17.420–22 [326–27])

In no country are dogs so valued as they are in England, yet English poetry has nothing to match the solemnity and beauty of this brief scene.

Odysseus goes in and begins plying his beggarly business. He asks Antinoos, the nastiest of the suitors, for a morsel to eat, getting in return a footstool thrown at him. Upstairs, Penelope hears the noise and asks Eumaios to fetch the new visitor—who knows, he may have some information about Odysseus. He is not far away, Eumaios tells her, up north in Thresprotia, collecting treasure on his way home. "Ah, if he comes again," she says,

> ". . . no falcon ever
> struck more suddenly than he will, with his son,
> to avenge this outrage!"

Ah, if he comes again . . . As though in answer to these words, something happens:

> The great hall below
> at this point rang with a tremendous sneeze—
> "kchaou!" from Telémakhos—like an acclamation.
> And laughter seized Penélopê.
>
> (17.705–11 [539–42])

Why does she laugh—because she hears her son sneeze? A sneeze is a disruption of the body's economy, to us a matter of small moment, but in Homer's world it can be something more; it may carry a message, it may be an omen. The Homeric omen, Norman Austin writes, "assumes order [in this instance disorder] and meaning in the external world, and sees in one small event a paradigm of the order. It is man's part to discern that structure from a single clue and then to modify his behavior in accordance with it." "Penelope laughs," he explains, "because Telemakhos' sneeze is an omen of the same sort that her laughter is to us. She has just felt some change in the atmosphere of her hall, and has sensed its connection with the stranger's arrival."[23] The atmosphere has indeed changed, for heaven is taking a hand in Odysseus's affairs, and the simplest action or event may be fraught with meaning. Homeric man lives in an intelligible world where things *mean*. His world does not have the omnipresent meaningfulness of the *Divine Comedy*, which can seem oppressive; it is rather one where man enjoys an open, companionable relation to natural phenomena in which he may sometimes detect a divine hand.

In comes a professional beggar, one Iros, who tells Odysseus to get off his turf. Odysseus accepts the challenge and with a single blow hooks him under the ear and shatters his jawbone. The suitors like this sort of thing—they "whooped and swung their arms, half dead / with pangs of laughter" (18.122–23). The Greek is stranger: literally, "they died with laughter" (18.100). They will before long, but not with laughter. The house is charged with Athena's presence and men are not masters of themselves. The suitors are grateful to Odysseus for giving them this fine sport and wish him the best—"May the gods grant your heart's desire!" (18.141 [112–13]). He "found grim cheer in their good wishes" (18.146), Fitzgerald translates, but again we need a more literal rendering: "he was pleased by the omen" (18.117). A verbal omen of this sort consists of any chance utterance that can carry a significance not intended by the speaker and may be a portent of what is to come.

Amphinomos, the most decent of the suitors and potentially a tragic character, hands the supposed beggar a fine plate of food and wishes him good luck. Another omen—they are coming thick and fast now. A design is at work, but not of man's designing. "You seem gently bred," Odysseus says and speaks gravely of the radical insecurity of the human condition:

> ". . . Of mortal creatures, all that breathe and move,
> earth bears none frailer than mankind. What man
> believes in woe to come, so long as valor
> and tough knees are supplied him by the gods?
> But when the gods in bliss bring miseries on,
> then willy-nilly, blindly, he endures.
> Our minds are as the days are, dark or bright,
> blown over by the father of gods and men . . ."

He adds:

> ". . . So I, too, in my time thought to be happy . . ."
>
> (18.161–72 [128–38])

This recalls the words that Akhilleus addressed to Priam in the final book of the *Iliad*, the highest point that poetry has ever reached: "We heard that you too, old man, were once happy" (line 543). The *Odyssey* has not sounded a note like this before, nor have we heard Odysseus speak at this reflective depth. Like the chorus in an ode of Greek tragedy, he stands back from and above the immediate action and looks beyond it to the universal laws that govern the lives of all men on earth.

Amphinomos listens to these solemn words, but they cannot help him. "Now his heart foreknew / the wrath to come, but he could not take flight, / being by Athena bound there" (18.194–96 [154–55]). He will die at Telemakhos's hands. The workings of heaven are like a landslide carrying all before it, innocent and guilty alike, creating the mental disturbance we sensed in the suitors' crazy laughter, and sense again as Penelope, prompted by Athena, says that she feels

> a wish to show herself before the suitors;
> for thus by fanning their desire again
> Athena meant to set her beauty high
> before her husband's eyes, before her son.
> Knowing no reason, laughing confusedly,
> she said:
>   "Eurýnomê, I have a craving
> I never had at all—I would be seen
> Among these ruffians, hateful as they are . . ."
>
> (18.202–10 [160–65])

No wonder she laughs confusedly, for the wish is not hers but Athena's; the goddess is using her to lead the suitors to their destruction. When she appears, her beauty is heightened by the goddess, and "their hearts grew faint with lust; / not one but swore to god to lie beside her" (18.266–67 [212–13]). Or can it be, for we should let the deliberate ambiguity in these lines play both ways, that she herself wishes to woo the man who might just be her husband by flirting with the suitors in order to make him jealous? Whatever in her confusion she may have in mind, Athena's intentions are made clear a little later when Telemakhos says to them:

> "Bright souls, alight with wine, you can no longer
> hide the cups you've taken. Aye, some god
> is goading you . . ."
>
> (18.495–97 [406–7])

For once the translation misses something essential. In the Greek, Telemakhos calls them δαιμόνιοι, literally "driven by a δαίμων," a more than human power. You are maddened, he goes on, driven by a *mania* sent by a god (μαίνεσθε). Understandably, Fitzgerald is trying to avoid taking us out of our depths, for divinity actively present in human affairs is beyond the compass of our thought and experience today, hard for the secular person even to imagine and disturbing to the Laodicean religious who are no longer taught that the *fear* of the Lord is the beginning of wisdom and suppose that should the divine take a hand in our affairs its purposes will be benign. The older world thought otherwise and knew how disruptive its inroads may be. It may manifest itself as light, a sudden more-than-natural radiance, as it does near the start of book 19 when Athena holds up a golden lamp. "Oh, Father," Telemakhos cries:

> ". . . here is a marvel! All around I see
> the walls and roof beams, pedestals, and pillars,
> lighted as though by white fire blazing near.
> One of the gods of heaven is in this place!"
>
> (19.47–51 [36–40])

Or it may make itself manifest as terror. Near the end of book 20, Telemakhos says that he does not oppose his mother's marriage, though he cannot pack her off against her will. At this

> Pallas Athena touched off in the suitors
> a fit of laughter, uncontrollable.

> She drove them into nightmare, till they wheezed
> and neighed as though with jaws no longer theirs,
> while blood defiled their meat, and blurring tears
> flooded their eyes, heart-sore with woe to come.
> Then said the visionary, Theoklýmenos:
>
> "O lost sad men, what terror is this you suffer?
> Night shrouds you to the knees, your heads, your faces;
> dry retch of death runs round like fire in sticks;
> your cheeks are streaming; these fair walls and pedestals
> are dripping crimson blood. And thick with shades
> passing athirst toward Érebos, into the dark,
> the sun is quenched in heaven, foul mist hems us in . . ."
>
> (20.387–401 [345–57])

The daemonic seizure that Athena impels on the suitors has collapsed the walls that shield mortals from the dread invasion of divinity. Our human earth has turned into hell, a reverse transfiguration—
Christian terminology can hardly be avoided. To find speech for this,
the poet must strain his language to a point where most translators
dare not go. The Greek words that follow "your heads, your faces,"
οἰμωγὴ δὲ δέδηε (20.353), "and groaning bursts into flame," are too
much for Fitzgerald, who substitutes a line of his own invention. Only
Chapman stands up to the wildness of the synesthesia: "shriekes burn
about you" (20.532). Theoklymenos sees—*sees*, not foresees; this is
vision, not prophecy—the suitors transformed into their shades, dead
living men on their way to the world below. The sun itself cannot look
on this horror and is "quenched," extinguished.

This vision from book 20 is still to come. Before the suitors are read-
ied for what they are to suffer, Odysseus, the human agent of their
fate on earth, must become what the whole poem has been preparing him to be, the husband of Penelope. The discord of their long
separation must be resolved into the harmony—in the Greek sense
of the word, a joining or putting together—of their marriage. This
is the matter of the decisive nineteenth book, which brings them together for the first time.[24] Sitting with him in the great hall, Penelope
asks him who he is and where he has come from. It is the practice of
this *rusé personnage*[25] when questioned to start talking about something
else. He did this in Phaiakia when Queen Arete asked him where he
had got the clothes he was wearing. He does the same thing here. He
begins by praising Penelope's fame and wisdom, in this way winning
her confidence so that she tells him about the trick she played to keep
off the day when she must marry one of the suitors. She would do so,

she assured them, when she had completed the web she was working on, an indefinite time ahead, since she unraveled by night what she had woven during the day.

She resumes her questioning, and Odysseus comes out with one more of his fictitious tales, describing how he once entertained her husband at home in Krete. He sounds so convincing that she is moved to tears. A delicately transparent simile reveals that her defenses are beginning to dissolve:

> The skin
> of her pale face grew moist the way pure snow
> softens and glistens on the mountains, thawed
> by Southwind after powdering from the West,
> and, as the snow melts, mountain streams run full:
> so her white cheeks are wetted by these tears
> shed for her lord—and he close by her side.
>
> (19.241–47 [204–9])

Her defenses nonetheless still just stand, and she asks the stranger for some proof of his story, not so much doubting it perhaps as asking for fuller confirmation of what she is coming to believe. What was Odysseus wearing? A fleecy purple cloak fastened by a broach depicting an elaborately wrought hunting scene. She remembers both the cloak and the broach, but still she resists: "I will not meet the man again / returning to his own home fields," she says mournfully, yet she has moved closer to him and just called him her "respected guest and friend" (19.306–7, 302 [257–58, 254]).

Odysseus, sensing that he has gained ground, presses on and tells her that he has positive news that her husband will soon be back in Ithaka. "Here is my sworn word for it," he says impressively:

> ". . . Witness this,
> god of the zenith, noblest of the gods,
> and Lord Odysseus' hearthfire, now before me:
> I swear these things shall turn out as I say.
> Between this present dark and one day's ebb,
> after the wane, before the crescent moon,
> Odysseus will come."
>
> (19.356–62 [302–7])

It is late, so she tells the maids to prepare a couch for her guest and a bath. But the old soldier will not have some sly flibbertigibbet girl touch him—let someone his own years give him a footbath. Penelope calls on her housekeeper:

> ". . . Come here, stand by me, faithful Eurýkleia,
> and bathe, bathe your master, I almost said
> for they are of an age, and now Odysseus'
> feet and hands would be enseamed like his . . ."
>
> (19.417–20 [357–59])

We should not take this to mean that she now accepts the stranger as her husband. Rather, she half thinks that this might be him and her thought inadvertently slips out into words. Odysseus sits down to have his feet washed, then suddenly realizes the risk he is running. There is a scar on his thigh that Eurykleia is sure to recognize; he must not let her see it or his identity will be known before he is ready to reveal it. To relax the tension, the poet now opens up a long, brilliantly narrated flashback to a day in the carefree time of youth when he was out in the hills on a boar hunt. In the lead, he was about to cast his spear as the beast was already charging and it gashed his thigh badly. Inevitably, Eurykleia does in due course recognize the scar and exclaims, "*You are Odysseus!*" (19.551 [474]). (Did she in fact recognize him all along, so that the scar merely affirms what she already suspected?) Penelope is nearby, but Athena bemuses her and she hears nothing. Late though it is, she cannot let him go, afraid of one more lonely night when "bitter thoughts and fears crowd on my grief." Like Desdemona singing her willow song, she finds relief by turning her sorrow into lyrical form, a lovely aria about the nightingale, once a mortal woman who in her madness killed her son:

> ". . . Think how Pandáreos' daughter, pale forever,
> sings as the nightingale in the new leaves
> through those long quiet hours of night,
> on some thick-flowering orchard bough in spring;
> how she rills out and tilts her note, high now, now low,
> mourning for Itylos whom she killed in madness—
> her child, and her lord Zêthos' only child.
> My forlorn thought flows variable as her song . . ."
>
> (19.600–608 [516–24])

We should not press this too closely and say that she fears that by holding out on the suitors she risks bringing about her son's death at their hands, for she knows that they have been planning to kill him. What fills her mind is the pure sense of loss, loss of her husband and the happiness she once knew with him. Her thought, as she says, flows variable, and in the effort to reach some solid ground she describes a dream she had, or—again we reach for the meaning that may lie just behind the words—has she just invented it?

"... Listen:
interpret me this dream: From a water's edge
twenty fat geese have come to feed on grain
beside my house. And I delight to see them.
But now a mountain eagle with great wings
and crooked beak storms in to break their necks
and strew their bodies here. Away he soars
into the bright sky; and I cry aloud—
all this in dream—I wail and round me gather
softly braided Akhaian women mourning
because the eagle killed my geese . . ."

(19.620–30 [535–44])

The Greek is brilliantly ambiguous here. The primary sense of her
words is probably as Fitzgerald has it. Or perhaps she means that the
eagle has killed the geese for her. Or has her tongue got ahead of her
conscious thought, as it does a little later, and made her say "my eagle," my eagle husband, Odysseus? It would not be possible to bring
this over into English, and Fitzgerald does not even try. At all events
she is revealing more than she means to do. If the geese feeding at
her house are the suitors, who have been doing that for years, why
does she delight to see them and why mourn their death? Because,
as Russo suggests in his note on this passage, "the lonely queen obviously derived some cheer from the attentions of the suitors, and would,
on an unconscious level, regret their sudden slaughter."[26] No doubt
some of them were presentable enough young men. The meaning of
the dream is clear, her guest says: Odysseus is coming back to deal
with your suitors. But no, she still won't have it. The dream was false,
one of the delusive night visions that come through the ivory gates, not
the horn gates through which true dreams come.[27] News of Odysseus's
return would be too good to be true. She resists, we may understand,
because accepting the news that her husband is returning would
mean giving up the defensive structure she has built around herself;
feeling relatively comfortable there, she is loath to step outside into the
cruel reality of her life. The Greek nowhere directly says this. Homer's
language was superbly equipped to present actions and the great primary emotions, but was scarcely required to depict the fugitive *mouve-
ments de l'âme*. All the more wonder then that using the resources at
his command he can let us see so far into the recesses of the mind.
He is doing something here, we may believe, that had never been
done before, moving into regions that the psychologizing novelists
of the nineteenth century were to make their own, fantastic though
it may seem to make such a claim for a poet composing nearly three
millennia ago. Yet as we saw with the words describing the danger that

94 CLASSICS AND TRANSLATION

Skylla represented, a great poet may on occasion stretch beyond the range of his time and culture.

Penelope now pulls herself together sufficiently to realize that the issue of her marriage must be decided at once. Why the sudden urgency? Her parents have been pressing her to remarry, and although Telemakhos is not going to force her hand she knows that he would be glad to see her take a husband, if only to prevent the suitors from devouring any more of his estate. What has precipitated the matter is the arrival of this fascinating visitor who might be Odysseus. The next day, she says, she will hold a contest:

> ". . . We have twelve axe heads. In his time, my lord
> could line them up, all twelve, at intervals
> like a ship's ribbing; then he'd back away
> a long way off and whip an arrow through.
> Now I'll impose this trial on the suitors.
> The one who easily handles and strings the bow
> and shoots through all twelve axes I shall marry . . ."
>
> (19.664–70 [573–79])

Bracketing off the much-discussed question of how one can shoot an arrow through an ax, let alone twelve axes (through the metal ring at the end of the helve allowing an ax to be hung on a wall, Bernard Knox suggests in a note to Fagles's translation), one wonders what she has in mind. Since she has seen Odysseus perform this feat, it might be a means of declaring him the winning man. But this cannot be right, for she does not yet know or cannot bring herself to admit that she knows him to be her husband. As the more perceptive critics have seen, this is a form of divination. As we might toss a coin to let it decide a difficult issue for us, she is letting the contest do it for her. It is to be held the next day, and with this their long parley is at an end.

Lying awake and wondering in his troubled mind how one man can take on a whole crowd, Odysseus does what Penelope has just done and turns to divination, asking Zeus for an omen, a double omen consisting of what Greeks called a φήμη or κληδών, some utterance that may carry a message, and a τέρας, a sign or portent from the outer world of nature. Zeus responds by thundering from a clear sky, and Odysseus hears the voice of a woman grinding barley. Old and tired, she has had to work late into the night to complete the stint imposed on her. She prays to Zeus:

> ". . . let this day be the last the suitors feed
> so dainty in Odysseus' hall!

They've made me work my heart out till I drop,
grinding barley. May they feast no more!"

(20.132–35 [116–19])

Since we do not practice divination today, the reader probably lets
this pass as one of the odd things that ancient Greeks did. If he is
industrious he may seek help from a commentary, but what he finds
there is likely to be so much academic lumber that lies inertly in the
mind. With a poem that can speak so directly to our human sympathies we would hope for more, something that helps us to understand
what Odysseus finds in these two chance happenings, as we would call
them. Are there traces of this ancient thinking in our minds today?
Surely there are. Suppose that a person contemplating some expen-
sive purchase hears someone say in answer to an improbable suggestion, "No, I won't buy that for a moment!"—might not this make him
wonder if he really wanted to make this purchase? The world of nature too we still find meaningful, so much so that in the form of
weather it can used as a structural device in novels. It plays a powerful part in an early modern classic like *The Turn of the Screw*. It is high
summer when the governess arrives at Bly; "the rooks circled and
cawed in the golden sky" and she enjoys "all the music of summer and
all the mystery of nature." As James begins to introduce intimations
of trouble (Quint appears at the top of the tower), it rains so violently
that she cannot walk the children to church on Sunday morning. A
darker intimation follows: Miss Jessel, a figure of "unmistakeable horror and evil," whereupon nature speaks again more decisively in a
brilliantly written sentence: "The summer had turned, the summer
had gone; the autumn had dropped upon Bly and had blown out half
our lights." A Greek would have known what the extinction of those
lights heralded. The literature of even the distant past need not always seem so remote from us and, curiously enough, relatively recent
work can be stranger than anything from antiquity. Greek poetry offers nothing so bizarre as the ironclad virtue of the heroines of Victorian fiction.

Reassured, Odysseus has to put up with more indignities in his own
house, thanks to Athena, who is still at her grim work and "had no desire now to let the suitors / restrain themselves from wounding words
and acts" (20.312–14 [284–85]). A bully called Ktesippos remarks
that Telemakhos's guest should have his share of the good things
going. "Let me throw in my own small contribution" (20.326 [296]),
he says wittily, and throws a cow's foot at Odysseus's head. He does not
have long to live. Book 20 ends with the vision of the suitors driven
to madness by Athena.

   The day of the contest dawns and Penelope goes to fetch the bow
from the storeroom. Standing among the suitors, she announces:

>   "My lords, hear me:
> suitors indeed, you commandeered this house
> to feast and drink in, day and night, my husband
> being long gone, long out of mind. You found
> no justification for yourselves—none
> except your lust to marry me. Stand up, then:
> we now declare a contest for that prize . . ."
>
>   (21.71–77 [68–73])

She will marry the man who can string the bow and send an arrow
through the twelve axes that have been lined up ready for the contest. Telemakhos pretends to try the bow himself, but stops playing at
a nod from his father. One Leodes, a decent-enough fellow and something of a prophet (this avails him nothing; he will die at Odysseus's
hands), steps forward and has a go but gives it up at once as hopeless.
Because you can't string it, Antinoos says angrily, you make out that
no one can. There are men here who can do the job. All the same he
proposes to have the bow greased to make it more pliable. Why not
let me try my hand? Odysseus breaks in, whereupon Antinoos turns
on him—a mere tramp daring to compete with the best men in the
island! Let him have the bow, Penelope orders. Odysseus picks it up,
examines it closely, and then, the moment we have been waiting for:

> the man skilled in all ways of contending,
> satisfied by the great bow's look and heft,
> like a musician, like a harper, when
> with quiet hand upon his instrument
> he draws between his thumb and forefinger
> a sweet new string upon a peg; so effortlessly
> Odysseus in one motion strung the bow.
> Then slid his right hand down the cord and plucked it,
> so the taut gut vibrating hummed and sang
> a swallow's note.
>
>   (21.460–69 [404–11])

Zeus thunders his approval, Odysseus picks up an arrow, sends it
clean through the socket rings of the twelve axes, and now, all perplexities cast aside, the poem stands in the clear light of battle.
Fitzgerald signals the new note by turning to a new meter, a longer
heroic line:

> Now shrugging off his rags the wiliest fighter of the islands
> leapt and stood on the broad door sill, his own bow in his hand.

He poured out at his feet a rain of arrows from the quiver
and spoke to the crowd:

> "So much for that. Your clean-cut game is over . . ."
>   (22.1–5 [1–5])

The meter remains the same in the Greek, but we feel the poet flex-
ing his Iliadic muscles.

Antinoos is the first to die, his throat pierced by an arrow as he raises
a cup of wine to his lips. Eurymakhos tries to come to terms with
Odysseus but soon gives it up and charges, only to fall in his turn. One
by one the suitors meet their fate. Athena lends a hand when help
is needed, deflecting arrows showered at Odysseus and at one point
driving the suitors mad with terror by revealing that fearful aegis (a
kind of shield dreadfully emblazoned?). For heaven approves of the
slaughter. This book, the twenty-second, is governed by the *lex talio-
nis*, the law of an eye for an eye, a tooth for a tooth, in all its archaic
severity. No one is spared: the goatherd Melanthios who played dogs-
body to the suitors in their dirty game is savagely hacked to pieces;
the servant girls who bedded with the suitors are taken out and hanged.
The celebrated Hellenist of an earlier day, Gilbert Murray, who found
a good deal in the Greek record to trouble his gentle spirit, noted
with relief the end of the line describing their death: "Their feet
danced for a little, *but not long*" [italics added] (22.526 [473]).[28] He
could have found more to comfort him in the high Hellenic note that
sounds in Odysseus's words to Eurykleia as she shrieks in triumph:

>   "Rejoice
> inwardly. No crowing aloud, old woman.
> To glory over slain men is no piety.
> Destiny and the gods' will vanquished these,
> and their own hardness . . ."
>   (22.460–64 [411–13])

Regrettably, a number of Homeric scholars have wished to delete these
beautiful lines.

Penelope has been kept upstairs away from the carnage and will
not believe Eurykleia when she tells her that Odysseus has killed all
the suitors. It cannot be, she says, it must have been some god who
punished them for their sins. She goes down uncertain how to behave. Keep her distance and question him? Or take his hands and kiss
him? Odysseus stands still, saying nothing; the moment of reunion is
coming but it must not be hurried. Very gently he lets her take her
time and silences Telemakhos, who reproaches her for being so aloof:
"Peace: let your mother test me at her leisure" (23.129 [113–14]). She

does so, cleverly testing the great tester. If he really is my husband, she says, we will recognize each other. "There are / secret signs we know, we two" (23.125–26 [109–10]). She orders Eurykleia to make up his bed for him: "Place it outside the bedchamber my lord / built with his own hands" (23.203–4 [177–78]). At this Odysseus flares up in anger, asking who dared, who could, move the bed that he had built, and goes on to describe it:

> ". . . An old trunk of olive
> grew like a pillar on the building plot,
> and I laid out our bedroom round that tree,
> lined up the stone walls, built the walls and roof,
> gave it a doorway and smooth-fitting doors.
> Then I lopped off the silvery leaves and branches,
> hewed and shaped that stump from the roots up
> into a bedpost, drilled it, let it serve
> as a model for the rest. I planed them all,
> inlaid them all with silver, gold and ivory,
> and stretched a bed between—a pliant web
> of oxhide thongs dyed crimson.
>
>   There's our sign! . . ."
>
>   (23.216–28 [190–202])

The loving detail is earned, for this bed, with all that it suggests of gentleness and peace, the bed where they first lay in love and where he begot his only son, is the still point to which the whole poem has been moving through the strange adventures in foreign parts of the first half on to the violence of the previous book. Penelope can resist no longer:

>   So they came
> into that bed so steadfast, loved of old,
> opening glad arms to one another.
>
>   (23.331–33 [295–96])

Two eminent Alexandrian scholars said or seemed to say that the poem ended here, or perhaps they meant that it came to its consummation rather than its actual conclusion, as Stanford suggests in his note on these lines. It has, at all events, reached its main goal: Odysseus has righted the great wrong by punishing the suitors for their crimes and setting his house in order. Above all, the loving unity of husband and wife has been restored. The reunion with Laertes is, however, still to come; the bond between father and son was far too strong in Greek culture for it to be left hanging. We may also wonder how the Ithakans are going to take the deaths of so many of their prominent men; they can hardly let Odysseus get away with it. Something more has to be done, but it is hard to believe that the final book as a whole is the best that could be done.

It begins with the shades of the suitors being led by Hermes to the world of the dead. Since Theoklymenos foretold that this was their destination, we might well have been left to suppose that the prophet knew what he was talking about. On their way they pass by some of the famous dead who fought at Troy: Akhilleus, Aias, Agamemnon. We met them in book 11—do we need to meet them again here? Agamemnon describes the great funeral held for Akhilleus, impressive but hardly relevant unless we suppose that the poet wished to link his poem with the *Iliad*. Agamemnon goes on to speak of his own wretched ending, done to death by his wife and her vile paramour on returning home. This is relevant, since the contrast between his return and that of Odysseus was introduced in book 1 and has been mentioned again intermittently, and the parallel between the false Klytaimnestra and the faithful Penelope is one of the poem's many doublings.

Looking at the shades that Hermes is conducting, Agamemnon recognizes one of them and asks what brought him to this sorry pass. The man relates, at considerable length, how he and his fellows tried to win the hand of Penelope, who kept them on tenterhooks for years by her clever trick with the web, eventually announcing that she would marry the man who could shoot an arrow—and so forth. Why go over all this again?

Now for Odysseus's visit to Laertes, miserably reduced and hardly more than a farmhand on his own property. Before identifying himself, Odysseus decides that he should test him, "draw him out with sharp words, trouble him" (24.265 [240]). This seems unnecessary and rather cruel, but Odysseus knows what he is doing. He is afraid that revealing himself at once, as he did with Telemakhos, might be too much for the old man, so he moves slowly, as he did with Penelope, letting Laertes gradually perceive that the man standing before him is his long-lost son. His intention, as Alfred Heubeck sees, is to release him from "the paralysis of emotion, lethargy and apathy" into which he has fallen.[29] So he relates one more fictitious story, describing how he once met a man called Odysseus and became fond of him. Much affected, Laertes asks the visitor his name. "My name is Quarrelman," Odysseus answers, "King Allwoes' only son" (24.335–36 [305]). Since his real name may in Greek signify Son of Pain,[30] this serves to put Laertes on the right track, and unable to keep the old man in suspense any longer, Odysseus throws his arms round him and cries, "Oh, Father, I am he!" (24.354 [321]). Like father like son: Laertes asks for a sign to confirm this, and is shown the famous scar.

Meanwhile the townsfolk are arming to take their revenge on the murderer. His bloodlust not yet quenched, Odysseus is about to set to and slaughter the lot of them, but at this point Zeus, prompted by Athena, intervenes:

> ". . . Odysseus' honor being satisfied,
> let him be king by a sworn pact forever,
> and we, for our part, will blot out the memory
> of sons and brothers slain. As in the old time
> let men of Ithaka henceforth be friends;
> prosperity enough, and peace attend them."
>
> (24.534–39 [482–87])

This would have made a fine ending—for a different poem (the *Oresteia* for instance), one in which Odysseus's relations with the citizenry had been a central theme and our attention had been directed to his Ithakan kingdom rather than his own house. As it is, the effect of Zeus's words, judicious though they are, cannot be very great.

Scholarship has cast doubts on the authenticity of book 24. However this may be, the general reader can hardly help wishing that the poem came to a more satisfying close. One could surely have been devised. Twice we have heard, first from Teiresias in book 11, then from Odysseus himself speaking to Penelope, about a mysterious final journey that he must undertake. He is to go overland on foot carrying an oar to a people knowing nothing of ships or seafaring, plant the oar there, then make sacrifices to his enemy the great god Poseidon (is not this an issue that should be settled?) and further sacrifices to the gods when he returns home. Could not this story, which is never developed, have been introduced here? The poem might then end like this:

> a seaborne death
> soft as this hand of mist will come upon you
> when you are wearied out with rich old age,
> your country folk in blessed peace around you.
>
> (11.148–51 [134–37])

This picture of the old soldier, seaman, traveler, in calm of mind all passion spent, could have provided the *Odyssey* with a noble ending. But the poem ends as it does, and Fitzgerald, who read his way into it as no scholar can, writes in his postscript that "in substance Book XXIV is fully 'Homeric' and that whoever composed it knew what he was doing." Let the final word rest with *le grant translateur*.[31]

4
Robert Fitzgerald as Translator:
The *Odyssey,* the *Iliad,* and the *Aeneid*

W<small>ITH</small> D<small>UDLEY</small> F<small>ITTS</small>, R<small>OBERT</small> F<small>ITZGERALD</small> <small>TRANSLATED THE</small> *O<small>EDIPUS</small>*
Rex, less successfully the *Antigone;* on his own, the *Oedipus at Colonus.*
But it is as translator of the three great classical epics that his name
will live.[1] Of these it was the *Odyssey* (his first labor) which called forth
his full strength, his happiest vein, and his version of the poem is the
most beautiful we have in English.

THE *ODYSSEY*

The translator of Homer must first decide on the line that he is going to use. For the age of Dryden and Pope the rhyming couplet was
the only candidate, but when the couplet fell from favor, the blank
verse of *Paradise Lost* came to be recognized as the English heroic
measure. Matthew Arnold opted for the hexameter, with the English
stress accent replacing classical syllabic length, but the specimen translations he offered did not help to commend his choice. Pound's first
canto, a translation of the opening of book 11 of the *Odyssey* in a disguised form of the Old English alliterative line, is masterly, but it
is hard to imagine it prolonged for many thousands of lines. The
same reservation applies to the treatment of a scene from *Iliad* 17 in
wiry sprung verse by the classical scholar E. R. Dodds, unfortunately
very little known.[2] Christopher Logue, with great metrical variety and
enough shock tactics to keep us on the edge of our seats, in his earlier versions from the *Iliad* brought over a number of passages with a
fire unequaled since Pope's great translation.

    The prevailing meter in modern times has been the six-beat line,
which seems to have been first used at length by the English poet C.
Day-Lewis in his translation of Virgil's *Georgics* (1940). He described

it as "a rhythm based on the hexameter, containing six beats in each line, but allowing much variation of pace and interspersed with occasional short lines of three stresses."[3] This is not a recognized line of English verse, but it suits an age when poetry has been taught not to put on airs, and in Day-Lewis's hands it has its modest virtues:

> I remember once beneath the battlements of Oebalia,
> Where dark Galesus waters the golden fields of corn,
> I saw an old man, a Corycian, who owned a few poor acres
> Of land once derelict, useless for arable,
> No good for grazing, unfit for the cultivation of vines.
>
> (p. 69 [4.125–29])

From England the six-beat line (minus the lines of three stresses) passed to America, into the hands of Richmond Lattimore, whose 1951 translation of the *Iliad* quickly assumed classic status and was used in classrooms all over the country. A Greek scholar himself, Lattimore was loudly praised by members of his profession for his ruthless fidelity to the original. "Professor Lattimore adheres to the literal at times," Guy Davenport unkindly observed, "with the obstinacy of a mule eating briars."[4] Certain defects this celebrated translation has. Lattimore's six-beat line lacks the rapidity that Arnold saw as the first of the qualities characterizing the Homeric hexameter, and does not provide what Schiller called "a language which does your thinking and poetizing for you."[5] On the contrary, the translator must work at his six-beater all the time to prevent it from turning into wooden prose arbitrarily chopped into verse lengths.

Robert Fitzgerald, unaffected by the fashion, saw that our classic English measure, the more or less iambic decasyllabic line, was the only choice, even though it was not in favor when he wrote and has often been very dull, as even Wordsworth can be when he is not inspired. Milton showed that it does not have to be dull and is capable of the widest metrical variety: "Into a Gulf shot under ground, till part"—a 4:4:2 rhythm, two choriambs, call them, plus an iamb, followed by a swift caesura-less line: "Rose up a Fountain by the Tree of Life" (*Paradise Lost* 9.72–73).

Fitzgerald made himself entirely at home with the iambic line, using it with a variety and flexibility it has always been capable of. He avoided the danger of monotony by counterpointing speech rhythm against the formal iambic rhythm ("too much iambic will kill any subject matter," Pound told him),[6] and succeeded in writing an English so easy and unforced that we look through the words, conscious of them only for their expressive felicity, to what is being done or said. He can be as casual and relaxed as this:

"... I hear the old man comes to town no longer,
stays up country, ailing, with only one
old woman to prepare his meat and drink ..."

(1.232–34 [189–92])

Almost prose? but turn to Rieu's version and see how much is lost when
Homer is really turned into what Greek called λόγοι πεζοί, "pedestrian's talk": "For I gather that he no longer comes to town, but lives
a hard and lonely life on his farm with an old servant-woman, who
puts food and drink before him."

Fitzgerald's lines are verse all right, narrative verse as fluent and
natural as any in our language, and can effortlessly modulate into
poetry as they do a little earlier on in this passage:

"... A man whose bones are rotting somewhere now,
white in the rain on dark earth where they lie,
or tumbling in the groundswell of the sea ..."

(1.199–201 [166–69])

He is helped by his exceptionally fine ear for dramatic utterance
and tones of voice, all-important in Homer, in whose poetry there is
so much speech. The range is very great, from the homely pathos of
Penelope's

"Oh, Nan, they are a bad lot ..."

(17.657 [499])

to the Olympian maestoso of Zeus's

"Hermês, you have much practice on our missions,
go make it known to the softly-braided nymph
that we, whose will is not subject to error,
order Odysseus home. ..."

(5.32–35 [29–31])

Listen now to the softly braided Calypso asking Hermes why he has
come to see her: "Tell me please, Hermes of the golden wand, why
have you come, an honored, dear friend? You have not visited me
much in the past. Say what you have in mind, for I am eager to do it
if I can and if it is something that can be done." But this will never
do. The lady must be allowed to speak her own beautiful language
(5.87–90):

"τίπτε μοι, Ἑρμεία χρυσόρραπι, εἰλήλουθας
αἰδοῖός τε φίλος τε; πάρος γε μὲν οὔ τι θαμίζεις.

αὖδα ὅ τι φρονέεις· τελέσαι δέ με θυμὸς ἄνωγεν,
εἰ δύναμαι τελέσαι γε καὶ εἰ τετελεσμένον ἐστίν . . ."

Fitzgerald hears what she would say were she speaking English:

> "O Hermês, ever with your golden wand,
> what brings you to my island?
> Your awesome visits in the past were few.
> Now tell me what request you have in mind;
> for I desire to do it, if I can,
> and if it is a proper thing to do . . ."

(5.92–97)

Homer gives the god his ceremonial epithet, χρυσόρραπις, "with wand of gold." These epithets are a problem for the translator, since English poetry is so much less free with them than Greek. Robert Fagles in his version of 1996 takes the bull by the horns and writes: "God of the golden wand, why have you come?" (5.98). Not very polite, nor is this a convincing form of address; neither in real life nor in a novel can someone say, "Man in the black mask, what are you doing in my house?" Fitzgerald solves the problem by making a point of it. He hears a coquettish half-mocking note in Calypso's voice as though she were saying, "I see you have brought your golden wand with you. You never leave home without it, do you?" Fagles has her call him "a beloved, honored friend" (99). Fitzgerald continues the note of mockery and keeps closer to the Greek αἰδοῖος with "your awesome visits." His "for I desire to do it, if I can" follows the original closely; "and if it is a proper thing to do" (can the god be asking her to do something *im*proper?) does not, but a great translator can occasionally lend his greater original author a helping hand, as Laurence Binyon does when he writes "thwart winds" for Dante's "contrari venti."[7]

Long narrative poems are hardly in vogue, and readers are easily put off by rank after rank of solid verse. Whether or not consciously avoiding this danger, Fitzgerald often breaks up lines into their constitutive elements, directing our attention now to this character, now to that, and introducing bits of speech so that we sometimes seem to be reading a scene from a play. Take a passage like this from book 17:

> Telémakhos,
> after the blow his father bore, sat still
> without a tear, though his heart felt the blow.
> Slowly he shook his head from side to side,
> containing murderous thoughts.

                              Penélopê
on the higher level of her room had heard
the blow, and knew who gave it. Now she murmured:

"Would god you could be hit yourself, Antínoös—
hit by Apollo's bowshot!"

                              And Eurýnomê
her housekeeper, put in:

"He and no other?
If all we pray for came to pass, not one
would live till dawn!"

                              Her gentle mistress said:

"Oh, Nan, they are a bad lot . . ."

                              (17.641–57 [489–99])

Fitzgerald's *Odyssey* was immediately recognized as a masterpiece, but it has not always pleased professional classicists, who complain that it pays no attention to the most influential contribution made to Homeric scholarship in this century, the demonstration by the American scholar Milman Parry that Homer's poems are oral compositions. The units of his poetry—to quote the formulation of Parry's theory by an enthusiastic adherent, Denys Page—

> are not words, selected by the poet, combined by him into phrases, and adjusted by him to his metre: its units are *formulas*, phrases ready-made, extending in length from a word or two to several complete lines, already adapted to the metre, and either already adapted or instantly adaptable to the limited range of ideas [*sic*] which the subject-matter of the Greek epic may require him to express. The oral poet composes while he recites; he must therefore be able to rely on his memory. He makes his lines out of formulas which he knows by heart, and which he has learned to use in this way as one learns to use an ordinary language.[8]

The facts, the elements of Homeric diction, are as Parry recorded them, and are not open to question. The inferences from those facts are very much open to question and have been questioned by scholars bold enough to go against the prevailing doctrine.[9] This, however, is not the place to go into the matter, since the oral-formulaic style cannot be adequately reproduced in translation. Even if the translator uses words semantically equivalent to the Greek, they will not have the same effect, or give the same pleasure, as they do in the original where we see or hear the recurrent phrases, πολύτλας δῖος Ὀδυσσεύς (long-enduring, noble Odysseus), πολύμητις Ὀδυσσεύς (the great planner Odysseus) and the like, fit into their appointed place in the Greek hexameter. Nothing of the sort can happen in English verse with its far freer metrical structure, and the recurrent phrases seem merely repetitious.

Fitzgerald at all events does not try to pretend that he is himself composing orally and allows himself the liberties that fine verse translators have always taken from the time of Dryden and Pope, on to Edward FitzGerald in the nineteenth century and to Pound, the greatest libertarian of them all, in the twentieth. These liberties are not licenses; they are necessary freedoms. When in *Iliad* 19 Achilles returns to the fighting, Pope translates:

> All bright in heav'nly Arms, above his Squire
> *Achilles* mounts, and sets the Field on Fire.
>
> (19.434–35)

These lines do not correspond to anything in the Greek words. What Pope, using his own words, has done is to make us feel the sudden surge of energy, greater than anything we have felt before, that *sets the field on fire* when Achilles goes into action.

The situation today is different. Translation of classical poetry is for the most part directed not to the lover of poetry or even the general reader but to the classroom, where it is taught by people who probably do not know Greek or Latin and want to be sure that the version they are using closely follows the original. They are going to be seriously embarrassed if, having praised Homer's wit for describing Athena disguised as a young girl as "the awesome one in pigtails" (7.44 [41]), they discover from a classical colleague that it is Fitzgerald's wit they should be praising, not Homer's; he speaks of Athena as "the dread goddess with beautiful hair." Good old Lattimore never lets us down like this, they mutter resentfully.[10]

Merriment of this sort Fitzgerald allows himself only now and then. This is a responsible translation, and we should hardly hold it against him that it makes very enjoyable reading. There are those who enjoy reading the *Odyssey* in Greek. He does, however, have his own angle on the poem, interpreting it rather than simply word-for-wording it into English. Consider a line like this:

> Aîas, it was—the great shade burning still

(Odysseus has just met his old enemy among the dead, 11.646 [543]). There is no burning shade in Homer's Greek, but there is in Virgil's Latin, in the scene in *Aeneid* 6 modeled on Homer when Aeneas meets the shade of Dido, whom he has deserted, *ardentem et torva tuentem*, "burning and glaring savagely." Fitzgerald lets the Latin speak through the Greek because his vision is synoptic; he knows that the *Odyssey* is part of a larger whole in which the poems of Virgil and Milton and the other great poets of our tradition have a simultaneous existence (to borrow words from Eliot's "Tradition and the Individual Talent"). He does what Pope does when, translating the *Iliad*, he lets Milton's "High on a throne of Royal State . . . Satan exalted sat" speak through his English Homer: "High in the midst the great *Achilles* stands," "High o'er the Host, all terrible he stands."[11]

Fitzgerald's translation is interpretative rather than literal because he understands that a phrase or line may in different contexts mean something different. Twenty-three times in the poem there is a line that introduces a speech by Odysseus. Lattimore follows Homer by using the same words each time: "Then resourceful Odysseus spoke in turn and answered him/her." Fitzgerald renders it in this and more than this variety of ways:

> To this the strategist Odysseus answered:

(Calypso has inquired if he thinks Penelope more attractive than herself, since he is so anxious to return to her, 5.223 [214].)

> The great tactician carefully replied:

(Queen Arete wants to know why he is wearing clothes that her daughter Nausicaa took that morning to the river to launder, 7.257 [240].)

> His mind ranging far, Odysseus answered:

(Athena has revealed herself in Ithaca and promised to help him; carefully he sifts her promises, 13.398 [311].)

> And the great master of invention answered:

(He is about to relate the fifth of his six fictitious life stories to Penelope, 19.194 [164].) A particularly fine example of Fitzgerald's care for context occurs in book 7, where Odysseus, safe at last in happy Phaeacia after so many harrowing adventures, is referred to as πολύτλας, "much-enduring," one of his most constant epithets. Fitzgerald translates: "Odysseus, who had borne the barren sea" (7.142 [133]). There is no barren sea in the Greek but a lot of it in Odysseus's mind.

One could continue to praise the variety of means whereby this resourceful poet-translator has brought over into English Homer's poem of the resourceful Odysseus. Often what he writes is simply translation in its fullest sense, as in the passage where Proteus comes stealthily ashore at midday, μελαίνη φρικὶ καλυφθείς:

> hidden by shivering glooms on the clear water.[12]
>
> (4.431 [402])

Sometimes he will force an obscure word into sharp Mediterranean focus, for example translating ἐς γουνὸν Ἀθηνάων ἱεράων (11.323) as "the terraced land / of ancient Athens" (374–75); or, rendering ἐνὶ γναμπτοῖσι μέλεσσι (11.394) as "in the great torque of his arms" (459), he will find a picture in a dull-looking phrase. With ease he takes over the compound epithets which in English normally stick out like the poetic aliens that they are:

> guests were arriving at the great lord's house,
> bringing their sheep, and wine, the ease of men,
> with loaves their comely kerchiefed women sent,
> to make a feast in hall.
>
> (4.664–67 [621–23])

"Comely kerchiefed" is as natural and lovely as the Greek καλλικρήδεμνος and calls up the same graceful, dignified picture.

Now and then we may think that he has taken the first pleasant word that came to hand—and so failed to see deeply or freshly into the text: "drooping willow" (10.566 [510]) for example, does not do justice to ὠλεσίκαρπος with its symbolic suggestions, needed by the context, of barrenness and early death; and, shortly after, "pale Perséphonê" (ἐπαινὴ Περσεφόνεια) is glib Swinburnian (10.545 [534]). On other occasions we may feel that he has gone too far, as when he writes

> ". . . the whole rondure of heaven hooded so
> by Zeus in woeful cloud . . ."
>
> (5.313–14 [303–4])

His only addition is "woeful," but the way he has combined the elements of the Greek sentence is Virgilian rather than Homeric. At 21.14 (12), one may find "quills of groaning" for στονόεντες ὀϊστοί, energetic if a touch too Icelandic, but when on its next appearance, the phrase grows into "the quiver spiked with coughing death" (63 [60]), some readers will be inclined to find such a verbalism to be outside the sphere of Homeric diction altogether.

I do not mean, in taking these single phrases out of context, to suggest that Fitzgerald has strained for energies of effect beyond the warrant of his author. It is, on the contrary, in its essential truth to Homer that the distinction of this translation lies.* For "that increasingly important if ill-defined person, the Greekless 'general reader,'"[13] in E. R. Dodds's just and careful words, this is the only translation. Those that preceded it have their interest but are not essential; those that have followed do not matter. The fortunate few who have some Greek, good Greek, any Greek, find their pleasure in the original quickened by meeting it reborn in their own language. Sometimes, even . . . listen to Nausicaa proudly describing her father in his great chair by the fire (6.328 [309]):

> there like a god he sits and takes his wine
>
> τῷ ὅ γε οἰνοποτάζει ἐφήμενος ἀθάνατος ὥς.

Is not the English almost as fine as the Greek, even if Fitzgerald cannot quite match Homer's swagger?

The *Iliad*

Of the many difficulties that test the translator of the *Iliad* two are worth singling out. Far more sharply than with the *Odyssey* he faces the problem of what to turn the poem *into*. Though the *Odyssey* is not "our first novel," there is just enough life in the cliché to allow translator and reader to collaborate in the pleasures of a narrative mode that has not been improved on. This has always been an amenable poem. Odysseus's series of encounters in books 5 through 12 will submit to a wide range of interpretation; the second half of the poem, though it has its longueurs, provides a narrative action—the hero's return and recovery of his home—that is exciting in itself and points to further levels of meaning, psychological, social, cosmological, that we can accommodate readily enough. The *Iliad* is a far more formidable

---

* These two sentences, and the previous three paragraphs, are taken from "Guslar with Rose-Tipped Fingers," *Arion: A Journal of Humanities and the Classics* 1, no. 1 (Spring 1962): 122–24.

"On Looking Into Fitzgerald's Homer," *New York Review of Books* 21, no. 20 (December 12, 1974): 3–8.

object, a huge uncompromising tragic masterpiece that must be taken on its own terms before it will speak to ours.

The *Odyssey*, moreover, could be thought of as awaiting its translator: until Robert Fitzgerald came along. No previous rendering was entirely satisfactory. But the *Iliad* has been translated, supremely well, and the new man has always to ask himself: Can I do this passage better than Pope? He may of course hope or assume that Pope's *Iliad* is so far out of cultural reach that his version will stand outside its shadow, in the direct light of the original. For what gives Pope's translation its supreme confidence has long proved its greatest liability: the belief he shared with his readers that Homer's epic form had been handed down through the ages and was still, in its latest reincarnation, living and usable.

Our notions of epic have changed and Pope's *Iliad* belongs to its period, yet it is far more than simply an Augustan classic. And certainly it is not a "pretty poem"; Bentley's mot is wide of the mark. Although Pope cannot respond to everything in the *Iliad*—he sophisticates where he should be plain and does not fully catch its tragic accent—the distinguishing feature of his translation is the way he meets Homer's power, the rage of being that drives through the poem, with an almost comparable power of his own. It is the greatest verse translation in English, and Johnson's praise in the life of Pope—"that poetical wonder . . . a performance which no age or nation can pretend to equal"—seems a good deal less extravagant than it used to.[14]

There is no question, though, that we need a modern *Iliad* of real poetic quality, and Fitzgerald brings many qualifications to the task. His work on the *Odyssey* taught him how to write verse narrative, how to convert the small change of Homeric diction into contemporary though not too contemporary English. He has an ear for the cadence of speech, a sense of the prose reality of Homer's action.

Though he takes his proper local liberties and avoids the word-for-word "fidelity" that so often caught his immediate predecessor in what Hugh Kenner has called lexicographic lockstep,[15] Fitzgerald meets the Greek closely and responsibly. In book 9 the man who loves civil war is said to be ἀφρήτωρ ἀθέμιστος ἀνέστιος (9.63), that is, excluded from fellowship in a clan, in violation of usage, denied access to the hearth. This is easier to gloss than translate, but Fitzgerald, catching the sense closely, comes up with resonant, convincing poetic speech:

> Alien to clan and custom and hearth fire
> is he who longs for war.

> (p. 205)

Or take the repeated, formular phrases that are so much discussed. Often, no doubt, they are mere metrical *remplissage*, yet they are dense with stored experience and may always spring to life—like a familiar object one passes every day that suddenly, one day, becomes a revelation. Thirteen times in the poem one of the words for "earth" is modified by an epithet meaning literally "that feeds many." Fitzgerald sometimes ignores the epithet and writes simply "earth," "ground," or the like; here and there he omits the whole phrase. But at one point (6.213), a lull in the fighting gives him time to look at this blood-stained Trojan earth and remembering what it once was, before the Achaeans came, he writes "the field where herds had cropped" (p. 148). This is how one reads Homer; no one, I think, has been able to translate him in quite this way.

And he is sensitive to the pace of the poem. When Homer stops you dead in your tracks, he tries to do so too. There is in the first scene a phrase used of the sea (πολυφλοίσβοιο θαλάσσης, 1.34) that, once heard, is not forgotten. Fitzgerald gives himself three shots at the sounding adjective: "by the shore of the tumbling clamorous whispering sea" (p. 12). This may not quite work and perhaps owes too much to another poet,[16] but it does serve to register a disturbance in the Greek. It might even drive someone to learn Greek and go and look for himself. Often, Fitzgerald's strokes do work. Here is Priam in book 24, half maddened by grief:

> The old man,
> fiercely wrapped and hooded in his mantle,
> sat like a figure graven
>
> (pp. 572–73)

where "fiercely" and "figure graven" brilliantly unfold a single packed word (ἐντυπάς [24.163], meaning, we are told, that he was wrapped in his mantle so closely as to show the contour of his limbs).

The poem's narrative business is lucidly presented. A moment in the fighting: "And near and nearer / the front ranks came" till a single figure "detached himself to be the first in battle— / vivid and beautiful, Aléxandros" (p. 68 [3.15–16]). In the domestic scenes, thanks to our greater knowledge of Homer's *Realien*, the modern translator can score over Pope whose culture loaded the clear Homeric world with the pomp thought proper to epic. Priam is thus credited with a residence worthy of a baroque monarch ("And now to *Priam*'s stately Courts he came, / Rais'd on arch'd Columns of stupendous Frame," 6.304–5 [242–43]) whereas Fitzgerald can write simply "Priam's palace . . . made all of ashlar, with bright colonnades" (p. 149).

There is much to admire and be grateful for in Fitzgerald's *Iliad*. Why then is one left with a certain sense of dissatisfaction? At his best, Fitzgerald can keep a powerful movement going, as in the battle with the river in book 21 and for much of book 16, the *Patrocleia*, where there are passages "composed" with something of Homer's monumental drive—for instance, the lines (16.765–76) culminating in the vision of the dead charioteer Cebriones "minding no more the mastery of horses" (p. 400). With the lyrical moments, as one might expect, he is particularly successful. The lovely ease and assurance that distinguished his *Odyssey* shine once again in (for instance) the lines describing the Cretan dancers on Achilles' shield.

And yet . . . In the preface to his *Iliad* Pope spoke of "that unequal'd Fire and Rapture, which is so forcible in Homer, that no Man of a true Poetical Spirit is Master of himself while he reads him." This is the challenge that every translator must meet. To an astonishing degree Pope did meet it; I have not yet found that Fitzgerald does. This *Iliad* does not overwhelm; it does not leave one, shaken and exalted, with the sense of an abounding, transfigured reality.

This relative failure is most apparent in the big military books, from 11 through the middle of 18, that span a single terrible day's fighting. They test the translator cruelly and are hardly less testing for the contemporary reader. The nature of war has changed beyond all recognition, and the "poetry of war" has not been the same since Fabrice stumbled into the battle of Waterloo. No one can suppose that Homer enjoys war, yet he confronts it, head-on, with a dreadful relish that easily offends us. As a metaphor for the human condition his battles are acceptable enough, but there are too many of them and they are too literal, too savagely particularized, to allow this easy way out. On a different level there is, to be frank, the danger of tedium in the many passages which, in English, seem to consist of not much more than "A killed B and C was killed by D," plus epithets and accouterment.[17]

I say "in English" because in the original the problem hardly arises. For two reasons, I think. First, the insistent realism of Homeric poetry persuades us that this is all actually happening. The fighting cannot be written off as so much literary slaughter and is often too frightening and too heartrending to leave time for boredom. There is no catching at our emotions in all this killing, and no consolation; no real cause to fight for, and certainly no promise of a future reward for fighting well. A man dies, that is all. With an accent not so much of pity as of absolute sorrow the event, in all its gravity, is caught and recorded again and again: the abrupt fall of an erect, flourishing creature.

Here, the Homer of the *Iliad* is strictly incomparable, but there is another factor in the making of these scenes that does not put them quite beyond the reach of a poet who, like Pope, was working in a great style. And that is the high formality of the verse and the meter itself. In chapter 18 of *Biographia Literaria*, Coleridge remarked on meter's power "to increase the vivacity and susceptibility both of the general feelings and of the attention . . . As a medicated atmosphere, or as wine during animated conversation, [the effects of meter] act powerfully though themselves unnoticed." Thanks to this metrically induced "atmosphere" through which and in which the action of the poem is presented, the battle scenes hardly ever, in the original, read like mere transcriptions of carnage. The formality of the verse form does not so much distance as heighten them, they are not less but more than usually "there," so that—our own powers of response enormously intensified—the narrative can blaze for hundreds of lines on end, seemingly at full stretch but with always enough energy in reserve to reach still higher and burst into almost intolerable splendor.

Fitzgerald's flexible blank verse line, though it is skillfully handled and certainly a far finer medium than Lattimore's laborious six-beater, lacks the resources of a great style. It cannot pace the steady hexametral drive of the Greek; it can, at a demanding moment (Achilles' return to the war), rise only to this:

> Automédôn then
> took in hand the shining whip and mounted
> the chariot, and at his back Akhilleus
> mounted in full armor, shining bright
> as the blinding Lord of Noon. In a clarion voice
> he shouted to the horses of his father.
>
> (p. 469 [19.395–99])

But in the original a passage like this makes us feel, in Cedric Whitman's words, "that all the surge and motion of the *Iliad* hitherto has been nothing, so far does the hero's roused vitality surpass all else." Pope, in his own terms, meets the challenge:

> The Charioteer then whirl'd the Lash around,
> And swift ascended at one active Bound.
> All bright in heav'nly Arms, above his Squire
> *Achilles* mounts, and sets the Field on Fire;
> Not brighter, *Phoebus* in th' Aetherial Way,
> Flames from his Chariot, and restores the Day.
> High o'er the Host, all terrible he stands,
> And thunders to his Steeds these dread Commands.
>
> (19.432–39)

Perhaps there is something in this poem that Fitzgerald could not quite stomach. It may be, too, that the nature of the present demand for translation puts an obstacle in the translator's path. Writing for people who mostly do not have the original, he is required to be what professors call "accurate." Though Fitzgerald does not work word for word or line by line, he is much closer to his text than Pope, whose unit was the whole paragraph, even the whole scene, which he then proceeded to recast and re-create in his own terms. Standing at this distance he was able, paradoxically, to enter into a closer, certainly a richer, relation with his original than most modern translators can. "What distinguishes Pope's accomplishment," Douglas M. Knight writes in the introduction to the Twickenham edition of Pope's Homer, "is that he is willing to allow his own world and Homer's a mutual or shared life, each providing a commentary on the other. Translations of Homer commonly founder because they will not risk such interplay."[18] Interplay, in this sense, means taking liberties that would raise academic eyebrows these days and rob you of the prize of classroom adoption. Yet is there any other way to *translate* great poetry—that is, to carry it across into the new language and time? It still demands of the translator that he bring his whole life, his whole cultural experience, to bear on the text.

Here are Pope's and Fitzgerald's versions of the death of Axylus (6.12–19), one of the many passages that poignantly juxtapose peace and war.

Alexander Pope:

> Next *Teuthras'* Son distain'd the Sands with Blood,
> *Axylus*, hospitable, rich and good:
> In fair *Arisba's* Walls (his native Place)
> He held his Seat; a Friend to Human Race.
> Fast by the Road, his ever-open Door
> Oblig'd the Wealthy, and reliev'd the Poor.
> To stern *Tydides* now he falls a Prey,
> No Friend to guard him in the dreadful Day!
> Breathless the good Man fell, and by his side
> His faithful Servant, old *Calesius* dy'd.
>
> (6.15–24)

Robert Fitzgerald:

> Diomêdês
> then slew Áxylos Teuthránidês
> from the walled town Arisbê. A rich man

and kindly, he befriended all who passed
his manor by the road. But none of these
could come between him and destruction now,
as the Akhaian killed him, killing with him
Kalêsios, his aide and charioteer—
leaving two dead men to be cloaked in earth.

(pp. 141–42)

Briefly but firmly, the man's kindly, useful life is set before us, then the terror of his death. The situation here is universal enough, it would seem, and one wonders why Fitzgerald makes so little of it while Pope is hardly inferior to the original. Perhaps it is because the universal, to affect us, must be given a local habitation and a name. Thanks to the interplay he allows between his own world and Homer's, Pope has more to do than simply match the Greek words with English. As Maynard Mack shows elsewhere in the Twickenham introduction, he colors the scene with later, and contemporary, cultural elements—Stoic, Christian, a new social awareness of the poor—and seizing on the emergent concept of *philanthrōpia* or *humanitas* which he found in these lines presents it in the more developed form it had taken in his own day. We know too much to permit ourselves these liberties now? But translation is not archaeology, and a true translation of a moving passage must itself be moving.

For various respectable purposes we need a reliable account of what Homer "says." Lattimore has provided one. Translation means more than this, though, and the question is whether the *Iliad* can be *translated*, in its entirety, today. Fitzgerald has tried his hand at it, but he is too fine an artist to fake, and his text reveals that all too often he has not been able to meet the challenge of the *Iliad*. The trouble may in large part be that he has failed to find an answer to the problem I began with: the problem of what to turn this poem *into*. Pope's strength is that he did have an answer. The late Renaissance or neoclassic heroic mode gave him the means to respond to about as much of the *Iliad* as was visible to his age. It gave him a great style through which to meet the still greater style of the original.

Thanks to Robert Fitzgerald, we will not need another *Odyssey* for a long time to come. Despite the interest of his new version there is room for another *Iliad*, and I think the next man (Christopher Logue or someone else) is going to have to take far greater risks and allow his own world and Homer's to come to grips with each other. It is not, as classical scholars invariably suppose, a matter of "modernizing" Homer. (Logue goes too far in this direction and does not maintain Pope's interplay between then and now.) What we need is rather a poet who will do for the *Iliad*, or parts of it, something of what Pound did for the passage from the *Odyssey* in his first Canto. Though this could only have been written in the twentieth century, diction and tone are decidedly archaic. Pound presents us with an ancient object: that somehow comes to light in a modern poem. He shows the past surfacing within the present, and preserves the tension between them. An authentic moment from a distant then *is* now.

THE *AENEID*

Secure in his lofty station for century after century ("the chastest and the royalest" poet, Bacon said),[19] Virgil began to lose ground in the Romantic period and today his position is deeply ambiguous. Although fewer and fewer people have the classical languages, Homer and the Greek tragedians are present to the literary consciousness; Virgil is not, or not to the same degree, partly no doubt because he survives translation so much less well. Tell the story of the *Iliad* and still more of the *Odyssey* and a good deal of what Homer has to say comes across. The *Aeneid* is also a narrative poem and Virgil's story is no less, in many ways far more, important, but the narrative action is refracted through a dense linguistic medium which conditions and controls the way we take that action. This medium, the incomparable language admired even by the poet's adversaries, is not represented in either of our classic versions (Gavin Douglas writes, splendidly, a different kind of poetry; Dryden's Augustan preconceptions are subtly, sometimes grossly, distorting) and has up to now defeated every modern translator.

Fitzgerald's *Odyssey* showed his command of a narrative style; if the *Iliad* proved less amenable to his genius, his version did suggest that here perhaps was the man uniquely qualified by taste and conviction to tackle the *Aeneid*. How has he met the challenge? How close does his version let us all come to this famous poem, and what, from its troubled past, does it have to say to our troubled present? Can the old claims, however rephrased, still be sustained?

A work of the past can possess the quality of "nowness" in two ways. It may treat so directly of what is permanent in the human condition that time can get no hold on it. The parting of Hector and Andromache in book 6 of the *Iliad* asks for no exercise of the historical imagination; the best poetry of Thomas Hardy will not date unless our species changes utterly. "Yes, this is true," we say of such writing,

"The Return of Virgil," *New York Review of Books* 30, no. 16 (October 27, 1983): 3–4.

"this is how it is." There is a second kind of nowness, timely rather than timeless, whereby an old author reemerges and is found to speak with a contemporary voice to the concerns of a particular generation. Donne and Góngora in the earlier twentieth century spoke in this way, until the academy stepped in and reclaimed them.

Though he has countless phrases and lines that touch the heart as immediately as any poetry can, Virgil does not possess the first kind of contemporaneity. His art is too distanced, his poem too much the expression of a certain moment in history, to be timeless in the sense that Homer's is. What of the second kind? Will Fitzgerald's *Aeneid* guide us, Latinists and Latinless alike, to uncover a timely *Aeneid*? Some classicists have been pointing in this direction for a while. The Virgil of R. A. Brooks's superb paper "*Discolor Aura*: Reflections on the Golden Bough"[20] struck a note distinctly contemporary with its time; there was nothing antiquarian about the *Aeneid* proposed by Ralph Johnson in *Darkness Visible*.[21]

If the poem is an epic of the foundation of Rome, its theme is the refounding, or possibility of refounding, the *res Romana* which Augustus (Octavian, as he was then) had in hand when Virgil began writing around 30 BC. The possibility and above all the cost of refounding: for while Virgil steadfastly believes in the city, the ordered human community, he is very conscious of the all but ruinous burdens it imposes, of how much it calls on us to renounce in the way of instinctual gratification. He has or at least understands our sense that any acceptable order should be not imposed but, as Wallace Stevens says, discovered—educed or allowed to emerge as the natural configuration of what has to be ordered. Where he goes beyond us is in his allegiance to the city and his willingness to accept the price that must be paid for it. If the poem is able to return its hesitant, brave "Yes" to the question "is the city worth so much suffering?" the answer would be worth little if it had not taken so fully into account everything that seems to cry "No."

Virgil announces his theme at the end of the prelude to book 1: "It was so massive, so burdensome a task [*tantae molis erat*] to found the Roman people." He begins to show what this means in the scene that follows, an example of the way he makes the old epic machinery serve new purposes, moral, social, and political. Aeneas is on the last leg of his voyage to Italy when he runs into a storm stirred up by Juno, the poem's principle not simply of discord but of positive evil, who has persuaded the wind god Aeolus to unleash the winds. Jupiter had imprisoned them in a huge cavern and charged Aeolus with guarding them, for were they to break loose "they would sweep away sea and land and high heaven." Fearing this, he imposed on them "the mass [*molem*] of great mountains." The winds must represent the passions and as such should be morally neutral, but the terrible century of anarchy and civil war from which Rome had only just emerged had shown what havoc the unrestrained passions can play. The passions, man's natural instincts, can no longer be trusted; he must be forced to behave decently. This is what Virgil seems to imply in some curious words in book 7 where the people of the golden age of Saturn are described as "righteous not by compulsion or law but of their own free will" (7.203–4). So perhaps it was once, but in the Iron Age the poem inhabits man must be policed into virtue, "righteous by compulsion."

The poem keeps asking how far this is morally possible. How much restraint and denial will human nature bear without being denatured and corrupted? In the figure of Turnus, Virgil presents the old unrestrained heroism of the Homeric world where the passions could enjoy themselves (as Nietzsche said of music)[22] with remarkably few prohibitions. But Turnus, the innocent tragic victim of Juno's malignant design, is broken and thrown aside, a man history no longer has any use for. In Aeneas, as everyone says, Virgil tries to portray a new, self-denying heroism, but from the Romantic period on many readers have felt that he is simply not a hero at all. "Bigob, I thought he was a priest," Yeats's Irishman reportedly said.[23]

The problem, the nearly insuperable problem of post-Homeric epic, is that this "new" hero must perform the old heroic actions, in the later books assume an Achillean, almost superhuman role. We have to try to see these actions as meaning something new and should I suppose say, "how sad that a sensitive person like Aeneas is forced to do such things." The danger is that we do not really believe he is doing them at all—as though we were asked to imagine a character from Henry James uneasily at large in a Western.

This new heroism is more convincingly represented by what is done to Aeneas, what he has to endure, than by what he himself does. His career is one of continual renunciation. He would sooner have remained at Troy, but is compelled to set out on the fated journey to Italy. He would have been willing to stay with Dido in Africa, a cherished, not altogether disconsolate prince consort; the divine command forces him to abandon her. His military activities in the second half of the poem are impelled by no lust for conquest but again at the bidding of his destiny.

One human attachment after another is denied him. How often do we see him stretch out his arms—to his mother, his wife, his father, the woman he loved and deserted—only to see them vanish. In book 8 he does finally embrace his divine mother, Venus, when she brings him the shield portraying scenes from the future history of Rome, most prominently the story of Antony and Cleopatra. What Aeneas sees there is a replay with a different ending of his own affair with Dido: a Roman who forsakes or so nearly forsakes his duty for love of an alien woman. Aeneas looks at the actions on the shield and "Knowing nothing of the events themselves, He felt joy in their pictures" (8.989–90 [8.730]). Literally this is true, otherwise quite untrue. He knows all too well and yet his destiny cruelly forces him to delight in the terrible thing he has done.

How are we to understand all this? A good deal in the poem seems to support the old Christian reading, above all perhaps in the sense that the world is simply too difficult and too terrible for man to find his way without constant divine guidance. This reading sees Aeneas as a man with a vocation (in some fashion he obviously is), a man under obedience called on to renounce his own will and carry out the will of God in which, as the Christian poet will say, we find our peace. If Aeneas demonstrably does not find his peace in the poem, it is because the Christian message was still struggling to emerge and could not yet be firmly articulated, least of all in the old unregenerate heroic form.

The *Aeneid* will take such a reading but it allows others, and there are those who prefer a tragic or rather a darkly pessimistic *Aeneid*. For them it is the story of a man who tries to collaborate with God and history and is very, very nearly broken in the process. This in essence is Brooks's interpretation ("Man does not fit in history," as he puts it),[24] which after half a century still seems to me the most convincing we have.

The argument will go on, for like *Paradise Lost* the *Aeneid* is a controversial poem and it is here that its greatness consists, not in its "success" but in the profound and perhaps insoluble issues it raises and explores with such passion and truth. No epic "succeeds" after Homer.

A work of this sort demands a great deal of the translator. He must tell the story in a way that holds our attention, as Virgil does, and, as Virgil does, tell it in a way that lets us see *through* the story to what so richly lies half unspoken behind it. For Virgil's narrative "means" in a sense that previous narrative does not. To make the old epic genre address his new Roman circumstance he had virtually to invent a new "polysemous" kind of poetry, as his commentator Servius called it, one with many levels of signification, and poetry has never been the same since. This of itself need pose no problem for the modern translator and indeed plays into his hands, since we now expect a poem to be polysemous. What makes Virgil almost untranslatable, in something more than the sense in which all good verse is untranslatable, is that his language, stylized, distanced, and yes, "poetical," is at the furthest remove from any modern manner and from the natural genius of English.

A soldier has drunk too much wine and lies at night on the battlefield snoring. Shakespeare would have had no qualms about this, nor would Aeschylus, who lets his Furies snore in the very temple of Apollo. Virgil, however, whose stylistic canon does not readily allow for such creaturely activities, writes, "he breathed forth sleep from his whole breast" (9.326), and was complimented by Servius for avoiding the low word. Fitzgerald, neatly taking care of Virgil's refined circumlocution and of our preference for calling spades spades, has the man "snoring loud, lungs full of sleep" (9.461). At times, inevitably, Virgil defeats him, as when he describes a pack of hounds as *odora canum vis*, literally "the keen-scented strength of dogs" (4.132), that is, strong dogs with a keen scent. This would be impossibly abstract in English and Fitzgerald sensibly lets it go with "hounds in packs keen on the scent" (4.185).

Inevitably again he sometimes gives his diction a more homely edge than the original strictly warrants. At the start of book 5, as a storm blows up the helmsman Palinurus says, "Father Neptune, what are you brewing for us?" (Virgil merely writes "preparing," 5.17 [14]), and he tells Aeneas that there is no "bucking" the rough weather ahead ("struggling against," Virgil writes, 5.27 [21]). Dryden would have thought such "village words,"[25] too mean for the occasion, but the habit of our language is against him, and admitted temperately, as Fitzgerald admits them, they are invigorating. Too strident or pervasive a colloquialism would turn the *Aeneid* into a different poem, too stylized a diction leave the translation dead on the page.

Here and there we feel that Fitzgerald had to keep himself in check, chastening to Virgil's sterner purposes the sprightly interventions which the *Odyssey* so readily allowed him. This is clearest in passages where Virgil is writing with the Greek poem in mind. In book 4 he describes how Jupiter sent Mercury to tell Aeneas that he must leave Dido and get under way again, just as in book 5 of the *Odyssey* Zeus sent Hermes to Odysseus with a similar message. Here is Fitzgerald's account of the Greek:

> No words were lost on Hermês the Wayfinder,
> who bent to tie his beautiful sandals on,
> ambrosial, golden, that carry him over water
> or over endless land in a swish of the wind.
>
> (5.48–51 [43–46])

Such vivacity, compound of delight and a kind of detached amusement, will not do for Virgil:

He finished and fell silent. Mercury
Made ready to obey the great command
Of his great father, and he first tied on
The golden sandals, winged, that high in air
Transport him over seas or over land
Abreast of gale winds.

(4.324–30 [238–41])

In Homer it is important for Odysseus and for his poem that he set out once more on the journey home; in Virgil the whole history of the world depends on Aeneas reaching Italy. For actions so momentous the translator must devise a weightier style; he cannot, as it were, take time off and enjoy himself en route. Not that Fitzgerald doesn't give us an occasional grace note, as when in the famous scene where Venus and Vulcan make love he describes her as "cherishing him in her swansdown embrace" (8.518 [388]).

This is not the tear-drenched nineteenth-century *Aeneid*, but it is a painful, even grievous reading, above all a deeply serious reading. Its greatest single virtue is that it does what translation can seldom do: force us to think about and into what we read as hard as the original does. This must be what makes the almost insurmountable problem of translating Virgil's marvelous language here seem less intractable. As Dryden knew ("I contemn the world when I think on it," he wrote in the dedication of the *Aeneis*, "and myself when I translate it"), it cannot be directly translated. You cannot, that is, meet it head-on: what sane writer could suppose himself capable of wielding "the stateliest measure ever moulded by the lips of man"?[26] Fitzgerald's achievement is that he has reached so deeply into *what* is said that the *how* of its saying comes to seem, almost, unimportant and his words take on their own sufficient dignity. Think of what Aeneas does and the kind of man he is, and the old dilemma of how to English *pietas* and *pius Aeneas* solves itself, by means that appear very simple. He is "a man apart, devoted to his mission" (1.16 [10]). So too with the opening words, hackneyed as a quotation from *Hamlet, Arma virumque cano*, where so many translators have come to grief. "I sing of warfare and a man at war," Fitzgerald begins.

Without consciously trying to be Virgilian, he sounds like Virgil— a minor Virgil, to be sure, but that is already a great deal—by feeling as Virgil does and taking seriously the things he takes seriously. The Virgilian *religio* is here, his sense of the piety of elder days: "I paid / My homage to that shrine of ancient stone" (3.115–16 [84]). The Virgilian note of sorrow for all those who fail and fall is truly struck again and again: "The Teucrians on the shore wept for Misenus, / Doing for thankless dust the final honors" (6.301–2 [212–13]). Virgil's tenderness is here: "And I could not believe that I would hurt you / So terribly by going" (6.624–25 [463–64]), Aeneas says to Dido in the underworld.

This is for many pages a quiet translation. (Sometimes it is salutary to turn back to Dryden for a harder, brisker Virgil.) Fitzgerald's language does not draw a great deal of attention to itself, yet how seldom in this long work does it go dead on him. His ear, practiced on so many thousand lines of Homer, is very cunning, his fingering consistently sure. Here is Cleopatra at Actium: "The queen / Amidst the battle called her flotilla on / With a sistrum's beat, a frenzy out of Egypt" (8.941–43 [696])—the slight metrical irregularity giving life to the picture. Here is the virgin warrior Camilla: "If she ran full speed / Over the tips of grain unharvested / She would not ever have bruised an ear, or else . . ." (7.1111–13 [808–9]—the beautiful hypermetric syllable conveying the lilt and lightness of her passage. A sudden dactylic thrust gives us a famously onomatopoeic line: "Hoofbeat of horses shaking the dust of the plain" (8.808 [596]). Small things, it may seem, but the success of a translation depends on many minute effects.

Fitzgerald's is so decisively the best modern *Aeneid* that no one will want to use any other version for a long time to come. Latinists, as they read it, will be led to consider their original afresh. Those without Latin are going to find, to their surprise, and I hope their pleasure, that the poem is still as good as anyone ever said it was.

5

A Mistaken Ambition of Exactness: Richmond Lattimore's *Odyssey*

THE TRANSLATOR OF HOMER FACES ALL THE CHALLENGES AND ALL the hazards of his art on the grandest scale. The two great poems have come down with us from the other end of time; they are central to our culture, very familiar and also very remote. Few now read them in the original, yet everyone has an idea of how Homer wrote. The translator must satisfy, that is, he must inevitably fail to satisfy, those who have never heard Homer's voice as well as those who have. And having heard it, find all other voices flat. The translator, writing within his own mortal means, must reckon on even the ignorant reader's knowledge that the original is the master of masters, the most famous poet in the world.

In 1967 another *Odyssey* took its place beside the more than thirty existing English versions.[1] But of course this was not simply "another *Odyssey*," for it was by Richmond Lattimore, who was at that time, "by general consent," a front-page article in the *TLS* claimed, "the most distinguished living verse-translator of the classics into English."[2] To step from the ranks and question what general consent has established is a desperate undertaking, but it must be said that even if Lattimore's many translations from the Greek have been justly praised, they have not been accurately described. His *Iliad* has become the standard version, the book to put into every beginner's hands. But no one, that I know of, has told the beginner that although this *Iliad* may be as good as general consent and his staff have claimed ("the finest translation of Homer ever made into the English language," Brigadier Arrowsmith once reported; "certainly the best modern verse translation," agreed Colonel Highet), it is a very eccentric version, perhaps the most peculiar *Iliad* in English. Consider these lines (16.180–83):

> Polymele,
> daughter of Phylas; whom strong Hermes Argeiphontes

"A Mistaken Ambition of Exactness," *Delos* 2 (1968): 171–97.

loved, when he watched her with his eyes among the girls dancing
in the choir for clamorous Artemis.

"When he *watched her with his eyes*": technically, this is pleonasmus, a
vice of language which Shakespeare mocked in *The Merry Wives of
Windsor* (act 1, scene 1):

Falstaff:	Pistoll!
Pistol:	He heares with eares.
Evans:	The Tevill and his Tam! What phrase is this? "He heares with eares"? Why, it is affectations.

Why does Lattimore write in this way? Because this is how Homer
writes, ὀφθαλμοῖσιν ἰδών, "seeing with his eyes," there is no deception.
But surely an expression that in Homer's full and easy manner may
be acceptable enough sounds awkward today and need not be reproduced? No, replies Lattimore, it is not the translator's job to correct his author. As Homer wrote, so must he write, above all avoiding
mistranslation, "which would be caused by rating the word of his own
choice ahead of the word which translates the Greek" (from Lattimore's statement of principles in the introduction to his *Iliad*, re-
affirmed in the introduction to his *Odyssey*).

Now this is certainly an interesting principle, but it is a curious one,
more curious than it looks and, followed as closely as Lattimore follows it, likely to lead to results that are very curious indeed. The critics have not, I think, been entirely candid in admitting how strange
is the world into which Lattimore leads us:

> and she, Eriboía, screamed

[she is being assaulted by someone]

> for the bronze-armored Pandíonid
> Theseus, who gave him a black
> and rolling eye from under brows.

Theseus gave Eriboía's assailant a black (and rolling?) eye? Not at all,
he observed what was going on and rolled his dark eyes wildly beneath
his brows. I do not necessarily object to this mode of translation—it
keeps us on our toes and reminds us how different the Greek world
was from our own—but I do object when a critic tells us (on the back
cover of *Greek Lyrics*, where these lines occur)[3] that "the lenses" which
Lattimore provides "are as clear as our language is capable of making them." This is not true; our language is capable of providing much
clearer lenses. Again, I am forced to protest when the writer in the

TLS, speaking of the "emphasis on individual characterization" in the *Odyssey*, observes how well the poem suits "Professor Lattimore's remarkable interpretative talent," for he does not go on to warn us how peculiar Lattimore's interpretation is. Consider the place in book 5 where Odysseus, sailing home on his improvised craft, is surprised by a sudden storm (line 299). In Samuel Butler's late Victorian, novelistic translation, he speaks like this:

"Alas," he said to himself in his dismay, "whatever will become of me?"

Rieu uses fewer words but is less idiomatic:

"Poor wretch, what will your end be now?"

Robert Fitzgerald writes:

Rag of a man that I am, is this the end of me?

None of these versions is very striking, but all three translators put into Odysseus's mouth dramatically credible words. And Lattimore?

Ah me unhappy, what in the long outcome will befall me?

This is not an isolated example of the kind of interpretative talent at work in this translation. All Lattimore's characters employ this severely stylized speech:

Dear wife, we both have had our full share of numerous trials

says Odysseus, waking up beside Penelope for the first time in twenty years (23.350). The Greek, so far as I can see, is both direct and stately. Butler tries for the directness ("Wife, we have both of us had our full share of troubles"), Fitzgerald is more stately: "My lady, / what ordeals have we not endured!" In their different ways, both translations are acceptable, and they both reveal what one may call a normal interpretative talent. The speech Lattimore gives his characters points to a much odder reading of the poem. However we think of Odysseus, as "the live man among duds," "ce rusé personnage," or even "naked Ulysses, clad in eternall Fiction,"[4] few of us imagined that he expressed himself like this. And not only Odysseus. Here is Zeus justifying his ways to man:

Oh for shame, how the mortals put the blame upon us
gods, for they say evils come from us, but it is they, rather,

who by their own recklessness win sorrow beyond what is given,
as now lately, beyond what was given, Aigisthos married.

(1.32–35)

It is impossible to read a couple of pages of this *Odyssey* without discovering that it is unlike any other translation one had read—unless one has read other translations by Lattimore, which are all, in differing degrees, governed by the same principle of absolute fidelity to the letter. Such a principle obviously makes it difficult to write shapely or idiomatic English, yet Louise Bogan, reviewing *Greek Lyrics*, praises "his feeling for the telling noun and verb, the simple yet poignant epithet, and the dramatic turn of syntax," and the *TLS* critic notes "the freshness and vigor of language described from first page to last" of his *Odyssey*. The latter critic does indeed admit that the language of this translation is not the language of English poetry. Let him make the point in his own very poetic way and then let me quote a passage to illustrate his point. The language, he says, "flows as crystal clear and swift-moving as a mountain stream; yet even as we read we know that this stream has its sources in no English hills." Now here is a stretch of the stream—a sample of Odysseus's table talk in Phaeacia (7.211ff.):

Whoever it is of people you know who wear the greatest
burden of misery, such are the ones whom I would equal
for pain endured, and I could tell of still more troubles
that all are mine and by the will of the gods I suffered.
But leave me now to eat my dinner, for all my sorrow,
for there is no other thing so shameless as to be set over
the belly, but she rather uses constraint and makes me think of her,
even when sadly worn, when in my heart I have sorrow
as now I have sorrow in my heart, yet still for ever
she tells me to eat and drink.

Such a passage (and one could point to many more of the same kind) certainly throws an original light on Homeric poetry and must make the reader with no Greek wonder what Matthew Arnold could have had in mind when he praised the "lovely ease and sweetness" of Homer's habitual manner.[5] Arnold's Greek, no doubt, was patchy and very likely he did not realize how primitive Homer's thought and how awkward his paratactic style often are. At all events, if this is how Homer writes, the truth should not be hidden from the Greek-less reader.

And yet is this really how Homer writes? To some people, his poetry has seemed stronger and more beautiful than anything in the world.

Pope, for instance—but has Pope any right to be heard? His Homer, the *TLS* reviewer says, "was produced for educated *cognoscenti*, and merely reflected the poetic fashions of the day: it is not till near the end of the nineteenth century that any significant progress becomes apparent." And yet Pope had some poetry in him, and he found in Homer an "unequal'd fire and rapture which is so forcible . . . that no man of true poetical spirit is master of himself while he reads him" (preface to his *Iliad*). A modern poet, who gave seven years to translating the *Odyssey*, tells us that Homer's verse is "as beautiful in itself as the verse of Yeats or Shakespeare" (Fitzgerald's postscript to his *Odyssey*). And not only poets have been affected in this way. It was a mere critic, C. S. Lewis, who spoke of "the unwearying, unmoved, angelic speech of Homer" (*A Preface to Paradise Lost*).

How then does Homer write? There is only one way of finding out. Here are some lines from the end of book 2, first in Homer's Greek, then in the prose translations by Butler and Rieu, followed by three verse translations—Lattimore, R. C. Onesti (an Italian translator who provides a useful yardstick for Lattimore since she works on similar principles),[6] and finally Fitzgerald. Telemachus, hard-pressed by the suitors, is taking a ship to seek news of his father:

ἱστὸν δ᾽ εἰλάτινον κοίλης ἔντοσθε μεσόδμης
στῆσαν ἀείραντες, κατὰ δὲ προτόνοισιν ἔδησαν,
ἕλκον δ᾽ ἱστία λευκὰ ἐϋστρέπτοισι βοεῦσιν.
ἔπρησεν δ᾽ ἄνεμος μέσον ἱστίον, ἀμφὶ δὲ κῦμα
στείρῃ πορφύρεον μεγάλ᾽ ἴαχε νηὸς ἰούσης·
ἡ δ᾽ ἔθεεν κατὰ κῦμα διαπρήσσουσα κέλευθον.
δησάμενοι δ᾽ ἄρα ὅπλα θοὴν ἀνὰ νῆα μέλαιναν
στήσαντο κρητῆρας ἐπιστεφέας οἴνοιο,
λεῖβον δ᾽ ἀθανάτοισι θεοῖς αἰειγενέτῃσιν,
ἐκ πάντων δὲ μάλιστα Διὸς γλαυκώπιδι κούρῃ.
παννυχίη μέν ῥ᾽ ἥ γε καὶ ἠῶ πεῖρε κέλευθον.

Butler:

They set the mast in its socket in the cross plank, raised it, and made it fast with the forestays; then they hoisted their white sails aloft with ropes of twisted ox hide. As the sail bellied out with the wind, the ship flew through the deep blue water, and the foam hissed against her bows as she sped onward. Then they made all fast throughout the ship, filled the mixing bowls to the brim, and made drink offerings to the immortal gods that are from everlasting, but more particularly to the grey-eyed daughter of Jove.

Thus, then, the ship sped on her way through the watches of night from dark till dawn.

Rieu:

They hauled up the fir mast, stept it in its hollow box, made it fast with stays, and hoisted the white sail with plaited oxhide ropes. Struck full by the wind, the sail swelled out, and a dark wave hissed loudly round her stem as the vessel gathered way and sped through the choppy seas, forging ahead on her course.

When all was made snug in the swift black ship, they got out mixing-bowls, filled them to the brim with wine and poured libations to the immortal gods that have been since time began, and above all to the Daughter of Zeus, the Lady of the gleaming eyes. And all night long and into the dawn the ship ploughed her way through the sea.

Lattimore:

and, raising the mast pole made of fir, they set it upright
in the hollow hole in the box, and made it fast with forestays,
and with halyards strongly twisted of leather pulled up the white sails.
The wind blew into the middle of the sail, and at the cutwater
a blue wave rose and sang strongly as the ship went onward.
She ran swiftly, cutting across the swell her pathway.
When they had made fast the running gear all along the black ship,
then they set up mixing bowls, filling them brimful
with wine, and poured to the gods immortal and everlasting
but beyond all other gods they poured to Zeus' gray-eyed daughter.
All night long and into the dawn she ran on her journey.

Onesti:

l'albero, un tronco d'abete, nel foro del trave mediano
piantarono sollevandolo, poi gli stragli legarono,
issarono le vele bianche con forti ritorte di cuoio.
Il vento riempí la vela e l'onda spumosa
urlava forte intorno alla chiglia, mentre correva la nave.
Correva sull'onda la nave, affrettando il cammino,
Cosí, legate nell'agile nave nera le funi,
posero in mezzo crateri coronati di vino,
e libavano ai numi immortali eternamente viventi,
ma, sopra tutti, alla figlia occhio azzurro di Zeus.
Tutta la notte corse la nave e all'alba compiva il cammino.

Fitzgerald:

They pushed the fir mast high and stepped it firm
amidships in the box, made fast the forestays,
then hoisted up the white sail on its halyards

until the wind caught, booming in the sail;
and a flushing wave sang backward from the bow
on either side, as the ship got way upon her,
holding her steady course.
Now they made all secure in the fast black ship,
and, setting out the wineboards all a-brim,
they made libation to the gods,
                              the undying, the ever-new,
most of all to the grey-eyed daughter of Zeus.
And the prow sheared through the night into the dawn.

The Greek lines provide a fair example of the perfect narrative
style of Homer. The passage is full of business-like prose detail presented with the greatest clarity and economy. We know exactly what
the sailors are doing as they prepare to set sail, we see and feel the
objects they are handling, the fir mast, the white sails, the twisted ox-
leathers. This professional activity gives way, in the next two lines, to
the action of natural forces: the wind that strikes full against the sail,
the surging wave that shouts around the keel as—at the end of the
fifth line—the ship moves on her way, νηὸς ἰούσης, leading naturally
to the next line in which the subject is the ship cutting her rapid
course across the waves. Then back to the men again, with two lines
showing them fastening the tackle and filling the wine bowls, line 430
as swift, rhythmically, as the sailors' performance of their familiar
duties, line 431 slowing down toward its heavy spondaic ending and
preparing for the next couplet, which lifts effortlessly to splendor
with the bright and solemn polysyllables that celebrate the gods, "the
great gray-eyed Athena" before all others. Then back to the ship once
more with the strong, adventurous thrust of the last line. (Note πεῖρε
κέλευθον chiming with διαπρήσσουσα κέλευθον at 429—observed
by Onesti but not by Lattimore—and also the patterning of couplets
and single lines, 2:1, 2:1, 2:2, 1. As often in such passages, there is the
ghost of a stanzaic structure here.)

The poet convinces us that he is presenting the whole scene, a total
registration, by the way he moves rapidly between three perspectives,
human, natural, and divine. These shifts of perspective are unifying
rather than disruptive because they are all felt to be part of a single
vital continuum. If the whole action leads us to the eternal present of
the gods celebrated in lines 432–33, the divine is equally the source,
the ground, of the energy that informs the passage, the vivid life of man
and wind and wave and ship, the eternal present of Homeric poetry.

But what can the translator do about all this?

I have printed the prose versions first in order to get them out of
the way. As poetry abandoned its old provinces before the victorious

advance of the novel, it was inevitable that Homer, too, should be appropriated for the dominant form. Samuel Butler, writing in the heyday of the novel, went seriously about the business of turning Homeric verse into narrative prose, and his *Odyssey* (if not his *Iliad*) can still be read with enjoyment. Rieu's version, appearing in the tired aftermath of the Second World War, sold widely and undoubtedly gave pleasure, but it has not survived the passage of two decades very well and it cannot stand up to Butler's. This is not merely because Butler wrote better prose (though of course he did: compare the easy run of his first sentence, and the natural way it falls into two parts, with Rieu's jerky asyndeton). It is rather that the novel has changed. Whether or not the *Odyssey* is "the first novel of Europe" as T. E. Lawrence and others have believed,[7] it is not at all like the kind of novel we prize today. Turning the *Odyssey* into fiction now means turning it into decidedly second-rate fiction—a price Rieu was quite prepared to pay. (Notice the way he fills out the action with cliché observation and cliché diction—"choppy seas," "forging ahead," "ploughed her way," and the like—in order to reassure the reader encountering the father of European poetry for the first time.)

Take a moment in the narrative just before the passage I quoted. Rieu, following the Greek words fairly closely, writes:

> And now, out of the West, Athene of the flashing eyes called up for them a steady following wind and sent it singing over the wine-dark sea.

Such writing belongs to no acceptable style of narrative fiction. This is travelogue prose called in to promote a confusion of genres. Butler, concerned to present a credible, realistic action, writes:

> Minerva sent them a fair wind from the West, that whistled over the deep blue waves.

Athena's (or Minerva's) flashing eyes have been suppressed since, as he says in the introduction to his *Iliad*, prose does not permit Homer's "iteration of epithet and title." (But he is sensibly inconsistent here and a few lines later admits "the grey-eyed daughter of Jove," a convincing enough figure and greatly preferable to Rieu's tinsel "Lady of the gleaming eyes.") Instead of Rieu's "wine-dark sea" (airline prose again), Butler has "deep blue waves," and the wind, instead of *singing* over them, merely *whistles*—somewhat to Butler's dissatisfaction, for he reminds us in a characteristic footnote that the wind "does not whistle over waves. It only whistles through rigging or some other obstacle that cuts it."

Butler at least knew what a prose translation of Homer cannot do. The question is, can it do enough to be worth the labor? Compare the first three lines of Fitzgerald with either of the prose versions: Fitzgerald presents the businesslike detail quite as effectively, and in addition he sets it to a vigorous verse rhythm which means that the mode of presentation is comparable to Homer's. More importantly, his good verse can shape the passage in a way that prose can do only by a conscious, and occasional, exercise of virtuosity.[8] It marks the shifts of perspective which I noted in the Greek and at least does something to suggest how the action rises to the celebration of the gods' eternal being and then returns to the ship cutting its way through the night sea.

Turning now to Lattimore (and at the same time training a lateral eye on Fitzgerald and Onesti), one may have to add that verse which fails to exercise its proper powers does not necessarily have the edge on good prose. Read Butler's or even Rieu's first sentence aloud and at least you know what is happening, whereas Lattimore contrives to obscure the action with unnecessary or ill-placed words and sentences set back to front. Why write "mast pole made of fir" instead of "fir mast," five words where two would suffice? (Though Italian is more prolix than English, Onesti manages it in three, but she proceeds to bungle the first line and a half by following the Greek word order too slavishly.) "In the hollow hole of the box" is a landlubberly way to speak of stepping the mast; Homer gives you the sense that he knows his way around a boat and his translator must do the same. In the third line, Butler, Rieu, Onesti, and Fitzgerald (and for that matter Lawrence, and Butcher and Lang, and Leconte de Lisle, and T. A. Buckley, the author of the Bohn version) all follow Homer in putting the important part of the action first: white sails hauled up. Lattimore makes us force our way through the tongue-tripping clutter of "and with halyards strongly twisted of leather" before we learn what is, literally, up. And the phrase itself is singularly awkward, hesitating as it does between two constructions: "strongly twisted [all fouled up? or plaited, twined?] halyards made of leather"—in which case why in this resolutely unpoetic style does the epithet follow the noun? Or is it a formation akin to the biblical "with coffers fashioned of bronze"? Since the Greek line is pellucid, it is hard to see the point of introducing this potential confusion.

The next line, 2.427, "the wind blew into the middle of the sail," besides contriving to do in nine words what the Italian does in five, is a schoolboy literalism that belongs to a prose trot. (The Bohn translator duly writes "and the wind swelled the middle of the sail.") The wind struck the sail full, that is all we know and all we need to know.

The blue wave at the cutwater is pleasant, but since the Greek construction is pregnant and exciting (Onesti follows it closely and is acceptable enough), why weaken the effect by telling us that the "wave *rose and* sang"? If it didn't rise, it wouldn't be a wave. Fitzgerald is excellent here:

> and a flushing wave sang backward from the bow
> on either side, as the ship got way upon her,
> holding her steady course.

He attends to every detail of the action quite as faithfully as Lattimore, and in addition he has taken the trouble to rethink the Greek into English words and constructions and rhythms, rather than following the original *mot-à-mot* in the hope that since it's good in Greek it is also going to be good in English.

2.429: Why write "cutting across the swell her pathway" instead of "cutting her / a path across the swell"? Perhaps it would spoil the rhythm? Lattimore's sense of rhythm is a subject I would sooner avoid, but since the "rhythmic subtleties" of this translation were praised in the *TLS*, it may be that something should be said, even at the cost of a digression. There is a recurrent Odyssean line which Lattimore renders:

> and sitting well in order dashed the oars in the grey sea.[9]

A close enough translation, certainly, but the trouble is that the reader can hardly help being reminded of a line from Tennyson's "Ulysses" which gets in the way:

> Push off, and sitting well in order smite
> The sounding furrows.

What happens is that Tennyson's strongly marked rhythm *invades* the indeterminate rhythm of Lattimore's "free six-beat line," with the metrically disastrous result that we are bound to read his first eight words as a piece of conventional blank verse ("and sítting wéll in órder dáshed the oárs"), which leaves the last four words dangling in an arrhythmic limbo and so destroys the meter of the whole line.[10]

The claims of the free six-beat line to be an acceptable medium for translating the classical hexameter have, I think, been granted a great deal too readily. It is about the same length, but its lumbering gait is at the furthest possible remove from the supplely articulated line of

Homer. Most of the time it is verse only by typographical courtesy, and its movement is so ill-defined that it falls a ready prey to any other meter whose path it chances to cross—and not only dignified meters like blank verse. Consider this line from the passage under discussion (2.433):

> but beyond all other gods they poured to Zeus' gray-eyed daughter.

Insert a caesura after "poured" and the line fractures into an ignoble doggerel couplet:

> But beyond all other gods they poured
>   To Zeus' gray-eyed daughter.
> But since the stuff went overboard
>   She said they didn't oughter.

2.430: Lattimore's accuracy has a habit of failing us just when it might be useful. Homer tells us, as he often does, that the ship was "fast" and "black." You may do as Butler does and leave both out, or as Fitzgerald, Onesti, and Rieu do and put both in. But if you are only going to include one, you had best keep "fast" and drop "black." Telemachus is setting out on what he knows is a potentially dangerous journey, and the speed of his ship is important. Lattimore, who seldom seems very interested in the story, chooses to tell us simply that the ship was black.

2.431: The "mixing bowls" to be found in Butler, Rieu, and Lattimore are certainly better than Onesti's absurd "craters crowned with wine," but they suggest a kitchen utensil rather than something to drink from. It damages our sense of the reality of Homer's narrative to introduce improbable objects and implements, unless they are required by the story. Fitzgerald's "winebowls" are more convincing.

2.432: "For modern man it is no easy task to attain a true understanding of ancient Greek religion." So runs the first sentence of Walter Otto's *The Homeric Gods* ([1929] 1954). And it is no easy task for the translator to make them convincing—and divine, yet unless he does so, he damages Homer's poems beyond repair. Of our five translators, it is obvious that only Fitzgerald and Onesti have thought about the matter. Butler's "the immortal gods that are from everlasting" is better than Rieu's chatty and inaccurate "the immortal gods that have been since time began" (inaccurate, since the gods did *not* exist "since time began"; we know how they came to birth), but it has a drowsy

Sunday morning ring about it. Lattimore, with "the gods immortal and everlasting," assumes as usual that if he sets down the dictionary meaning of a word, he is absolved from thinking about what it means. Fitzgerald's "undying" is better than "immortal" because it emphasizes the gods' one absolute prerogative: unlike men, they do not die. Lattimore's "everlasting," for αἰειγενέτῃσιν, is of course respectable, but what prompted Onesti to write "eternamente viventi" and Fitzgerald to write "the ever-new"? The answer is surely that "everlasting" confuses the mode of everlastingness enjoyed by the Greek gods with that of the Christian (or Hebrew) god. God, or Jahveh, extends from before the beginning of time to after the end of time, whereas a Homeric god exists in an eternal present—as Onesti's rendering suggests. Fitzgerald's solution is more daring. Presumably he had in mind the very late philosophical word ἀειγενεσία, "eternal generation." To intrude such a concept into the simplicities of Homeric theology may seem wanton, yet Greek philosophy is the child of the Greek language, and the Greek language owes more to Homer than to any other author. It seems to me not unreasonable to suppose that a Homeric word may contain, *in posse*, the unconceptualized seeds of later meanings. Fitzgerald has at any rate taken the kind of risk which the good translator will always take in order to penetrate the life of his text.

2.434: Lattimore's "she ran" leads us to suppose that it is Athena, the subject of the preceding line, who ran. Since it is almost certain that in the Greek the ship ran, not the goddess, it seems pointless to end on this disagreeable ambiguity.

A fair comment on these performances would I think have to be that Fitzgerald is superior to all his competitors on all counts, that Onesti (who in her own country, so far as I know, had been credited with nothing more than a useful job of work) is on the whole superior to Lattimore *in the same genre of translation*; and that Lattimore is sometimes but by no means always superior to Rieu and usually inferior to Butler.

But perhaps a single passage does not do Lattimore justice. It is the staying powers of a long-distance runner that Homer demands of his translator, and it may be that over a stretch of several hundred lines Lattimore outdoes his more showy rivals. We shall perhaps find that his workmanlike honesty and his accurate knowledge of Greek present the reality of Homeric narrative as no other method can. It would be laborious to transcribe hundreds of lines, so let us instead take a number of passages from one book—the fifth will serve as well as any other—and study the conduct of the narrative, the sense of scene, and the handling of dramatic speech.

5.47–48: Here is Hermes, about to set off for Calypso's island in order to compel her to release Odysseus:

> He caught up the staff, with which he mazes the eyes of those mortals whose eyes he would maze.

It does not do to sophisticate Homer's style and pretend that he wrote with the careful artistry of Virgil. One assumes that it is Lattimore's resolve to write exactly as Homer writes that has led him into the very clumsy repetition of "maze." But no, Homer does not repeat the verb. He says, a little loosely, perhaps, but with no real awkwardness: "he picked up the staff with which he enchants men's eyes," and then, at the start of the next line, adds two qualifying words to make clear the Hermes does not enchant *all* men's eyes: "of those he wishes"—that is, to enchant. Onesti retains this qualifying afterthought without making Homer sound like a man who cannot put words together properly:

> e prese la verga con cui gli occhi degli uomini affascina,
> di quelli che vuole.

5.57–58:

>   he came to the great cave, where the lovely-haired
> nymph was at home, and he found that she was inside.

Again, one assumes that Homeric narrative sounds a trifle ridiculous now and then: if the nymph was "at home," clearly she was "inside" (her cave). But again one finds this turn of phrase is Lattimore's, not Homer's. The Greek says, sensibly enough: "he came to the great cave in which the lovely-haired nymph lives [i.e., that is her settled place of residence] and found that she was inside" (i.e., she happened to be at home on this particular occasion).

5.97–98:

> "You, a goddess, ask me, a god, why I came, and therefore
> I will tell you . . ."

Calypso has just asked Hermes the reason for his visit. The juxtaposition of the two key words, θεά / θεός, "goddess/god," easily enough handled in an inflected language like Greek, makes it plain that Hermes' answer, or question, is politely ironical. He says in effect, "Look, we gods understand each other clearly enough—we are of the same race. You know why I've come, so why bother to ask me?" English cannot readily manage the juxtaposition, but there are plenty of ways to bring the point over. Fitzgerald sets the two words closely enough together and catches the cool, quizzical tone of the god's question:

> Goddess to god, you greet me, questioning me?

To attempt simply to copy the Greek construction, as Lattimore does, is to show disrespect for the structure of English and a lack of care for the tone of the Greek.

5.118–20:

> "You are hard-hearted, you gods, and jealous beyond all creatures beside, when you are resentful toward the goddesses for sleeping openly with such men as each has made her true husband . . ."

Calypso, having learned that she must give up Odysseus, lashes out angrily at the Olympians. There is a great deal of dramatic speech in both the *Odyssey* and the *Iliad,* and it presents the translator with a major challenge. Ezra Pound described one of the two unmistakable qualities of Homeric poetry as "the authentic cadence of speech; the absolute conviction that the words used . . . are in the actual swing of words spoken."[11] One of the reasons why Fitzgerald's translation succeeds so well is that he has an excellent ear for the difference of personal style. Lattimore has not, and it is difficult to believe that these words are spoken by an angry woman who sees her lover being taken away from her. Apart from this, it is eccentric to describe the gods as "jealous beyond all *creatures.*" "*When* you are resentful" is unidiomatic, and so is the "*the*" before "goddesses." "With such men as each has made her true husband" is simply incompetent writing. Onesti, keeping quite as close to the letter, comes up with a natural run of words:

> voi che invidiate alle dee di stendersi accanto ai mortali
> palesamente, *se una si trova un caro marito.*

5.145–55:

> By nights he would lie beside her, of necessity,
> in the hollow caverns, against his will, by one who was willing.

The Greek is extremely neat; there is a mocking elegance in the phrase describing Odysseus's erotic servitude—παρ' οὐκ ἐθέλων ἐθελούσῃ. English cannot handle the hyperbaton, but there are various ways of getting a similar effect. Chapman's is, I think, the most pleasing:

> At night yet (forc'd) together tooke their rest,
> The willing Goddesse and th'unwilling Guest.

Onesti is fairly dextrous:

> Certo la notte dormiva sempre, per forza,
> nella cupa spelonca, nolente, vicino a lei che voleva.

Lattimore naturally disregards the elegance and is content to drag the key words into some sort of proximity. Possibly he took a hint from the Bohn translation: "But during the nights he slept indeed even by necessity in the hollow caves, against his will, near her who was willing."

5.192–94:

> So she spoke, a shining goddess, and led the way swiftly,
> and the man followed behind her walking in the god's footsteps.
> They made their way, the man and the god, to the hollow cavern.

The Greekless reader is going to need all his wits here. He has been told that the god Hermes has just left the island, and so far as he knows it is now inhabited only by Calypso and Odysseus. Who then is the god in whose footsteps Odysseus walks? The explanation of this interesting little trap devised by the master translator is that Greek can use the word θεός to mean both "god" and "goddess." Since there is no definite article to indicate the sex of the particular deity, Lattimore, refusing to intrude into Homer's text his sense of what the word must mean, observes the Greek θεός and translates "god." It makes nonsense of the scene, of course, but what does that matter? First things first.

In his refusal to allow that the translator is even minimally concerned with interpretation, Lattimore, so far as I know, stands alone. (Even the literal Bohn version here admits that the θεός must be female.) Let me take another example. Three times in the poem Athena performs for Odysseus the minor miracle of making him appear larger and more impressive than he really is. The relevant lines are 6.230, 8.20, and 23.157. Lattimore renders them all indifferently as "taller and thicker" even though the Greek (a minimal point but just worth noting, since his absolute accuracy has been praised so often) describes him as "bigger," μείζονα, on the first and third occasion and "taller," μακρότερον, only on the second. The excellent Onesti duly distinguishes between *più grande* and *più alto* and also, one may feel, devises a more acceptable translation than "thicker" for the second epithet in the formula, πάσσονα, which means "stout," in the old sense, or "robust," the word she herself selects. Lattimore's translation is not very idiomatic, for though we may say that a man is thickset, we do not usually say that he is thick. However, by the standards he has set himself, it will pass. The interesting point occurs at 18.195 when Athena performs a similar kindness for Penelope. Homer, in his usual economical way, employs the words he has used for Odysseus, μακροτέρην καὶ πάσσονα, assuming that we can be trusted to interpret them correctly. An easy enough task, since the context makes clear that her appearance has notably improved. Homer obviously now finds her, with Edwardian relish, a "fine figure of a woman," and translators have had no difficulty in getting the point. "Grandeur she gave her, too, in height and form" (Fitzgerald), "she made her taller and of a more commanding figure" (Butler), "elle la fit paraître plus grande, plus majestueuse" (Leconte de Lisle), "e più alta, maestosa la fece a vedersi" (Onesti), and so on. And Lattimore? Professor Lattimore responds in this way:

> She made her taller for the eye to behold, and thicker.

5.252–59: Heroic poetry delights in realistic descriptions of the everyday business of life—eating and going to bed, cutting up a pig or sailing a ship. Homer watches Odysseus very closely as he builds the boat that is to take him away from Nausicaa's island, and although the meaning of the Greek is in places obscure, there is no doubt that we are meant to know exactly what he is doing. Lattimore's translation runs like this:

> Next, setting up the deck boards and fitting them to close uprights
> he worked them on, and closed in the ends with sweeping gunwales.
> Then he fashioned the mast, with an upper deck fitted to it,
> and made in addition a steering oar by which to direct her,
> and fenced her in down the whole length with wattles of osier
> to keep the water out, and expended much timber upon this.
> Next Kalypso, the shining goddess, brought out the sail cloth
> to make the sails with, and he carefully worked these also.

As usual, Lattimore's words stand between us and the action. He has not thought seriously about what Odysseus is doing nor even, it would seem, looked very closely at the Greek. What, for instance are "*close* uprights"? Answer, close-*set* uprights. "He worked them on" is vague, and it is not clear how one "sets up" deck boards. In the way one sets up a ladder? (It has been suggested to me that the translation would make better sense and keep closer to the Greek if one understood the word usually in Homer taken to mean "deck"—or more strictly, poop—in its later sense of "scaffolding." Odysseus would not then be required to *set up* the deck, or deck boards; he would be doing something more sensible—namely, *constructing the hull.* Translate: "And he made it [that is, the ship] by setting up a frame, fitting it with close-set ribs.") Lattimore's "closed in the ends with sweeping gunwales" is very peculiar. The Greek verb τελεύτα cannot mean "closed in the ends," and the noun here translated as "gunwale" (defined as "the strengthening piece at the top of the hull" in the Penguin *Dictionary of Sailing*) is understood by the Liddell-Scott-Jones lexicon to mean "long planks bolted to the upright ribs" and by J. S. Morrison, an expert on Greek ships, as "longitudinal timbers."[12] Probably translate: "and he finished it off with long strakes."

A "mast, with an upper deck fitted to it" is even more extraordinary. The word translated "upper deck," ἐπίκριον, might theoretically, I suppose, bear this meaning (as sideboard might mean a board by the side), but the lexicon thinks it means "sailyard" and so does J. S. Morrison, and whatever Homer takes the word to mean it can hardly be anything so bulky as an upper deck, since later on, when the mast is snapped by the wind, he tells us that the ἐπίκριον and the rope attached to it (σπεῖρον) "fall far away into the sea" (line 318). But even if Lattimore's translation should be right, it is grotesque to speak of a deck fitted to a mast when you mean a mast fitted to a deck.

"A steering oar by which to direct her": Lattimore's usual neglect of English idiom—an oar, or rudder, does not *direct* a ship; and his usual readiness to make the least possible sense of what Homer wrote. What should a steering oar do but—steer? Compare Fitzgerald: "and shaped a steering oar to keep her steady."

In the next line and a half, Lattimore manages to convince us that neither Homer nor Odysseus knew much about shipbuilding. "Wattles of osier" do not sound seaworthy, and "to keep the water out" suggests a depressingly minimal ambition on a shipwright's part. What Homer says is that "the wattles of osier" (assuming this is the best translation: how many of Lattimore's readers would recognize a wattle of osier when they saw one?) are designed to provide a protection against the waves. A passage in Bowra's *Heroic Poetry* makes the phrase perfectly clear. Odysseus, he says, "puts a fence round the boat to prevent it being swamped, and this device is still used in Greece. Leake saw a gunwale enveloped with withies 'to protect it from the waves or from the danger of a sudden heel.'"[13] In point of fact, a translator who reads the Greek carefully and thinks for a moment about what it must mean can make perfect sense; thus Butler: "He fenced the raft all round with wicker hurdles as a protection against the waves."

"And expended much timber upon this." Only in the world of Lattimore could a shipwright *expend timber upon wattles*. Although some have taken the timber to mean ballast, the sense is almost certainly that Odysseus backed or supported the wicker sides with wood. Calypso, finally, is made to add her quota of folly to this extraordinary passage of bringing out (where from?) sailcloth. Why? Why, to make sails with. What Homer says is that she brought φάρεα, "large pieces of cloth," so that Odysseus, resourceful man that he was, could make a sail in addition to everything else. Rouse translates, "Then Calypso brought him cloth to use for a sail, and he made that too." An elementary-enough sentence, yet how shapely it stands beside Lattimore's.

It must, I am afraid, be admitted that Lattimore is frequently very clumsy and that he is less interested in the realities of emotion and action than we might have expected from so eminent a translator. Still, even if the critics have let us suppose that all was well in these important areas, their emphasis has fallen elsewhere. The central claim made for Lattimore's translations is that they are above all else *accurate*. He gives you more of the Greek than anyone else and he gives you only what is in the Greek. Let me quote in full the blurb (it is by Moses Hadas) from which I have already taken a sentence: "The significant quality of Mr. Lattimore's versions is that they are pure. The lenses he provides are as clear as our language is capable of making them."

This must mean that Lattimore's versions are (in Gogol's complimentary sense) colorless; his words, instead of drawing attention to themselves, are so transparent that we can look through them to the Greek words.[14] His scrupulous, self-effacing fidelity must reveal something of the inner life of the Greek language, the delicate play of meanings and half-meanings which is lost on most translators and indeed on most readers of the original. I have already offered one or two bits of evidence suggesting that this is not so, or not so without qualifications, but the claim must nevertheless be taken very seriously. The laboratory test I propose to employ may at first seem trivial, even captious, but I think we will find that it takes us to the heart of the matter. I want to look at Lattimore's use of a single English word and at the Greek word, or words, which it translates. Since Homer's world is so full of brightness, the reader is not surprised to find the adjective "shining" occurs very frequently. He may however be surprised to learn that at least sixteen Greek words are rendered by this one English word.

The matter must now be pursued in tedious detail.
1. "Shining water" (ὕδατι λευκῷ), 5.70.
The water running from the four springs near Calypso's cave. A possible translation, but not very specific. Literally, "white," "clear," or "limpid" would perhaps be better. Or is the picture more vivid? Bearing in mind that the same adjective is used in the *Iliad* (14.185) of Hera's beautiful veil which—in Lattimore's translation—"glimmered pale [λευκόν] like the sunlight," and in the *Odyssey* (6.45) of the "white radiance" of light which quivers over Olympus (see item 15 below), we should perhaps take our courage in both hands and guess that what Homer sees is something as beautiful as Eliot's

> And the pool was filled with water out of sunlight . . .
> The surface glittered out of heart of light.
> *(Burnt Norton,* section 1)

(Though Eliot's water is still, unlike Homer's flowing springwater.) Rash, no doubt, yet we are told the place was so beautiful that even a god would marvel at it.

It is often difficult to know in which single word or phrase one should locate the sense of abounding life a passage of Homer gives. It is even more difficult to cut off the expanding suggestions of his language at a determined point and say that this is "all" it means. Meditate on a phrase and it turns into an epiphany.

2. "Shining son of Nestor" (Νέστορος ἀγλαὸς υἱός), 4.21.
Meeting the same phrase again at line 303 (and the same adjective used of someone else's son at 188—where "shining" is already on duty for another Greek word), Lattimore seems to have sensed the risk of an unwanted ambiguity and instead wrote "*glorious* son of Nestor," the version which he uses on the four subsequent occasions when the word is used of a male offspring. However, he did not see fit to go back and correct 4.21 (or another "shining son" at 3.190). One should perhaps notice that φαίδιμος, a word of roughly similar meaning (see item 7 below), is rendered "shining son of" at 15.2 and 16.395, though elsewhere it appears as "glorious son."

3. "Shining among divinities" (δῖα θεάων), 5.116, etc.
A clumsy rendering of the very common Greek formula, failing even to make clear that the "divinities" in question are female. Lattimore

has, however, other versions: "shining among the goddesses," "shining among goddesses," "bright among goddesses," and, best and simplest, "a shining goddess." (Cf. Onesti's "la dea luminosa.")

4. "Shining sun" (ἠέλιος φαέθων), 5.479, etc.
The Greek adjective certainly means "shining" and, yes, the sun shines. At 11.16 it is heightened to "the radiant sun . . . with his shining." But Homer's "strong vertical light"[15] calls for a more potent luminary.

5. "Shining clothes" (εἵματα . . . σιγαλόεντα), 6.26.
Of Nausicaa's dirty laundry. The adjective, in Homer's usual way, describes the normal state of the clothes. Since the English present participle almost inevitably suggests something present, Lattimore's choice is unfortunate. What is needed is a good neutral adjective applicable to fine clothes in general—"tes belles robes" (Leconte de Lisle), for example. (Onesti's "le vesti vivaci" has agreeable Cretan suggestions, but perhaps specifies too closely.) When Lattimore meets the word at 15.60, used for Odysseus's tunic, he does better with "shimmering" (compare Victor Bérard's "linge moiré").

6. "Shining lash" (μάστιγι φαεινῇ), 6.316.
Used by Nausicaa to get her mule under way. Lattimore follows Bohn, Butcher and Lang, and Lawrence; Rieu and Fitzgerald translate "glistening," which perhaps better suggests the flash of supple leather.

7. "Shining Odysseus" (φαίδιμ᾽ Ὀδυσσεῦ), 11.202.
The phrase is also rendered "glorious Odysseus" (at, e.g., 10.251 and 11.100). Is "shining" used here because the speaker is Odysseus's dead mother in Hades, her eyes full of tears as she speaks to her son? An interesting possibility, but then why does Lattimore make Circe, whose eyes are not full of tears, address Odysseus in the same way at 12.82?

8. "Shining red wine" (αἴθοπα οἶνον ἐρυθρόν), 12.19.
The adjective is in the *Odyssey* applied mainly to wine (sometimes coupled with a second adjective, e.g. γερούσιος at 13.8, "for or befitting elders"), also to bronze and once to smoke mingled with flame. Since the basic meaning seems to be "fiery-looking," the wine is probably a spumante, hence Rieu's "sparkling" and Lawrence's "red wine with a fiery sparkle to it" (which draws too much attention to itself). Fitzgerald's "ruby-colored wine" unpleasantly suggests Australian port.

9. "Pigs with shining tusks" (ἀργιόδοντας ὗας), 8.60, etc.
Also "with shining teeth," 14.416, 532, etc. Reduced at 14.423 and 438 to "white-toothed pig"—an example of Lattimore failing to preserve

"the formulaic practice of the original." In the Greek, such epithets have a so to say heraldic effect. The specifics of this world minister to a brilliant stylization, and yet retain their specific quality. Lawrence's "white-tusked boars" is preferable to Lattimore's different versions, and to Rieu's "white-tusked porkers," which might do in another context, but is too *rustre* for Homer.

10. "Shining eyes" (φάεα καλά), 17.39.
Of Telemachus's eyes, as Penelope kisses them. Literally "beautiful eyes," an excellent translation. (At 16.15, rendered "beautiful shining eyes.")

11. "Shining sheep" (ἀργεννῆς ὄϊεσσιν), 17.472.
Lattimore's translation of the same expression at *Iliad* 6.424, "white sheep," perhaps meets the case sufficiently.

12. "Shining veil" (λιπαρὰ κρήδεμνα), 18.210, etc.
Worn by Penelope. A fair enough translation, but in this context (Athena has magically heightened her beauty), and in the present debilitated state of the word, something stronger would have been welcome. "Glistening," perhaps, or "glinting."

13. "Shining bright as the sun shines" (λαμπρὸς δ' ἦν ἡέλιος ὥς), 19.234.
Of a very grand tunic once worn by Odysseus. (Still incognito, he is describing his own imagined appearance to Penelope.) "Shining" is certainly an acceptable rendering of λαμπρός, but since a different Greek adjective, applied to the tunic two lines above, has been translated by the same word, the effect is not very strong.

14. "Shining basin" (λέβηθ' ἕλε παμφανόωντα), 19.386.
A grand, resounding word that needs leaning on. This basin, obviously, takes dominion everywhere. And the occasion is almost ritual in its gravity, as the old servant washes the feet of her master, back at last in his house. Fitzgerald responds with "her basin glittering in firelight," which is nice but too Dutch Domestic. Pater perhaps suggests a better approach with his description of Verrocchio, "designer . . . of all things for sacred or household use . . . making them all fair to look upon, filling the common ways of life with the reflexion of some far-off brightness."[16]

15. "Shining Olympos" (αἰγλήεντος Ὀλύμπου), 20.103.
The root word, αἴγλη ("radiance," I suppose one translates), takes us into the secret places of Hellas, the mystery of light, the Greek Holy of Holies. Pindar, beyond all other poets, has made this word sacred

to the imagination. In the great description of Olympus in book 6, a "white radiance" of light quivers, or glances, literally *runs* over the divine dwelling ("candida scorre la luce," Onesti writes, finely). Fitzgerald translates:

> Never a tremor of wind, or a splash of rain,
> no errant snowflake comes to stain that heaven,
> so calm, so vaporless, the world of light.
>
> (6.49–51 [43–45])

(Note how he has taken advantage of the English poetic tradition, borrowing a phrase from Vaughan's great vision of the Christian heaven—"They are all gone into the world of light"—and taking a verb from the lines of Shelley which were presumably inspired by this passage: "Life, like a dome of many-coloured glass, / Stains the white radiance of Eternity," *Adonais*.) Lattimore, however, registers no more than placid approval:

> Olympos, where the abode of the gods stands firm and unmoving
> forever, they say, and is not shaken with winds nor spattered
> with rains, nor does snow pile ever there, but the shining bright air
> stretches cloudless away, and the white light glances upon it.

16. "Shining bronze" (νώροπα χαλκόν), 24.467.
"Gleaming" or "flashing" would perhaps be closer.

In a number of these passages "shining" is an acceptable, even the best, rendering. But even if it were the best rendering every time, it would still be desirable to cast about for other words, if only to suggest the lexical plenty, the abounding sensuous life of Homeric poetry. There are occasions when Lattimore's insistence on this particular adjective becomes almost hypnotic. Imagine how the intelligent student with no Greek would set about looking for thematic relations in a passage like this (18.206–10):

> So she spoke, and made her descent from her shining [σιγαλόεντα]
>   chamber,
> not all alone, since two handmaidens went to attend her,
> When she, shining [δῖα] among women, came near the suitors,
> she stood by the pillar that supported the roof with its joinery,
> holding her shining [λιπαρά] veil in front of her face.[17]

The famous accuracy, I am afraid, amounts to a good deal less than the critics have claimed. Although Lattimore seldom attributes to a word a meaning not supported by the lexicon, he does not seem to care for the life of words, either Greek or English. He is accurate only in the sense that he takes the Greek words more or less in the order they occur and ties round their necks the appropriate dictionary meaning. The language of Homeric poetry, that can fill even the beginner with dreadful joy, seems to interest him as little as the action and the characterization of Homeric poetry. His inert, approximate diction, the insensitive movement of his lines, the trailing, shapeless sentence structure, and above all the prevailing low pressure, the absence of any poetic or even human excitement—everything points to a radical refusal to meet the challenge of the Greek.

I can imagine a reader who has had the patience to follow me so far saying something along these lines: "Yes, you have scored some points. You could hardly fail to do so. Few translators could stand up to the kind of inquisition you have seen fit to direct against Lattimore. A number of the passages you quoted were certainly rather unfortunate, though I imagine that there must be better ones which you refrained from quoting. It may indeed be that Lattimore has been overrated and that in spite of his general accuracy he does not always attend as closely as he should to the nuances of Greek poetry. Still, nuances are—nuances. He may fail in this or that respect, but his achievement is still a solid one. He has brought Greek poetry to a great many people who would otherwise not have been able to read it, and brought it *in a form they can trust.* This counts for more than you seem to realize. You are unsympathetic to Lattimore's methods and aims—all right. But what you don't sufficiently take into account is that the 'creative' translations you admire belong to a period when most educated people could read the Greek for themselves. Such work demands of the reader a good knowledge of the original, not merely so that he can 'check' the translation but so that he can gauge, and enjoy, the element of personal style and personal interpretation. The point, and the wit, of Fitzgerald's description of Athena, metamorphosed into a little girl, as 'the awesome one in pigtails' is lost on the reader who doesn't know that in the Greek she is her usual august self, 'the dread goddess with beautiful hair.' No doubt there is still room for Fitzgerald's kind of translation, and even perhaps for the rogue versions by poets like Christopher Logue. In the past, such re-creations were acceptable because the reader could measure them against Homer. If they are still acceptable today, it is because the reader can measure them against Lattimore."

And of course there is something in this. A translator who allows himself even the controlled liberties of a Fitzgerald does conceal

from the Greek-less reader certain aspects of Homeric poetry which
he has every right to know about. (Though nothing that I can see prevents him from setting the poetic translation beside a prose trot.) To
take the single most notable example, Fitzgerald pays no consistent
attention to the formular character of Homeric diction. In introducing a speech by Odysseus, he will write "The great tactician carefully
replied" or "To this the strategist Odysseus answered" or "His mind
ranging far, Odysseus answered." The reader is not to know that these
are all variants on a single, unchanging line which Homer uses no less
than forty-five times in the *Odyssey* and which Lattimore almost always
renders in this way:

Then resourceful Odysseus spoke in turn and answered him / her.[18]

The formular style of composition, observable on every page of the
Iliad and the *Odyssey*, makes Homer's poetry different in kind from
all the great poetry of later ages, and the translator who fails to observe it, as almost all translators before Lattimore have failed, can
hardly be said to translate Homer at all.

That at least is one way of putting it. And Lattimore's attempt to
"follow, as far as the structure of English will allow, the formulaic practice of the original" (from the introduction to his *Odyssey*, p. 22) is
certainly one way of translating Homer. This formulaic (or formular)
practice is so obvious and continuous a feature of Homeric poetry
that one may wonder how any translator ever ventured to ignore it
(or observe it only when it suited his purposes). It could hardly have
been through ignorance, for the practice was always apparent, even
if the world had to wait for Milman Parry before it understood the
theory. And presumably it was not from mere wanton disregard of the
text. Is there perhaps something about Homer's repeated formular
lines and phrases which cannot be carried over directly into English?
Let us look at another line. Twenty times in the *Odyssey* the coming
dawn is announced in this way:

ἦμος δ᾽ ἠριγένεια φάνη ῥοδοδάκτυλος Ἠώς.

It ought to grow monotonous, but somehow it does not. It is as if
Homer can render the essential life of things whereas other poets can
only describe them. It seems that his line is not "about" the coming
of dawn, it is the coming of dawn and hence can sustain eternal recurrence. Fitzgerald tries a number of translations, straining to catch
something of the heavenly candor of these sixteen Greek syllables:

When primal Dawn spread on the eastern sky
her fingers of pink light—

                                        (2.1–2 [1])

When Dawn spread out her finger tips of rose—
                              (3.436 [404] and elsewhere)

When the young Dawn with finger tips of rose
came in the east—

                                    (9.181–82 [170])

When the young Dawn came bright into the east
spreading her finger tips of rose—

                                        (17.1–2 [1])

Lattimore, however, follows Homer and uses the same words every time:

Now when the young Dawn showed again her rosy fingers.

And in so doing he provides the reader with an interesting fact about Homeric composition. Does he also provide the truest translation? The reader who finds that Lattimore's line, on its twentieth repetition, "gives him as much pleasure as he can bear"[19] may answer, "Yes."

The aesthetic question aside, one may wonder if it is technically possible to create in English anything like the very complex formular system that is found in Homer. The externals can certainly be reproduced, at whatever cost to the expectations one brings to a poem written in English, but what of the inner necessities, the "laws," which govern them? The reader of Lattimore's *Odyssey* repeatedly finds the principal character described as "long-suffering great Odysseus." Ah, he says to himself, formular composition—how very interesting! But inevitably he misses the point, and therefore the pleasure, of this recurrent phrase—namely, that it is the particular noun-epithet formula for Odysseus's name (when used in the nominative) that fills the space between the trochaic caesura of the third foot and the end of the line. In Lattimore's loose six-stress line, the phrase is not necessary, as it is in the Greek; it can therefore only seem otiose. The Greek hexameter sets up exact expectations, and there is great formal pleasure in observing how it meets them. We cannot, in English, know the special satisfaction of hearing a phrase lock into its appointed place, nor can we sense how a metrical pattern breeds countless new phrases of similar structure. For even though a group of words may be repeated as often in English as in Greek, Lattimore's line does not cut it into time, and hence into memory, as precisely as the Greek hexameter does. If the Greek poem is like a great hall of echoing shapes, of the English translation we can only say that it is full of awkward repetitions.

In keeping to the externals—or most of the externals—of formular composition, the translator hobbles himself and does not really serve the reader, who can get all the information about Homer's technique that he is capable of absorbing much more conveniently from a critical essay. Here again, the celebrated accuracy lets us down, for it is only an accuracy of the surface. The reader of Lattimore is like a traveler in China: he observes the curious practices of the natives, but does not really understand why they behave as they do.

In point of fact, he could learn considerably more about Homer's method of composition if Lattimore paid closer attention to the text. Astonishingly, he sometimes contrives to miss powerful effects which the formular style allows Homer to make and which could easily enough be accommodated in English. Every reader of the *Iliad* has observed that the poem begins with a scene in which a father tries to win back his child from a powerful man (Chryses begs Agamemnon to give up his daughter Chryseis) and is brutally rejected; and includes near its close a scene in which a father tries to win back his child from a powerful man (Priam begs Achilles to give up Hector's body) and is mercifully granted his wish. Homer marks the thematic point (or the formular style marks it for him) by using an almost identical line on both occasions:

1.13: to win back his daughter and bringing gifts beyond number

24.502: to win [him] back from you I bring gifts beyond number.

("His daughter" and "from you" are metrically equivalent in the Greek; so are "and bringing" and "and I bring.") Here is a windfall for the translator who seeks, like Lattimore, to preserve the formular practice of the original. And yet he manages to muff it, rendering the first line

to ransom
back his daughter, carrying gifts beyond count

and the second

to win back from you, and I bring you gifts beyond number.

The person who attacks a *fable convenue* is under some obligation to show how and why it won acceptance in the first place. To oppose the consensus of informed opinion and question Lattimore's achievement in the field of Greek translation must seem a mere critical violence unless one undertakes to explain how the great reputation was gained and what need his translations have met.

The immediate point to make is that his success has been primarily a success of classroom adoption. Whatever one may say against Rieu's *Odyssey*, there is no doubt that a lot of people bought it because they thought they would enjoy reading it and presumably a good many of them did. The main reason for buying Lattimore's translations has always been that you had to take—or teach—a survey of Greek or world literature. They came at exactly the right time, a time when Greek literature, read in translation, was starting to play an important part in undergraduate education all over the country. Since the instructors for the most part knew nothing of the ancient world, the need was for translations of certified philological accuracy with scholarly, informative introductions. And these translations had to be written in the kind of undemanding English that ordinary students could understand. Whatever its merits or demerits, the Lang, Leaf, and Myers *Iliad*, with its pseudobiblical diction, is no use to those who have never read the Authorized Version. A poetic translation like Pope's (or like Christopher Logue's) is equally useless, since it demands of both instructor and instructed a knowledge of English and Greek poetry. Something new was required by these new conditions, a kind of translation that kept close to the original (raising no awkward questions like "Is this in the Greek?"), that reduced the intervention of the translator's personal style and interpretation to the minimum, and was neither too stuffily traditional nor too brashly modernist. If it were written in verse, or at least printed in verse lengths, so much the better, for this sustained the fiction that it was Greek poetry one was studying and also made it easier for the instructor to point to a particular line. Lattimore's *Iliad* (1951), the cornerstone of his reputation, exactly met all these demands. It was essentially a new kind of translation, directed neither to the cultivated reader who wanted to see the great original caught in the contrived distortions of an English mirror nor to the more general reader who thought it might be fun to take a look at Homer. It was directed to a classroom of students and their instructor who had to meet for an hour on MWF to study Greek Lit. A glance at the introduction to his *Odyssey* shows how deftly Lattimore has learned to minister to his public. It begins (the italics are mine):

The Odyssey as we have it is an epic of over twelve thousand lines.

(Three points here: 1. "as we have it": this will serve to introduce a few comments on the problems of Homeric authorship. 2. "is an epic": ask what an epic is, etc. 3. "of over twelve thousand lines": useful piece of arithmetic.)

> *It has been divided, like the Iliad and probably at the same time, into twenty-four books.*

(Dictate this to the class, most of whom, having had to scramble through the first twelve books over the weekend, won't have read the introduction. If time permits, discuss the difference between the structure of single books and the structure of the whole poem.)

> *The contents can be, very broadly, divided as follows:*

(And the division follows, one, two, three, four. This can go straight on the blackboard.)

> *I begin by summarizing the bare facts of the story.*

(The instructor does likewise.)

And so on. It is clear what is happening: Homer is being softened up for classroom consumption. Compare the very unhelpful way in which the postscript to Fitzgerald's *Odyssey* begins: "The ship on which I sailed from Piraeus one summer night approached Odysseus' kingdom from the south in the early morning."

Classical scholars, not perhaps always sensitive to the niceties of English, were glad to know that Homer was now available in a philologically accurate translation and praised their colleague enthusiastically. His books began to win acceptance and the literary world, not too sure of itself where classical literature was concerned, assumed that the professionals knew what they were talking about. Lattimore, it seemed, was the man to go to should the time come for a dip into Greek poetry. Since he wrote, in a kind of verse, fairly dignified English (with an occasional, reassuring touch of poetry), he saved one from the uneasy fear that must have come upon those forced to visit the Bohn Classical Library: that one belonged to the underprivileged classes. True, he was not very lively, but presumably his originals were even deadlier. To the critic who knew no Greek, and yet needed to discuss a passage of Greek verse, Lattimore's translations were invaluable. Their neutral diction and avoidance of personal idioms and of the English poetic tradition in general allowed him to pretend that he was talking about the original (merely printing a translation for his reader's convenience), whereas if he had used Fitzgerald, not to mention Pope, he would have been forced to admit that he was dealing with an English poem that demanded attention in its own right. In gratitude for this civilized fiction, the critic commonly added a few words in praise of Lattimore's superb translation.

And so the great reputation grew. It could not of course have grown, let me be quite clear on this, were Lattimore not a man of talent. The modest but genuine gift for language revealed in his original poetry can sometimes be seen in his translations—in his *Oresteia* (specifically, I think, the *Agamemnon*), in some of the versions from the elegiac writers in *Greek Lyrics* and sometimes in his *Iliad,* which, though marked by the same literal-mindedness that disfigures his *Odyssey,* is a stronger and more vital piece of work. Then, at least, he seemed to believe in what he was doing and there are passages, like the fight between Achilles and the river Scamander in book 21, which reveal a genuine energy of language and even a kind of vision.

Yet the performance never remotely matched the reputation, and more than a decade passed before it was required to face any serious critical inspection.[20] Criticism might have helped him to resist his dangerously simpleminded approach to the art of translation and encouraged him to give his genuine poetic gifts their head. But instead of criticism he has received praise, praise often so extravagant in tone and so out of proportion to the achievement that it is sometimes hard not to question the good faith of those who have offered it. His *Odyssey* displays all the vices of his method without any of the conviction which once gave his writing a certain gray dignity. When the time comes to speak the final words about this melancholy episode in the history of classical translation, it will be found that Samuel Johnson provides the appropriate text. In his essay on Denham, he remarks that this writer seems to have been one of the first to understand "the necessity of emancipating translation from the drudgery of counting lines and interpreting single words." The great critic continues: "How much this servile practice obscured the clearest and deformed the most beautiful parts of the ancient authors, may be discovered by a perusal of our earlier versions; some of them the works of men well qualified, not only by critical knowledge, but by poetical genius, who yet, by a mistaken ambition of exactness, degraded at once their original and themselves."[21]

6

Structural Translation:
Christopher Logue's *Patrocleia*

TRANSLATION IS OFTEN SADDLED WITH AN IMPROPER OBLIGATION: IT is supposed to "give you the original." I don't question the attractions of this doctrine. To get enough Greek to read Homer with some sort of understanding is going to take you anything up to three months, so why not spare yourself this labor and believe, with Professor X, that Professor Y's new version of the *Iliad* is "a true representation," "the essential Homer," and so forth? Moreover, this belief underpins the World Lit. in Translation courses which play an important part in the teaching of the humanities in the United States. It would not do to admit that so much time is being spent reading Lattimore, Fitts, and Arrowsmith (estimable men though these are). No, it is Homer, Sophocles, and Euripides that the young men and women are sharpening their sensibilities on.

The point about good translation is not that it "gives you the original." It doesn't and can't and shouldn't try to. There is one place to get Homer's *Iliad* and only one place: in the fifteen thousand lines or so of the Greek text. What a translation does is to *turn* the original into something else (*vertit anglice*), and the interest of the operation is in the essentially critical comparison which is thereby set up between the two objects. The difference may be slight (with modern prose) or very considerable (with ancient poetry), but it is always there and it is what distinguishes the translation from the literate trot designed for people who don't have the language of the original. The distinction is as nearly absolute as such things can be, and until it is grasped the present low standard of translation is not likely to improve.

I don't think that Dryden or Pope or Edward FitzGerald would have had much difficulty with Logue's *Patrocleia*,[1] but it cut an odd figure when it appeared. The main purpose of these notes is to try to discourage the reader from laying it beside Lattimore's *Iliad* and ask-

"Structural Translation: Notes on Logue's *Patrocleia*," *Arion* 1, no. 2 (Summer 1962): 27–38.

ing, "Where is this in the Greek?" Of this method of judging a translator, E. M. W. Tillyard has some good remarks in a chapter on Pope's
Iliad: "critics of translation usually fix their eye on the small detail,"
he writes, "on the accuracy of the phrase or the short passage. The
better tests of a long work are whether the translator has a durable
rhetoric and whether he can follow the main undulations of his original."[2] I'm not sure about "a durable rhetoric"; I would have supposed
that the translator must devise the best rhetoric he can and hope it
will prove durable. But otherwise Tillyard's comment is helpful. It will
be my argument that Logue's version does follow the undulations
of his original, and that the liberties he has taken are not capricious
but stem from a conception of Homeric translation both serious and
responsible.

He seems, first of all, to have taken the trouble to consider what he
could *not* do. He realized that he didn't have a hope in hell of taking
on Homer at his own game. He saw, I mean, that a modern translator
could not create a formal equivalent for Homer's diction; nor could
he reanimate the heroic convention within which Homer wrote. Pope
was luckier in this respect, for he still believed in the epic tradition
and he was writing in the immediate afterglow of the last great epic
poem which the West was to produce. He could animate the convention, in the terms in which his culture understood it; and with Milton
at his back, he could rise to Homer's high style as no other translator
has ever done.

The modern translator is, by comparison, out on a limb. The only
great form which he can use in place of the epic is the novel. Since
the time of Butler it has often been supposed that Homer could be
treated most vitally by being turned into a novelist, but Robert Fitzgerald's translation has shown how much we were losing when we accepted even the *Odyssey* as a novel; with the *Iliad* we lose almost everything. Logue's *Patrocleia* insists that the *Iliad* is a poem, and if it is
unlike most versified Homers, that is because Logue believes, like
Pope, that a translation must stand in a responsible relation not only
to its original but also to the literary situation of the translator's own
day. There is of course no rule that a translation must be "modern."
Binyon's Dante is not written in a contemporary idiom, yet he shows
himself aware of the modifications which a number of poets from
Swinburne on have made in the traditional ten-syllable line. How far
the resources of modern poetry are to be used is a matter for each
translator to settle for himself; but that he should ignore them altogether and still succeed is almost unthinkable. While Logue's version
is in no real sense "the *Iliad* in modern dress," it is written in the belief that no translationese should be allowed to muffle the impact of

the original. Such a belief more or less commits him to a modern diction and to modern methods of presentation, and Logue has sensibly taken what help he could from the only long modern poem by a writer of distinction. Obviously he could not use *The Cantos* as Pope had used *Paradise Lost,* and it would be wrong to call his version Poundian. Nonetheless he has kept Pound in mind, taking from him the variety of metrical effects, the abrupt changes of tone, the presentation of a scene in terms of sharp visual images, the occasional use of prose, and other devices.

If the intelligent modern translator, then, knows that he cannot revive the epic convention, and that any attempt to take on Homer at the verbal level is going to lead to defeat, not to say massacre, what can he do? What aspects of Homer are not out of his range? To such a question, Milman Parry's work on the formulaic tradition provides an immediate, very encouraging answer. The oral poet, we understand, uses an inherited diction, builds his lines and paragraphs out of an organic body of traditional formulas (Zeus-who-delights-in-thunder and rose-fingered-Dawn and so on). This situation surely plays straight into the hands of the enterprising translator. Instead of wasting his time trying to reproduce the unreproducible diction, he can concentrate his energies on that aspect of the poem which is most truly Homeric: on the relation of incident and episode within a massively organized total action.

My argument is that "structural translation," as I think one may call it, while it looks capricious and arbitrary, holds out the hope of an essential fidelity.

The design of book 16 is strong and simple:

1. Achilles and Patroclus, lines 1–256
2. Patroclus's exploits, lines 257–418
3. Death of Sarpedon, lines 419–683
4. Death of Patroclus, lines 684–867

Logue retains this design, and within each section substantially follows the sequence of incident and episode, here and there transposing, adding, and cutting. Within the single scene, his aim is to present Homer's action and Homer's picture with the maximum intensity; to do this, he does not always use Homer's words, and on occasions he adapts Homer's similes or replaces them with new ones of his own. The task of the translator of Homer, Pope wrote in his preface, "is above all things to keep alive that Spirit and Fire which makes his chief Character." If he is to do this, his translation must generate its own life; it cannot batten parasitically on the life of the original.

Within its own terms, Logue's account of the scene between Achilles and Patroclus in the first hundred lines follows Homer closely. We note that he cuts the first simile comparing Patroclus's tears to water running down a rock face. In the great books of the *Iliad*, similes are used with a constant, careless profusion; we are continually being made aware of the whole life of man and nature of which any one action is merely a part. Such is the energy of this poet that we accept his similes even when they have only a rather general relevance. No other writer has been able to command so great an energy, and later poets have had to use their resources more sparingly, more functionally. By post-Homeric standards, the initial simile (a fairly conventional one, repeated from 9.14–15) detracts from the homely, rather Dantesque simile a few lines later in which Patroclus is compared to a little girl running along beside her mother (cf. *Purgatorio* 30.43–45). Logue therefore cuts the first one and concentrates on the second.

His additions are slight but interesting. Phrases like Patroclus's description of Thetis as "your sainted Mother"[3] serve to remind us of the long familiarity between the two men. No doubt Achilles invoked this singular authority just a shade too often. (One recalls 9.410: "My mother Thetis tells me.") His ironic explanation of Agamemnon's folly in taking away Briseis ("He was a sick man at the time") adds something different to the scene—not the human reality within the poem but the reality of the translator's own time. To Logue's first British readers, at least, Achilles' remark distinctly suggests a Tory doing his best to defend Eden's Suez policy. *What is this doing in the text?*

Brecht found he could present a dramatic action more effectively by dropping the conventional theatrical illusion. Logue wants us to believe in the reality of Homer's action, but he does not ask us to believe that he, Christopher Logue, is anything other than a modern Englishman writing a translation of Homer in a small mews flat in London. If he is ready to let modern references find their way into his translation—as Pope, it has been suggested, brought into his rendering of the quarrels between the Greek leaders something of the contemporary vitality of parliamentary debate between the Whigs and Tories[4]—it is because he believes that the translator cannot get to serious grips with his text until he detaches the label inscribed "Very Ancient—Please Don't Touch." The mere act of translation brings the old work into the confusions of the present; it has got to take its chance there. The translator of, say, *Aucassin et Nicolette* might well feel dubious about exposing his fragile charge in such a way; Homer's poem, which penetrates the life we lead, can without danger be penetrated by it.

The Achilles-Patroclus scene is followed in the Greek by an "intercut" reminding us of the fighting (lines 102–24), which Logue follows in substantial detail. Homer then briefly returns to the two friends, and the arming of Patroclus follows (lines 130ff.). Logue omits this passage, for he has worked the most significant detail (the anticipatory pathos of Achilles' spear being too heavy for Patroclus to handle) into the previous scene. The arming of the hero is a feature of the epic tradition which faces the translator with a severe problem. A film director might make effective visual play with that heap of outlandish gear taking shape, piece by glittering piece, around the hero's person; what hamstrings the translator is the terminology, the naming of the parts. Start talking about baldrics and corselets, not to mention greaves, those disastrous heroic spats, and you are involved in a game of charades. (Logue has a theory about the properties of the heroic age. Certain objects—sword, cup, horse, for instance—have kept their vitality fully charged through the ages; they are as much at home in our world as in Homer's. We may not personally have handled a sword, but instinctively we know all about them.)

Logue returns to the scene in Achilles' camp via a thirteen-line passage which turns out to be a simile comparing the Trojan War to a campaign of the Chinese imperial army ("October. / The hungry province grows restive.").[5] We find it easy now to move from one historical culture to another, and of course in *The Cantos* Pound regularly makes analogies between Greece and China. But why does Logue bring in this Chinese cross-reference here? Because, I think, he is all the time trying to present these scenes of archaic warfare with the maximum sensuous reality and excitement. Ancient Greece, for many people, has been staled by long cultural contact, whereas in Chinese art and poetry, a relatively recent acquisition, "le passé revit à l'état neuf" (to quote Yourcenar on Cavafy's use of unfamiliar Greek history).[6]

The simile of the wolves follows in both Homer and Logue, then the muster of Achilles' troops under their five commanders.[7] In Homer, the first two men are sprung from amours between gods and mortal women. This is a little hard for us, and Logue accordingly cuts the first story, providing instead a detail of the man's military qualifications. But this is not, I repeat, the *Iliad* in modern dress; he is not doing with Homeric epic what the Augustans did with Roman satire, systematically transposing it into contemporary terms. If he cuts the first story, it is because he wants to present at least one such parentage in all its strange beauty. When we read the lines in the Greek (lines 179ff.), we accept Homer's account instantly; the words sing the action into our minds in all its sensuous candor. Pope toned it down, telling us merely that Hermes saw the young woman dancing in "Diana's quire." Lattimore has no such misgivings:

> lovely in the dance, Polymele,
> daughter of Phylas; whom strong Hermes Argeiphontes
> loved, when he watched her with his eyes among the girls dancing
> in the choir for clamorous Artemis of the golden distaff.

I can't myself make much of this. Was Artemis bawling instructions—keeping the time with her distaff, perhaps? Lattimore, concerned with avoiding "mistranslation, which would be caused by rating the word of my own choice ahead of the word which translates the Greek," has no time for these delicate mysteries, and we are driven back to the Greek text for enlightenment. The lines must mean something, however; Logue writes:[8]

> When young this woman was so beautiful
> She joined Artemis' dancing nuns
> Who lived together in the House of Spindles.

Is this what Homer had in mind, this gay Mycenean sorority? I don't know, but at least it gives us a picture and an action. It exists in its own right, and I think it may exist in Homer's too.

Anyone who turns from the spacious, echoing lines in which Achilles prays to Zeus for the safe return of Patroclus (lines 231ff.) is going to feel cheated by the tame version of the Lord's Prayer which Logue offers in their place. What has happened to Pelasgian Zeus, wintry Dodona, and the curious Selli? A poet with different sympathies might, I fancy, have made more of this passage, but Logue is not going to risk losing his reader's attention by bringing in strange religious practices which have to be glossed from Pausanias or Farnell. He knows that a modern translator cannot count on what Pope called "a competent knowledge in Antiquities" (cf. Pope's note on book 5, line 449). Throughout, he uses the basic terminology of Christianity on the grounds that it provides the only religious koine we still possess. (Thus libation is summarily turned into communion.) Compare Glaucus's prayer to Apollo later in the book.

With line 275, the *aristeia* of Patroclus begins. The first man he kills is a certain Pyraechmes.[9] Homer deals with the affair in three lines (lines 287–90); Logue devotes over thirty to it. Why? Involved, I think, is a question of some importance. Homer presents his battle scenes with incomparable power and immediacy; we are in the thick of it, the spearheads dangerously close to our diaphragms. But he feels no need to maintain a consistent authorial position, and he combines direct presentation with more summary description. When we read Homer's Greek text, we read it in Homer's terms; when we read the versions which X and Y hammered out on their typewriters and key-boards, we read them in the light of the gains in narrative method which have been made in the last two and a half thousand years. Since at least the time of James, the relation of an author to his work has become a critical question of some delicacy—we are very conscious of the ways in which a story gets itself told, we want to be sure where the author stands in relation to that story—and a modern poet who undertakes to write narrative poetry cannot afford to neglect the nar-rative skills which the novel has made available. Logue, like Homer, varies his point of view, but in scenes like these he finds that a con-sistent eyewitness account will be the most effective. Homer's brief statement to the effect that Patroclus struck Pyraechmes in the right shoulder will therefore not suffice; we must be made to see how the thing happened, and this may take time. (So a film may take five min-utes to present something that novelist may describe in a couple of sentences. The analogy with the cinema is relevant; Logue sees his task as in some sense parallel to the transposition involved in turning a literary narrative into a movie.)

Lines 306–50 present a segment of fighting. The passage is formally introduced and concluded:

306–7: Then man killed man in the scattered fighting of the captains.

351: So these Greek captains each killed his man.

The details of Homeric combat are always vigorous, but the total effect sometimes seems haphazard. "Homer poses a battle," Logue writes, "and then flicks about inside it, so what you get—or should get—in the end is the *knowledge* of a vast field of action, even though the item at which you are looking is no more than a—perhaps replaceable—detail." This method of presentation is obviously not the only one. A film director might decide to present—against a background of gen-eral fighting—one or two actions and follow them closely. This is what Logue has done:[10]

Out of many battles, consider two.

In both episodes (Cleobulus and "Little Ajax," Peneleos and Lycon) Logue follows the action, though not of course the words, of the original quite closely, while including some extra detail—the two soldiers drinking at the pool,[11] for example. He uses a slightly different technique in a later section of the battle, the fighting over Sarpedon's body (lines 550–640). Homer again presents a sequence of brief individual combats. This business of "A killed B and then C was killed by D" is nobody's favorite reading, and it proved a serious embarrassment in the subsequent epic tradition. (See, for example, *Aeneid* 9.569–76 for the thing at its most tiresome.) If we are honest, I think we may admit that Logue's handling of the scene is a distinct improvement on the original. It has much greater variety, for one thing; we are given close-ups of this or that detail—the torn horse, for example—and then the camera moves back for a synoptic vision of the action as a whole—the banners, the shields, the oppressive sense of light and heat.

Returning to the segment lines 306–50, we find that Homer concludes it with a simile which serves to transpose the action onto a different plane. (He likes this device—not dissimilar in effect from an ode in a Greek play; cf. the placing of the woodcutter simile in lines 633ff., after the fighting over Sarpedon's body.) The Greek slaughter of the retreating Trojans is compared to wolves ravaging a flock of sheep. The reality of this is easy enough to imagine, but it is in fact something that most of Homer's modern readers haven't seen. Logue tries to use similes that are as immediately centered in our experience as we may suppose Homer's to have been for his original auditors. Thus, in his rendering of the beautiful simile describing how Sarpedon falls, mortally wounded, he adds one contemporary touch (lines 482ff.):[12]

> He fell as a tree falls—oak, say, or pine—
> Slowly at first and then, with the bright
> Commercial axes at its heart,
> The tall hurt trunk lies down
> Among its leaves, resentfully.

Why spoil the elegiac tenderness of the original by reminding us that the axes were "commercial"? In the Greek, the simile serves to soften, just a little, the bitterness of this young death. A tree is cut down, but it continues in a kind of life as part of a ship; Sarpedon falls, but his body will be spirited away to Lycia where he will be given a handsome memorial.[13] The ultimate purpose of Logue's change of emphasis is part of his different conception of war about which I shall have something to say in a moment. At the immediate level, he brings in the word "commercial" because, as usual, he wants to set the action of the simile firmly within our own experience. To see a great tree being cut down must always have been a moving sight for an imaginative person, but for us it is something more. The bright commercial axes point not only to the contrast between the slow organic growth of the tree and the mass-produced instruments that destroy it, but also to the ends, the commercial ends, for which we usually cut down trees. We devastate forests to produce lying newspapers. Our pleasant vices have brought an extra touch of indignity to Sarpedon's death.

In the passage from which this discussion set out (lines 352ff.), we find Logue replacing Homer's simile of wolves and sheep with a new one of his own. He compares the Trojans retreating across the ditch surrounding the Greek ships to lemmings on their march to mass suicide. Most of us have not, certainly, seen this happen (except perhaps in a Disney movie),[14] but we have read about it, and the very strangeness of the act stirs the imagination as the fairly conventional wolf/sheep simile doesn't. And, I think, it allows Logue to pass another concealed comment on the nature of war: a freely elected form of mass suicide. This is an essential element in his translation and one that, for some readers, is likely to raise the most serious difficulties. It deserves a section to itself.

The scene in which the Trojans pile into the ditch (lines 367ff.) is considerably expanded in Logue's version. As with the earlier Pyraechmes episode, it is full of effective visual detail; again, too, he brings in several touches of his own, notably the camp followers who

> Nipped down into the ditch to strip the dead
> And cosh the wounded into hell.[15]

Over the business of killing and being killed, the *Iliad* extends a total clarity. "The passage from life to death is veiled by not the least reticence" (Simone Weil).[16] Nonetheless, Homer writes from within a convention by which war is, genuinely, "man-ennobling." In the courage with which man confronts the terror of battle, life finds its supreme assertion. Today, not only do we have no heroic convention, but in treating of war our only valid convention is deliberately anti-heroic. And to our sense of the squalor, the sheer folly and waste of war as presented in the literature of 1914–18, we have something quite new, namely the knowledge that war, one of our uniquely human activities, threatens the race itself. Logue knows that in the *Iliad*, the only great poem about war, the battles are not play-acting, and he makes no attempt to keep out his own disgust at the fact of war.

But what right has the translator to bring all this into his version?

Pope's *Iliad* is seldom considered seriously as a translation. A fine Augustan poem maybe (now that Pope is critically fashionable), but of course—you mustn't call it Homer. Aristarch avenged himself better than he knew for his handling in the fourth section of *The Dunciad*. Nonetheless, the fact that a great English poet devoted twelve years to a translation should surely give later practitioners something to think about. What principles did he follow, what conclusions did he come to? It seems to me worth urging that Pope's *Iliad* is not merely a brilliant poem, but perhaps the most completely serious translation in the language. Pope had far too much sense of history, and of course of poetry, to suppose that he could translate Homer by word-for-wording him into English. He knew that whatever he was able to produce was going to be, superficially, very unlike the original. He had a double vision of the poem, as existing in its own right, and as existing—and *developing*—within the long tradition which it initiated. His task, as Douglas Knight shows in a useful study, was to reconcile these two visions.[17] Thus, in a note on Achilles' appearance in book 9, Pope remarks that it is interesting for the reader to be shown how simply great men lived "in the earliest Ages of the World." But in his translation of this passage (9.245–54 [186–91]), the stress is different, for in Augustan epic a prince must be presented in a more elevated manner if he is to be imaginatively credible. "The poetry, as opposed to the annotation, must hold our attention for Homer in another way" (Knight). Pope does not try to repeat in English what Homer has already done, unrepeatably, in Greek. He recreates the thought, sometimes even the action, of the original in terms of the cultural, philosophical, moral, and to some extent social conditions of his own time. Thus, to show Zeus as representing little more than nearly unlimited power would for Pope be mere wanton archaizing. With the *Aeneid* and, even more, *Paradise Lost* in mind, he presents a Zeus who has acquired a sense of cosmic purpose and justice quite foreign to his great Ionian predecessor. (See for example Agamemnon's complaint against Zeus's "vile deception" in 9.17–28 with Pope's version, lines 23–38, in which, despite a sharp reference to "partial Jove," the stress is on the inscrutable mystery of the divine action.)

A modern translator—to return to Logue—does not write in the light of an expanding epic tradition and when he changes the emphasis of the original, his changes are bound to be more arbitrary. His only guides are, negatively, his sense of the present literary situation; and, positively, his full human response to the experience presented by Homer. He knows, for example, that it is pointless to try to revive a heroic convention of war, for that would lead him into mere fancy-dress translationese. He must do with Homer's military matter what Pope did with his divinity: concentrate on those aspects of it which are within his literary and moral range and adjust the rest in

162   CLASSICS AND TRANSLATION

accordance with the new focus. Logue can no more let "glorious" war into his text than Pope can admit amoral deity.

This is perhaps the moment to suggest a distinction between the translator's duty towards the action of the poem and towards what one may call, loosely, its thought. His duty towards the action is almost absolute. (Logue's liberties are merely a matter of presentation.) Towards the thought, it is more problematic. But if he is responding to the total human seriousness of the *Iliad* he cannot, it seems to me, ignore his own terms of reference. *Even if this involves importing into the text something that is not there at all?* (I am talking of substantive matter, not of detail.) The question is delicate, and I am thankful I do not have to defend Pope's deity; I feel happier with Logue's war. Let me quote a single passage and ask the reader if it is really as "un-Homeric" as it looks. In one of the scenes of general combat, these lines occur:

> The captains in their iron masks drift past each other,
> Calling, calling, gathering light on their breastplates.

This answers to no particular place in the Greek text, but it calls up a picture of Homeric warriors—solemn, remote, antique—that we can easily accept. Logue, however, sets this noble vision in savagely ironic light by means of the simile which immediately precedes it:

> And over it all,
> As flies shift up and down a haemorrhage alive with ants,
> The captains in their iron masks drift past each other,
> Calling, calling, gathering light on their breastplates.[18]

This particular device, the sharp juxtaposition of attraction and repulsion, belongs to modern literature or perhaps one should say to seventeenth-century literature; it is anyway quite outside the range of Homer's poetic means. Is the passage therefore un-Homeric? Nietzsche may provide an answer in a passage from *The Genealogy of Morals* (essay 1, section 11) where he speculates on the motives which led Hesiod to present cultural history via his myth of the Five Ages: "He could cope with the contradictions inherent in Homer's world, so marvelous on the one hand, so ghastly and brutal on the other, only by making two ages out of one and presenting them in temporal sequence: first, the age of the heroes and demigods . . . and second, the Iron Age, which presented the same world as seen by the descendants of those who had been crushed, despoiled, brutalized, sold into slavery" (trans. Golffing).

Logue juxtaposes the two "ages" more abruptly than Homer; but the juxtaposition is Homer's, not his. Although the violence in Logue's changes of tone and the abrupt shifts between attraction and revulsion are not to be found in Homer, they are inescapably part of our reading of Homer, and the translator who seeks to make the *Iliad* live in the modern world cannot exclude them.

In the *Patrocleia* and in the best of his subsequent Homeric fragments, Logue has come as close to certain aspects of the *Iliad* as we are likely to get now. Though the tragic seems beyond him, he conveys, better sometimes even than Pope, the energy and terror of this poem and, more fleetingly, the glory. Like Homer, he can convince us that it is all really happening. In *Pax* (his version of book 19) he describes the scene when Thetis brings Achilles the armor made by Hephaistos:[19]

> And as she laid the moonlit armour on the sand
> It chimed;
> And the sound that came from it
> Followed the light that came from it,
> Like sighing,
> Saying,
> *Made in Heaven.*
>
> And those who had the neck to watch Achilles weep
> Could not look now.
> Nobody looked. They were afraid.
>
> Except Achilles: looked,
> Lifted a piece of it between his hands;
> Turned it; tested the weight of it; and then
> Spun the holy tungsten, like a star between his knees,
> Slitting his eyes against the flare, some said,
> But others thought the hatred shuttered by his lids,
> Made him protect the metal.
>
> His eyes like furnace doors ajar.

He is too decorative here, and the passage hardly shows him at his best, but if it fails it fails valiantly, in the line of duty. For the translator of a scene like this has somehow to make us believe the unbelievable: here, now, beautiful, terrifying things created by the hands of a god are in the hands of a man more terrifying and beautiful than they are.*

* This paragraph is taken from "On Looking Into Fitzgerald's Homer," *New York Review of Books* 21, no. 20 (December 12, 1974): 6.

Logue's principle is to reproduce, substantially, Homer's action while responding to it in his own terms. In this respect he is in the position of the Homeridae, who would have felt free to retouch their great inheritance. One line of development was over when the poem was first set down on paper, but did it thereby reach its perfect form and "stop"? Obviously it didn't. Through the medium of the epic tradition, Europe continued to "rewrite" Homer, in original poems and in translations, until the end of the eighteenth century. When that tradition died, an attempt was made to graft Homer onto the new tradition of the novel, but this proved a boring failure. Not only was the novel an inherently unsuitable form, but the poem itself, thanks to modern scholarship, lost its old flexibility and hardened into a dead philological exhibit. Logue, unencumbered by Greek scholarship, has managed to get inside the poem again and has discovered that, after all these years, it is still breathing.

7

The Gaiety of Language: Bacchylides and the Translation of Greek Poetry

"WE NEED AN EYE WHICH CAN SEE THE PAST IN ITS PLACE WITH ITS definite differences from the present," T. S. Eliot wrote, "and yet so lively that it shall be as present to us as the present."[1] An eye for the present moment of the past, for those aspects of an old author that most call for attention today, is by and large the critic's eye. It is even more the translator's eye. It is not the scholar's eye. Many contemporary classical scholars, indeed, alarmed by the impurity of method they detect in a Murray or a Verrall, are above all concerned to avoid importing modern interests into their reading of an ancient text. Their business is with those many and complex questions which only an exact scholarship can handle; what remains may be left to the dilettante or perhaps the scholar himself in his private hours. Such "purity of method" is no doubt admirable in itself, but when it involves ignoring whatever it is in an author that made him worth reading in the first place, it is time to start asking questions. Denys Page, in his edition of Sappho and Alcaeus, is serious and intent when he is trying to establish the true reading, to sort out some linguistic difficulty, or castigating the blunders of his predecessors; when he comes to the experience offered by Sappho's poetry, the body of realized life, this seriousness gives way to an easy, dismissive irony that is often not far from contempt. "Here, at the height of her suffering, she devotes a quarter of her poem to such a flight of fancy, with much detail irrelevant to her present theme." So Page concludes his analysis of the great poem which the Alexandrian editors placed first in their collection of her work. His task, as he himself allows, is "the difficult and doubtful task of *interpreting* at least the longer . . . pieces."[2] My italics point to something that the bland, hard surface of Page's prose rather consistently refuses to do. He makes little attempt to engage with Sappho's *poetry* (as distinct from her dialect, meters, historical

"The Gaiety of Language," *Arion* 1, no. 3 (Autumn 1962): 65–88.

references, and so forth), and whenever she fails to conform to his notion of what a poem should be, it is always Sappho who is at fault.

In reading Sappho one does not have to look for "the present moment of the past." Everything is present. More completely than any Greek poet except Homer, she cancels the intervening centuries. But much Greek poetry is far more specialized—in its formal procedures and in the qualities of its sensibility—and it is here that the critic, and the translator, show what they are made of. Attic tragedy, despite its present vogue, is in many ways a strange, remote form. We are perhaps rather too easily assuming that it has been domesticated. Choral lyric is stranger still, the most distant province of Greek literature. Of the two choral poets who work has survived in some bulk, Pindar, superficially the more remote, might I think prove the more accessible —given a critic or translator who could wake him into life. Perhaps our approach to Pindar starts at the wrong end; we try (as finally of course we must) to make sense of a Pindaric whole, of a complete ode, even of his entire remaining work, chattering nervously the while about formulae of break-off and transition, gnomic bridge passages, ring composition, and the like, in the effort to make ourselves feel at home in his curious world. It might be better if we started with the immediate donnée, his diction. The furious pressure to which Pindar subjects language, the incessant dislocations of normal usage, the extraordinary play of metaphor, the systematic exploitation of the sensuous confusions of speech, the way abstract nouns are wrenched into the sphere of sensation (to *taste* toil, to *flame with* excellence, to be *clasped*—or blended, mingled, wedded, almost *bedded*—with praise)— all this induces a state of heightened response in which the facts of everyday experience are dissolved, "destroyed," and then re-created in a new sensuous fullness. His poems "live or die as physical objects radiating the freshness and pleasure of a transformed reality."[3]

But if Pindar offers something that could excite the student of modern poetry (in a sense, of course, all poetry is modern poetry), it is not at all clear that Bacchylides, who shares with him many of the procedures of choral lyric, could be approached in this way. There is nothing in his language, I suppose, that is particularly close to us today, no single aspect of his poetry as a whole that strongly engages our creative or critical interests. The critic should no doubt be supple and imaginative enough to deal with texts that do not bear on his immediate preoccupations—though in fact little of literary interest seems to have been said about Bacchylides since the sands of Egypt yielded up some fifteen hundred lines of his poetry more than a century ago.[4] But what is the translator to do? What sort of modern English equivalent can he devise for this poet, a good one but not, like Pindar, a great one, working in a difficult remote genre?

The attempt to approach Bacchylides critically has promptly led me in to the standard critical cliché, the comparison with Pindar, a cliché as old as Longinus (33.5) and probably much older. Bacchylides is a delightful, interesting author—so the critical writ runs; his work is full of bright, vivid imagery, he has his moments of suggestive pathos, but—he cannot be compared to Pindar. Adam Parry, in his introduction to the Robert Fagles's translation,[5] offers his own (negative) version: "To blame Bacchylides for not being Pindar is as childish a judgment as to condemn Vermeer for falling short of Rembrandt, or Marvell for missing the grandeur of Milton." And the comparison duly follows. Now, I don't at all want to quarrel with Parry; he has a number of good things to say in his commentaries on individual poems, and I suspect that his insight contributed substantially to the success of this volume. Of course he means no more here than that it is foolish to blame chalk for not being cheese. He is just clearing his throat. Nonetheless, the relaxed critical tone is all too representative of the patronizing way in which classical scholars like to address the general public. For if it is foolish to blame Bacchylides for not being Pindar, that is just what is always being done, whereas who has ever blamed Marvell for not being Milton? Why bother to make so trivial a point?

But if the critic is to deny himself this Pindar/Bacchylides comparison, what is there left for him to do? What other point can he make? Taking translation to be a form of criticism, let us take this question to Fagles's versions and see what sort of answer emerges.

Bacchylides presents the translator with a number of problems. I will single out two: the fragmentary state of the text, and the *embarras* of compound epithets. These are not the most obviously significant problems, but they will serve my present purpose. For the first has a general interest extending beyond Bacchylides, and the second can I think lead us to the heart of his poetry. Or at least to its surface, which may prove to be what he principally offers.

The poem which stands first in most editions, the epinician ode to Argeius of Ceos, has not reached us intact. We have lost (according to Blass) the first 110 lines, of which 46 can be partly reconstructed from separate fragments. It was a clever stroke of the zeitgeist to let Egypt start revealing its tattered treasures just at the moment when a taste for the fragmentary was developing in the arts. An earlier translator would not have made much of the odds and ends assembled by Blass and would probably have started where Jebb's text starts, at line

111. But to someone familiar with modern verse there is often a genuine pleasure to be found in these ruined syllables. The lack of connection we can altogether take in our stride—we are used to establishing connections for ourselves. Pound's little poem "Papyrus," which aroused the scholarly indignation of Robert Graves and Laura Riding, shows, playfully, how readily the fragments of Oxyrhynchus can be assimilated:[6]

> Spring . . . .
> Too long . . . . . .
> Gongula . . . . . .

One's eye, coasting down the column (how much of her technique did H. D. learn in this way, one wonders), is first caught by a couple of lines which are not in the papyrus at all—

> oh godbuilt gates / of Pelops' shining island—

but were retrieved from the scholiast's comment on Pindar *Olympian* 13.4. At line 48 we find two words which can be reconstructed as ἱστουργοὶ κόραι, "girls at the loom," and at 50, μελίφρονος ὕπνου, "of sweet sleep." The whole section 49–55 is quite promising. I quote Jebb's synopsis: "One of the maidens, on awaking from sleep, speaks to another about quitting their ἀρχαίαν πόλιν, and seeking a new abode 'on the verge of the sea' (ἀνδήροις ἁλός), in the full 'rays of the sun.'"

From these bits and pieces, Fagles produces the following lines:

> O gates flung up by the gods
> On Pelops' shining island . . .
> Girls at the looms . . .
> Delicious sleep . . .
> A fine old city . . .
> And dunes where the combers
> Crash under searing sun . . .

It was clever of Fagles to have made this πρόσωπον τηλαυγές for himself out of such shaky material.[7] But of course, you say, this is not what Bacchylides wrote. It proves, does it not, what you had always supposed, that translation is hardly a serious business. What a contrast between this light-fingered fellow Fagles raiding the apparatus, magpie fashion, for whatever gauds may take his fancy, and Lobel (to invoke the most terrifying name in the business) austerely dipping into his baskets.

This is not, I agree, the facade that Bacchylides designed. That facade is ruined. What then is the translator to do? He may reconstruct radically (and produce something like those restored "medieval" palazzi the Italians used to build); he may skip and start halfway; or he may do what Fagles has done and create, out of the old stones lying here and there in the grass, an attractive little archway of his own. It pretends—the notes make clear—to be no more. But it achieves its purpose. It catches our attention for Bacchylides; it makes us want to read on and discover what happens next on this sunlit island. It was simply chance that allowed Fagles to introduce Bacchylides to us speaking our own fragmentary poetic speech; but it was creative intelligence that turned this chance to good ends.

Before I show him dealing with something that Bacchylides really did write, let me point to one more passage in which he takes advantage of a break in the papyrus. Near the middle of the ninth ode, in his translation, this passage occurs:

> Harpinna foamed in a sheen of robes
> To mix with sturdy Mars?
> Corcyra curved in wreaths?

To these attractive lines, the papyrus contributes no more than:

> υπεπλον[
> ανελικοστεφα[

But this is more promising than it looks, for it yields two likely adjectives, εὔπεπλος and the beautiful ἑλικοστέφανος. And the context helps to establish the owners of these charming costumes. The poem was written for one Automedes from Phlius, a small Dorian state in the northeast of the Peloponnese; and in the passage in question, the poet is celebrating the matrimonial successes of the daughters of the local river god, Asopus. It was Bacchylides' third editor, Jurenka, who drew attention to a passage in Pausanias (5.22.6) describing how the Phliasians dedicated statues to these river nymphs and to the gods they lay with: "Their images have been ordered thus: Nemea is the first of the sisters, and after her comes Zeus seizing Aegina; by Aegina stands *Harpina*, who, according to the tradition of the Eleans and Phliasians, *mated with Ares* . . . after her is *Corcyra*." Which of these four ladies is to be brought into the poem is a matter of choice, governed by meter and space. Edmonds, whose text is the most fully—and, in his usual manner, the most hazardously—restored of the five which I have been able to consult, plumps for Harpin[n]a and Corcyra, but the second name seems unlikely on metrical grounds.

The larval purist in me regrets, dimly, that Fagles's translation here cannot, perhaps, quite be squared with the meter. It is nonetheless a genuine recovery, not a clever substitute like the opening of the first poem. For even if the names were different, Bacchylides must have written something very like this. "It is the charm of his ode," Jebb writes (p. 206), "that it takes us into the heart of these Peloponnesian uplands," delicately evoking the pious fancy of this remote Greek people who turned the springs and streams of their land into nymphs whose beauty drew down the shining presences from Olympus. Fagles's "Corcyra curved in wreaths" (an admirable translation of ἑλικοστέφανος), with its suggestions of at once rustic piety and archaic haute couture, has created for us, out of a few battered syllables and a scholar's footnote, an image of the garlanded statue of the eponymous river nymph, or the nymph herself as local folklore conceived her. His success in releasing the picture enclosed in the compound epithet leads me to my second point.

The imperfect state of Bacchylides' text puts the translator on his mettle; faced with this challenge, Fagles reveals himself an agile, ingenious man, ready (as all good translators must be) to take his *bien* where he finds it and now and then, maybe, when he thinks no one is looking, to add a little *bien* of his own. (This is, nonetheless, to use the sacramental word, an *accurate* translation; its freedoms are dictated by insight into the original.)

The state of the text is an accidental difficulty; the compound epithets are an essential one. The wealth of such epithets seems to have been a characteristic of earlier choral lyric; they are sown thickly in much of what we have of Ibycus, and an ancient critic comments on their "abundant use" in Stesichorus. Pindar's epithets are of course very numerous and often of breathtaking power, but he does not use them as Bacchylides does, heaping up three and even four around a single noun, as at 5.98–99, for example, or 10.37–39. We find over ninety epithets in Bacchylides which do not occur elsewhere in extant Greek; they are probably the most striking single feature of his style, and they face the translator with a serious problem. (By "the translator," I mean the man who wants a picture and a meaning and does not suppose that a literal English equivalence is automatically going to bring over the picture and the meaning in the Greek.)[8]

The English language forms simple vernacular compounds easily enough—long-legged, mealymouthed, and so on—but the elaborate, "poetic" compound is another matter. If we turn to the 858 lines of the General Prologue to *The Canterbury Tales,* as clean and strong a draft of our native speech as exists, we find that it yields no more than three compounds, "gat-tothed" (468), "short-sholdred" (549) and "fyr-reed" (624), all of the straightforward vernacular kind. But if we look next at the prelude to book 5 of *Troilus*, where Chaucer, with an eye on classical poetry, wants to be rather fine, we discover him talking about "gold-tressed Phebus" (after *auricomus*, I suppose). One might just imagine a critic of the school of Leavis, much concerned with the vital relation between poetry and everyday speech and determined to preserve the purity of our native tradition from alien presences, finding here the first sign of those classicizing tendencies which were to reach their dark florescence in *Paradise Lost.* Maybe we should not have tried to enlarge the mold of English by raiding the classics, but that is what our poets have in fact done, and the attempt to anglicize Greek compound epithets—and their far less numerous Latin progeny—is simply one small aspect of this long endeavor.

The natural way in English to deal with the more elaborate type of Greek compound is to expand it into an adjectival phrase or clause. Thus the translator who had to render Ζέφυρος ἡδύπνοος would not go far wrong in adopting Chaucer's "Zephirus . . . with his sweete breeth" (General Prologue, line 5). Thus Robert Fitzgerald avoids "rosy-fingered" (an unattractive word in English, bequeathed us by Spenser, *Fairie Queene* 1.2.7) and writes instead

> When Dawn spread out her finger tips of rose.

This avoids any wrenching of English usage, but as a method it is open to one or two at least theoretical objections. An elaborate adjectival phrase or clause ("Zeus who delights in thunder") tends to obstruct the run of your sentence; and, arguably, it lacks the poetic force that a good compound can have. (How greatly would the "too-and-fro-conflicting wind and raine" of *Lear* be weakened if the compound were replaced by a clause.) Moreover, in a sense it sidesteps the problem instead of facing it and thus fails to perform one of translation's most valuable functions, which is to enlarge the formal and expressive possibilities of the new language.[9]

The compound epithet is a regular feature of the poetic, or elevated, style in Elizabethan poetry, and such it has remained, even into the twentieth century; Dylan Thomas wrote of "the heron / Priested shore" ("Poem in October"). Yet between its use in Shakespeare, who developed it as magnificently as he developed every other aspect of our language, and Gerard Hopkins, the poet who exploited its resources most completely, there is relatively little systematic development. The subject is so central to the translation of Greek poetry that I think it is worth glancing at its place in the English poetic tradition.

W. H. Gardner, in the course of some valuable pages on this particular feature of Hopkins's style, suggests that the compound epithet in English may be divided into two main types, the "poetical-descriptive" and the "dramatic or rhetorical."[10] The first type, deriving through Spenser and Milton from the Greeks, "reaches its fine flower in the 'soft-conchèd ear' and 'far-foamèd sands' of Keats." As examples of the second type, Gardner offers Shakespeare's "steepe-downe gulfes" (*Othello*) and "to-and-fro-conflicting winds and raine" (*Lear*).

This distinction fits the facts, but in its place I would propose, as neater and no less accurate, "Greek" and "English." In the first category I would place Shakespeare's "fiery footed steedes" (from *Romeo and Juliet*), in the second the two examples from his mature style cited by Gardner, or Chapman's perhaps less powerful but very interesting "care-and-lineament-resolving Sleepe."[11] In the first category, again, I would place Milton's "flowry-kirtl'd Naiades" (*Comus*), a compound which very exactly re-creates the pleasure of the more decorative and ceremonious Greek formations; Shelley's "eagle-baffling mountain" and "isle-surrounding streams" (from the first act of *Prometheus Unbound*); and Tennyson's "many-fountain'd Ida" ("Oenone"). The latter, although a direct translation from the Greek, is warmed into life by the moving rhythm of the lines in which it occurs; Shelley's compounds, apparently more enterprising, are too anxious to demonstrate their Hellenic stock; they have not been sufficiently felt into English.

We reach a point of greater interest when my two categories (and also, I think, Gardner's) begin to break down. Tennyson's "golden-rinded," for example, from an early poem, "Eleanore," feels Greekish, but what about this a line or so further on, the description of the bower "Grapethickened from the light"? The formation has a genuine sensuous life, and though Tennyson may still be partly thinking in Greek, he is emphatically writing English.[12] What again of the very charming compound from Browning's "A Pretty Woman," "That fawn-skin-dappled hair of hers"? In a sense, this falls into Gardner's "poetical-descriptive" and hence into my "Greek" category, but it feels wholly English and anticipates some of Hopkins's compounds.

It is no part of my purpose to analyze the enormous wealth and variety of compound epithets in Hopkins. I refer the interested reader to Gardner, who discovers no less than fifteen distinct types of formation (*Hopkins*, 1:286). What I am concerned with here is the way in which Hopkins was able to extend the formal possibilities of English poetry by his creative insight into the procedures of Greek poetry. The attempt to bring the English and the Greek poetic traditions into the closest possible relation was of course common to many

nineteenth-century poets, but whereas in works like *Merope* and
Erechtheus we see the writer depriving himself of most of the native resources of English poetry without being able to call on the resources
of Greek poetry in their place, in Hopkins the Greek influence has
the effect of making him even more exuberantly English.[13] Hopkins
was of course interested in many aspects of Greek poetry, most of all
perhaps in the "beautiful variety" and "infinite flexibility" of the Greek
lyric forms, but also, as Gardner shows (*Hopkins*, 2:98–100), in the syntax. His strange adjectival phrases ("the rólling level únderneáth him
steady áir," "The Windhover") seem to be attempts to re-create in English something equivalent to the way in which fifth-century Greek
poets weld a sequence of words into a single rhythmic and sense
unit.[14] But nowhere is Hopkins more Greek than in the loaded vehemence with which he piles up epithets.

> Wíry and white-fíery and whírlwind-swivellèd snow
> Spins to the widow-making unchilding unfathering deeps.
> (*The Wreck of the Deutschland*, stanza 13, lines 7–8)

Does this not read like an inspired translation of some unknown fragment of Aeschylus?

The daring, the sensuous fullness, of so many of Hopkins's coinages
provides a way—strangely little exploited—of dealing with the feature
of Greek poetry that has most consistently defeated translators. Surely
the "evil leisuring hungering dangerous-harboring winds" at *Agamemnon* 192–93 would play straight into the hands of the translator who
had gone to school to Hopkins? Hardly less so the sequence of six epithets at *Suppliants* 794–96 with which Aeschylus builds up the image
of a mountain. Or the "untimely-at-midnight clamor" (ἀωρόνυκτον
ἀμβόαμα) at *Choephoroe* 34. Or Sophocles' "oxsummering meadow"
(βουθερὴς λειμών) at *Trachiniae* 188. The field is wide open.

But the interest of Hopkins's use of Greek poetry extends beyond
the business of translation. What he did was to show, as Arnold and
Swinburne were unable to show, that Greek and English poetry could
be brought into a close critical relation. This relation is still there—
if we want to use it. One is told to leave one's modern preoccupations
at the door before one approaches a Greek author, but there is surely
a difference between bringing an anxiety about the historicity of mir-
acles or votes for women to an ancient author, and bringing a decent
interest in the problems of poetic expression. For different in so many
ways as the Greek and English poetic traditions are, there is a lingua
franca of poetry which unites them. (It is this that allows a person with
good literary sense to be excited by poetry in a language he hardly

understands.) The English-speaking reader, more than any other, with his immediate access to the only body of poetry in the West that can compare with Greek, should not hesitate to use his native literary experience to help him get at Greek poetry. Surely the man who has ever really read Shakespeare could not say, as Page says in his comment on *Agamemnon* 1180–83, that "image and reality are confused, as often in Aeschylus." Surely he is going, unlike Page, to understand how in the second stasimon of the same play Helen can be both the gentle lion cub and the "priest of ruin," both the "spirit of windless calm" that first came to Troy and the "fiend whose bridal was fraught with tears," the νυμφόκλαυτος Ἐρινύς which later destroyed it. (See Page's comment at 744ff.) To the grammarian, such procedures are puzzling and annoying, but, unfortunately for the grammarian, that is how some great poets write. This may be the tactical moment to call Coleridge to my aid. He is describing, in the first chapter of *Biographia Literaria*, his literary training at Christ's Hospital under the Reverend James Bowyer: "At the same time that we were studying the Greek tragic poets, he made us read Shakespeare and Milton as lessons . . . I learned from him, that poetry, even that of the loftiest and, seemingly, that of the wildest odes, had a logic of its own, as severe as that of science; and more difficult, because more subtle, more complex, and dependent on more, and more fugitive causes."

This kind of interrogation of whatever is relevant in our own poetic tradition is something that the translator should surely undertake before he attempts the peculiarly difficult task of turning Greek poetry into English poetry. A study of the particular feature I have been looking at will not, certainly, tell anyone how to form English compounds. *D'abord il faut être un poète.* But it could provide a few rules of thumb—be concrete, be specific, create an image and so on—and, negatively, it might suggest the kinds of compound that will not do. Hardy's "brown-shawled dame" ("Signs and Tokens"), for example, will not do; it is too dull. Shelley's "eagle-baffling mountain" will not do; it is too Greek. Anybody's "deep-girdled woman" will not do; it offers no picture and next to no meaning. Positively, one can I think say that a compound should "give pleasure," as Hopkins' "dappled-with-damson west" gives pleasure (*The Wreck*, stanza 5, line 5); and there should, usually, be some energy in its formation (Shakespeare's "steepe-downe gulfes"), some intensity of perception or variety of sense data that demands the tightest possible juxtaposition. A minor point is that the simpler compounds, at least, are stronger when they are not hyphenated. Tennyson's "grapethickened," the original spelling of the 1832 edition of his poems, has surely more sensuous life than "grape-thickened," the form to which he reduced it in the 1842 volume, perhaps a result of adverse criticism.[15] The hyphen points to the construction and as it were apologizes for it, thus weakening its poetic force. Hopkins tends in fact to hyphenate his adjectival compounds but not, usually, his noun compounds (wolfsnow, Amansstrength, etc.). Who would want to parcel out Joyce's grand formation into a run of little words?

Beside the rivering waters of, hitherandthithering waters of. Night!

At this point I return to Fagles and his dealings with the adjectival Bacchylides. One may not invariably like what he does, but he has got seriously to grips with his text. Take a single example, the passage at 5.172 where Meleager describes his sister as χλωραύχην. This is one of Bacchylides' most charming strokes, but it is hard to translate. χλωρός is partly an adjective of color and means something like "pale green" (the green of young plants); it can also mean "yellow" and (of the complexion) "pale." But along another line of meaning it is used, with no sense of color, of living, growing, glowing things: of fresh sappy wood as against dry, of dew, of a field full of flowers, even of a glistening tear. The sense in Bacchylides, as Jebb says, is "with the freshness (the fresh bloom) of youth upon her neck." It may be worth comparing Fagles's version with the one offered by Lattimore in his translation of this ode:[16]

> Deïaneíra, her throat still green
> with youth.

I don't understand this. I have seen a girl with green eyebrows but never with a green throat. Once again I ask: where has Lattimore seen one? Berni, in an anti-Petrarchan sonnet, writes of a woman with a *blue* mouth ("bocca ampia *celeste*" in "Chiome d'argento fine ..."), but the reference there is plainly to some gap-toothed hag, whereas Bacchylides wants to paint a picture of a young and beautiful girl. Fagles's translation is:

> Her neck glows
> With the gloss of youth.

Unfortunately this won't do at all. "Gloss" is too hard, too metallic, for χλωρός, and it hasn't anything like the right sensuous suggestion. What was needed was something as new and imaginative as Browning's "fawn-skin-dappled hair" or Hopkins's "brown-as-dawning-skinned" sailor ("The Loss of the Eurydice"). But earlier on in the same ode

he manages one of Bacchylides' most notable adjectival clusters with
some success (5.98–99):

> Constrain the goddess,
> Whose arms are white
> Under wreaths of buds.

Fagles quite often unfolds his epithets in this way, working them
into the run of the sentence. But he also coins a number of compounds, and here I think he has been skillful. Almost always he employs the type of formation adopted by Hopkins in his "silk-sack
clouds," "dare-gale skylark," "sea flint-flake, black-backed," "baldbright
cloud"[17]—a pair of monosyllabic verbs, nouns, or adjectives (unhy-
phenated in Fagles). Thus he writes "stormpace stallion" (πῶλον
ἀελλοδρόμαν, 5.39), "cragtooth hound" (καρχαρόδοντα κύνα, 5.60),
"riptide tusks" (of the Calydonian boar, an energetically compressed
treatment of πλημύρων σθένει . . . ἐπέκειρεν ὀδόντι, 5.107–8) and
"bluebraid Nereids" (17.37–38, which sensibly takes advantage of our
uncertainty about the Greek color sense to avoid the hackneyed rendering of ἰόπλοκος as "violet-crowned" or something of that sort).

These are all accurate translations, in the conventional sense; they
are also good, forceful English and if there is nothing specially "modern" about them, they are at least words that a contemporary poet,
given a similar context, might use without loss of face. Let me take
one further example, from 9.47–52, this time setting it in its context:

> Roads fan out to the world
> That carry word of your clan,
> Those sleeksash girls the gods
> Made flourish as founders
> Of streets that block invasion.

(The last line gives the sense of the Greek very well, but stylistically
it "specifies" too vigorously for Bacchylides, whose poetry does not
engage so closely with our everyday world.) "Sleeksash girls," for
λιπαρόζωνοι θύγατρες, is distinctly a *trouvaille*. It certainly observes, as
a compound epithet should, the third law of Wallace Stevens's universe, "It Must Give Pleasure." In a paper on "The Criticism of Greek
Tragedy," William Arrowsmith complained that there has been a "failure to realize turbulence."[18] There has. There has also been a failure
—in our approach to Greek poetry as a whole—to realize *gaiety*. Major
Greek poetry is, heavens knows,

> Vested in the serious folds of majesty.

It is also "crested / With every prodigal, familiar fire."[19] We have forgotten, somehow, in our dreary translations, in our dreary chatter about the culturally uplifting value of Greek civilization, the enormous brightness, the αἴγλα διόσδοτος, with which Greek poetry recreates and celebrates the entire phenomenal world. Do we tell our students, as they plough their way through their paperbacks, that a huge period of Aeschylus or Pindar can be as light on its toes as a dancer?

Bacchylides is, certainly, a long way from the great masters who give Greek poetry its claim to be our "proper study." Yet in the formal procedures of his verse, he touches their high manner. His λιπαρόζωνοι θύγατρες are, the syllables as they glitter by tell us, very charming. And this charm Fagles has caught with his "sleeksash girls." Any sensible man would obviously be delighted to take a sleeksash girl out to dinner. But if his adjective meets the Greek on the ground of gaiety, it is distinctly jaunty, whereas λιπαρόζωνος is stately and ceremonious too, recalling as it does similar formations in earlier Greek poetry— λιπαροκρήδεμνος, for example, in the beautiful passage near the beginning of the Hymn to Demeter, to which Pater drew attention ("The Myth of Demeter and Persephone"), where the goddess Hecate sits, withdrawn, in her cave, "half-veiled with a shining veil," listening to the cries of Persephone.

We get none of this in "sleeksash." How should we? If we want these pleasures of association, we must read Bacchylides in Greek. Fagles was quite right to concentrate on one element in his original and go all out for that. Had he tried for everything, he would probably have missed everything. He has, nonetheless, here and often elsewhere, been faithful to an important element in Greek poetry. And he has approached it with the proper sensual relish.

> Natives of poverty, children of malheur,
> The gaiety of language is our seigneur.[20]

Fagles has taken Bacchylides' gaiety seriously. There is a suggestion, in his versions, of festal glitter. He has got αἴγλα into his lines. He has also taken the meters seriously. Translators of Greek lyric poetry, profiting by what they feel to be the liberties of modern verse, have mostly abandoned meter altogether and offer a series of irregular, vaguely cadenced lines which sometimes *look* a little like a page of Greek lyric. Fagles has gone about his job more seriously.

What characterizes Bacchylides' metrical composition, it has been noted, is the tendency "to divide his periods rhythmically into short kola, usually of two or three *metra* each" (Jebb, p. 94). Translated into the common speech, this gives the effect of "quick and nervous . . . rhythm" to which Parry alludes in his introduction. Fagles has tried to create an English equivalent by using a short line; I suppose his average line is of about six syllables, and if he now and then stretches to ten, he often contracts to three. There is a good deal to be said for the use of short lines in translating Greek lyric. The unit of English poetry, lyric as much as narrative, is the line—even where, as in developed blank verse, there is regular enjambment. The metrical unit of Greek lyric is the kolon. The difficulty is that English does not take readily to a series of very short lines. The short line requires great rhythmical variety if it is to be effective, the kind of variety which (to take an example) the Scots poet W. S. Graham achieves in his fine poem *The Nightfishing* (1955). Graham uses a line with strong, almost hammered, irregularly placed stresses, clever variation of rising and falling rhythms and of masculine and feminine endings. I don't at all know if Fagles consulted this poem, but should the occasion of a second edition give him a chance to revise—or if, as we must hope, this is merely his pioneer venture in the field of Greek lyric—I think he might find Graham helpful.

He is often, in fact, successful. Take the opening of Ode 17:

> Black at the beak that craft
> With Theseus braced for war
> And fine Ionian sons and daughters,
> Seven of each aboard her
> Cutting the Sea of Crete,
> As Athena armed with the aegis
> Bellied her shining sheets
> With a wind from north.

Isolated, this is not remarkable; in its context, it works. Here and elsewhere Fagles uses alliteration and assonance to pull his lines together; they have thrust and shape, and the movement seems to me right for Bacchylides. But take the opening of the fifth ode:

> Splendid in destiny,
> Marshal of men
> Where chariots
> Whirl through Syracuse.

I don't know how εὔμοιρε should be translated, but the vapid "splendid in destiny" is the kind of thing that would have put an epinician poet out of business. And the third line, getting off to a limp start and then stopping before it has established any sort of rhythmic raison d'être for itself, is a feeble affair. The short line, to be interesting, needs a tight play of stresses; and whereas Bacchylides could draw his diction from a great and still vital tradition, his twentieth-century translator has got to put a spin on his words if he wants them to reach our side of the net. In looking at these translations, one or two general points about Bacchylides have come up. Can we now—thanks to Fagles—go on and say anything more interesting about his poet than that, though good, he is not so good as Pindar?

It is extremely unfortunate for Bacchylides' reputation, and for our critical sense of his poetry, that in the absence of any other choral lyricist whose work has survived in bulk, we are forced to compare him with Pindar—even while insisting, like Parry, that the comparison is foolish. The best things in Bacchylides are fine, Edmonds writes, but—they do not, "like Pindar's three-word apocalypses, stir thoughts too deep for tears" (*Lyra Graeca*, 3:647). Well, no. But still, there are things that a poet may do besides stirring thoughts too deep for tears with three-word apocalypses, so it would surely be worth inquiring if Bacchylides does anything else that, in its slighter way, may be worth our attention.

The vice of this Pindaric comparison, apart from its obvious injustice, is that it draws attention to what in Bacchylides is, in some respects, questionable, and away from what he has more valuably to offer. It is, for instance, generally agreed that the fifth ode, in which he tells how Heracles meets Meleager among the shades, is his best poem. "Carmen egregia arte compositum rebusque et verbis splendens facile principem locum inter epinicia tenet," Blass declares. "A favourable instance" of his talents, Rose allows.[21] "This is Bacchylides' most impressive work," Parry agrees. Let us take a look at it.

After the opening address to Hiero, Bacchylides points to himself preparing to send his song of praise to Syracuse (lines 9–16). My expression "points to himself" is I think a fair comment on the very deliberately raised tone of this passage. It feels rather "Pindaric." Given the frequent difficulty, or impossibility, of dating these poems, it is of course very hard to say when Bacchylides is imitating Pindar or vice versa. At line 9, for example, we find him using an expression which Pindar was to employ two years later. Equally, in a passage where we think we detect a debt, the poet may simply be drawing on a fund of expressions common to the epinician style as a whole. Nonetheless, there is a very marked style, exalted often, sometimes homely, but almost always characterized by an intense poetic concentration, which we recognize as Pindaric. It was quite different, so far as we can judge, from the more playful manner which Simonides adopted in his epinicia;[22] and different, too, from the lighter, more relaxed style we recognize as Bacchylidean. The present passage seems to me one in which Bacchylides is not so much imitating Pindar as allowing himself to be influenced, to be perhaps a little bullied, by the new elevation and intensity which Pindar had brought into the victory ode.

The celebrated comparison of the poet to an eagle follows (16–30): the eagle soars high in the limitless inane while lesser birds cower below. It is a fine anthology piece and duly found its niche in *The Oxford Book of Greek Verse*. To the obvious criticism that it is absurd of Bacchylides to describe his poetry in terms that belong rather to Pindar, we may reply that he is not thinking of himself but of the poet, any poet, writing in the high epinician way. Or we may say, with Blass, that what is being compared is the "ampla materies carminis cum immenso aeris spatio in quo volat aquila"—for he goes on to say that "a boundless course" is open to him on every side. The fact remains that the pomp of this extended simile leaves us uneasy; if it were being used functionally, it should prepare the way for a story told with a certain majesty, *modo Pindarico*, whereas the scene which follows is marked rather by a vivid pathos. But before he comes to his myth, Bacchylides adds another short passage in which, with what seems a remarkable emphasis, he calls the earth to witness that no horse has ever reached the winning post ahead of Pherenikos. The manner may again be strained, and Lavagnini's comment sounds reasonable: "Tanta solennità sembra fuor di proposito per elogiare le virtù di un cavallo."[23] (Bacchylides uses a very similar expression at 8.19–20, but there he is at least speaking of a human victor.) Of course, to attempt to be at all inward with a genre as remote as this is very hazardous—who has the faintest conception of what the performance of an epinician ode was really like? It is often hard enough to be sure of the tone of the older poetry in one's own language. All the same, unless one is to accept passively whatever the poet offers—and in that case why bother to read him?—one must at least try to catch his tone of voice. And I think one can say here that while a similar elevation of manner in Pindar is felt to be acceptable, given his exalted conception of the significance of a victory in the games, it is not equally acceptable in Bacchylides; and that, moreover, he has other ways of writing which do not raise these misgivings.

The myth itself is beautiful and has been justly praised. I want to look only at one point, the lines in which Heracles replies to Meleager's long story (lines 160–69). The shade has described his early death, and Heracles is for once affected. Ah well, he says, in his gruff Dorian way, best for a man never to be born, I expect. Still—no use talking about that. By the way, you don't happen to have a surviving sister, do you? If she looks anything like you, why, I'd marry the girl!

This question, coming at the end of Meleager's touching narrative, is surely very odd indeed and seems as badly out of place as Montano's question at *Othello*, act 2, scene 1—"But good Lieutenant, is your Generall wiv'd?"—which aroused Thomas Rymer's indignation. The immediate purpose of both queries is the same: to introduce a description of the lady in question, and certainly Bacchylides' picture of Deianeira, with the fresh grace of youth still about her, is very charming and balances the previous account of her brother's young death. More important, no doubt, it serves as a further indirect illustration of the gnome which introduced the myth: "no mortal man is blessed in everything" (lines 53–55). Heracles will return to earth and marry Deianeira, and suffer in his turn.[24]

My point is not so much the clumsiness of the plotting—though I think it is clumsy—as Bacchylides' failure to use myth, as Pindar and the major Greek poets use it, as a means of inquiring into the structure of man's fate. This is what he attempts to do here: the story of Meleager is meant to open out, through the concluding hint of what is to happen to Heracles, and bear generally on the human condition. In fact, we are left with a touching story to which a not particularly interesting moral is loosely attached.

My purpose in pointing to what I think is Bacchylides' relative failure here is to get at what I take to be his success elsewhere—success in a kind of writing we do not find in Pindar. The thirteenth epinician has not reached us intact. The opening is missing and a few lines and part-lines have been lost in the course of the poem. But there is quite enough to be getting on with. The ode begins, as we have it, with a description of Heracles' victory over the lion at Nemea, where the young Pytheas has just been victorious. A general statement on the unquenchable brightness of victory is made and then transposed into the actual brightness of the κῶμος, the festive glitter of the welcome which awaits the young man as he comes home to Aegina. This is in the usual epinician manner, but a more interesting transposition, or modulation, follows. Aegina (the eponymous nymph, not the island) is gracefully invoked—

> Girl of the rapid river,
> O gentle Aegina,

and then—to quote from Parry's excellent commentary—"the joy and brightness are condensed in the figure of the dancer," the ὑψαυχὴς κόρα, a distinctly Yeatsian young woman with a proper sense of the ancestral glories of her race who goes off with her friends to sing and dance on the hills. Fagles's translation has just the right suggestions:

> When she goes gay
> With her famous friends
> Who live nearby,
> Crowned in reds and reeds
> For their island rite
> They sing your strength,
> O Queen.

They sing of Aegina herself and of the legendary heroine who bore Peleus (father of Achilles) and Telamon (father of Ajax)—and there follows a passage of heroic narrative drawn from the *Iliad*. It is tiresome that the text is doubtful at this point. According to Jebb's conjecture, accepted in their editions by Kenyon, Blass, Jurenka, and Edmonds, the ensuing narrative is sung by the girls. According to the supplement proposed by Wilamowitz and Housman, which Snell adopts in his Teubner edition and Fagles follows, there is a transition here: the girls' song ends and the poet takes over and tells the story in propria persona. From the literary point of view, Jebb's text is greatly preferable. There is a most suggestive contrast between the voices of the girls and the grim Homeric scene which they present— a contrast which I find present in the actual mode of the narration. And even if there is a transition here to the poet, the point is not altogether lost. The young women have done their job, for the lyrical prelude to the narrative conditions the way we take it.

I called it a "grim Homeric scene," but that only does for one aspect of it. Bacchylides presents, with genuine power, the violence of Hector's assault against the ships, the terror of Achilles' raging over the plains of Troy; a number of epithets and phrases remind us of the *Iliad*, and there is even a full-blown simile in the epic manner. But beside—or rather, below—all this is something that is not at all Homeric. There is of course the basic modulation from the powerful Homeric hexameters to Bacchylides' light, glancing dactylo-epitritic meter. But there is more than this. The sentence which describes Achilles raging over the plain ends by presenting him as "the fearless son of the Nereid wreathed in violets" (lines 122–23):

ἰοστεφάνου
Νηρῇδος ἀτρόμητος υἱός.

This is the kind of elaboration, so common in choral lyric, of a Homeric phrase, in this case "child of fair-haired Thetis" (*Iliad* 4.512, 16.860). But in fact this way of describing Achilles is very rare in the *Iliad*. Of the 190 or so times in which his name, or one of his patronymics, is qualified by an adjective, phrase, or clause, only on the two occasions mentioned above (or four, counting "whom an immortal mother bore" at 10.404 and 17.78) is an expression employed which relates him to the gentle world of Thetis. Elsewhere, except for neutral terms such as δῖος, ἀγαυός, ἀμύμων, and the like, his name is always qualified by words or expressions belonging to the masculine world of war and leadership. I am not concerned here with the metrical reasons which may have made these forms more convenient, but simply with the impression made on the reader or listener by their constant use.

The question is whether this rather unusual way of presenting Achilles is just a pleasant variation, or whether it is being used more purposefully to modify (in some way) the heroic context in which it occurs. A point perhaps worth noticing is that the epithet ἰοστέφανος — and the variant εὐστέφανος—is regularly used not of Thetis but of Aphrodite.[25] But in calling this a point, one immediately wonders if in fact it is a point. How closely should one read Bacchylides? Are we justified in questioning one of his numerous epithets in this way? I think we are, for although he may sometimes throw in an epithet simply to glitter an otherwise dull line, he often uses them far more functionally. (Parry provides a few examples, pp. xxii–iii.) We should in fact expect nothing less, for he was a careful artist and well before his time Greek poets had turned the "ornamental" epithet, which Homer employed with such tireless profusion, into a very precise poetic tool. "By the end of the sixth century . . . and probably a great deal earlier," A. E. Harvey observes, "the lyric poets were fully conscious of the conventional associations of Homeric diction. Consequently it seems unlikely that they will have used purely ornamental epithets indiscriminately."[26] If this is true—and Harvey offers some convincing stylistic analysis—it is quite reasonable to suppose that Bacchylides is conscious of the fairly well-established associations of ἰοστέφανος and that he is using the word for a definite reason. The function of this "ornamental," very unmilitary epithet, occurring in a passage of heroic narrative studded with warlike Homeric epithets, is surely to lower and gentle the tone. It would come very well off the lips of the girls of Aegina; they would naturally welcome any opportunity of celebrating the softer side of their hero.

It would be silly to make so much of a single word but for a rather similar effect a few lines later on in which the associations I have claimed for ἰοστέφανος are very much to the point. After the epic simile (lines 124–32), the poem describes how the Trojans took heart "when they heard that the warrior Achilles was keeping to his quarters because of the soft limbs of blonde Briseis":

εἵνεκεν ξανθᾶς γυναικός,
Βρισηΐδος ἱμερογυίου.

Once again, Bacchylides has Homer in mind. In the course of the Catalogue of Ships, there is a comment on the absence of the Myrmidons; the reason they were absent was that their leader, Achilles, "was lying among the ships, angry because of Briseis, the girl with the lovely hair" (2.688–89):

κούρης χωόμενος Βρισηΐδος ἠϋκόμοιο.

Once again, then, we have the customary choral *réchauffement* of an epic phrase; and once again, and more strongly, there is a perceptible change of tone. In Homer, it is of course a slighted sense of heroic honor that keeps Achilles away from the fighting. So it is in Bacchylides—ostensibly. But the epithet ἱμερόγυιος is not only not Homeric (the nearest thing in the *Iliad* is χροὸς ἱμερόεντος, which occurs, appropriately, in the sensual context of the Deception of Zeus, 14.170); it takes us right out of the sphere of Homeric sentiment and into that of seventh- and sixth-century lyric.[27] If we did not know Bacchylides' Homeric original here, we would surely suppose that he was presenting Achilles as a romantic lover pining for his mistress.

Harvey, in the article I have already mentioned, points to the existence in archaic lyric of a convention whereby the poet, in certain contexts, notably in dealing with matter belonging to the heroic world, borrowed elements of Homeric diction which he would not normally have used. By the time of Anacreon, we find something much more sophisticated—namely, the deliberately "witty" use of Homeric diction in lighthearted poems about everyday life. Harvey shows with how delicate a stylistic control Anacreon introduces Homeric echoes to produce an effect of mock solemnity. Bacchylides, I suggest, is working the other way round. Where Anacreon had brought a solemn Homeric word into a gay love poem, Bacchylides, with an equal stylistic finesse, introduces a word more proper to love poetry into what claims to be a rather solemn piece of epic narrative. He is not, like Anacreon, witty, yet I think we may find some of the qualities which constitute wit in the way he can hold two levels of style in his mind and move so easily between them. The particular pleasure which his poetry, at its best, can offer is present here in the way, without ever quite denaturing it, he turns the Homeric original into something subtly different. His poetry sets up a contrast—the sort of stylistic contrast which the Greeks, we know, enjoyed: witness their exorbitant taste for parody—between two kinds of poetry, and so between two ways of life. The matter of Greek poetry, one might very roughly say, is sometimes fairly simple, but the manner is usually highly sophisticated. (I have in mind not mere sophistication of *technique*, which can be found in quite primitive poetry, but a sophistication of emotional attitude.) And that is what we have here, the perfection of manner.

Adam Parry, in his commentary, approaches the ode quite differently. He shows how the initial "brightness," present in the victory itself and in the festivities that celebrate it, is taken up in the myth and revealed on a deeper level of meaning. "The Greek heroes who overcame the Trojans have died but 'excellence flaming to all' . . . is bright even in that darkness. It is the same excellence that 'honors Aeacus' island, harbor of fame.'" Everything he points to can be found in the text, but I wonder if this is what should take the critical stress. Isn't Bacchylides here doing simply what was expected of an epinician poet, relating today's bright achievement in the games to some legendary achievement in the past? Moreover, as Parry analyzes it, the poem sounds remarkably like a poem by Pindar. To me, it is, in the best sense, much more lightweight, and it seems to me that the critic should try to point to what is original in the poem—the very skillfully handled stylistic level—rather than to the normal features of the epinician which Bacchylides was paid for. As Parry reads it, the poem is rather solemn; I think it is pretending to be solemn while contriving to be distinctly gay.

Even if my point is not critically valid as applied to this particular ode, it may still be worth making insofar as it bears on the way we read Greek poetry. Our reading is still markedly influenced by the nineteenth-century thirst for high seriousness. What Eliot said of traditional taste in English poetry—that it had been "largely founded upon a partial perception of the value of Shakespeare and Milton, a perception which dwells upon sublimity of theme and action"[28]—is true also of our taste in Greek literature, substituting Homer and Attic tragedy for Shakespeare and Milton. But thanks to the critical revolution which took place in the first half of the twentieth century, we ought to be equipped to appreciate a great deal in poetry apart from sublimity.

The pity is that the areas of Greek poetry which might to some extent have ministered to a fresh critical approach—the work of the seventh and sixth centuries, most of all, perhaps, the great Archilochus—has reached us in so fragmentary a state that the literary critic tends to be shouldered aside by the papyrologist and the philologist. Yet here is a body of writing with which the modern critic might have felt thoroughly at home: poetry that takes much of its material from the everyday circumstance of life, and poets, like Archilochus and the Lesbians, who generally write somewhat in the language they speak.

But with the major exception of Guy Davenport's Archilochus, and to a lesser degree his Sappho, very little of this poetry has been brought to life or critically engaged.

Something of the old prejudice, the high-minded insistence on elevation, has blocked a proper understanding of Bacchylides. A Pindaric ode can at least partly be approached in terms of sublimity. An ode of Bacchylides cannot. But the critical observation is, surely, not that Bacchylides failed to rise to Pindar's heights, but rather that Pindar, in giving the victory ode a great burden of religious emotion, was doing something new and very strange. With Simonides' epinician poetry, so far as we can judge, the tone was gay and lighthearted. And properly so. However seriously the Greeks took their athletics, it would probably not have occurred to anyone except Pindar that a victory in the games was quite the occasion for a kind of divine epiphany. Bacchylides was influenced, at the formal level, by Pindar, sometimes to his cost, I think, but at his best he retains the lighter manner of much earlier choral lyric. As such, he is the last accomplished voice of the beautiful tradition which flourished between the grandeur of Homer and the grandeur of Attic tragedy. We should think of him not as a lesser Pindar, but as the successor of Simonides, Ibycus, Stesichorus and, more distantly, of the enchanting Alcman. He retains the element of epic narrative which Quintilian's phrase may point to in Stesichorus,[29] while not usually attempting to rival the Stesichorean gravity; and, at his best, he writes with a grace and a formal intelligence greatly in advance of anything that Ibycus could achieve in the ode—if the unfortunate Polycrates poem, so inferior to the rest of his fragments, is really by Ibycus (fr. 282 PMG).

For Bacchylides' qualities at their best we should look to a poem like the seventeenth, the dithyramb about Theseus's quarrel with Minos on the ship bound for Crete. The "epic" tone of the angry speeches which the two men level at each other is admirably done (compare, for example, lines 29–36 with *Iliad* 20.206–9); there is just the right stylistic elevation—note, for instance, at lines 24–28, the grand Hellenic way in which Theseus accepts the dispensations of fate. But, as Parry says, "the moral and tragic elements alike are subordinate to a mood of patterned gaiety and intricate delight . . . In no other of [his] poems do we feel so strongly the stylized grace of his lyric narrative." That seems to me the right way to talk about Bacchylides.

8

Polygram: Pindar's Pythian 12 in Translation

Eᴛᴛᴏʀᴇ Rᴏᴍᴀɢɴᴏʟɪ ᴛʀᴀɴꜱʟᴀᴛᴇᴅ Pɪɴᴅᴀʀ'ꜱ ᴏᴅᴇꜱ ɪɴ 1921.[1] Hᴇʀᴇ ɪꜱ his version of Pythian 12:

Te invoco, città di Persèfone, città la più bella fra quante
albergo son d'uomini, oh amica del fasto, che presso Agrigento
ferace di greggi, ti levi su clivo turrito: oh Signora,
gradisci benevola, e teco si accordino gli uomini e i Numi,
5   da Mida le foglie del serto di Pito gradisci, e lui stesso,
che vinse gli Ellèni nell'arte cui Pàllade
un giorno rinvenne, intrecciando
la nenia feral de le Gòrgoni.

La nenia che giù da le vergini cervici di serpi tutte orride
10   stillare con misero spasimo udiva Persèo, quando l'una
spengea della suore trigemine; e il capo fatale, dei Sèrifi
all'isola addusse. Le Fòrcidi così nella tenebra immerse;
così di Medusa bellissima la testa rapì; di Polìdete
all'epula pose funereo fine;
15   e sciolse sua madre dal giogo
perenne, e dal talamo ingrato,

il figlio di Dànae, cui padre, si narra, fu l'oro piovuto
dall'ètere. Or Pàllade, quando l'eroe prediletto ebbe salvo
da questo travaglio, sul flauto compose un multisono canto,
20   volendo il lungo ululo lugubre dal fitto guizzar delle fauci
sprizzante, imitare. La Dea compose quell'aria; e ne fece
presente ai mortali, la disse canzone
dai capi molteplici; e fosse
compagna all'agon popoloso.

25   Sgorga essa, dei balli compagna fedel, fra la tenüe lamina
di rame, e la canna che cresce nei prati cui bagna il Cefíso,
vicino a la bella contrada d'Orcòmeno, sacra a le Càriti.—

"Polygram / 1: Pindar's Twelfth Pythian," *Arion* 7, no. 2 (Summer 1968): 249–263.

Se prospera sorte è tra gli uomini, da pena non mai si scompagna.
Ma fine alla pena oggi stesso può un Nume segnare. Non s'evita
30   la sorte. Ma un giorno verrà che imprevisto
colpendoti, un bene ti niega,
e l'altro, inatteso, t'accorda.

But why read Pindar in Italian?

Consider what happens when a musician transposes from A major to B major. The relationships remain exactly as they were, but the atmosphere and the implications change. Transpose Pindar not into English but into German or Italian and something of the same sort happens. A foreign translation can bring to a familiar text that sudden air of strangeness in which we seem to see it for the first time. It "says" the same things, but it sounds different.

The use of foreign translations is liberating, again, in that it keeps us from the parochialism of believing that our own language (and culture) stands in a specially privileged relation to antiquity. When we say that a classical author "cannot be translated," what we usually mean is that he cannot be translated into English. Yet just as no single language embraces the whole of reality, so no language matches Greek at every point and provides the perfect vehicle for translation. That first "totality" of the Greek language (to adapt, and reduce, Walter Benjamin's lofty concept) can only be recovered by bringing together the different tongues into which its spirit and its form have passed.

And there is a more obvious reason for approaching a difficult author like Pindar via another modern language. In reading an English translation, we are constantly worried by the way the writer, in trying to follow some turn of his original, distorts English idiom or syntax. With a foreign translation, the chances are that we catch the approximation without being troubled by the distortion. Read, in the version by Richmond Lattimore,[2] the beginning of that passage in the third Pythian which prompted Arnold to exclaim that "the grand style in its simplicity is inimitable":[3]

> But a life unshaken
> befell neither Peleus called Aiakidas
> nor godlike Kadmos, yet men say these two were given
> blessedness beyond all mortals.
>
> (*Pythian* 3.86–89)

Inimitable? The grand style in its simplicity? What can Arnold have been thinking of? But read the same passage in Romagnoli's Italian:

Ma incolume vita non ebbe
nè d'Êaco il figlio, nè Cadmo divino,
che pure sortirono, dicesi, fra gli uomini eccelsa fortuna.

Is the inversion "nè d'Êaco il figlio" awkward, the Latinate "incolume"
a trifle mannered? That is for Italians to worry about. The English-
speaking reader receives the impression of pregnant, memorable
utterance, a genuine stylistic elevation. Again, if you have no Greek
and want to gain some sense of the famous lines from the same ode
which provided Valéry with the epigraph for "Le Cimetière marin,"
you would be well advised to go not to Lattimore's version:

> Dear soul of mine, never urge a life beyond
> mortality, but work the means at hand to the end
> (Pythian 3.61–62)

which is flat and uninteresting, nor to the Wade-Gery/Bowra version:[4]

> Dear soul of mine, for immortal days
> Trouble not: the availment that is to be had
> Drain to the last

which is painfully clumsy, but to Romagnoli:

> Non chiedere, oh cuore diletto, la vita perenne,
> ma esercita l'opra concessa.

This is nobly sententious; it is also believable poetic speech. The English translators, struggling to follow the form of Pindar's invocation
("O dear soul"), come up with a phrase that could only be found in
a translation. "Oh cuore diletto" does not belong to the Italian poetic
tradition, but it is convincing and it is elevated. From Romagnoli, the
English-speaking reader gains some sense of the way Pindar writes,
the high, severe manner of this poet. Even if the reader possesses the
lines in the original Greek, he possesses them more fully when he has
heard them re-created in a living language.

Not of course that Romagnoli gives us everything. His sententious-
ness is perhaps more in the Roman than the Greek manner, and he
fails to suggest both the strangeness of Pindar's language and the fact
that the Greek advances an intellectually interesting proposition. If we
want as much as this from the translator, we must go to Hölderlin:[5]

> Nicht, liebe Seele, Leben unsterbliches
> Suche; die thunliche erschöpfe die Kunst.

Apart from the dislocations of German word order and usage—
which in themselves serve to transport us to an unfamiliar world—
the phrase "erschöpfe die thunliche Kunst" is as pregnant as Pindar's
τὰν δ᾽ ἔμπρακτον ἄντλει μαχανάν and claims a kind of attention that
Romagnoli's "esercita l'opra concessa" does not.

Romagnoli offers a more readily approachable Pindar (Hölderlin's
versions are likely to be of value only to the fairly advanced reader),
and I think he offers more of him than any English translator. He may
well have been helped by his language—Gildersleeve, it will be remembered, considered Italian "an exceptionally good medium for
translation of Pindar."[6] Literary, poetic Italian enjoys an extremely
fluid word order, and it preserved, well into the twentieth century, the
freedom to use words and constructions from the older literary language which allows the translator to suggest the formal, ceremonious
quality of Pindar's diction. Above all, Italian possesses a high poetic
style which, as Coleridge remarked, has been distinguished from the
language of prose very much in the Greek way.[7] Romagnoli can draw
with full conviction on this tradition (fortified by a number of rather
gaudy Greco-Latin neologisms inspired by Carducci and D'Annunzio),
whereas an English translator like C. J. Billson, whose versions of Pindar appeared within a decade of Romagnoli's, cannot draw on the
older tradition of England without falling into absurdity.[8] Italian, however, is weak in one respect that matters very much to the translator of
Pindar, the power to form compound epithets. Romagnoli faces the
problem intelligently, sometimes turning them into adjectival clauses
("le spiagge di Cuma, ch'àn siepe di flutti" for ταί θ᾽ὑπὲρ Κύμας
ἁλιερκέες ὄχθαι; "la diva che glauche ha le ciglia," etc.) or, less often,
but more strikingly since it is not an Italian usage, treating them as
appositional noun clauses—"il Dio chioma d'oro," "Corònide peplo
leggiadro," and the like.[9]

Before getting down to his version of the twelfth Pythian, which
does not, I think, show him at his best, it may be interesting to quote
a strophe from the third Pythian and watch how he handles the formidable problems it presents. Pindar devotes a great wandering period to the healer Asclepius:

τοὺς μὲν ὦν, ὅσσοι μόλον αὐτοφύτων
ἑλκέων ξυνάονες, ἢ πολιῷ χαλκῷ μέλη τετρωμένοι
ἢ χερμάδι τηλεβόλῳ,
ἢ θερινῷ πυρὶ περθόμενοι δέμας ἢ χειμῶνι, λύσαις ἄλλον ἀλλοίων ἀχέων
ἔξαγεν, τοὺς μὲν μαλακαῖς ἐπαοιδαῖς ἀμφέπων,
τοὺς δὲ προσανέα πίνοντας, ἢ γυίοις περάπτων πάντοθεν
φάρμακα, τοὺς δὲ τομαῖς ἔστασεν ὀρθούς.

(Pythian 3.47–53)

How difficult this is to translate Lattimore conveys very well:

> They came to him with ulcers the flesh had grown,
> or their limbs mangled with the gray bronze, or bruised
> with the stone flung from afar,
> or the body stormed with summer fever, or chill; and he released each
>   man and led him
> from his individual grief. Some he treated with guile of incantations,
> some with healing potions to drink; or he tended the limbs with salves
> from near and far; and some by the knife he set on their feet again.

"If a man should undertake to translate *Pindar* word for word," Cowley wrote, "it would be thought that one *Mad man* had translated *another*." Lattimore's version is close, but it is not word for word (arguably he is too free with this author), nor is there anything about it that suggests insanity, either the poet's or the normal kind. Indeed, it is too level, too pedestrian, and fails to convey the habitual strangeness of Pindar's Greek. Cowley continued: "as may appear, when he that understands not the *Original*, reads the verbal Traduction of him into *Latin Prose*, than which nothing seems more *Raving*."[10] This does not seem to me true of Boeckh's translation into Latin prose which, particularly if printed in verse lengths, gives one the sense of the Greek at a glance and blocks out the structure in a way that an English translation cannot:[11]

> Eos igitur, quotquot advenerant sponte natis
> ulceribus affecti, aut cano aere membra vulnerati
> aut saxo eminus iacto,
> aut aestivo igni corpus laesi aut frigore, liberans alium alius generis
>   doloribus
> exemit: hos quidem mitibus incantamentis curans,
> illos lenes potus bibentes, vel membris circumligans undique
> medicamina; alios vero sectionibus constituit rectos.

And here, finally, is Romagnoli's version:

> E quanti giungevano afflitti
> d'ingenite piaghe, o trafitti da lucido bronzo le membra,
> o dall'avventar di macigni,
> o sfatti dall'alido estivo, o dal gelo,
> mandava disciolti dai varî travagli, di blandi scongiuri
> cingendo talun, beverato quell'altro di miti pozioni,
> o tutte di farmachi succhi fasciando le membra;
> ed altri rimisene in piedi con abili tagli.

The long Greek sentence is very beautiful. It is elaborate, yet it does not feel "constructed" in the way a Latin period usually does. Its contours have been molded by the stress and tension of growth. It is orderly and symmetrical, because order and symmetry are the natural form of the material in the poet's mind. And it delights in variety: the cola are irregular and the construction changes, notably with the verb πίνοντας in the sixth line. It contemplates, in loving detail, a wide range of sickness and cure (three kinds of sickness, two of them subdivided; four kinds of cure), and yet contemplates it with a kind of prescientific (but in no sense primitive) wonder—wonder at the variety of human suffering and, equally, at man's power to heal. To get anything of this sort from a translation, we must go to Hölderlin, but Romagnoli is in his way satisfying and certainly superior to any English translation I know. He still breathes something of the same air as the Greek, he seems to belong to the same family. In the second line Romagnoli can use, quite naturally, a "Greek accusative" ("trafitti le membra"—though I do not know why πολιός, "gray," becomes "lucido"); his third line is monumental like Pindar's and moves to the same stately dactylic tune. He does not attempt the change of construction in line 6, using instead a causative verb, "beverato" (where Hölderlin dares to follow the Greek: "dass linderndes sie / Tranken"), but he has kept the shape of the whole period:

τοὺς μὲν ὦν, ὅσσοι μόλον   :   e quanti giungevano
(eos igitur, quotquot advenerant)

λύσαις . . . ἔξαγεν   :   mandava disciolti
(liberans . . . exemit)

τοὺς μὲν μαλακαῖς . . . ἀμφέπων   :   cingendo talun
(hos quidem . . . curans)

An English translator would of course not be well advised to retain this periodic structure, but my point is that the Italian translator, without violating the norms of the literary language, can and Romagnoli does, and in so doing he brings the reader to within hailing distance of Pindar's way of writing.

Romagnoli's Pindar seems to me to represent an acceptable level of translation—the level we ought to be able to count on. If Lattimore leaves Pindar quite dead, Romagnoli undoubtedly gives him a kind of life. He conveys something of the movement and tone and what one may call the outward aspect of a Pindaric ode. Further than that he does not try to go. He hardly attempts to re-create, or reproduce, in Italian the inner life of Pindar's speech. It may be wondered, of course, how far this is possible, or even desirable, in a modern language. Take a typical Pindaric phrase from the tenth Nemean (line 43), which J. E. Sandys translates: "But from Sicyon, they returned with silver wine-cups."[12] What the Greek says is

Σικυωνόθε δ᾽ ἀργυρωθέντες σὺν οἰνηραῖς φιάλαις ἐπέβαν

—that is, they were "silvered with wine cups." There is no doubt about the picture; even a pedestrian commentator like Fennell sees that what Pindar means is "with a gleam of silver shining on them." But the picture is a function of the language—here, at least, intuition and expression are one. Pindar transfers the dazzle of the wine cups onto the men who carry them. But it is on the linguistic level that this happens: the moment of hallucinated vision is made possible by a kind of explosion that took place within the sentence as it was forming. When the dust settles, the elements are found to be differently constituted and it is the men, not the cups, that shine. What is the translator to do? He cannot simply copy Pindar's phrase into English ("silvered with wine cups") as I did, for this will give no sense of the pressure at work in the language. And yet even this is better than doing what Lattimore does, and placidly restoring Pindar's sentence to apple-pie order:

From Sikyon they departed[13] with silver of the wine goblets.

Risk nothing, win nothing. Romagnoli at least has the decency to suggest that the Greek is exciting:

Li recinse fulgore d'argento quando essi, le fiale del vino recando, tornâr da Sicione.

He tries hard for the picture, but he unfolds it into something far too immediately comprehensible, and into far too many words, and so fails to startle us into vision.

Take another example, the splendid phrase from the sixth Isthmian, οἰνοδόκον φιάλαν χρυσῷ πεφρικυῖαν, "a wine bowl shuddering with gold." The scholiast's comment, illustrating his refusal to face complexity and turbulence in Pindar, offers two lines of interpretation:

1. The bowl is carved in high relief so that the surface seems rough or bristly (like a boar's back, Aristarchus says).
2. The bowl shines or glitters.

This failure of insight is carried over into Virgil's version of the phrase, "aspera signis pocula" (*Aeneid* 9.263–64) which marks an imaginative decline. Pindar's bowl is closer to the pewter dish with the sun shining on it which revealed to Jacob Boehme the being of God than it is to Virgil's embossed cups, which are no more than decorative objets d'art.

Where the tradition of interpretation and even Virgil fail us, it is not surprising that translators should do no better. Lattimore writes "a wine goblet cut in shuddering gold," keeping Pindar's word but not risking his construction. Romagnoli wanders off into verbiage and loses the object altogether:

> una coppa
> di vino, di guizzi tutti aurei
> corrusca.

There is more poetry, and more Pindar, in Boeckh's quite literal "phialam auro horrentem." A word-for-word rendering gets far closer to the original than a translation into second-rate verse (the point Coleridge made to the company of sensible and well-educated women puzzled by Cowley's dithyrambic treatment of the second Olympian).[14] But of course we want much more. If Pindar is ever to become a force in English poetry—and until he becomes a force in English poetry, we cannot really read him in Greek—we need a translator who can write with this sort of power:

> Stanching, quenching ocean of a motionable mind;
> Ground of being and granite of it: pást áll
> Grásp Gód, thróned behínd
> Death, with a sovereignty that heeds but hides, bodes but abides.
> (*The Wreck of the Deutschland*, stanza 32, lines 5–8)

He would not of course imitate Hopkins's mannerisms, but he could hardly fail to learn from the way Hopkins wrenches words out of their usual relationships, fusing them into new torrential units of speech, locking them into almost asyntactic confrontations where they explode into meaning. (A phrase like "past all / Grasp God" invites, entirely in Pindar's manner, a variety of interpretations: "God who is past all grasp," or, yoked into a convulsive compound, a "past-all-grasp God"; or "when all is passed, grasp, take hold of, God.")

Hölderlin, with whom the true Pindar first enters the European literary tradition, is the only translator who satisfies these conditions. He did not, unfortunately, tackle either the tenth Nemean or sixth Isthmian, but the first sentence of the passage from the third Pythian which we examined dislocates relationship in a comparable way and presents the translator with a similar test. Romagnoli, as we saw, wrote "E quanti giungevano afflitti d'ingenite piaghe." (And Lattimore, "They came to him with ulcers the flesh had grown.") But what Pindar says, literally, is "They came the companions of self-grown wounds." On this curious expression Gildersleeve comments: "The sphere of partnership and companionship is wider in Greek than in English. We usually make the disease, not the sufferer, the companion."[15] Hölderlin, however, follows his usual practice and reproduces the Greek exactly:

> Die nun, so viele kommen eingeborner
> Wunden Gefährten.

Were the translator not a great poet, writing in the belief that Greece was being reborn on German soil, we would put this down to crass literal-mindedness. What we have here is obviously something different. This is not an example of the translator allowing the original to violate the normal structure of his own language; rather, Hölderlin has allowed the Greek to impose its own view of reality, its own means of handling and disposing the data of experience. We all say that we want to get as close as possible to the Greek, but few of us care to get as close as this. In reading Greek we try, as best we can, to "think in Greek," that is, we enter the Greek world and accept its different structuring of reality. In so doing, we preserve the essential separation between the Greek world and our own. Hölderlin, driven by his myth of rebirth, moves in the opposite direction: instead of going to Greece, he brings Greece to Germany. He tries to think-in-Greek-in-German. To translate Pindar, on this view, means to become Pindar, and this is a higher price than most translators are prepared to pay.

"Beyond Gadara towards the darkness we must not pass" (*Nem.* 4.69). It is a relief to turn back from this frontier of translation to the sensible middle ground where Romagnoli operates. Although his version of the twelfth Pythian does not show him at his best, it has its points of interest and there is something to be learned from his errors.

1–3. He begins with the verb of invocation which establishes the poet's presence, and the urgency of his presence (unlike Lattimore, who puts it at the end of the third line). And "amica del fasto," for φιλάγλαε ("fasto" = pomp, splendor), is quite attractive, but it was a bad mistake to hold the phrase over till the middle of the second line. The shine needs to be up front. (So that the poem may start and end with brightness: the unhoped-for, god-revealed moment of the conclusion is in Pindar always associated with αἴγλα, "brilliance"; cf. the αἴγλα διόσδοτος of his last poem.) "Città la più bella . . ." has too many words ("albergo" in poetic Italian simply means "dwelling-place") and fails to catch the way Pindar glances at the topos—if it was one then—that cities too have their death. Hölderlin's literal "Schönste der sterb-lichen Städte" (or for that matter the Wade-Gery/Bowra's "fairest of mortal cities") is the only rendering. "Ferace di greggi" is a mere state-ment—the place is rich in flocks, whereas the Greek is momentary, and visual. Lattimore's "where the sheep wander" is better.

4–8. The repetition of "gradisci" would pass in a translation of Me-leager, but it will not do for Pindar, who wastes no words. However, "intrecciando," the literal sense of the Greek, has the right concen-tration and leaves the reader to work out the meaning, as Pindar means him to do, unlike Lattimore's "followed in song," which lodges an enfeebling gloss in the text. (Wade-Gery and Bowra compromise with "wove to a tune.") Gildersleeve is sound here: "The hardness of Pindar, not to say his obscurity, is not to be outdone, but it is not to be done away with. There are to be no periphrases for the sake of clearness." The Loeb translation by Sandys, he adds, "sometimes goes too far in helping the student to follow the text" (*Brief Mention*, 351).
   In lines 6–8 Romagnoli, like all translators except Hölderlin, fails to frame the action between Pindar's two terminal points, *Pallas* and *Athana.* See comment on 20–21.

9–11. The diction is not very attractive, though Romagnoli does suggest something of the movement of the Greek and something of the strangeness of the action. But he spoils the rest of the strophe by changing the order of events. He presents a more or less linear se-quence, moving from Perseus's killing of Medusa to his liberation of his mother Danaë from Polydectes, whereas in the Greek the action is framed (again) by the "heads" of the first and last lines, the snake-wreathed heads of the Gorgons, the lovely head of Medusa (herself one of the Gorgons). Within this constructed space Pindar moves about freely, touching now on this detail, now on that.

17–18. The first line has a shine on it and is rhythmically stronger than Lattimore's "born of the raining gold," but Romagnoli's "l'oro piovuto dall'ètere" hasn't the power of Pindar's "self-flowing gold." Hölderlin scores again by being literal and scores doubly since his extraordinary epithet "selbstentströmtem" outdoes the Greek in ele-mental power. Romagnoli, by telling us that the gold which *fathered* Perseus *rained* from the *aether* (three pieces of information which Pindar omits), weakens the image and moves halfway to the familiar anthropomorphic story of Zeus descending in a shower of gold and lying with Danaë. The Greek contemplates a far more ancient mythological event: a child begotten by gold streaming of its own volition, ἀπὸ χρυσοῦ . . . αὐτομάτως καταρρέοντος, as the scholiast says. Note also φαμεν: not "si narra" but the Yeatsian "I declare" ("Blood and the Moon"). *Credo quia mirabile est.*

20–21. "Il lungo ululo lugubre" hasn't the stridency one hears in Pindar's ἐρικλάγκταν γόον (cf. Hölderlin's etymologically incorrect but very powerful formation, "streittönende"), but there is some energy, and imagination, in the words that follow—the lament spurting ("sprizzante") from the flickering jaws ("fitto guizzar delle fauci") of the monster. However, neither Romagnoli nor Hölderlin nor anyone else can suggest the remarkable way Pindar's sentence grows in the space between the definite article, τόν, near the start of line 20, and its substantive, γόον, at the end of the next line.

Note that while you can speak of this sentence "growing" between these two points, it is equally possible to say that it is placed, or "held," between them—as lines 7 and 8, more obviously, are held between the two names of the goddess, Pallas and Athana, set at the beginning and the end of the couplet. The translator's problem here is not primarily one of syntax and word order. It is rather that the effect of the Greek is partly visual, whereas Western poets have traditionally been committed to the temporal nature of their art.[16] Pindar sets out his meaning in space, visually, in addition to developing it through time: the Gorgons are contained within the limits established by the divine names. This is a dimension of Greek poetry to which we are very insensitive; with our classroom habit of construing we reduce it to the limitations of our own syntax, and there would be great value in a translation which used the typographical resources of modern poetry in order to make us *look at* an ode of Pindar. Of Mallarmé's "Un Coup de dés" Valéry remarked, "Il me semble de voir la figure d'une pensée, pour la première fois placée dans notre espace."[17] A translator might learn a good deal from the way the four elements of the main sentence (UN COUP DE DÉS / JAMAIS / N'ABOLIRA / LE HASARD), first given in the title, are held in suspense through several pages of smaller type and "released" bit by bit.

25–27. Romagnoli goes badly wrong, again, by changing the sequence of phrases and putting "dei balli compagna fedel" (his not particularly happy translation of πιστοὶ χορευτᾶν μάρτυρες, "faithful witnesses of the dances") at the start of the strophe rather than at the end of the period. Pindar's phrase is the culmination of a process which started at line 19, if not before: Athena created the music of the flute in imitation of the fearful cry wrenched from the jaws of the monster Euryale; created it and gave it to men, naming it, by an etymological pun, "the many-headed tune." The flute's music calls men to war and also, as in this case, to the games (mimic war, strife transformed into play), as it passes through (compare the cry that passed through the jaws of Euryale and, earlier on, the death cry that "poured" from the bowed snake heads) "the slender bronze and reeds"—that is, the flute with its bronze mouthpiece, hendiadys marking the conjunction of artifact and natural object and developing the poem's movement from "nature" to art, from savagery to order, from barbarous dissonance to musical sound and, equally, the poem's theme of art's sources in the daemonic. (The reeds through which the music passes were, in the myth, the snake necks of the Gorgons.) These reeds, the poems continues, grow—the Greek says "dwell," the verb used of the tutelary goddess's habitance of her city in line 3, a recurrence preserved only by Hölderlin—in the dancing grounds by the city of the Graces, in the precinct of the nymph Cephisis. We have come a long way from the dark business of the central part of the poem, the crying snake heads, Polydectes' cruelty and Danaë's suffering, the people of Seriphus frozen into stone. Now, the dancing grounds, the city of the Graces, fostering spirits of growth and bloom and fruit, sanctified territory. It is at this point, as the sentence comes to a full close, that the reeds emerge as "the faithful witnesses of the dancers." Note the suggestions: (1) the reeds (we may think of them as surrounding the dancing grounds) separate wild from cultivated land; (2) as witnesses, the reeds remind us of the ring of spectators in whose presence Midas won his victory with the flute; (3) as the source of the flute's music, the reeds bear faithful witness by keeping the time— the measure of art, as against the lawless clamor of the monster world which Athena has subdued.

28–32. The quality of the writing suggests that Romagnoli is not very interested. One assumes he accepts the genial old view that Pindar trots out a few gnomes to bridge a gap or bring the evening's entertainment to a decorous close. But Pindar is very intent: the series of statements that chart the twists and turns of vicissitude may confront each other with little intervenient discourse, but they are certainly not punctuated by yawns. In fact, their function is clear enough. First, the play of unexpected reversals enacted in the myth must be met or "held" by an equally active play of maxims. Much has happened "beyond, or against, expectation"—for Medusa, Polydectes, Danaë, Perseus, and of course for Midas who broke the mouthpiece of his flute, we are told, but won all the same. And, above, and beyond, all expectation, we have witnessed the unpredictable inrush of divine grace, the sudden gold that flowed for Perseus's begetting. Second, and perhaps more importantly, the last three lines of the narrative have moved from mythological violence into a world of harmony and order. A gracious, divinely sanctioned interlude: that must not be prolonged. The jostling assertions that bring the poem to a close duly conduct us back to familiar territory, to our world of chance and change and labor.

Pindar's gnomic passages have defeated every translator. Lattimore's conclusion is as dull, intellectually, as Romagnoli's and not so well written. The last seven lines of the Wade-Gery/Bowra version, however, are not without accomplishment, even though the fingering is too light for Pindar:

> Any bliss that man may win
> (And without labour, none) God shall perfect,
> To-day, perhaps! yet Fate must be abided.
> Then lo! Time's hand
> Throwing at you the unforeseen
> Turns calculation upside down, and gives you
> One thing, but another not yet.

And yet perhaps the light touch is appropriate. The solemnity with which the aging poet will contemplate the god's gifts and man's uncertain fate is still far ahead. Here the note is buoyant, confident: "This he gives, that not yet." The master is still not out of his twenties.

9

The Beastly House of Atreus

Τ I: εὐηγεσίας χάριν

1.

HALFWAY THROUGH THE *CHOEPHOROE*, THAT IS, AT THE CENTER OF the whole *Oresteia,* is an ode that for Aeschylus may seem a little un-enterprising, despite some poetic splendors. Orestes, now returned from exile, has joined forces with his sister Electra and the loyal cho-rus, and together they have summoned to their aid the powers of the dead but still active Agamemnon. The plot whereby the guilty pair, Clytemnestra and Aegisthus, are to get their deserts and Orestes re-gain his inheritance is taking shape. It is at this point that Aeschylus gives the chorus an elaborate ode on some legendary female crimes, all pointing to Clytemnestra's. Why female crimes? a modern reader may wonder rebelliously. Surely the male members of the house of Atreus are at least as much at fault. It is a mistake, though, to ques-tion an old poem too bluntly from today's prepared positions, as mis-taken as the historicist attempt to bracket off contemporary interests altogether. A work that does not speak at all to the strong concerns of the present we can't of course in any real sense read; but it is likely, if it speaks from the past, to address them obliquely, perhaps an-swering our question by means of another question or even shifting the whole ground of the debate. The most fertile situation, in our early encounters with a great text, is when we are engaged along a very wide front but do not really understand what is happening there; when we are moved and excited, without yet knowing why we are moved or what exactly it is that excites us. Step-by-step text and reader move closer together and the dialogue that leads to understanding can begin. The position we want to reach, I shall be supposing, is one

"The Beastly House of Atreus," *Kenyon Review* 3, no. 2 (Spring 1981): 20–40.

that contains, and thus transcends, both our own cultural perspective and that of the text: what Gadamer calls the fusion of horizons.

The ode starts with a ranging look at the terrors of the natural world and then moves to comparable terrors in the human world:

> Many are the strange and baneful shapes earth breeds. Monsters that hate our kind teem in the arms of the sea. Torches hung in the heavens burst into flame, and beasts on wing and afoot can tell of the wind's tempestuous rage.
>
> But of man's too-daring spirit who shall speak, and women's reckless passions, all-daring, mated with mortal ruin? Loveless, the female's mastering passion subverts the yoked and stabled coupling of beast and man.
>
> (*Choephoroe* 586–601)[1]

"Too-daring" and "all-daring," awkwardly compounded in English, are formed from the noun τόλμα. The word is used in a good sense ("courage") and in a bad, usually translated "overboldness," "recklessness," and the like. In the *Oresteia* the word regularly indicates violation of a cultural norm, some disruption of a precarious and hence precious equilibrium. It is first heard when Agamemnon, faced with the demand that he sacrifice his daughter in order that the Greek fleet may sail for Troy, is said to "change his purpose and resolve on τὸ παντότολμον (*Agamemnon* 221)—"a totally transgressive act" is perhaps the nearest prose equivalent. Plato uses the verbal form in speaking of the bestial side of the psyche which breaks loose in dreams and "shrinks from no transgressive act" (πάντα . . . τολμᾷ ποιεῖν), not even from incestuous union with the mother (*Republic* 571c). The *Oresteia* has shown, by the time this central ode has been reached, a series of atrocious crimes committed within the family, and the stage is set for a further act of τόλμα when Orestes will kill his mother (*Choephoroe* 1029).

The ode goes on to exemplify three instances of passionate female transgression: a mother who destroys her son, a daughter who betrays her father, and the famous horror story of the women of Lemnos who killed all the men on their island. And now, our moral ear attuned, we are ready for the crime to which the whole composition points, Clytemnestra's murder of her husband, Agamemnon, on his return from the Trojan War. The text is here unfortunately corrupt, and even the sequence of strophes is not quite certain. We make out a hateful marriage that is an abomination to the house, a woman plotting against her warrior husband. There is another compound of τόλμα, this time negatived, but the sense can only be guessed at. The design of the ode as a whole is, however, clear. It is cast in the form of what is now called a priamel, an archaic compositional device whereby the poet begins with a series of foils which are discarded one after the other as he moves toward the real focus of attention. But although this is technically the form Aeschylus uses, we read badly if we suppose that the powerful opening stanza, or pair of stanzas, is to be dismissed once it has served its purpose. On the contrary, it reverberates all through the ode, setting up a parallel between two kinds of terror: monstrous beasts and forces in nature which, though fearful, are nonetheless natural; and monstrous actions in the human realm of culture which we find supremely unnatural. The two realms must be kept distinct; as we shall see, one of the main forms which τόλμα takes is precisely the overriding of this distinction. And yet they are very close, with events in one realm constantly mirroring or matching events in the other or interacting in some way. Agamemnon and Menelaus set out across the sea to recover the latter's stolen wife; vultures "oared by their wings" search for the young stolen from their nest. In the present ode human marriage and the mating of animals are shown as subject to the same disruptive forces. It is because the two realms are so close that the distinction between them has at all costs to be preserved.

Two other passages exhibit a similar pattern of thought and suggest that the relation between nature and culture is important in the trilogy. (We may find that this distinction, familiar to us from anthropological studies, cuts deeper than the apparently similar Greek distinction between φύσις and νόμος, nature and custom or law.) The subject of both passages is again Clytemnestra, not because she is necessarily the greatest sinner but because her crime is the one most fully presented. After he has killed her, Orestes says in a powerfully dislocated speech:

> Against her husband she plotted this vile thing, he whose children she had carried beneath her girdle, a burden once dear but now, as the event shows, a deadly hatred. What do you think—was she born sea-snake or viper whose very touch corrupts though it bite not? Such was her τόλμα, such her lawless spirit.
>
> (*Choephoroe* 991–96)

Earlier on the prophetess Cassandra, brought from Troy by Agamemnon and soon to be killed by Clytemnestra, said of her:

> Such is her transgressive daring (τολμᾷ)—the wife, the killer of the husband. What should I rightly call this hateful monster? An amphisbaena, or a Scylla living among the rocks for sailor's ruin? A raging hell-mother breathing truceless war against her kin? How she raised her cry of tri-

umph, the all-daring one (παντότολμος), as though at the turning-point of battle.

(Agamemnon 1231–37)

τόλμα again, in verbal and adjectival form, framing the passage. Again, dreadful beasts, and dreadful actions in the realm of culture (and with the hell-mother, some folklore horror or witch, a hint of the daemonic), but this time, instead of keeping them separate, the poet lays them side-by-side as though he were starting a simile. And this time unnatural human behavior—a mother introducing war into the family (bella matribus detestata), a woman usurping man's military role —is matched with unnatural creatures in nature: the amphisbaena, a fabled monster with a head at each end; Scylla, a marine horror encircled with yelping dog-mouths and acting with a malignant human intelligence. It looks as though disorder in one realm has spilled over into the other.

In her fragmented, appalled vision of Agamemnon's death, Aeschylus's brilliant invention replacing the normal messenger's speech after the event, Cassandra begins by sensing some frightful thing taking shape in the house. A woman is bathing her husband, she reaches out to him, hand stretches after hand. There is something resembling a net, a hell-net, a wife-net. Then:

Aah . . . look! Keep the bull from the cow. In the folds . . . with a black-horned thing—she has caught him, she strikes!

(Agamemnon 1125–28)

It is supremely horrible that the kindly ceremony of the bath designed to solace the tired limbs of the traveler should be the occasion for murder, and not just for murder but for this animal goring. And the violation of cultural usage is compounded by inversion of nature's usage, for it is a cow that has turned on the bull, nature horridly confused with culture since the cow entangles its victim in a bathrobe, a cow that uses its black horn like a sword or axe. (As we might expect, though some eminent commentators, oddly, seem not to, this confusion is enacted at the primary linguistic level with the participial clause breaking disruptively into the main clause.)

Cassandra next sees Clytemnestra—the adulteress plotting her husband's death with the aid of her lover, Aegisthus—as "a two-footed lioness bedding with a wolf in the noble lion's absence" (lines 1258f.). Violation of cultural norms again, and another inversion of nature's usage: lions do not mate with wolves. A little earlier (lines 1224f.)

Aegisthus was called "the cowardly lion tumbling in a bed, keeping house against the lord's return." This too has troubled scholars. Wilamowitz deleted the line, Paul Maas wanted to replace the lion with a wolf. Eduard Fraenkel in his great commentary, finding a cowardly lion "hard to swallow," objected that "it would be for a Greek . . . an offence against the laws of nature to call a lion—of all creatures—[cowardly]."[2] Exactly! Just as a lion minding the house is an offence against the laws of culture. Violation in one realm has led to disorder in the other.[3]

The evil spreads. The *Agamemnon* began with a flaring light that split the dark and a cry of ambiguous joy. At the start of the *Choephoroe* we hear of a cry of terror at dead of night and later learn how Clytemnestra woke from a nightmare, screaming, and torches blinded by darkness sprang up in the palace at the queen's behest. She dreamed that she had given birth to a snake and suckled it at her torn breast. Accepting the omen, Orestes declares: "She bred this monstrous thing; let her die by violence. I will turn snake [ἐκδρακοντωθείς, a tremendous formation; compare Dante's *indracarsi*] and kill her" (*Choephoroe* 548–50). Later in the play, flanked by his silent companion Pylades, Orestes goes into the palace to carry out his deadly task, and the chorus sing in triumph that justice is being done at last (lines 937–38):

> There has gone into Agamemnon's house
> a double lion, a double Ares.

Whatever the force of "double"—the two men who have just passed inside or, surely less likely, two sets of killing, first Agamemnon and Cassandra, now Clytemnestra and Aegisthus—the point is the inappropriateness in a household of lions (natural violence) and "Ares" (the god's name standing for an act of human violence, perhaps with something daemonic about it). That this is indeed Aeschylus's point is shown by some words he puts into the mouth of the avenging Furies in the third play. Their chosen role, they announce, is the overthrow of houses "whenever Ares, tamed, strikes down a kinsman" (*Eumenides* 355f.). Violence human or daemonic in the household again, and in the oxymoron tamed (or domesticated) Ares there is the further suggestion of a wild beast reared there. Aeschylus can be so economical because earlier on in a great ode we shall soon have to turn to he has dealt at length with this matter of domesticating lions.

After the murder, Orestes stands over the bodies of Aegisthus and his mother (as she in the *Agamemnon* stood over the bodies of her husband and Cassandra) and defends his action, calmly at first but then, as the madness in the breed takes hold of him (earlier we saw it take hold of Clytemnestra), his speech becomes disjointed and fearful. It was at Apollo's bidding that he carried out his transgressive act (τόλμα, line 1029), he declares, but he knows that the home he has recovered at such cost can be no home for him and that he must go into exile to Apollo's sanctuary and purge himself of the kindred blood he has shed. The faithful women of the chorus try to reassure him. You have liberated the city, they say, with one happy stroke lopping off the heads of a pair of snakes. At this ill-omened word, the horror that has lain just below the action for so long, working its way forward through imagery, intermittently heard as the pulse of a deadly chant, now for the first time takes visible shape and Orestes sees them, the Erinyes or Furies, women shapes, black-robed, their heads wreathed with snakes. He screams in mortal terror and after a brief exchange with the chorus runs headlong from the stage pursued by his "mother's angry hounds," still visible only to him. In the first half of the next and final play, where the Furies assume the role of the chorus so that we too see them, the imagery persistently depicts Orestes as a hunted animal, with the Furies as hounds following the scent of their prey. Sometimes the language suggests uglier creatures. They breathe withering fire, like dragons; they suck blood, like vampire bats, and devour their victims; at one point they take the form of a single "dreadful snake." Heir to all the transgressions of his family, Orestes is exposed to the full fury of these elemental beings whose human aspects are crossed with the bestial and the daemonic.

In our proper desire to take fullest possession of an acknowledged masterpiece like the *Oresteia*, we seize gratefully on those parts of the whole which we can understand without having to adjust our scheme of things. There is no difficulty in responding to the soaring blasphemy of Clytemnestra's words as she stands over her husband's body:

> As he struck me with the dark spatter of bloody dew, I rejoiced no less than the sown field brightens with god's gift of rain when the sheath is in labor with the ear.
>
> (*Agamemnon* 1390–92)

Perhaps, though, we do not hear her blasphemy with Greek ears as blasphemy against the divine fertility of nature. And probably we do not fully register the disturbance the poet would have counted on when, in the opening scene of the trilogy, the watchman Clytemnestra has stationed on the roof of the palace describes her as a woman who plans like a man. It is likely again that we don't make enough of the fact that immediately after his magnificent description of how he passed the time during his year-long vigil ("I have come to know well the assembly of the stars of night, those that bring winter and those bringing summer to mortals, shining masters glorious in the sky"), the watchman goes on to announce that he is on the lookout for a beacon, the last of a chain of fires arching across the Aegean, Clytemnestra's contrivance to get the news of Troy's fall before anyone else. When she herself later compares these beacons to the heavenly bodies, sun, moon, and perhaps comet, we admire her poetry but do not instinctively sense any crossing of forbidden lines. For we have tranquilly inserted our own contrivances amid the heavenly bodies which we do not see, with Aristotle, as far more divine than man. (We think it odd of him to say that man is obviously "not the best thing in the universe.")

It is not a matter of abandoning our cultural horizon as we read the *Oresteia* and pretending, quite vainly, to be fifth-century Athenians, but rather a kind of tactical ceding of home ground in order, later, to be able to reach more deeply into the poet's. To bring the older text close, we must first push it away. The first step is to remove the patina of familiarity that lies dullingly on the masterpieces of our tradition and uncover, even at the cost of some violence of interpretation, whatever is strange and alien there. Classical scholars do of course insist on the foreignness of Greek civilization and tell us that we must try to see antiquity as it really was, not as we would like it to have been. And yet one sometimes feels that their frame of reference is not so unfamiliar after all and that antiquity as it really was bears a curious resemblance to Oxford and Cambridge and other such haunts of the learned.

For the moment, then, let us leave Clytemnestra whom we think we understand—as the first of drama's great villainesses—and turn to her sister Helen. She was taken from her husband, Menelaus, by Paris and brought to Troy, a grave crime for which the Trojans received exemplary punishment. (Troy provides Aeschylus with a clear paradigm of the working of crime and punishment from which he can at any moment pass to their more complex operation in Argos.) In the first stasimon or ode (*Agamemnon* 355ff.) we hear how Paris "came to the house of the Atreidae and violated the hospitable board by the theft of a wife" and how Helen, "daring things that should not be dared" (τόλμα again), followed him. The second ode (lines 681ff.) turns directly to Helen herself, the harlot "woman of many men" (*Agamemnon* 62) and at the same time a mysterious half-daemonic figure— "terribly she resembles the immortal goddesses," Homer's old men said of her—whose very name suggests destruction (ἐλεῖν, to destroy). She is called ἐλέναυς in the series of coinages which fascinated Pound, Helen destroyer of ships, ἐλέπτολις, destroyer of cities, ἕλανδρος, destroyer of men. There is a poetry in these Aeschylean odes as developed in its formal and expressive means as any known to us, yet much of the time we have to admit if we are honest that we read in a state of exalted bafflement. The problems of interpretation they raise have hardly yet been sighted, let alone faced. Consider the relation of the first five stanzas of this ode:

1. Helen of the dreadful name went to Troy. Her avengers followed in hot pursuit.
2. The Trojans celebrated her union with Paris, but soon the marriage song turned into a song of mourning.
3. "It was in this way that a lion-cub was reared by a man in his house," a charming creature beloved of young and old.
4. "But in time it showed its true nature. Paying its scot to those who reared it, with ruinous slaughter of cattle it made a feast unbidden, and the house was fouled with blood . . . By god's design a priest of ruin (ἄτη) had been bred in the house."
5. "At first there came to Troy—call it a spirit of windless calm, jewel of tranquil riches, gentle javelin of the eye, love's flower that stings the heart. But bending the marriage awry she brought it to a bitter end, hurt to hearth and fellowship, rushed on the sons of Priam by Zeus the lord of guest and host, a fury whose bridal was fraught with tears."[4]

I take it that the thinking here is difficult for us. Bringing someone like Helen into your house, Aeschylus seems to say, is like bringing a lion there. Yet despite "in this way," the lines in stanza 3 about the lion cannot be taken as the vehicle of a simile whose tenor is Helen's abduction and presence in Troy. There is no formal marker to introduce the tenor, for one thing; the story of the lion is simply pursued for a while, it turns into a priest of ruin, a new sequence of images suggests the figure of Helen, and then she too is transformed and becomes a fury or Erinys. It is best to take the lion's story as a fable (the word I translated "in this way" really means "once upon a time," Fraenkel shows) or more exactly a parable: it is laid beside the account of Helen's career in such a way that the two set up free-floating relations with each other. But what relation is being proposed? The abduction of Helen, it is made clear, was a grave crime, whereas bringing up a lion in your house may be rash but is surely not wicked. Perhaps no very close parallelism is to be sought: "Helen was only the instrument, not the agent, of the destruction of the Trojans. Clytemnestra's career is far more similar to the lion's."[5] Yes, but then why spend a whole stanza on the innocent charm of the cub? What light does that throw on Clytemnestra?

The parable may speak to something in *both* sisters: what they have in common is that neither can safely be lodged in a household. Applied to Clytemnestra (the two-footed lioness) we understand this as a poetic or metaphorical way of depicting her lawless savagery. Yes again, but bear in mind the theme that Aeschylus constantly associates with her, the introduction into the human realm of the terrors of the wild. The poet's stress falls where we least look for it, on the confusion between animal and human, on the transgression which overrides the distinction between nature and culture. It is not to our minds a moral distinction, since it applies equally to acts which we agree with the Greeks in calling wicked and acts we regard as merely unwise. Nor does it distinguish as we do within the animal realm, since it groups the charming lion cub with monsters like the amphisbaena. The exquisite Helen too belongs to this forbidden company, a no less dangerous and alien presence than her sister, not because she is wicked but because she is daemonic, something other than human. As Aristotle tells us, there are two kinds of being who cannot live in a city: animals and gods (*Politics* 1253a29). What is threatened by both Helen and Clytemnestra and all they embody or symbolize is the space of human dwelling which must be preserved from the perils which surround it, whether they take the form of the bestial or the daemonic.

God's dangerous intrusion into our world is a great theme which Euripides was to dramatize in the *Bacchae*. (Recall how in that play Pentheus at one point sees Dionysus as a bull.) The threat to the house of Atreus takes a different and odder form, a *grotesque* form we might be inclined to say if Aeschylus's violent text could once and for all be freed from inappropriate notions of classical decorum. Consider the strange goings-on in this tragic mansion. Lions and wolves mate in the bedroom, in the bath chamber a cow gores a bull to death. A lion is minding the house, a pair of lions stride into the house. "Ares," domesticated (like a wild beast kept as a pet), strikes down a kinsman, while across the water in Troy the consequence of giving house-room to an Atreid princess can only be compared to the shambles of a rampaging lion. We hear of Scyllas and amphisbaenas—creepy-crawlies with a head at each end, of snakes that putrefy a man without even biting him. A woman dreams she has given birth to a snake and her son says he will turn snake to kill her. He duly kills both his mother and her lover (You have cut off the heads of two snakes, he is told) and is then driven offstage by things resembling women with snakes sprouting from their heads, after which, like an animal running for its

life, the heir to the throne of Argos is chased halfway round Greece
by a pack of hounds that can at will turn into dragons or vampire bats.
It hardly does to dismiss all this as poetic imagery, and it is no help
to say that Homeric similes too are full of animals. So they are, but
Homer's animals stay in their proper place, illuminating the human
realm, not invading it.

We are often warned not to look in Greek tragedy for characterization in the Shakespearian or modern sense. The warnings are very
much in order but have been less than effective because it is seldom
made clear what should centrally command attention if the plight of
the tragic hero must take second place. It is among the many merits
of John Jones's book, *On Aristotle and Greek Tragedy*, to which I am obviously much indebted (see note 3), that it indicates so clearly where
the stress should fall in the *Oresteia*. It falls on the *house* of Atreus itself, a psychic unity not merely greater than its individual component
members but possessing its own, greater identity. The poet shows his
hand in the opening scene of the *Agamemnon* when he has the watchman say, "if the house could speak." The primal offence in the *Oresteia*
is whatever threatens the stability of the house, Aeschylean shorthand
for the human community (culture), and violates the norms which
sustain it. The norms, on which the happiness and well-being of the
community depend, govern social usages and roles and a host of carefully observed differentiations—between man and woman, parent and
child, old and young, master and servant, stranger and kinsman. They
govern the relation between living and dead, for the dead remain part
of the ongoing life of the house. The norms control the balance of
forces within culture and secure the human space from the intrusions
of nature. They also regulate the proper interplay between culture
and nature, a very important theme which will come to the fore in
the second part of this paper. On such a view, the reestablishment of
order, once it has broken down, involves not or not primarily the punishment of the wicked, still less the enforcement of abstract justice,
but rather, as Jones shows us, the restoration of the shattered norm.
    Although we can respond to the power and passion with which
Aeschylus dramatizes these themes, they no longer in themselves touch
us directly. Differentiation today spells discrimination and is being
ironed out in the interests of social justice. Order we too easily see as
dull, negative when not actively repressive. And Aeschylus's fears about
the danger of confusing animal and human escape us almost entirely.
We live in a country where crocodiles are sold commercially and one
hears of people who keep a baby croc in the bathtub. More generally,
we are only too eager to refresh a jaded civilization with whatever

infusions of savage energy we can lay our hands on. We do so without misgiving because we no longer see the forces threatening the human artifice as Aeschylus and so many of our older authors did. Confident in his steadily growing powers, Western man has for several centuries been assuming that culture had finally got the better of its old adversary. Nature might strike back in this or that way, but the *regnum hominis* was secure, even impregnable. This is still the official view; nature is regarded as a human resource and any remnants of the original wild not yet under our control (weather, death itself) will be before long or at all events should be. There are signs, though, that nature may be staging a comeback, most obviously through the environmental crisis (to which we respond by saying that we should use *our* resources more wisely) but no less through the return of *human* savagery in social and political conduct. We take this in our stride nowadays and have most unwisely allowed the momentous reversal whereby the city has become the jungle (in earlier, Romantic imagery, the wild ocean) to be dulled into a cliché. There is nonetheless a sense of shock in the air, we are no longer quite certain we are going to make it, and Yeats's lines written in 1919 still speak representatively to a modern anxiety ("The Second Coming"):

> Things fall apart; the centre cannot hold;
> Mere anarchy is loosed upon the world.

There is however another way of conceiving the relation between Yeats's two terms. What if the center (culture, the city), to hold together and flourish, *needs* to be faced by something that from its perspective looks like anarchy? Is there a point of view from which "anarchy" (nature, the wild), while always to be feared, has also to be accepted, as our old and permanent adversary, our partner even? The polarity between nature and culture may be the condition of our well-being: it is nature's embracing threat that keeps culture trim. Culture cannot extend its rule too far without nature striking back and culture itself growing arid (prompting "returns" to nature which deny our identity as beings whose nature is to create and be created by culture). If there is anything to this, our older authors, speaking from worlds which knew nature and loved culture as we no longer do, might provide more than aesthetic pleasure or an academic exercise. We might find that we were striking against something hard there, some permanent bedrock of experience, and that earlier habits of mind were stirring in us and providing a new way of understanding and facing some current perplexities.

The forces that threaten our civilization today are too complex to be brought into a single focus. For earlier societies the threat was far more direct. A student of myth, Joseph Fontenrose, puts it in this way: "The cosmos has been won from the chaos that still surrounds it, as a cultivated plot from the surrounding wilderness."[6] Even if the opposition between cosmos and chaos is not Greek (chaos means something different in Greek), Aeschylus at least would have understood what it involved—if not as immediately as the poet of *Beowulf,* for instance, would have done. I say "at least" because while Greeks of the classical and earlier period show an acute sense of the insecurity of the human condition, they for the most part experience it directly in the form of civil strife or military disaster or δαιμόνια like famine or plague, "acts of God" over which man has no control. Something prevented them from looking far into its cosmic or metaphysical ground. Perhaps that something was the *Iliad.* It was the achievement of Greece's foundational poem to propose an intelligible—not a "rational"—universe, one that has no special care for man but provides a hospitable space for his enterprise. Homer steadily faces the worst that can befall us, but he knows that the outer frame of things is secure. Danger, suffering, disaster of every kind, yes. The city will fall in the end. But chaos will not come again.[7] The darkness pressed harder against the great fifth-century Athenian poets, and they guessed at something worse than the irrational black horse skewing things awry, not only in the psyche but in the universe, which Plato was eventually forced to allow for. But even they never dared to imagine Grendel, an embodied principle of cosmic malignity.

And yet familiar images like the ship of state must have arisen from a vision of life akin to that described by Fontenrose. But for the city walls, protecting us like the sides of a ship, we would be exposed (like that most wretched of beings, the ἄπολις or man without a city) to the terrors of the wild that lie all around. Myth recorded that somewhere at the roots of the world lay the old forces of chaos, Titans and the like. They had however been decisively defeated by the Olympians before man arrived on the scene and there was not much danger that they would return. This great theme finds its tempered expression (censored, a Norseman would say) in Pindar's first Pythian ode, which binds into a mighty harmony the founding of a new city in Sicily, the victories won by a Sicilian prince over Carthage and Etruria, thus securing the western frontiers of Hellas against barbarism, and Zeus's cosmogonic victory over the chaos demon Typhos, imagined as a vast body pressed down by the volcanic Mount Etna, at whose foot the new city lies. Structurally the relation of Typhos to the new city is identical with that of Grendel to Heorot, which has also just been built. But whereas in the Old English poem the new settlement lies open to the monster's nightly assaults, helplessly until the arrival of the hero Beowulf, the Greek monster, though still spouting fountains of unapproachable fire and rolling down rocks to the sea in spirals of flame, has been thoroughly subdued and may seem to be providing the citizens of Etna with a grandiose display of *son et lumière*.

In the plays of Aeschylus's latest period (judging at least by what has survived), the theme of cosmic war emerges in a new and far more menacing form. The *Oresteia* shows the human conflict within the house of Atreus swelling to universal proportions, with the Furies ranged against the new gods, Apollo and later Athena, and threatening, if they are denied their right to punish Orestes for matricide, to blast the fertility of life, natural and human, and give the world over to anarchy. Behind the Furies stand the Fates, the ultimate Apportioners; behind Apollo and Athena, Zeus. And as the imagery of the plays insists, behind these figures loom still more primary oppositions: dark against light, below against above, old against new, female against male. Everything is at stake. C. J. Herington has discussed this theme of cosmic cleavage as it occurs in the *Oresteia*, and may have occurred in the *Supplices* trilogy and the *Prometheia*, in terms of Aeschylus's response to the cultural crisis of the mid-fifth century. "When archaic man runs headlong into classical free enquiry," he writes, "when a tradition of static authoritarianism in politics and religion comes face to face with classical democracy"—when, to use words from the same paper, the old tribal consciousness confronts the New Learning, and late-archaic religious thinking glimpses the advent of philosophy: "when these confrontations occur all at once, the world will in fact seem to split; from the microcosm of the mind, through the state, to the divine macrocosm."[8] By an immense effort Aeschylus ends the *Oresteia* by pulling his universe together, but it has been a very near thing. Or perhaps he only claims to have pulled it together; the cleavage may have gone too far even for his unifying powers.

The concept of cultural crisis is one we are all too familiar with. Aeschylus, it has to be remembered, possessed no such concept; he simply sensed that the universe man had always known was being rent in two. Hence it was not merely the necessities of dramatic form that made him present this cleavage, in the first two thirds of his trilogy, in the form of transgressive τόλμα destroying the equilibrium of a household. He dramatized what was new and only intuitively grasped ("cultural crisis") in the form which the tribal consciousness had always experienced the forces threatening its persistence. When social roles are confused and forbidden lines crossed and the rules that keep nature and culture separate are set aside, then it seems as though the whole frame of things is shaken and people cry in bewilderment, "Where shall I turn when the house is falling?" (*Agamemnon* 1532). Faced with the unfamiliar dangers confronting the Athens of his day, a society loosed from its moorings and moving very fast in a direction no one could foresee, Aeschylus turned instinctively to the old theme that, until modern times, has always come alive when the community feels itself threatened: The wild is moving back, chaos is invading a hard-won patch of cosmos. See to the walls.

2.

And yet what strikes us, as we look out from our man-centered world to the worlds of the old poets, is not the separation between man and nature but the closeness. As though the filial bond whose rupture Romantic poets were to lament at the beginning of the modern period had not yet been severed. Leopardi, addressing a girl who, in death, has become emblematic of the lost unity of being, says: "Your native land sees you no more. That window from which you used to speak is empty and reflects [only] the sad glitter of the stars" (*Le ricordanze,* lines 140–44). Sad, because the stars are now meaningless points of light. The heavens are as dead as the earth has become now that the blessed presence has withdrawn. For the watchman at the start of the *Agamemnon,* the stars that meet in their nightly assembly and bring round the seasons in unfailing sequence are the visible, living embodiments of the great world of nature whose beauty and regularity contrast so strongly with the strife-torn instability of the little world of man. For that is what nature provides. Not simply food, not simply raw material for the human artifice, but paradigms of order. It was the great teaching of the Homeric similes that man's ephemeral works and passions achieve such dignity and order as is granted them by being brought into the self-renewing, undying round of natural process.

What is the relation between this nature and nature as a source of violence from which the human artifice must be protected? There seems to be an abrupt contradiction here. We might hope to find some explanation in the fifth-century Sophistic distinction between φύσις, nature, and νόμος, the laws or conventions governing the community. The nature envisaged here is, however, almost exclusively *our* nature, that of the "natural man" whose instinctual demands are controlled (shackled, some said) by the accepted usages of society. The φύσις/νόμος distinction forms part of a political—or social or moral —debate and hardly reaches out beyond the world of man. More fruitful for our present purposes, I think, is the anthropologist's distinction I have been using between nature and culture which, as G. S. Kirk and some other scholars have seen, can be brought to bear on aspects of Greek experience.[9] For although this distinction was never formulated by Greeks, it finds expression in their mythology, most clearly in the stories they told about centaurs. Hybrids of one sort or another are found in the myths of many peoples. Greek myth has not only its centaurs, composite horse/man creatures, but its satyrs and silens, northern European folklore its spirits of the forest and wilderness, like the wodwos against which Sir Gawain fought in the Middle English poem and which Ted Hughes reimagined for us. What is curious about centaurs is that while they are treated as alien and hostile—shaggy beast-men (or simply beasts), Homer calls them with distaste—they are not just animals. At one time they were admitted into human households but showed a riotous penchant for women and wine and had to be violently expelled. In *Odyssey* 21 we hear about a centaur called Eurytion who visited Peirithoos, king of the Lapiths, on the occasion of his marriage and got very drunk. He was thrown out and had his ears and nose chopped off into the bargain. Stronger measures were apparently needed, for the *Iliad* knows of a campaign against centaurs in which a number of heroes, including the wise Nestor, took part. In some powerful lines in book 1 (lines 266–68) Nestor says of his companions: "They were the mightiest men on earth. The mightiest, they fought the mightiest, the beast-men who live in the hills, and terribly they destroyed them." In Sophocles' *Trachiniae* we are shown Heracles dying in agony from the poison smeared on his shirt by his wife, Deianeira, a poison given her years before by the centaur Nessos after he had tried to rape her. That is, a deadly gift received from a beast-man dying from the culture hero's poisoned arrow, a poison made from the blood of the Hydra, a monstrous water snake harking back to the early days. This "gift" from nature was introduced into the human realm by a woman who used it to destroy her husband. It looks as though the theme dramatized in the *Oresteia* was felt to be important enough to require further treatment.

While most centaurs were savage, lustful creatures against whose inroads culture had to be defended, there were however one or two centaurs, most notably Cheiron, who were wise and humane. Cheiron was the teacher of heroes, of Peleus and Jason and Asclepius and Achilles and Heracles himself, instructing them in morals and medicine and music and prophecy. Yet even Cheiron retained his hybrid aspect, and a detail in a story told by the late mythographer Apollodorus of another wise centaur, Pholos, suggests that his civilizing power depended on his retaining his basis in nature. Entertaining Heracles once, Pholos served the hero cooked meat while he himself ate it raw. Since horses and hence presumably centaurs are not carnivorous, this nonrealistic detail seems a way of emphasizing that, in Kirk's words, the centaurs "embody raw nature" (*Myth*, p. 161). And yet a benign centaur can teach humans the arts of culture. I don't know if it is permissible to try to interpret this contradiction in the light of a South American myth on the origin of fire related by Lévi-Strauss.[10] Remote as this material is from the Greek, it is possible to see similar concerns at work there, the more clearly since it has not been refashioned by poets. The problem faced in the South American myth is (I suppose) that of understanding how a destructive and sometimes terrifying natural power can take its place within the fragile artifice of culture. The flame that tears through the heavens and can lay waste a forest and burns me if I touch it is safely lodged amid our hearthstones, cooking our food and warming us when we are cold. How did this elemental natural force provide the means to create one of the central institutions of culture, the cooking of food?

Lévi-Strauss records six versions of the Indian myth. The first version (told by the Kayapo Indians of southern Brazil), supplemented by a few details from the others, will serve our present purposes. At a time when man did not know the use of fire and ate his food raw, a boy met a jaguar who took him home and offered him meat cooked on a fire. He also taught him other important cultural skills, the use of bow and arrows for hunting and the spinning of cotton. The jaguar took a liking to the boy and being childless decided to adopt him. His wife, however, who was human, did not welcome the newcomer. She scratched him and in one version held him in her paws [*sic*] and frightened him by her growls, even threatening to eat him. The boy ended up by killing her, apparently not to the jaguar's displeasure. In due course the boy returned to his village with some cooked meat, and the villagers resolved to help themselves to the jaguar's possessions (in one version turning into animals to do so) and came back from their raid with his fire, bow and arrows, and spun cotton. Disgusted by this ingratitude, the jaguar conceived a hatred for the human race and became purely animal. He no longer had his human wife and henceforth "only the reflection of fire shone in his eyes. He hunted with his fangs and ate his meat raw, having solemnly renounced grilled meat."

The features of this myth bearing on the Greek material I take to be the following: essential elements of culture came to man from a well-disposed member of an otherwise hostile and dangerous species belonging to nature. The jaguar is an animal, but he possesses skills that will later be recognized as characteristically human. He also has a human wife (to whom he is not closely attached) who is his exact opposite: human, with animal habits. That is, his natural or animal traits are preserved but transferred to his wife. The jaguar thus occupies an intermediate space between nature and culture, and this crucial theme is repeated in his adoption of the boy. Had the couple had children, these would presumably have been half human, half animal; the boy temporarily assumes this intermediate status and it is in this guise, as the human son of an animal, that he goes back to his village, which is still in a state of nature, with his cultural gift. The villagers, not to be outdone, by a most elegant reciprocity temporarily assume animal form themselves as they go from the village to carry out their cultural theft. The transaction completed, the jaguar assumes his natural state and the villagers reassume their human state. The transition from nature to culture has thus been achieved, by means of this subtly orchestrated process of give-and-take, and culture's differentiation from, and continued dependence on, nature firmly established. (Continued, because of course myth conveys not a past event but a present reality.)

The Greek stories are less bold and less elaborate. Here the cultural skills come not from a wild beast but from a creature already at least partly human in aspect. Nor is the process of give-and-take worked out so carefully; we find, for instance, no equivalent of the Kayapo transformation of human into natural in order to acquire nature's gifts for culture. The process itself is, however, similar and the same interests are at work, that of accommodating the paradox of man's differentiation from and dependence on nature. The centaur myths, too, emphasize the essential role of mediator with the wise Cheiron poised, like the jaguar, between the two realms, retaining his animal basis while imparting his civilizing skills. The explanation of the differences, admittedly considerable, is likely to be that the Greeks, certainly at the time when these stories took the form we know, were already far more securely entrenched in culture than the Indians who must maintain their precarious existence in the wilds of tropical America. The Greeks could even then cautiously assume some rights over nature and were thus content with a single mediator, whereas for the Indians, faced with a far more potent adversary, the transaction is correspondingly more hazardous and complicated.

The centaur myths, clarified by the South American material, may then do something to show how two apparently contradictory attitudes to nature complement each other and form part of a larger whole. If the *Oresteia* has (until near the end) more to say about nature's hostile aspects than of its bounty and the closeness of our commerce with it, this is because of Aeschylus's theme, which emphasizes

transgressive τόλμα introducing into the human realm a natural violence that there is unnatural. But of course the other attitude was part
of the thinking of his society and is indeed present in his own writing. It is found in his similes, where a curious interaction between natural and human has often been noted. In the typical Homeric simile
the two parts, vehicle and tenor, are more or less self-contained: just
as lions do something or other in their world, so do men in theirs.
Aeschylus prefers to let one part run into the other, blending (some
have said confusing) vehicle and tenor. In the long simile I have already referred to near the start of the *Agamemnon*, the two sons of
Atreus set out in pursuit of Helen like vultures robbed of their young.
The action of the vultures is described, and the poet continues:
"From on high some god . . . hears the shrill bird-cry of these resident
aliens and sends against the transgressors a late-avenging Erinys"
(lines 55–59). There are several things here which belong not to the
vultures (vehicle) but to the human world of the tenor. Resident alien
(μέτοικος) is an administrative term used of foreigners living in Athens.
("The birds . . . are μέτοικοι in the heavenly πόλις," Fraenkel explains.)
"Transgressors," to our ears at least, applies more to human offenders
like Paris than to wild animals, and the task of the Erinyes or Furies
in the trilogy is to punish human crime.[11] Again, "late-avenging" suits
"the punishment of Paris, delayed ten years, but not . . . the matter to
which it is applied—requital for the vultures."[12] A more striking case
of interaction is found in the parable of the lion cub where Aeschylus devotes eighteen lines to the animal's career, presenting it in
purely natural terms except for one significant detail: "It made a *feast*
unbidden" (line 731). In the powerful final couplet he then moves
into the cultural realm of morals or theology as the lion becomes a
priest of ruin.

The most complex example of this interaction is found in the
speech Clytemnestra makes as she watches Agamemnon walk slowly
across the tapestries to his death in the palace. Hailing his return
from Troy, she says:

> If the root lives the leaves come home, stretching their shade against the
> Dog Star's heat. You, back to home and hearth, signal warmth coming in
> winter. And when Zeus makes wine from the bitter grape, then at once
> there is coolness in the house as the lord and master moves within.
>
> (*Agamemnon* 966–73)

Behind this comparison of Agamemnon's homecoming to a vine
spreading its leaves over the roof is the ancient, widespread identifi-
cation of the lord of house and the welfare of the house. What has

dislocated the figure (and perhaps, though not necessarily, disturbed the text—Aeschylus may simply be forcing language to his purposes) is the dramatic intensity of the lines, the enormous joy that blazes just beneath Clytemnestra's words as she sees her long-laid plans for vengeance at the point of fulfillment. "The comparison and the thing compared mix together," A. W. Verrall noted in his late nineteenth-century commentary. The vehicle (living root) is stated but is at once given tenor language—men come home, not leaves. Back to vehicle with the vine-shade, then the tenor breaks in again with Agamemnon, who however signals not his return (tenor) but warmth in winter (vehicle). The beacon also signaled his return—not a message of much warmth for the household. The second lobe of the vehicle, coolness in summer, is then inserted between a clause properly belonging to it ("when Zeus makes wine"—in midsummer) and a tenor clause ("as the lord . . .").[13]

The passage has caused scholars considerable discomfort and some, like Wilamowitz, have even rewritten bits of it into their notion of sense. What troubles them is the apparently chaotic way Aeschylus fluctuates between human and natural, hardly seeming to distinguish them. The same failure to distinguish—or ability to connect—is however found in other passages of Greek poetry which, lacking the deliberate dramatic ambiguity of Clytemnestra's words, have not been found difficult, though perhaps they should have been. In the *Odyssey*, for instance, we hear of "a god-fearing king who upholds right and the dark earth bears wheat and barley, trees are heavy with fruit, ewes drop their young without stint, the sea grants fish and under his good rule the people prosper" (19.111–14). Homer can take it for granted—his paratactic style effortlessly enforcing the connections while seeming to ignore them—that there is a direct causal relation between human virtue and natural fertility. So can Hesiod: "For those who give straight judgments to strangers and citizens and stick to right, their city flourishes and the people flower"—and once again we hear that nature yields her richest bounty (*Works and Days* 225ff.). The same causal relation is working in Sophocles' Thebes, where, thanks to Oedipus's (unwitting) transgression, all nature is sick: the earth cannot bear fruit, women are barren.

In his commentary on Hesiod, M. L. West notes that the metaphors of flourishing city and flowering people happen not to be found in Homer. Is it quite certain, though, that Hesiod is being metaphorical? What if he thinks in terms of larger unity embracing man and nature? Metaphor, like simile and other uses of language we call figurative, seeks to span a rift that has opened up in experience between different kinds of reality, in the modern period mainly between the scientific and imaginative kinds. The rift between man and nature is more fundamental, the most momentous of all our great divides. Aeschylus, who still stands on the other side, can assume a reciprocity between man and nature—"this very primitive conception," a classical scholar calls it[14]—that is grounded in the archaic sense of the unity of being. What this involves is very clearly stated by Norman Austin, though he does not use the actual term, in his book on the *Odyssey*: "The animal world and the human, the physical and the spiritual, the organic and the social, the contemporary and the historical, are all part of a single unity and any fragment from one sphere can act as a paradigm both for its own sphere and for any other sphere."[15]

The unity at work in Aeschylus's similes, as in a more straightforward way in Homer's, is shown no less forcibly in the use which both poets make of omens. An omen, as similes often are, is usually an event in nature which illuminates some aspect of the human world. Unlike the simile (the Homeric simile, at least) the omen may be prophetic; it also conveys a message to man and tells him how he must act. Omens are plentiful in both Homeric poems, but they play a larger role in the *Odyssey*, where they consist of a striking and on occasion deviant (unnatural) event in nature pointing to a deviation in culture, which must be corrected. Some are of considerable complexity, like the double omen sent by Zeus at Odysseus's request, composed of a seemingly chance human utterance and thunder rumbling portentously from a clear sky (20.98–121). No Homeric omen, however, is so puzzling, even baffling, as the one which Aeschylus presents in the *parodos* or introductory song of the *Agamemnon*. But first we need to take a few steps back in the story.

The trouble in the house of Atreus began, for Aeschylus's purposes anyway, in the previous generation. Thyestes, the father of Clytemnestra's lover and accomplice, Aegisthus, seduced the wife of his brother Atreus, the father of Agamemnon and Menelaus. Atreus in return killed Thyestes' children and served them to him in a meal. These two crimes had no further consequences until the next generation when a crime was committed against the family from outside. Paris, a visitor to the house of Agamemnon and Menelaus (here represented as living under the same roof), seduced Menelaus's wife, Helen, and took her off to Troy. The external offence—we may note that it repeats in part the first, internal offence—might have united both branches of the family and put an end to the danger of further feuding, had not something very unfortunate occurred as the Atreidae were about to set sail in pursuit of Helen. Two eagles appeared and seized and devoured a pregnant hare with all its young. This was instantly recognized as an omen, a favorable one since the eagles appeared on the

right-hand side, and an important one, since eagles are the minis-
trants of Zeus: Zeus who sanctioned the punitive expedition against
Troy. The prophet Calchas interpreted the eagles, "the warlike feast-
ers on the hare," as the two Atreidae, and the hare and its unborn offspring as Troy and its inhabitants. He also saw that the omen carried
the possibility of grave trouble, since "pure Artemis [protectress of
young wild creatures] out of pity is angry with the winged hounds of
the father, sacrificing a hare with all its young before it gives birth.
She hates the eagles' banquet" (*Agamemnon* 134–38). He went on to
pray that the goddess might not bring about "another sacrifice, one
against law and usage, accompanied by no feast" (ἄδαιτον, from δαίς,
"feast," often "sacrificial feast"). The prophet's fears quickly proved
well-founded, for the fleet was confined to harbor by adverse winds,
and he revealed that Artemis would grant them good sailing weather
only if Agamemnon sacrificed his daughter Iphigeneia. In agony of
spirit he brought himself to do so.

Probably no passage in Greek poetry has caused such critical dis-
array. The only reason given for Artemis's anger is that two eagles
devoured a pregnant hare. This, we are plainly told, is what induces
her to punish Agamemnon by forcing him—should we say?—to commit an atrocious crime. The difficulty may seem to vanish if we pass
at once from the portent to what it portends, the sack of Troy, and
say that this is what angers the goddess, since in the *Iliad* she is on the
Trojan side. But although the poet may for his purposes make passing use of her old pro-Trojan sympathies, they have no bearing on
his theme, and some critics have understandably looked for a profounder explanation. The pitiful goddess, they maintain, revolted by
the prospect of the destruction of a great city and the slaughter of
its innocent inhabitants, punishes the man guilty of such cruelty.
But Agamemnon has not even sailed for Troy, and what senseless injustice is it that demands punishment for an offence not yet committed? The difficulty is compounded by the fact that myth provided
an adequate if to our minds trivial occasion for the goddess's anger:
Agamemnon had offended her by boastfully killing one of her deer.
Aeschylus, however, ignores this convenient tale, and we are certainly
not to assume that he means us to understand it. Alternatively, he
could have made matters clear by invoking the theory of inherited
guilt: the son is being punished for the sins of the father. This doctrine was in the culture and is stated briefly near the end of the *Eumenides* (lines 934–37). We may find that it is at work here too, but if
so, Aeschylus for some reason goes out of his way to say nothing about
it at this stage. We do not hear about Atreus's crime until much later
in the play. The fact is that Aeschylus is disappointingly uninterested

in something we very much want to know: Did Agamemnon do what he did of his own free will or was he compelled, "predestined," to kill his daughter? The poet devotes only an equivocal sentence to the matter. Agamemnon, he says, "put on the yoke-strap of necessity" (*Agamemnon* 218). He who *puts on* the yoke of necessity, explains one school of interpreters, might have declined to do so. Yes, replies the other, but what he put on was the yoke of *necessity*. The use of this word (ἀνάγκη) makes it clear that he had no freedom of choice.[16]

We need first to try to see the situation as Aeschylus saw it. (First. Not abandoning our own cultural position but letting the Greek position interact with and challenge ours, so that in time we may reach common ground.) Beyond all doubt he is much concerned with guilt and retribution, but it may be that our way of concentrating on the moral responsibility of Agamemnon and even on the justice or injustice of heaven does not raise the kinds of question the poet is disposed to answer. He is more interested in the act than the actor. Like a stone dropped into a pool, transgressive action—whether or not "voluntary"—sets up a disturbance within the psychic community of the family or group that will widen and give rise to further disturbances unless corrected. This is where the poet's main attention goes; his eye is fastened on the dreadful autonomy of the self-reproducing event. Our perspective, burdened by its inherited Christian preoccupation with personal guilt and the more recent humanist obsession with the inner world of the individual, blinds us to what really matters for Aeschylus's kind of thinking: the maintenance of the human realm against the forces that threaten it. Certainly the offender must be punished, *because*—Jones gets the emphasis right—"the punishment of the wicked is the restoring of the shattered norm" (*On Aristotle and Greek Tragedy*, p. 121 n. 3).

And the stone dropped into the pool may send its ripples further, outside the family and the human world and into the world of nature—that is, into a region where our concept of justice does not hold. We saw how in the *Odyssey* something untoward in the heavens like Zeus thundering from a clear sky pointed to something rotten in the state of Ithaca. To see the relation pointing *only* in this direction, from nature to man, is however to yield to our ingrained anthropocentric bias. For a society possessing the sense of the unity of being the relation would point equally in the other direction: human deviation or crime may act out into the greater world of nature and cause a disturbance there. This is shown very clearly in the Aeschylean omen. I am not thinking so much of the fact that for two eagles to feed on a single victim is, the authorities tell us, "utterly untrue to nature" (Fraenkel produces this useful piece of information), but of the way the eagles' action is described in human terms—they *sacrifice* the hare and *banquet* on it—and colored with our sense of pity for the new life destroyed in the womb. (The same confusion occurs in reverse when Clytemnestra's actions are described in animal terms.) And more than this. Deviation in nature should call for the correction of human deviation. In the *Agamemnon*, however, the deviant natural event shown in the omen points to an action that will immeasurably worsen the human situation. We may have gone astray in our attempt to understand this passage by concentrating too much on the plight of the characters; what we were shown, after all, was something happening "out there," in the animal world. Preoccupied with our questions about guilt and justice, we fail to do what the poet does—mark first the violation of the laws of nature and *then* ask what transgression against the laws of culture can have occasioned it.

We need to look more closely at the poet's—or the prophet's—difficult words. Calchas has just stated that Artemis is angered by the eagles' sacrificial banquet. He goes on (lines 140–44):

> Although she is so kindly to the young of all wild creatures, she asks that the ξύμβολα, favorable and yet inauspicious, of these things be fulfilled.

"These things" refers to the event we have just witnessed, the killing of the hare. *Sumbola* (ξύμβολα) are literally the matching halves of any objects; break a stick and the two parts will be the *sumbola* of each other. The word can simply mean sign or token, as in the watchman's speech where the beacon is the prearranged *sumbolon* announcing the fall of Troy. It can also be used of that special kind of sign, an omen. Clearly it has that meaning here, but nothing prevents it from bearing its literal meaning as well: the two parts of the omen, the event in nature and what it portends in the human sphere, are the *sumbola* of each other. The word thus provides Aeschylus with an exact and economical way of expressing the theory of reciprocity. The *sumbolon* of the eagles' kill must then, since the prophet calls it favorable, be the destruction of Troy, and the meaning of the lines must be that the goddess, though angered by the fate that awaits her city, bows to the will of Zeus and asks that the expedition go ahead as planned.

But if so, why is there the danger that she may bring about a second more terrible sacrifice? It is this danger that makes Calchas call the omen inauspicious (a deliberately vague term, literally "not faultless"). We are forced to look at his words, riddling as prophetic utterance is, once again. For the Greek allows and perhaps prefers another rendering:

Since she is so kindly . . .

The referent of "these things" is the same but their *sumbolon* has changed. *Since* the goddess cares for the young of wild creatures, she is angered by the "sacrifice" of the hare and its unborn young and, desiring that the offenders be punished, asks that the *sumbola* of these things be fulfilled. The matching equivalent of the eagles' banquet is now no longer the sack of Troy but the "other sacrifice" which the prophet goes on fearfully to foresee, a lawless one accompanied by no feast. In plainer words, the sacrifice of Iphigeneia.

Has this thrown any light on the problem we set out from, the baffling fact that Artemis is angry with Agamemnon because . . . two eagles devour a hare? A possible source of confusion is removed if we keep in mind that the goddess is not to be thought of as a power outside nature. She is part of, in some sense *is*, offended nature itself, nature whose otherwise orderly course has been disrupted, contaminated, by grave disorder in the human realm. Put it this way, press the question I raised: What transgression against the laws of culture has occasioned this violation of the laws of nature? and we can now safely answer: Crimes committed a generation ago.[17] For the gods can bide their time and nature's world is timeless. Atreus's murder of his brother's children and the act, violating every conceivable social norm, of serving them to him in a meal have spilled over into nature and produced their *sumbolon* or matching equivalent there, the eagles' unnatural sacrificial banquet. This in turn is about to act back into culture as Agamemnon prepares to commit his unnatural crime, treating his daughter as a sacrificial animal, bidding the attendants to hold her over the altar "like a goat" (232) while her throat is cut. Commentators have wondered why Aeschylus introduces into this terrible scene something that seems needlessly to conflict with social usage, the ornately beautiful description of how Iphigeneia used to be present at her father's table and sing the chant that accompanied the libation. "It is unheard of in Attic society that the daughter of the house should join the company of men at table in the [dining hall]," Denniston and Page protest. The explanation must surely be that Agamemnon's supremely transgressive act (παντότολμον), the first in the chain of crimes within the trilogy itself, thematically the overriding of the distinction between the human and the natural realm, has to be firmly associated with feasting, with *eating*, the primal offence. Agamemnon's crime sets in motion Clytemnestra's, with its spreading confusions between the two realms, and throughout the first of the three plays the poet keeps stressing the motif of unnatural or monstrous eating. The lion makes a feast in the house where he is so rashly brought;

Cassandra in her trance sees children "bewailing their murder and the roasted flesh their father ate . . . holding their own meat for food" (lines 1096f., 1220); Clytemnestra, in the state of daemonic possession which takes hold of her after she has murdered her husband, feels that she has actually become the fiend that haunts the house, "the ancient savage Spirit exacting vengeance on Atreus, that cruel banqueter" (lines 1501f.); and finally Aegisthus tells how Atreus played host to his father, serving him a "feast (δαίς) of his children's flesh . . . food that was ruinous to the race" (lines 1593, 1597).

We may and indeed must still ask why, if Atreus's old crime is to be understood as the prime mover at its deadly work behind the omen, did the poet fail to tell us so? Why, to put it with Denniston and Page, instead of tracing the criminal sacrifice of Iphigeneia "back to the mortal's offence against divinity, or otherwise linking it to the destiny of the house of Atreus," does he present it as due to Artemis's anger against a pair of eagles? Once more, it seems to me, the answer is forthcoming if we get our question right. What concerns the poet is transgression itself, and at this crucial initial stage of his drama he will let nothing, no mention of individual guilt, obscure it. We are to be shown transgression, now out of control, moving like cancer cells across the boundaries separating nature from culture and destroying all the carefully drawn rules governing their interplay. Our queries about Agamemnon's freedom of action or about the justice of the gods' treatment of him are beside the poet's point. The situation is one not so much of moral or theological as of biological chaos in which all distinctions between different forms of life, human and animal, are overthrown and the larger unity embracing both has been shaken—has become, it may be, no longer a source of strength and assurance but a deadly trap from which there seems to be no escape. In our concentration on the plight of the individual victims—dreadful though it is, and Aeschylus, great dramatist that he is, does not play down their anguish—we lose sight of what in his eyes is far more dreadful: the threat against the stability of the human realm, in the largest terms the danger that a hard-won patch of cosmos may be swallowed up by chaos.

It was a profound instinct that led Aeschylus to choose the Atreid banquet as the primal transgression whose horror reverberates throughout the first great act of his trilogy, subverting one after the other all the norms by which culture maintains itself. Since we continue to find cannibalism horrifying, the motif still works but (once again) not quite in the way Aeschylus intended. We see the eating of the children as a barbaric outrage, as he did, but not or not so clearly as the transgressive destruction of a central institution of culture. One of our most beautiful human achievements has been to transform the ingestion of food, a simple biological necessity imposed on us as on all other animals by nature, into cultural ceremony, from the homely family dinner to the high formality of the banquet. Greek piety attributed a special sanctity to the meal, which "knits the partakers together in a sacred community," and a poet can speak of "the great oath by table and salt."[18] Lévi-Strauss has shown the social conventions governing the kinds of food and methods of cooking that fit each occasion, the clothes that must be worn, the rites to be observed—but of course the poets have always known this. The feast is a great Shakespearian theme and a no less great Homeric theme. The *Odyssey*, a poem that ends with the restoration of order in a household, begins (as *Paradise Lost* also does) with transgressive eating: the criminal folly of Odysseus's crew in devouring the cattle of the Sun, the suitors' lawless conduct in his own dining hall. The *Iliad* begins with an anger that made men's bodies the prey of wild beasts, reaches down to encompass the animal horror of Achilles' threat to hack off the flesh of his enemy and devour it raw, and ends with a ceremonial banquet in the palace of King Priam, the last of a series of measures by means of which a high civilization takes the shock of nature's supreme assault against culture, death. No less a theme, primitive enough to call up the oldest memories and fears in the tribal consciousness and yet far-reaching enough to involve the very continuance of life, could serve to carry Aeschylus's sense of the dangers threatening the Athens of his day.

3.

After Calchas has spoken of the other sacrifice which Artemis may demand, the tone becomes increasingly somber with huge dactylic lines full of abstract-looking words moving slowly across the page like thunderclouds ready to settle on any horror past or future. He describes the sacrifice as an inbred maker of strife, one that fears no man (or no husband). Anger remains, he says, and—as the sentence used to be taken—the noun is qualified by no less than six adjectives. It is a fearful anger, that rises up again; home-keeping, treacherous; an anger that remembers, and is child- (or children-) avenging. Then abruptly, magnificently, Aeschylus changes his tune to brave trochaics and from this tangle of foreboding makes a direct, vertical appeal to Zeus:

Zeus, whoever he be, if this name is dear to him, by this name I call him. There is nothing I can compare as I weigh all things in the balance—only Zeus, if I am truly to shake off from my mind the vain burden of care.

(lines 160–66)

The poet goes on to speak of Zeus's predecessors—Ouranos, deposed (castrated, according to Hesiod's account) by his son Kronos, whom Zeus in turn overthrew. The savage old cosmogony does not trouble the religious consciousness, which sees in it confirmation of the high god's supremacy. They have gone, Zeus remains, and "he who cries *Zeus is victor!* hits the mark of wisdom square." It is Zeus

who puts men on the road to wisdom by establishing this for certain law, that they must learn through suffering. In sleep falls drop by drop before the heart the aching memory of pain and even against men's will true wisdom (σωφρονεῖν) comes—a harsh and gracious favor granted us somehow, surely, by the gods on their high helmsman's bench.

(lines 174–83)

An unfortunate controversy has arisen in the profession as to whether passages of this sort constitute advanced thinking.[19] What, it is asked, does the celebrated doctrine of learning by suffering (πάθει μάθος) amount to? Surely no more than that you must pay for your sins. Well, yes. It may be agreed that Aeschylus's thinking here is no more advanced and no less than Dante's when, in a comparable agony of spirit, he turns to his supreme god and cries, *O sommo Giove / che fosti in terra per noi crucifisso, / son li giusti occhi tuoi rivolti altrove?* (*Purgatorio* 6.118–20, and the great lines that follow). There is poet's thinking, of course, and philosopher's, and perhaps some distinctions should be drawn. As to the question about πάθει μάθος, must not the response be that, while the characters in the play do not learn anything (a case might just be contrived for Orestes), the work as a whole has its lesson for those capable of experiencing it? In the central ode of the *Eumenides* the Furies, whom we had taken simply as incarnate spirits of vengeance, deliver a great hymn to cosmic justice and affirm that it is good for men to "learn wisdom (σωφρονεῖν) under pressure" (line 521). In the final ode of that play, addressing the assembled citizens of Athens, they promise (in George Thomson's translation):

Joy to all the people, blest
With the Virgin's love, who sits
Next beside her Father's throne.
Wisdom (σωφρονοῦντες) ye have learned at last.

(*Eumenides* 997–1000)

The meaning of πάθει μάθος, E. R. Dodds writes, is "no longer illustrated in the life history of individuals but writ large in the destiny of a whole people and ushering in a new age of understanding."[20] The traditional reading of the *Oresteia*, as scholars like Dodds and Herington have rephrased and refined it, seems to me substantially correct, in this sense: that it accurately describes what Aeschylus set out to do. His purpose was to show how a chain of crimes can be broken, harmony wrested out of discord, and the threatened cosmos reknit, with Zeus emerging from chaos as the final arbiter. How far Aeschylus can be said to advance a new conception of Zeus I do not know. Certainly the structure he struggles so mightily to hold together admits elements of the new; he was conscious of the profound changes coming over his society. The structure itself, however, was a very ancient one, and the question is how far it could still be held together.

The prayer to Zeus breaks sharply into the chorus's agonizing fears for the future and from the past. When it is over, the poet returns to the story, telling how the fleet was detained in port and Agamemnon sacrificed his daughter. The reason for the appeal to Zeus at this point is I think not that since he sent the omen only he can avert the event it points to. The chorus do not ask Zeus to intervene in the action. Rather, they speak of him as in some sense the answer to things; he can lift from our shoulders the burden of care and put us on the way to understanding. If the poet runs from μαντική, the interpretation of omens, to what can properly be called theology, it is because something has gone fearfully wrong with the whole system of relationships of which omens are a part. The prayer to Zeus is Aeschylus's way of breaking out of a situation that has come to seem intolerable. In an earlier play, the *Persians*, the queen sees a hawk attacking an eagle (lines 205ff.). This is a sign that Persia's overweening presumption has angered heaven and is to be punished by the defeat of her expedition at the hands of diminutive Greece. The deviant natural event points to an action that will affirm the just and orderly governance of the universe. In the *Agamemnon*, we found, the deviant event in nature points not to the restoration of human order but to still worse deviation or disorder: father murdering daughter and, as the chorus dimly foresee, some fresh retaliatory crime in the household.

So the poet turns away from omens and appeals directly to Zeus, not because Zeus is in any sense outside nature but in the hope that he alone may be powerful enough to hold things together and provide some new principle of unity and meaning. The possibility that Zeus, working through his daughter Athena, may be able to fulfill this hope does not emerge fully till near the end of the trilogy, but there is a passage in the *Choephoroe* which throws some light on the matter.

It is spoken by Orestes, who, as a character, is immersed in the action and hence lacks the chorus's power to see beyond it. What he expresses is not hope of a new unity but fear that the old unity may be lost.

Orestes has returned to Argos and revealed his identity to Electra and the loyal women of the chorus. In a moving little speech Electra tells him that he is all the family that is left her and must stand in lieu of murdered father, mother now justly hated, cruelly sacrificed sister. The burden of restoring the house rests solely with him: "Only let power and justice be on your side," she ends, "and Zeus, greatest of all." Orestes takes up her prayer and appeals to Zeus:

> Behold the orphaned brood of the eagle father who died in the meshed coils of the dread viper! . . . If you let the young of such a father perish, one who honored you greatly with sacrifices, from what hands will you receive feasts so lavish? Let the eagle's brood die and you will be unable to send men signs they can believe in.
>
> (*Choephoroe* 244–59)

Unless you help Agamemnon's children, Orestes says, you will not be able to send any more omens. A step in the argument seems to be missing. It was not Agamemnon who conveyed Zeus's omens; he uses eagles for that purpose. There is an implied simile here: Agamemnon is or was *like* an eagle, we would have to put it, but for Orestes, still thinking within the old unity, there is a real sense in which the king *is* an eagle. The danger which his words envisage is that this unity may be failing and that nature may cease to be what it has always been, a forest of signs, and become meaningless. Where once the eagles brought clear indication of god's purpose, men will look up and see only birds screeching overhead, as Oedipus will say.

"Raise the fallen house to greatness," Orestes ends (lines 262–63), and less than fifty lines later the *kommos* or choral lamentation is under way, an intricate musico-dramatic composition scored for three voices and designed to restore the shattered fabric of the house of Atreus by enlisting for the avengers the powers of the dead king. Merely read, these are among the mightiest pages in literature. The effect of full performance, with the words bodied forth in chant and dance, one hardly dares imagine. Yet the unaided words are potent enough to make us experience, to the fullest we are capable of, the archaic unity of being for which living and dead form part of a single community. The great antinomies meet head-on as the living son and daughter appeal from the world of light above to their murdered father in the dark world below. Slowly the enearthed presence gathers strength from the passionate need of his descendents until the chorus leader can cry, "They have helpers underground" (lines 476–77). The prayer has worked, the old bond still holds, and Orestes can now complete his task and—murder his mother. By a massive structural irony the effect of the *kommos*, designed to repair the fortunes of the house, is to plunge it in even deeper ruin. Once again the poet has shown that the unity which was once a source of strength and assurance has become a deadly trap.

The received view of the *Eumenides*—that it achieves a reconciliation of discordant elements—finds support in the dramatic structure which itself enacts reconciliation. Early in the play Apollo, finding the Furies in his temple, violently dismisses them, but in the long central trial scene, though still alien presences they are admitted into the city and are willing to accept its legal institutions. Finally, won over by Athena's persuasions, Furies no longer but Eumenides, Kindly Ones, they are led in a blaze of light to their new home below the Acropolis, dressed (textually uncertain but dramatically surely probable) in crimson robes. The metaphorical net which entrapped Troy and so often expressed the characters' entanglement in their fate, the purple tapestries across which Agamemnon walked to his death in the palace, the robes which Clytemnestra wound round him in the bath and which, in her speech after the murder, become the metaphorical net of ruin she fenced about him—become in the next play, as Orestes holds them up, once again the bloodstained robes in which his father died: all these stage properties (properties dissolving into symbolic images, images embodied in concrete objects) appear before us for the last time as the crimson robes which signal the goddesses' new status as honored foreign residents in Athens.

One way of putting it is to say that Aeschylus imposes the idea of reconciliation on us by showing just how much there was to reconcile, so that *unless* he brought off some grand final resolution his dramatic structure would have collapsed before our eyes and the trilogy ended in chaos. He seems to reach out for all the conflicting or antithetical elements he can lay his hands on, using every oddity or violence of language and stagecraft, intensifying the discords of the two earlier plays and opposing them schematically against each other. Take the presentation of the Furies. To bring them on stage at all was I suppose sufficiently bold and must have created interesting problems for the poet-producer, first of all the question of what they *looked like*. (Like something out of a story by M. R. James would presumably be the quick answer.) A more prudent dramatist, intending to transform them eventually into Kindly Ones, would have begun by playing down their unprepossessing aspects. Aeschylus goes the other way about it, stressing the most repulsive features of their appearance for all he is worth. The play opens in the Greek holy of holies, Apollo's temple at Delphi, with a speech by the priestess, thirty-three slow, solemn, liturgical lines. Then Aeschylus lets off his first bomb. The old woman goes into the shrine, leaving the stage empty for a few moments (an unusual, even unique occurrence in Greek tragedy).[21] She comes out crawling on all fours babbling of horrors she has seen inside—a bloodstained man clasping the sacred navel-stone, around him a troop of sleeping . . . women? No, more like Gorgons. Or perhaps Harpies? No, not quite Harpies either, but anyway indescribably dreadful. Enter Apollo seemingly in conversation with Orestes (characters in tragedy do not normally come on stage in this informal fashion, least of all gods), promises him his support and tells him to go to Athens to seek the help of Athena. He refers to the sleeping Furies with loathing. Exit Apollo and Orestes after thirty lines.

This remarkable little scene, or pair of scenes, serves two purposes. It introduces the play's central opposition between the Olympian gods and the Furies, and it prepares for the resolution of one of the trilogy's pervasive conflicts or discords by restating it in a new key. A major theme of the *Agamemnon* was the introduction of the wild into the human realm which I discussed in terms of the culture/nature polarity. Doctrinally, this polarity has little bearing on the Furies, who can operate in both realms (see note 11). Visually, however, and dramatically, we are made to feel that it has everything to do with them since they are constantly described in animal imagery, bestial presences that, thanks to Orestes' transgressive act, have invaded the human realm. The first thing we learn is that they have lodged themselves in (of all places) Apollo's temple. Begone, the god tells them, the proper place for you is the den of a bloodthirsty lion (lines 193f.)—a creature we have heard a good deal about. And they are imagined in other forms, as hounds and snakes and what Malory would call less-natural beasts. The change begins when they encounter Athena in Athens just before the trial. She sees them hunched round Orestes and remarks that they don't look like gods or like mortals, adding politely that it is not right for neighbors to speak ill of someone for being unsightly (lines 413f., keeping the reading of the manuscripts). After this tactful remark nothing more is said about their appearance. For the duration of the trial they are accepted within the human community, and the question arises: What is to be done with them? To drive them away, as Apollo wants, would be too dangerous, but they cannot simply be left there, since, as Aristotle will say, there is no place in the city for either animals or gods. Athena comes up with a very clever solution. They are to remain as honored, fearful presences, neither in the land nor outside it but *under* it, in a cave on the slope below the Acropolis where, in a great reconciling image, they are conducted at the end of play. It is Aeschylus's last word on the problem of domesticating the irreducibly alien.

The conflict, however, is too profound to be settled by even the grandest dramatic image, and the relation of the wild to the human realm is only one of the trilogy's themes, even if for my purposes I gave it special emphasis. We need to return to the early scene as Apollo and Orestes leave the stage and the ghost of Clytemnestra appears (rising from some kind of pit, as though from the underworld?) and addresses the Furies, still probably offstage and represented by "blood-curdling noises" (Taplin, *Stagecraft*, p. 371). She delivers herself of a remarkable opening line—"Sleep, would you . . . oiee! What do I need with sleepers?" (line 94)—and pointing to her wounded breast succeeds in rousing them to frenzied activity. Briefly but unforgettably the poet has brought before us the figure in whose name they are to make their supreme case, the figure of the murdered mother. This may be the point when the chorus finally enters. Aeschylus, who seems also to have been a great choreographer, brought them on not in the usual orderly fashion but "scatteredly," the ancient biography of the poet says—in ones and twos, darting here and there, searching, sniffing, for Orestes and yelping disjointed encouragement to each other in the wildest of Greek meters. Exit Clytemnestra, by whatever means, enter Apollo again, and there is a short exchange leading to total deadlock. Briefly:

FURIES	You told Orestes to kill his mother?
APOLLO	To avenge his father, yes.
FURIES	We punish those who kill their mothers.
APOLLO	What about a woman who kills her husband?
FURIES	That does not involve the shedding of kindred blood.
APOLLO	Does marriage mean nothing to you?
FURIES	We shall never let this man go.
APOLLO	I shall not desert him.

Setting up the central opposition of the final play in this fashion, Aeschylus goes on to make it expressive of some of the most potent antinomies of experience. As the language ceaselessly insists, the Furies are old powers belonging to the darkness of the world below, whereas the Olympians are new or young gods whose home is in the brilliance of the upper air. The opposition between old and new is stressed particularly hard. The Furies are "the mind of the past" (παλαιόφρονα, line 838, Lattimore's translation); three times they complain that the new gods have "ridden roughshod" over them (lines 150, 731, 778f.); twice during the trial Athena has to assure them that a youthful deity like herself respects their venerable antiquity (lines 848f., 881f.).

The conflict between male and female, which may seem to bring the trilogy within welcome reach of current debate but in fact reveals the most archaic level of Aeschylus's thinking, is no less central. The crimes of the first two plays were committed by members of one sex against the other: a father killed his daughter, a wife her husband, a son his mother. The question at issue in the trial is whether the murder of the male or the female is the graver offence. The female case is represented by the Furies behind whom stand the Moirai or Apportioners, conceived as female in nature. The male side is represented by the children of Zeus, Apollo and more effectively Athena, whose ambiguous sexual status, female but sprung directly from Zeus without female intervention and favoring the male in all save marriage (lines 736ff.), allows Aeschylus to reach for his final solution. Where Apollo rejected the Furies outright, Athena the mediator, mistress of the arts of persuasion, comes to terms with them and when, after the verdict of the trial has gone against them and cleared Orestes, they threaten to visit the Athenian land and people with pestilence, it is her patient persistence that brings them round. She induces them to change their curses into blessings and promise their future hosts an inclusive well-being in which the fertility of the earth and all life on it will be combined with political stability and hard-won wisdom. With this great transformation, the penultimate line of the trilogy can announce that Zeus and the Moirai have come together.[22]

We seem here to find confirmation of the standard reading of the *Eumenides,* which runs something like this: Two conflicting conceptions of justice (perhaps we had better say δίκη) have met and been reconciled. The "goddesses of revenge" have been won over by Athena, and the savage old rule of "blind retribution" and family vendetta has been elevated to a concept of "Justice, rooted in holiness, governed by reason."[23] The old powers are not, however, excluded or denied, for it is only with their collaboration that the new foundation can arise. There are I believe solid objections to such a reading, but first we should listen to the poet *showing* us reconciliation at work. Through the words of the Furies' final song of blessing, all that remains of a greater whole, there breathes a note of solemn and yet festive joy as of a Bach chorale. Translation can only be a broken reed here, but George Thomson has done better than anyone else, and I draw gratefully on his version.[24] "What song shall I chant over the land?" the leader of the Furies, or Eumenides as they are becoming, asks, and Athena answers in words that have something of Cordelia's appeal to the "unpublish'd Vertues of the earth" (*Lear*, act 4, scene 4):

A song of faultless victory: from earth and sea,
From skies above may gentle breezes blow,
And, breathing sunshine, float from shore to shore;
That corn and cattle may continually
Increase and multiply, and that no harm
Befall the offspring of humanity.

(lines 903–9)

And then they begin their song, praying that "the sun's brilliance
may make all that prospers life burgeon from the earth in a rushing
stream" (lines 924–26). They continue:

Ne'er may foul winds be stirred to touch with blight
Budding tree—a grace from me;
Ne'er may parching droughts that blind the newly
Parted blossom trespass here;
Ne'er may blasts of noisome plague advance across the fields;
Rather, Pan in season due
Grant that flocks and herds may yield
A twin increase of yearly wealth.

(lines 938–46)

They pray that the madness of civil strife may never arise in the city,
and then, the note of joy swelling and growing deeper-toned, come
the verses I have already quoted in part:

Joy to you, joy of your justly appointed riches,
Joy to all the people, blest
With the Virgin's love, who sits
Next beside her Father's throne.
Wisdom ye have learned at last.
Folded under Pallas' wing,
Yours at last the grace of Zeus.

(lines 996–1002)

And now they put on their crimson robes (surely) as the torch-lit pro-
cession forms to escort them to their chamber underground and the
final Benedicite resounds:

Peace to you, peace of a happy communion,
People of Pallas. Zeus who beholdeth
All with the Fates is at last reconciled.
        O sing at the end Alleluia!

(lines 1044–47)

The Greek sound represented by Thomson's Alleluia is *ololū*, first heard at the start of the trilogy as Clytemnestra is bidden to raise her cry of triumph to salute Agamemnon's homecoming and in sinister contexts intermittently throughout the first two plays. One final reconciliation.

In the face of this (readers without Greek must replace the translated words with the best poetry they can imagine) it is hard to deny that Aeschylus has done what he set out to do and brought off a grand reconciliation. Hard, and perhaps illicit? Is it proper to require of a dramatic poem the sort of demonstration we look for in a treatise? But Aeschylus's poetry does not need to be indulged, and with a work of this order we not only may but should ask what exactly it is that has been reconciled. The old rule of vendetta and the new covenant based on justice, we are told. Once again we must listen to the text. Immediately after the Furies hold their first conversation with Athena, during which she inquires about their complaint against Orestes and promises to establish a new court of law to look into the rights and wrongs of the matter, they come out with a magnificent hymn to cosmic justice, painting a picture of the chaos into which society will fall if the matricide is allowed to go free (lines 490–565). In accents that to some have suggested an Old Testament prophet, they tell how every man's hand will be turned against every other, neighbor helplessly learn of calamities befallen neighbor, and parents struck down by their children cry in vain for redress. Fear, fear of punishment that follows wrongdoing, must have its place in men's minds, they say (Athena will repeat their words during the trial scene, lines 698–99). It is good to learn wisdom under pressure, they declare, echoing as we saw the lines from the hymn to Zeus near the beginning of the trilogy. Then these strange half-bestial beings start speaking like pupils of Aristotle, though the doctrine they preach is in fact old: "Praise neither the life of anarchy nor one ruled despotically; to the middle course in all God gives the palm" (lines 526–30). (Athena will later say exactly the same thing, lines 696–97.) They end with two stanzas of the weightiest Aeschylean on the plight of the sinner who "runs aground on the reef of Justice." There is no blind or primitive retribution here, nor do we have any grounds for supposing that it is thanks to the civilizing influence of Athena that they have come to a more elevated view of their duties. This is the justice they have always stood for. What we heard so often in the earlier plays about a blow for a blow and a death for a death represented only one aspect of their rule, as revealed to the tormented gaze of mortals. If this is so, there can be no great difficulty in harmonizing their code with that of Athena, nor of getting them to underpin the new legal body she is setting up in Athens with their own moral authority. In short, as regards general principle there is not a great deal that needs reconciling.[25]

In terms of the particular question at issue, however, there is, and it is hard to see what happens as reconciliation. The issue in the lengthy trial scene is whether Orestes has committed justifiable homicide or murder. For Apollo and Athena, the killing of the father and lord of the house, still more of a great king like Agamemnon, is so terrible a crime that Orestes was fully justifiable in putting the murderess to death (no other form of legal redress being available), though of course he had to undergo the appropriate purifications afterward, as he has done. From the point of view of the Furies, defenders of the older system where the mother is supreme, the paramount crime is the killing of Clytemnestra. To let the murderer go free would in their eyes mean destroying the whole fabric of society. The legal issue is clear and admits of no compromise. One side must lose, and it is the Furies who lose. When the votes for and against Orestes are counted and turn out equal and the casting vote stands with Athena, she whom they had accepted as an impartial arbitrator gives her vote for the defendant, on grounds that conflict with everything they stand for. "I will not allow first place to the death of the woman who killed her husband" (lines 739f.), she declares. Although she manages with consummate tact to calm them down and save their collective face by promising them great honors to come, they have nonetheless been squarely defeated. And yet they are persuaded to change their curses to blessings and accept a home beneath the Acropolis from where they will lend their subterranean sanction to a court that, with this verdict as precedent, can be expected to hand down judgments to which they are totally opposed.

In view of what they have to renounce, moreover, it is hard to see how they will be able to give what they promise. In agreeing to become part of a city that denies their absolute claim for the mother, they have renounced the very ground of their being, as goddesses of the earth and its fruitfulness. For archaic Greece, the conception of Earth the Mother still held with a literalness that in our late industrial world is very nearly impossible to enter into.[26] It is this ancient conception which the Furies represent that gives them the power to bless and to curse, to grant life and to withhold it, to ensure the continued yield of the land and the life-giving course of the streams and to preside over the well-being of the community. For Aeschylus's dramatic purposes, their threat to visit the land with pestilence is treated as an act of vengeance for their defeat in the trial, but it is of course simply their normal way of responding to transgression in the human world. What they threaten to bring about in Athens if Orestes' offence is allowed to go unpunished is exactly what they do bring about in Thebes when Oedipus's offence goes unpunished. The δίκη embracing both worlds takes its inevitable course. No mere legal decision can put such a situation to rights, and whatever his motives or justification the transgressor must be punished if the shattered equilibrium is to be restored. And yet Orestes goes free, and they are made to promise that all nature will blossom.

I see no means of avoiding the conclusion that Aeschylus is trying to have it both ways. The reconciliation he so magnificently dramatizes is a reconciliation not simply of discordant but of incompatible elements. He is asserting that the old unity of being can continue to exist in the new order of things—in the rapidly changing Athens of the mid-fifth century. Once again he makes his point through the dramatic structure. As everyone has noticed, the trilogy seems to enter a new dimension as it moves, in the second half of the *Eumenides*, from legendary Argos to contemporary Athens. Political references, not wholly absent but certainly unobtrusive in the first two plays, begin to thicken as the third gets under way. There are several clear allusions to the alliance of 462–61 BC between Athens and Argos, a victory for the reforming party over the conservatives who favored friendship with Sparta, and perhaps to Athenian military action in Egypt and the political situation in the Troad. Athena's speech announcing her new court, explicitly directed to "the people of Attica," refers unmistakably to the contemporary reform of the Areopagus, the old aristocratic assembly, and her warnings and later those of the Furies against civil war point to what seems to have been a real danger after the murder in 461 of Ephialtes, the leading spirit of the reform movement. Worth noting too is the means of avoiding this peril which the goddess recommends. "Do not incite my people to civil strife," she says. Rather, "let there be foreign war which comes readily enough to him in whom [or "while"] there is the dread ["mighty," some translate] passion for glory" (lines 863–65). It is hard to be sure of her attitude, but she seems to be thinking of her city's growing imperial ambitions.

The impression on Aeschylus's first audience of this shift from the legendary past to their own world must have been very great, and we can still respond to the poet's powerful localization of his argument in his own historical here and now. What concerns my argument is the effect of placing the final song of blessing in this sharply politicized context. Simply by so doing he can assert with the utmost force and economy that the ancient virtues of the earth will continue to nourish the physically and intellectually mobile man of the new imperial city which Athens was becoming. The old bond is strong enough to contain the turbulent contemporary world. It will fall to the last great archaic master to show why this could not be and to pronounce the end of the unity of being which Aeschylus had striven to preserve. And Sophocles will go further and show that transgressive τόλμα which tears the fabric apart cannot be corrected, for it is written deep into our being and is indeed the condition for the creation of the human artifice, at least in any form we can now conceive it.

The rift which opens up in the later fifth century BC, that fateful period so heavy with consequences for the future, was not to become apparent for a very long time, not indeed until the rise of the natural sciences in the seventeenth century AD. The first signs are nonetheless there; the fact that the rift which was to set culture apart from nature in such a way that culture came increasingly to dominate nature opens so early in our tradition must give pause to those who see hope only in some more equable relation between culture and nature, in some relaxation of the dynamic thrust of the will to more knowledge, more power (two words for the same drive?). For how is culture, having fought so long and successfully against nature, voluntarily to relinquish any of its domain to the old adversary? How should we relax the imperial will and live creaturely again in the little world of man without sinking into a vegetable stasis against which our whole tradition and our very being would cry out? And even if the old creative sense of limit could somehow be recovered, where is the strength to put brakes on our planetary juggernaut which moves on almost mindlessly of its own huge momentum, taking the next step, whatever that step may involve, because the means to take it have been found? No one knows the answers to such questions, but it would be something at least to get the questions right. It is possible that the modest comeback, even revolt, which nature is now staging (the nature "out there" and the unreclaimed, still half-savage nature in our own breasts) might help us here. So long as we see our troubles exclusively from the familiar cultural, anthropocentric perspective, they can appear only as problems awaiting a technical or political solution. But what if we tried not so much to overcome our problems as to understand them and listen to what is speaking there? Nothing in today's civilization encourages so seemingly passive a stance, but if we were able sometimes to look at our situation through older eyes and with their aid relearn the power of limit (the *limes* or boundary line separating the human settlement from the wild, whose encroachments must always be resisted, whose rights must always be respected), then the more equable relation between culture and nature which some are looking for might seem less unattainable. A reach into our past might prove to be not a step back but a way of facing the questions that come at us from the future.

10
Greek Tragedy in Modernist Translation:
H. D., Louis MacNeice, and Robert Lowell

ANCIENT LITERATURE MUST ALWAYS BE RE-CREATED. THERE IS NO
middle way between poetic re-creation and crib. Faced with a different organization of language, a great many idioms which approach
familiar experience with an unfamiliar strategy, a set of key words—
particularly in Greek—for which there are no precise, or constant,
equivalents, the translator's work begins many stages further back
than with a modern language. The sentence, sometimes the word,
has to be dissolved, atomized, and its elements then reconstituted in
a new form.

At its highest, a translation comes into existence in the same way
as a work of original literature: a man experiences something—in this
case, a foreign text—which he has got to find words for if he is to have
any peace. More often, of course, a translation arises from an act of
will. A better occasion is perhaps a summons. With the more ambitious sort of translation, it is encouraging to feel that someone wants
your work, that it is going to serve some public purpose. I am sure
that it would help the translator of Greek tragedy, for example, if he
could feel that he was providing the text for a stage production. Some
possibility of regular production, indeed, not just the occasional amateur performance, would be a great thing. For the problems involved
in translating a Greek play are not literary problems alone. The un-
reality of so much translated Greek drama—on the page or on the
stage—is due partly to the difficulty of finding equivalents for a set of
conventions which are theatrical as well as literary.

Take the case of the messenger's speech which turns up in almost
every Greek tragedy, the big formal narration, lasting anything up to

"Translation and Transposition," in *The Craft and Context of Translation,* ed. William Arrowsmith
and Roger Shattuck (Austin, TX: The University of Texas Press for Humanities Research Center, 1961): 5–11; "Aeschylus in Translation," *Arion* 5, no. 1 (Spring 1966): 76–79; and "Lowell
and the Furies," *New York Review of Books* 26, no. 3 (March 8, 1979): 23–27.

a hundred lines, describing the disaster which has just overtaken the hero. The translator's problem is that there is so little precedent in his own literary tradition to draw on—there is the messenger's speech in Milton's *Samson Agonistes*, of course, and Pirithous's description of Arcites' fatal accident in *The Two Noble Kinsmen*, but not much else. The problem of the producer and of the actor is that they too lack any precedent, any theatrical precedent, to draw on. They cannot even relate the convention to any familiar human reality of the English-speaking world. As things stand, this brilliant artistic convention, one of the high moments of almost every Greek tragedy, defeats the translator and leaves the actor, should the thing ever be performed, with a long and embarrassing piece of versification on his hands. The problem is one that could only be solved by a corporate effort. The translator, having done his best to devise an effective rhetoric, should submit his text to actor and producer and modify it according to their technical criticism; actor and producer would have to devise a style of performance to fit the words the translator was giving them and to express the spirit he detected behind those words. With the additional help of musician, and ideally, of choreographer, the big choral odes would have to be tackled in the same way. And so on with the rest of the elements of the play. (I put it in this way, not because I can quite envisage so complex a corporate effort being mounted success-fully, but because I think the difficulties are on this scale and of this sort. They are emphatically not difficulties which can be solved by a single man sitting down with a typewriter and a copy of Sophocles.)

We must not think of translation as a substitute for the original, something "to send one's students to," a relatively painless way of ac-quiring cultural background. True translation is a commentary on the original, not a substitute for it. Like criticism, to which it is closely allied, its role is interpretative. Every age has to work out its own re-lations to the creative achievements of the past, and the task of the translator, like that of the critic, is to define those works of other times and places which are most living and reveal those aspects of them which we most need today.

Only when translation is seen in this way, as an essential instrument of criticism, is it going to be allowed the liberty it needs. Where it is seen as a substitute for the original, the stress is likely to fall on literal accuracy. If we are looking for a faithful account of the letter of the original, we should use a crib, not a translation. (There is of course no reason why a crib should not be decently literate. John D. Sin-clair's prose version of the *Divine Comedy* is a crib, but a crib that is well enough written to teach one something about Dante's poetry.) The accuracy of translation is of a very different kind. A great deal of

local distortion, of amplification and even excision, may be necessary
if the translator is to follow the curve of his original faithfully.

It is a pity that the revolutionary decades of the twentieth century,
the second and the third, did not produce more good translation.
For when taste changes, existing translations begin to seem either
opaque—they have solidified into literature in their own right, the
transparence of true translation lost—or unreadable. The new van-
tage point seemed to offer a chance of tackling the masterpieces of
the past with a new hope of success.

One can detect this note in a venture like the Poets' Translation
Series published by the Egoist Press just after the First World War. In
his celebrated little essay on Gilbert Murray, T. S. Eliot commented
on H. D.'s translations from Euripides and remarked: "allowing for
errors and even occasional omissions of difficult passages, [they are]
much nearer to both Greek and English than Mr. Murray's. But H. D.
and the other poets of the 'Poets' Translation Series' have so far done
no more than pick up some of the more romantic crumbs of Greek
literature." None of them, Eliot went on to say, has "yet" shown himself competent to attack the *Agamemnon*.[1] The suggestion, however,
was distinctly that this was going to be done soon. Ezra Pound, with
his belief that modern poetic techniques were in some way akin to
those of Greek poetry since the Greeks employed a kind of vers libre
in their choric odes,[2] was probably the presiding figure in this as in
so many ventures, not only through his actual translations, but also
through the Greekish lyrics in *Ripostes* and *Lustra*. "A brilliant impro-
visator translating at sight from an unknown Greek masterpiece,"
Yeats called him.[3]

In the field of Greek translation, however, the most promising
work was done not by Pound but by H. D.,[4] most successfully in her
fragmentary sketches from the *Iphigeneia in Aulis*, published by the
Egoist Press in 1919. Here, to my mind, she suggested certain elements in the Greek lyric better than they have been suggested before
or since. She leaves out an enormous amount. She is not interested
in the syntax, in the elaborate weave of the Greek lyric; and she shows
little dramatic feeling. She is hardly concerned with the "sense"; it is
the picture—the "image"—that she is after, and that is what she presents, a sequence of images as fresh and unexpected as though they
had just been disinterred from the sands of Egypt. The Imagist technique was particularly well equipped to present certain aspects of the
Greek lyric. The legato English line is too soft for the fiercely edged
musical phrases out of which the Greek lyric is built. The Imagistic,
Poundian insistence on clarity of outline—avoiding the English, or
anyway the late Victorian muzziness which Eliot rightly objected to

in Murray—and the whole mystique of perfect phrasing, composing "in the sequence of the musical phrase, not in sequence of a metronome"—all this provided the happiest promise of turning Greek lyric into English:[5]

> I crossed sand-hills.
> I stand among the sea-drift before Aulis.
> I crossed Euripos' strait—
> Foam hissed after my boat.
>
> I left Chalkis,
> My city and the rock-ledges.
> Arethusa twists among the boulders,
> Increases—cuts into the surf.

In her complete version of the *Ion* of Euripides, published a good many years later, in 1937, H. D. tried to stretch the fragmentary Imagistic discipline to cover a complete play. I suppose it is a failure—the lack of rhythmical and syntactical continuity makes it very hard to read on—but if so, it is a failure that is worth a good many successes. One sees her, in the translation itself and in the rather mannered prose notes between the sections—really grappling with the problems a Greek play presents: what to do about the big bland speech from the god at the beginning, how to handle the rapid crisscross exchange of stichomythia, trying to decide how much this or that passage really means, working her way to the reality of gesture and emotion behind the stiff, splendid words.

H. D. took the *Ion* to pieces, broke it down to a preverbal level, and then set about reconstituting it in her own terms. MacNeice's *Agamemnon* (1936)[6] was the work of a poet and a scholar, but it started very much further along the line. He took the words as they came and turned them into the best English words he could find. There was little trace of the effort which I believe every Greek play demands, to "make it new," to devise a new set of formal equivalents. Where H. D.'s *Ion* is modern, MacNeice is content to be modernistic. The diction is in fact quite often old-fashioned academese, slightly tightened up ("The altars are destroyed, the seats of the gods, / and the seed of all the land is perished from it" [*Agamemnon* 527–28]) and fitted out with some contemporary trimmings. The watchman, for example, is made to speak of the stars as "shining Masters *riveted* in the sky" (line 6). Industrial imagery was of course popular in the poetry of the thirties, but the adjective "riveted" is nonetheless badly lacking in propriety. It destroys the overtones of religious awe which the original carries, and it is wrong visually, since stars are essentially moving, flickering points of light whereas "riveted" suggests something immobile. Yet even if it did not advance the search for a genuinely modern translation of Greek tragedy it is far superior to many failures.

Compare, for example, MacNeice's version of a passage from the *Agamemnon* with Richmond Lattimore's.[7] Cassandra is speaking (lines 1114–18):

> ἒ ἔ, παπαῖ παπαῖ, τί τόδε φαίνεται;
> ἢ δίκτυόν τί γ᾽ Ἅιδου;
> ἀλλ᾽ ἄρκυς ἡ ξύνευνος, ἡ ξυναιτία
> φόνου. στάσις δ᾽ ἀκόρετος γένει
> κατολολυξάτω θύματος λευσίμου.

Lattimore:

> No, no, see there! What is that thing that shows?
> Is it some net of death?
> Or is the trap the woman there, the murderess?
> Let now the slakeless fury in the race
> Rear up to howl aloud over this monstrous death.

MacNeice:

> Ah God, the vision! God, God, the vision!
> A net, is it? Net of Hell!
> But herself is the net; shared bed; shares murder.
> O let the pack ever-hungering after the family
> Howl for the unholy ritual, howl for the victim.

The Greek lines strike the note of terror. (It is one of Aeschylus's unique achievements that he can create, on the level of great poetry, the shudder that a very good ghost story produces.) Lattimore is far too cool about it; he doesn't frighten in the least. He shows himself insensitive to the demands of dramatic speech. "What is that thing that shows?" What indeed? Nothing shows, if you insist on translating τί τόδε φαίνεται like this. MacNeice goes all out to suggest that Cassandra has seen something frightful, and even if he uses too many words on it, he has tried hard to respond to Aeschylus's fearful concentration. One may think that "she," in line 3, would be better than the Irishism "herself," and in fact this change would give quite a strong line:

> But *she* is the net; shared bed; shares murder

which is altogether superior to Lattimore's leisurely, discursive line:

> Or is the trap the woman there, the murderess?

Maybe it is, maybe it isn't, one's curiosity is not greatly stirred.

MacNeice's line is, admittedly, not great poetry. It does not have the accent of, say,

> That my keene Knife see not the Wound it makes,

but it does try for one element of Aeschylus's poetry, and in so doing suggests how a man who writes less well than Shakespeare may approach this poet. MacNeice had the good sense to see that he could not really hope to write Aeschylean poetry. (The failure of his version is that he left too much "poetry" in it.) He also saw, I think, that within the totality of the *Agamemnon* is an *extractable* stage play of colossal power. It should then be possible to retain the structure of this play—the narrative line, the curve of the dramatic action, the characterization—and transfer at least some of its poetry, much of it wholly untranslatable, into nonverbal forms—dance, mime, music, and so on. Let me try to make the point clearer by looking at the last three lines of the Greek. The first of these lines and the beginning of the next are iambic. Cassandra is describing, with whatever indirections, what she has seen. This is the language of statement, and as such it can be translated; MacNeice made a reasonable attempt. But then there is a startling change of perspective, and Denniston and Page, in their commentary, duly register perplexity: "it is natural that *Clytemnestra* (1054) should refer to the murder of Agamemnon as a 'sacrifice,' as if it were a religious duty; on *Cassandra's* lips the word is pure metaphor."

It is not "pure metaphor" (whatever pure metaphor may, in poetry, be). What has happened is that Cassandra, fluidly open to the spiritual atmosphere of the scene, has become possessed, momentarily, by the Furies who are so soon to possess Clytemnestra when she axes her husband. The Greek registers the suddenness of this daemonic seizure by switching from iambics (not that Aeschylean iambics are particularly staid . . .) to the frenzied dance of dochmiacs. How do our translators respond? Lattimore, for reasons best known to himself, responds with a flat iambic line—

> Let now the slakeless fury in the race

although elsewhere he usually tries to suggest the original meter. Mac-Neice is very prosy and uninspired. What is the difficulty? The difficulty, quite simply, is that English poetry cannot enact this sudden switch from statement to the cadence of daemonic possession. Our metrical effects are insufficiently varied and, more serious, insufficiently firm; they are not clearly enough cut into time.[8] Yet if English words and meter cannot establish this transition, dance and music could. A passage like this cannot be translated into English, but it could be performed; and if the dance and the music were right, it would hardly matter what words Cassandra was given to speak.

Robert Lowell was the last of the great modernists, in the sense that he claimed all the past for his own, or at least as much of it as he wanted. He was learned in poetry in a way few poets now are, and behind the literatures of modern Europe and America he always heard the ancestral voices of antiquity. With Roman poetry he felt very much at home. ("English is a half-Latin language," he once said, "and we've done our best to absorb the Latin literature.")[9] He translated a satire of Juvenal and made several goes at the odes of Horace, the least translatable and among the least exhaustible of poems, centered forever on their steady middle ground of human experience. And there is the version from Propertius in *Lord Weary's Castle*, "The Ghost," one of his most formidable things, pure Lowell and yet extending our sense of Propertius's range as Pound's *Homage* had done.

Greece was not nearly so close to him ("there's nothing like Greek in English at all . . . Greek wildness and sophistication all different, the women different, everything").[10] Lowell knew or once knew "some" Greek, but the version from Homer in *Imitations* suggests little feeling for the style of Greek poetry, hence perhaps his decision to do the *Prometheus* in prose. Yet this debt too had finally to be paid, and in his own medium, verse, and he left behind him a translation of the *Oresteia*.[11] It did not receive a final revision and is not quite complete, but there is enough to show Lowell at work on a major Greek text.

There is no use pretending it isn't a sad disappointment, the more so since Aeschylus is the one Greek poet Lowell might have come to grips with. His old poetic shock tactics would have stood him in good stead here and worked, at least on the level of diction, even if the result might have sounded more like Seneca than Aeschylus. The poet who saw the Aegean "flowering with corpses" (*Agamemnon* 659) could have spoken to the poet of "Atlantic, you are fouled with the blue sailors" ("The Quaker Graveyard in Nantucket"). Orestes' nightmare vision of the Furies squinnying at him, "working their eyebrows in the dark" (*Choephoroe* 285), or however the extraordinary line should go, might have played into the hands of the author of "Night Sweat." The translation is in fact more lively here than usual, but most of the time he does not seem to be hearing Aeschylus at all.

The explanation is not or need not be simply that he made no direct contact with the Greek but worked, as he tells us in a prefatory note, from other translations. Though no substitute for the original, the right translation might have given him much that he needed: a literate word-for-worder that set down the explosive particles of Aeschylus's great mix one by one and challenged him to recompose them from the ground up. And encouraged him to nose around the Greek on his own. Poets pick up a good deal this way. Browning's brave, mad version of the *Agamemnon* might have helped ("At night began the bad-wave-outbreak evils" [line 653], or "Back shall he come—for friends, copestone these curses!" [lines 1282–83]). Instead, Lowell relied mainly on the version by Richmond Lattimore, praising it for being "so elaborately exact." Well, yes, but the trouble is that Lattimore is often not exact or close enough to provide Lowell with what he wanted. Clytemnestra, dreaming that she has given birth to a snake, woke screaming (Lattimore writes) "as torches kindled all about the house, out of / the blind dark that had been on them" (*Choephoroe* 536–37). Evidently feeling that this was too wordy, Lowell reduced it to "Torches were lit all over the house." But Aeschylus speaks of torches blinded by darkness, and the words, combining literal and metaphorical, physical and metaphysical, have the whole weight of the trilogy behind them. No one could guess from Lowell's flat line that there is a dramatic poetry here comparable to "light thickens" in *Macbeth* (act 3, scene 2).

In the lyric dialogue between Clytemnestra and the chorus after Agamemnon's murder they speak of Helen, who caused so many deaths at Troy, and say something like "Now you have flowered, or garlanded yourself, with a final garland that will never be forgotten, [through?] blood not to be washed away" (*Agamemnon* 1458–59). The text is corrupt, a headache for the scholar but for the poet an opportunity. Robert Fagles, in his energetic version,[12] writes: "Now you are crowned / with this consummate wreath, the blood / that lives in memory, glistens age to age." Lattimore is briefer: "You alone, to shine in man's memory / as blood flower never to be washed out." This is vivid. What is wrong with it, for Lowell's purposes, is that having already achieved its own poetic form it gives him no basis to build on. So he took the easy way out and snatched at a trite image: "Ah Helen, Oh scarlet rose, / you are stained with our blood." Trite, and also foolish. If the flower is already scarlet, the stain of blood will not show.

The same sad story could be told of passage after passage. Though the verse is mostly workmanlike and in its unadventurous way dramatically speakable, there are crucial moments when Lowell simply doesn't give the actor (or the reader, for that matter) what he needs.

Orestes, seeing the snake-enwreathed Furies for the first time, is made to say "No, no, Attendants on Electra, / look closely" (*Choephoroe* 1048–49). But he is screaming in mortal terror and these words won't scream. If Lowell had had the right kind of translation (or worked in tandem with someone who knew Greek), he would have learned of two acceptable emendations which remove these unwelcome attendants from the text and replace them with "what women" or "grim women."

The introductory note suggests another reason why he failed Aeschylus. His aim, he wrote, was to "trim, cut, and be direct enough to satisfy my own mind and at a first hearing the simple ears of a theater audience." Eliot was I think responsible for this dispiriting view of dramatic poetry (poetry, he said, must be put "on a thin diet in order to adapt it to the needs of the stage"),[13] and it led him down from the *Four Quartets* to *The Cocktail Party* and down further to *The Confidential Clerk*. Aeschylus did not think of the language of verse drama in this way, nor did Sophocles, nor did Shakespeare, nor did Yeats, who might have provided a better model than Eliot. The language of *Purgatory* is immediately effective on the stage and though bare it has not been watered down. The consequence of this doctrine is that, all too often, our simple ears have to make do with this sort of thing— Lowell's version of the start of the tremendous speech when Cassandra comes out of her visionary trance and talks straight (*Agamemnon* 1183–87):

> No more circling, I'm on the scent.
> I hear the choir of your Furies.
> Do not try to conceal them from me.
> They are established here as your closest friends.
> They will not leave the house of Atreus.

Faced with so much hobbled writing, one longs for a touch of the old wanton Lowell, even the Lowell of *Phaedra*, disrupting the text with his own preoccupations but at least bringing it violently alive. There is only one example of this license here, and it is wholly disastrous. In the long opening lyric of the *Agamemnon*, the chorus, moving between the former crimes of the house of Atreus and the new crimes they dimly foresee, suddenly make a direct, vertical appeal to Zeus. Earlier readers found this passage singularly sublime. Some learned critics have preferred to see Aeschylus as a fine poet to be sure but no great thinker. Whatever view of Aeschylus's theology is taken, few have held that it amounts to as little as this, Lowell's three lines answering to twenty-four very dense lines of Greek (lines 160–83):

> Glory to Zeus, whatever he is:
> he cut off the testicles of his own father,
> and taught us dominion comes from pain!

Reduce the religious thought of the trilogy to this and you are left with not much more than the story of a wife who murdered her husband and was in turn murdered by her son. Lowell seems not to have thought seriously about the theme of the *Oresteia,* or about the form in which that theme is embodied, hence his treatment of the long choral odes in the *Agamemnon,* which are rearranged and cut to pieces. Certainly these odes are very hard to bring powerfully over into English, since they correspond to nothing in our own poetic tradition and draw allusively on patterns of thought which are strange to us. Yet they are the bedrock on which the whole trilogy is built, the groundswell of lyric meditation and vision on which it moves.

Lowell seems to take a curiously old-fashioned view of theater as primarily the verbal interaction of actors advancing the plot, a plot constantly interrupted by odes. Artaud, who wanted to rescue drama from "its servitude to psychology and 'human interest'" and spoke of a "unique language halfway between gesture and thought," might have helped here.[14] For the *Oresteia* is not simply one of the greatest of literary texts. It is the sole Western survivor of a lost form that built dramatic action, chant, and dance into a whole that we can only barely guess at but may still strive in some shape to recover. It is significant that Lowell's chief success is with the choral lament over Agamemnon's tomb in the *Choephoroe,* a musico-dramatic composition scored for three voices designed to restore the shattered fabric of the house of Atreus and enlist the buried powers of Agamemnon for the avengers—and thus shatter the fabric once again. Here Lowell cuts only glancingly and preserves the sequence. Because, I think, he saw this as dramatic action contributing to the plot, not just "poetry" unsuited to our simple ears.

That we need a fine translation of the *Oresteia* can presumably be granted. What is perhaps less obvious is the role that the poet-translator could play, not merely in ensuring that this great poem continues to shine in the life of the world but also in advancing the task that is thought to belong purely to scholarship. With a work as textually corrupt as the *Oresteia,* the scholar must spend much of his time coaxing into intelligibility battered syllables beneath which an overwhelming poetry may lie waiting to be released. Working by the strict rules of his craft, he can however go only so far. Often he must simply give up and clamp his despairing obeli on a passage he judges incurable.

This is where the poet-translator might come to his aid. The text of Aeschylus as we read it in any printed edition is to an unusual extent a construct, sometimes almost a fiction. It is based on a manuscript tradition where the true reading may be buried beyond recovery or garbled into nonsense, and draws on four centuries of scholarly emendation ranging from the very rash to the very pedestrian. The editor's instinct, in such a situation, is to play it safe; by temperament and training he is reluctant to admit into his text strained turns of speech or extravagant images. ("Odd and unusual, perhaps corrupt," a British editor remarks of a word in the *Agamemnon*.)

But with a poet as boldly inventive as Aeschylus, playing it safe is not necessarily the road to truth. It is unwise, with an author who when the fit is on him will write almost anything, to assert "Aeschylus could not have written this," even though no parallel usage occurs or has survived, even though Professor X proved conclusively in the *Rheinisches Museum* that the construction is illicit. The poet-translator might reach out or down for meaning in places where no self-respecting scholar would tread and find beauty in what duller eyes had taken for gibberish. A poet possessed of some learning, or with access to learning; a poet who wanted to live his way into Aeschylus's poetry, not use it as the occasion for his own.

In a desperately corrupt ode from the *Choephoroe* Lattimore writes:

> Much else lies secret he may show at need.
> He speaks the markless word, by
> night hoods darkness on the eyes
> nor shows more plainly when the day is there.
>
> (815–18)

This is not only good poetry (better than what Lowell gives us); it helps toward the interpretation of the Greek. Lattimore is of course a classical scholar, but it is poetry, not scholarship, that guides him here. His lines make sense, and make poetry. Whatever the manuscript tradition offers, or conjecture can provide, that brings the Greek closest to what Lattimore has written may well be what Aeschylus wrote. A better poet than Lattimore might go further and retrieve other passages that learning has had to abandon.

Amazed at Clytemnestra's brazen triumph over the death of her husband, the chorus ask what poison she can have taken, earth-bred or sprung from the [———] sea (*Agamemnon* 1407–9). From the "flowing" sea, our editions read, ῥυτᾶς, a seventeenth-century emendation. The tradition, however, offers ῥυσᾶς, "wrinkled." For several reasons this is probably wrong, though that intrepid conservative Douglas

Young accepted it in his translation. Probably wrong, but with a poet like Aeschylus you cannot be sure, and "wrinkled," with its suggestion of the monstrous, is poetically attractive. ("The wrinkled sea beneath him crawls," Tennyson wrote in "The Eagle.") Few scholars would wish to take "wrinkled" into their text, nor I imagine should they. But the poet-translator, with his special commitment to language (to his own language and that of Aeschylus and to the mysterious linguistic region where they might fuse), could afford to take this sort of risk. And in so doing, even though he is wrong in one place or another, would protect scholarship from its tendency to cut great poetry down to its own measure.

Facing death at her son's hand, Clytemnestra says, "I feel like someone who laments to a tomb." "Yes," Orestes replies in most of our editions, "for it is my father's fate that establishes your death" (*Choephoroe* 927–28).The word "establishes" is conjectural, and also dull. The single manuscript on which the *Choephoroe* depends first read πορίζει, which hardly makes sense, corrected to σ'ὁρίζει which with a further slight change yields the word most editors print. The late nineteenth-century scholar Verrall, a rash, brilliant, maligned man, proposed συρίζει, "my father's fate *hisses* your death." The Greeks associated snakes with tombs, and Orestes has said that he will turn snake to kill his mother. "Alas, this is the snake I bore," Clytemnestra goes on to say. Verrall's conjecture seems to have sunk almost without trace. Very likely it deserved to. And yet perhaps a poet should look into the matter. Poets sometimes understand poetry better than scholars do, and even classical poetry does not actually *belong* to classical scholars. What is needed, though, is collaboration, not competition, and the point is simply that scholarship should not be left in sole possession of this field.

11

Introduction to *Antigone*

IN *MIDDLEMARCH* GEORGE ELIOT SET HERSELF THE PROBLEM OF CRE-
ating a heroic woman whose course is set in a society that allows her
heroism no outlet in public action. Eliot's Dorothea Brooke is close
kin to Sophocles' Antigone, but she is an Antigone who is denied the
opportunity "to spend her heroic piety in daring all for the sake of a
brother's burial." Women now lead less sequestered lives, and to that
extent the *Antigone* is more comprehensible today than it was in the
nineteenth century. Yet the nature of heroism in the play, the particular form it takes in Sophocles' hands, does not fit easily into our frame
of things. "The heroic will to defy the world," a critic calls it.[1]

That will, the intractable resolve that sets the play in motion, is
clearly defined in the opening scene as, just before dawn, Antigone
and Ismene, the two daughters of Oedipus, speak in urgent under-
tones outside the royal palace in Thebes. The city has just gone
through a time of trouble. After Oedipus's disaster, his two sons Eteocles and Polyneices for a while ruled alternately, but they quickly
quarreled, and from nearby Argos Polyneices led an army against his
native city in the attempt to gain sole possession of the throne for
himself. The Argive army was defeated, but in the fighting—the day
before the play begins—the two brothers fell by each other's hand.
Antigone has just heard that the new ruler, her uncle Creon, has decreed that one of her brothers, the defender Eteocles, is to be buried
with full honors. The other, Polyneices, is to lie unburied on the plain
outside the city, a prey to birds and dogs. No one, on pain of death,
may touch the body.

This she cannot accept. Bound to her family by a fierce, instinctive
loyalty, Antigone cannot grant the city the right to enforce a loyalty
that would mean disloyalty, treachery, to her own kin, her own dead.
"I am going to bury my brother" (lines 80–81), she says flatly and

"Introduction" to Sophocles, *Antigone*, trans. Elizabeth Wyckoff ([Haarlem]: Limited Editions
Club, 1975): 7–17.

asks Ismene to help. The enormity of what she proposes is measured against Ismene's response. Ismene is not disloyal or cowardly, merely normal. She knows that as a private person she cannot defy the state nor, as a woman, defy men. "I shall obey the men in power" (line 67), she says resignedly, and Antigone turns on her in something like hatred. We have to remember that Antigone is very young, still probably in her teens (she is called παῖς, "child," throughout), and she has youth's uncompromising moral clarity. She has pared the issue down to the bone and sees no obstacle in the way of her great act of civil disobedience, "the crime of piety" (line 74) as she calls it in the play's central paradox. "You are in love with the impossible" (line 90), Ismene tells her. What of it? The penalty is merely death.

The two sisters go their divided ways, and as the sun rises the chorus of Theban elders marches in to sing a triumphant victory song which serves to set the preceding scene in a new perspective. The brother whom Antigone so cherishes was after all a traitor; he had sought to destroy his native city. And this is not all the chorus does. With great splendor of diction and imagery (to which in imagination we must add music and dance, the pulse and glitter of impassioned spectacle) they transpose the recent military conflict into the grandiose terms of a death struggle between an eagle and a dragon, a struggle in which the gods themselves take part. That destructive forces should, poetically, be compared to a ravening bird of prey, is understandable enough. But in what sense does the threatened city (threatened first by Polyneices and now perhaps by Antigone) resemble a dragon?

Let the question rest till the next choral ode, for Creon is now onstage dressed in royal robes and about make his inaugural speech. He is a little prosy here and there—politicians often are—and we may think his tone authoritarian, but in the circumstances his speech makes good political sense. For it will take a strong hand to pull the state together again. Only with the announcement of his proposed treatment of Polyneices' body—which violated ordinary Greek sentiment—do we begin to see that Creon is in his way as much an extremist as his niece. Antigone declares: I must honor my dead—that duty comes before everything. Creon replies: We must all obey the city, for on its safety everything depends, even our ability to form relations of love and friendship.

Between these two extreme positions there is no possible compromise. And every potential for disaster.

Enter a guard, ancestor of a long line of prolix yet shrewd-minded rustics, with the news that Creon's edict has *already* been defied. Some one has sprinkled dust on Polyneices' body, in symbolic token of burial. Antigone has set her match to the fuse. Creon duly explodes. They are violent people, these Theban princes.

How does the chorus respond? With an ode (among the most famous in Greek literature) on the greatness of man and the growth of civilization. We should not see these choral odes as decorative arias that hold up the action but rather as the poet's means of extending, ramifying, deepening, the action. "Many things are strange, uncanny but nothing stranger than human kind," they begin (lines 332–33). Sophocles uses a single word here, δεινός, which means wonderful, and strange, and also fearful, and perhaps even awe-inspiring. In what sense is man δεινός? Because of what he does, of what he dares, to create the human artifice. Sophocles starts with two forms of activity that look innocent enough, navigation and agriculture. That earthborn, earthbound man should take ship and venture across the alien seas: this, for early thought, was often seen as a kind of trespass. And what is agriculture, seemingly the most peaceful of pursuits, but the imposition of man's will on Earth, the eldest, the primal, of things? In building the human artifice man violates, *must* violate, an aboriginal repose that was there before he came and will outlast him.

After subduing sea and earth, irresistible man goes on to bend the wild creatures to his purpose. He teaches himself the arts of civilization, speech and thought and what Sophocles calls ἀστυνόμοι ὀργαί (lines 355–56), "the ways of life in the city," the dispositions that make life in the community possible. Man has now achieved his greatest triumph, the city, the polis. Then comes the first check, the first limit to his powers: Death. And in the last stanza we are told, more obscurely, in generalized moral terms—rather dull at first sight—of another danger that threatens the polis. Reading between the lines perhaps we might paraphrase: the daemonic energies that create the human artifice can also destroy it. *Without* these energies the polis cannot be created or remain in effective existence. *With* these energies, it is perpetually threatened.

Threatened by Antigone's civil disobedience? Or by Creon's high political hand? The next scene which brings them together in the confrontation we have been expecting takes us a step further. Did you bury the body? Creon asks her. Yes. Did you know this was forbidden? Yes. "And still you dared to transgress these laws?" (line 449). Yes. And in words of great moral splendor Antigone goes on to ground her action in what she sees as the nature of things:

> it was not Zeus who made that order.
> Nor did that Justice who lives with the gods below

mark out such laws to hold among mankind.
Nor did I think your orders were so strong
that you, a mortal man, could over-run
the gods' unwritten and unfailing laws.
Not now, nor yesterday's, they always live,
and no one knows their origin in time.

(lines 450–57)[2]

Moral splendor, indeed, but there is something else in her speech.
Note that she ends by deliberately insulting Creon ("And if you think
my acts are foolishness / the foolishness may be in a fool's eye," lines
469–70). She had no need to insult him. Yes, but had she not done so
she would not have been Antigone. "The girl is bitter. She's her father's
child" (line 471), the chorus comments. Sophocles has a stranger word
for her—ὠμός, violent, savage, even cruel. This child is not simply
brave. She has the harsh, imperious temper of her father, Oedipus.

So we must not soften Antigone as nineteenth-century critics did
(and some critics still do) by dwelling on her "tenderness." And
though we may if we wish call her a martyr—that is, the witness to an
order of things beyond the reach of the state—we must on no account see her as a Christian in disguise, not even when she says her
famous line, "I cannot share in hatred, but in love" (line 523). This
is not "Love your enemy." For her enemy Creon she has a proper
Greek hatred.[3] What she means is that she will not think in Creon's
political terms and hate one brother and love the other. She loves
them both, traitor and patriot alike, for both are her own flesh and
blood.

So Antigone is condemned and along with her, quite unjustly, Ismene. They are led inside the palace, and the chorus again steps
forward to meditate on the fortunes of this family. The ode starts with
the Aeschylean theme of a hereditary curse, but this, I suspect, is not
what Sophocles has most deeply in mind here. We are not to think
that his characters are compelled by some external force to act as they
do. ("Fate" plays a far smaller role in Greek tragedy than is sometimes
supposed.) Rather, the buffeted seascape to which, at lines 584–91,
they compare the house of Oedipus provides the appropriately
somber backdrop to the present action. Perhaps we can best understand what Sophocles is saying by concentrating on a few moments
in this ode. First:

So now the light goes out
for the house of Oedipus, while the bloody knife
cuts the remaining root. Folly and Fury have done this.

(lines 599–604)

The "light" is of course the hope that the new generation will fare better than the old; the "knife" belongs to the gods of the underworld (the Greek text is doubtful here, however), and the two daughters are "the remaining root." But what of "Folly and Fury"? The words need unfolding a little, and a fuller translation (by E. R. Dodds)[4] may help us: "The unwise mouth and the tempter who sits in the brain." The unwise mouth, we suppose, is Antigone's, and also Creon's. But what of this tempter who sits in the brain? What temptation, and who is being tempted?

The next line provides a clue, though again it needs unfolding. "What madness of man, O Zeus, can bind your power?" (line 605). Madness, yes, but what Sophocles says is ὑπερβασία, a going over or across, a trespass. Creon used the verbal form of this word when he accused Antigone of transgressing, of overstepping, the law (line 449), and she countered a few lines later with a similar word, accusing him of "over-running" (line 455) the law of the gods. The force of ὑπερβασία, however, extends beyond these particular instances and reaches deep into the heart of Greek tragic thought. Man, as the earlier Greeks saw him, is a limited creature whose nature drives him beyond limit, a mortal creature who aspires to immortality. He is haunted by dreams of transcendence, by the supreme temptation— at once the mark of his greatness and the high road to ruin—to pass beyond the human condition. This is ὑπερβασία, trespass, literally a going across and invading someone else's territory: the territory of the gods. So—to paraphrase the line in the ode—Sophocles cries through the mouth of his tragic chorus: No ὑπερβασία of man can bind the power of Zeus. And, at the end of the next stanza, a com- plementary statement: "Any greatness in human life brings doom" (lines 613–14).

But what does *this* mean? The play has shown us two forms of human greatness: the daring that goes into the creation of the city and the unquestioned heroism of Antigone's defiance of the city. What life- denying pessimism is it that finds such actions inevitably threatened by "doom"? Even if, as we saw, there is a kind of trespass involved in the creation of the city, what trespass against the divine order of things can there be in Antigone's "crime of piety"? A law-and-order man like Creon naturally disapproves. But do the gods? does Sophocles?

Passing over the next scene for the time being (between Creon and his son Haemon), let us move forward to Antigone's final appear- ance. She is on her way to death, a lonely, horrible death—Creon has decreed that she is to be buried alive in an underground vault—and for the first time she laments her fate. She has not weakened, she is not feeling sorry for herself. Nonetheless, her heroic act accomplished, we sense, momentarily at least, some slackening of the tensed will. She has come to realize the full cost of what she has done and feels the utter loneliness of her position. Lyrically she compares herself to the legendary Theban princess Niobe, the granddaughter of Zeus who (for her sins . . .) was transformed into a mountain eternally shrouded in tears of mist and rain. Quickly the chorus reproaches her: "God's child and god she was. / We are born to death" (lines 834–35). They cannot, that is, allow her to come so close to godhead, even though they admit her greatness. "Laughter against me now" (line 839), Antigone cries fiercely (or perhaps, "You mock me"). She will not listen to their conventional prudence, for she feels that through her great deed of transgressive reverence and because of the strange fate that awaits her—a living being immured in the house of the dead—she is passing into a region where the ordinary restraints on human aspiration no longer hold. The chorus reproaches her again (lines 853–56):

> You went to the furthest verge
> of daring, but there you found
> the high foundation of justice, and fell.

The furthest verge, limit: this is Antigone's home ground. In thus going to the verge, the chorus tells her, she has come up against "justice." Their next words make it clear that they are thinking primarily of human justice, Creon's justice. But Antigone knows another justice, "divine justice" (line 921), and with this she believes she has kept faith. Yet in the very extremity of her daring (her "love of the impossible," as Ismene put it), has she not gone beyond the limits assigned to mortal action and thereby transgressed against divine justice itself?

The play will hardly allow us to think this; yet it is well to ask the question, for it takes us close to the center of Sophocles' thought. What gives his tragic poetry its peculiar moral sublimity is the spectacle it offers of heroic figures facing temptations pitched so staggeringly high that ordinary men and women would not be tempted by them at all. The endeavor to transcend the human condition—Malraux, from our post-Nietzschean perspective, calls it "the visionary disease . . . the will to godhead" (*Man's Fate*, part 4): this is man's final temptation, his ultimate transgression. And also his greatest glory? Or is this only man's view? The conclusion of Sophocles' last play, the *Oedipus at Colonus*, where the gods admit the old hero to their company, suggests that it may the gods' view as well.[5]

So, at this lonely pitch of glory, this perilous but surely also triumphant verge of things, Antigone goes to her death. All is well with her, we must believe. What meanwhile of Creon? In the previous scene with Haemon, encouraged by what he took to be his son's proper submissiveness, he opened up his mind, and what he showed revealed that with Creon all was far from well. First, impiety or blasphemy. Let Antigone go to her tomb, he shouts, "Let her sing her song of Zeus / who guards the kindred" (lines 657–58). It does not become the man who had set himself up as the guardian of the state religion to speak thus of Ζεὺς ξύναιμος, Zeus of kindred blood. Next, tyranny. The ruler's command must be obeyed, he asserts, "when it is right, and even when it's not" (line 667). And finally, in his terror of being worsted by a woman, he gives way to something like hysteria.

Haemon, deferentially, takes his father to task and tells him that the city does not approve of what he is doing. Listen to the other side, he urges, "do not have one mind, and one alone," (lines 705–6), vainly preaching plural vision to a one-eyed family. "Yield your wrath, allow a change of stand" (line 718). The tree that bends with the torrent is not uprooted, the sailor who shortens sail in a storm gets safely home. Yielding, however, is precisely what the true Sophoclean hero cannot do. He will sooner haul down heaven on his head than give way an inch. "She cannot yield to trouble" (line 472), the chorus said of Antigone earlier on. Can Creon? The answer comes suddenly in the later scene when the prophet Teiresias warns him of the gods' anger. By consigning a living woman to the tomb and denying a dead man the rites of burial, he is inverting the natural order of things. Creon storms his defiance and then, without warning, cracks and gives way completely. "What must I do? Speak, and I shall obey" (line 1099), he says to the chorus with a strange and rather horrible humility.

So Creon yields, too late, and his world abruptly falls into ruin with an *embarras* of mortality that some critics have found "Elizabethan." Antigone, whom he had decided to release, hangs herself; both his son and his wife also commit suicide. Greek dramatists are usually more thrifty. Perhaps Sophocles could have done with one less corpse, but he evidently felt that the point had to be made with all force. What point exactly? That impiety against the gods is punished? Yes, but Creon's deepest offence lay in a different quarter. His trouble was that he aspired to heroic status without possessing the heroic temper. He had not understood that for the likes of him, moderation is the best policy.

Where does the play leave us? It leaves Creon as annihilated as any character in Beckett. ("I . . . am nothing more than nothing now," line 1325.) The city is hardly better off. At the end of *King Lear* Kent and Edgar, at least, live on to sustain the gored state, but heaven knows who is going to pick up the pieces in Thebes.

And yet as we stand back from the play and try to possess our experience, we may find that the final effect is not depressing or desolating. Though Sophocles has spared us no extremity of suffering and loss, it is closer to exaltation. Like his heroine, Sophocles has gone to the verge, and at that final reach of things he has discovered not defeat but triumph.

12

The *Anthology* Transplanted

Peter Jay's aim in *The Greek Anthology*[1] is to let the general reader inspect the more than millennial span of the Greek epigram redone into a variety of contemporary verse forms and idioms. His translators are almost all practicing poets, rather than classicists who do a little versing, and with their aid he has skillfully deployed the fiction that minor Greek poets spoke as minor poets speak in England and America today. Various questions might be put to this attractive book. Wondering how many of Jay's forty-seven translators actually read Greek, one might ask what effect the decline of classical education is having on the translation of classical poetry. Loss there must be, and yet the versions from the *Anthology* in *The Oxford Book of Greek Verse in Translation* (1938), whose authors presumably knew Greek well, are for the most part markedly inferior to those offered in Jay's book. Or, since the ancient world presents a new face every generation or so, one might inquire what aspects of Greek poetry are today open to English poetry. (The "obscene" poems, for example, that once had to be smuggled through in Latin prose, can now take the air as English verse.) I propose to put a different question to Jay's *Greek Anthology*: a question about poetic form.

A. C. Graham, in the introduction to his Penguin *Poems of the Late T'ang*, sets out the elements of a Chinese lyric in this way:

Tartar	horn	tug	North	wind,
Thistle	Gate	white(r)	than	water.
Sky	hold-in-mouth	Kokonor	road,	
Wall	top	moon	thousand	mile.

"The English reader of a poem in Chinese constantly discovers that several lines have almost translated themselves," Graham remarks. Yes, and into something that sounds like modern verse:

"The Anthology Transplanted," *Arion* n.s. 3, no. 4 (1976): 507–17.

A Tartar horn tugs at the North wind,
Thistle Gate shines whiter than the stream.
The sky swallows the road to Kokonor:
On the Great Wall, a thousand miles of moonlight.[2]

The contemporary translator of the short Greek lyrics we so mis-leadingly call epigrams is less fortunate. Take these elegant verses traditionally ascribed to Plato (*AP* 6.1):

ἡ σοβαρὸν γελάσασα καθ᾿ Ἑλλάδος, ἡ τὸν ἐραστῶν
    ἑσμὸν ἐνὶ προθύροις Λαῒς ἔχουσα νέων,
τῇ Παφίῃ τὸ κάτοπτρον· ἐπεὶ τοίη μὲν ὁρᾶσθαι
    οὐκ ἐθέλω, οἵη δ᾿ ἦν πάρος οὐ δύναμαι.

The bare bones might be disposed like this:

She : haughtily : (who) laughed : at Hellas : she : that : of lovers
crowd : at her doors : Lais : (who) had : of young (sc. lovers),
TO THE PAPHIAN : THIS MIRROR. "Since : what (I am) : see
I will not : and what I was : before : I cannot."

To try to reproduce the complex word-order and the syntax allowed by a highly inflected language like Greek would be a hopeless un-dertaking. At the same time the translator who ignores the form and goes straight for what he takes to be the emotional center of this poem—the loss of beauty or cruelty of time's passing—will find that he returns empty-handed. In work like this, form and poetic emotion are indistinguishable, the form is the poetic emotion, and the trans-lator who doesn't suggest that his original has at least the balance and poise of, say,

The Tortoise here and Elephant unite,
Transform'd to Combs, the speckled and the white
                    (Pope, *The Rape of the Lock* (1714), 1.135–36)

has failed. And yet how is he to convey the formal elegance of the way the two participles ("laughed" and "had" in the Greek) depend on the main verb ("I offer"), which, in a way that is standard for dedica-tions, is omitted and has to be understood? The balance of οἵη/τοίη in the last line and a half, as Lais herself speaks, is also pleasing and goes nicely into Ausonius's Latin (Epigram 60):

              quia cernere talem,
qualis sum, nolo; qualis eram, nequeo.

It goes well into Prior's early eighteenth-century English:

> Venus, take my Votive Glass:
> Since I am not what I was;
> What from this Day I shall be,
> Venus, let me never see.

But none of this formal elegance goes at all well into modern English; There is a version by Jay in this anthology (no. 310) which I shall not quote, since it seems to me quite unsuccessful. Dudley Fitts tried in his *Poems from the Greek Anthology*. The last two lines read:

> For I will not see myself as I am now,
> And can not see myself as once I was,

but this is insufferably flat.[3]

The poetry or verse of the *Anthology* is overwhelmingly literary, strict in metrical form, stylized in language, distanced often to vanishing point in its rendering of experience, constantly ringing the changes on a relatively slender repertoire of themes and motifs. Translation, to succeed, must at least appear to meet the Greek on this formal front, and since the eighteenth century English poetry has hardly had the formal resources to do so. The one great exception is Landor, who suggests certain aspects of the Greek epigram better than anyone has ever done, even if his carefully caught regrets are more romantic than classical:

> Stand close around, ye Stygian set,
> With Dirce in one boat conveyed!
> Lest Charon, seeing, may forget
> That he is old and she a shade.

It follows that "free verse" of the anything-goes, shovel-it-in variety is doomed to failure from the start. Perhaps there is too much of it in Jay's book. There must be a discernable form or at least the ghost of a form, and since there is no real modern equivalent to the elegiac couplet it has to be a different or new form. (Robert Bridges's quantitative version of Ptolemy's beautiful poem on the stars, *AP* 9.577, printed by Jay alongside a modern one by Fitts, is an exception: highly mannered but memorable in its way.) In Italian Salvatore Quasimodo now and then succeeds in creating such forms, as in this version of a poem by Alcaeus of Messene (*AP* 7.55) where he dissolves the structure of the original, consisting of three couplets, and rebuilds it into two differently articulated quatrains:

In un ombroso bosco della Lòcride,
a riva delle loro acque, lavarono
le Ninfe il corpo di Esiodo, e là
alzarono il suo tumulo.
I caprai lo bagnarono di latte
e biondo miele; e miele era la voce
di quel vecchio che si era dissetato
alle pure sorgenti delle Muse.[4]

In English Pound provides an obvious model, not so much in his actual translations from the *Anthology*, which are never I think very successful, but rather in some of the Chinese fragments in *Lustra* and above all in the wonderful formal resourcefulness of *Homage*. No one can write like Pound now, but directly or indirectly his influence is felt in one "school" of translators in this collection. In some of Peter Whigham's versions from Meleager, for example (*AP* 7.196):

Cicala stoned with dew,
making your loud meadow-music
                    alone
hidden somewhere
                    among high leaves
the sunburnt skeleton,
                    its thin serrated
legs scratching
          a lyre's melody!
—Sing something fresh
for the tree-nymphs
          maelid & heliad
a *responsus* for Pan in the meadows.

Whigham is a most accomplished performer, and the thirty versions from Meleager included here are among the undoubted successes of the book. Perhaps he makes him more brittle and foppish, wittier but more weightless, than he really is. He does not seem to have heard the "hauntingly liquid and delicate rhythm" that Mackail could catch in Meleager.[5]

And there is Alan Marshfield, whose translations from Rufinus are very stylish, sometimes quite sumptuously done. This piece, for instance (*AP* 5.36), an updated Judgment of Paris staged for the poet by three hetaerae:

Rhodope, Melite and Rhodoklea
                    contested

to see who possessed
     the best quim
I was the judge
    and like those three
         famous seraphs
they stood naked
     damp with wine
between Rhodope's thighs
       gleamed the one eye
like a rosepatch cut
     by a foaming stream
(and Melite's
    like watered silk
between frills folded
    an aching dark)
while Rhodoklea's
     was like clear glass
        its wet surface
like a newly minted
     temple carving
but I knew what Paris
     suffered for his choosing
so I at once did the honours
      to all three angels.

Except for the bracketed lines where a break in the Greek has allowed Marshfield to show his own paces, this is as close to the original as one has any right to expect, and it matches Rufinus's etiolated elegance with an elegance of its own drawn from the modern manner.

One more example of what is certainly not "school of Pound" and yet shows the translator bringing to the re-creation of ancient poetry modern poetic resources in a way Pound taught poets to do. It is a version by Andrew Miller of a very minor piece by Paul the Silentiary, a description of a building in the manner then fashionable in Byzantium and which Paul himself handled at greater length and sometimes splendidly in his ekphrastic poem on Santa Sophia. The building speaks in the first person:

On a High House in Byzantium

On three sides
    the sea's
broad, blue back
shot with light—
    the sun

that dawn scattered
against the wide windows
clings there
    till dusk.[6]

Johnson held that the translator should not seek to surpass his author; for scholarship, a classical text is what it is and must not be tampered with. But translation is a collaborative, maieutic enterprise that can reach across time and joining forces with its original complete what was there merely latent. Should we censure Miller because he has been able to uncover a poem lurking in Paul's pedestrian verses?

Another school in Jay's *Anthology* is on the face of it more traditional, but "modern traditional." I have in mind several poems in couplets by Edwin Morgan, an astonishingly skillful man who can translate stylishly from half a dozen languages ancient and modern; and, perhaps even more spirited, some translations in a similar form by Peter Porter. Porter, who has translated (or imitated) Martial very well, is more a Roman than a Greek; the harder, wittier Roman manner comes more naturally to him, with the result that perhaps his Greek versions are more witty than they have any business to be. This poem for instance by a very minor Hellenistic practitioner called Nicarchus, about a girl who, deciding to abandon the service of Athena, burns her shuttle and loom and proclaims allegiance to Aphrodite (*AP* 6.285):

Instead, our little Nicarete set up
    The lyre, the garlands and such proper emblems
As Violettas use to grace their calling,
    Her humble prayer to her Goddess running:
"Be my protector, Cypris, and I offer
    You ten per cent of all I make: I'm changing
My trade from upright to the horizontal."

Porter can claim at least a hint of justification from an ambiguity in the last line, "Take one trade and give me another in its place," where the word for trade (ἐργασία) can also be used of prostitution.

Not everything is as achieved as this (Philodemus, at moments the most startlingly original poet in the whole *Anthology*, is I am afraid distinctly too much for William Moebius), but all in all this is a useful and enjoyable book which prompts a few further thoughts. A poem by Meleager begins, in Whigham's version (*AP* 5.166):

Night & Night's longing
cruel tears at crueller dawn.

More literally the first line read: "O night, o my sleepless longing for Heliodora." The problem is the second line:

καὶ σκολιῶν ὄρθρων κνίσματα δακρυχαρῆ.

κνίσμα means "chafing" or the like and can refer to lovers' quarrels, here perhaps to lover's pains. The last word ("delighting in tears") is not quite certain but seems acceptable enough. The difficulty is the adjective governing ὄρθρων, "dawns": σκολιός, meaning "curved" or "bent," literally or metaphorically. Brave but rather desperate attempts have been made to translate the phrase: "perfidi diluculi cruciatus" (Dübner); "eyes that sting with tears in the creeping grey of dawn" (Mackail); "tortures of the crabbéd morns" (Headlam). Perhaps we should read σκότιος, dark, an easy and not unattractive conjecture. The real problem, Page writes in his commentary, is that it "may be doubted whether even Meleager, *though a bold phrase-maker,* would have written σκοτίων ὄρθρων κνίσματα in the sense suggested."[7] The real problem, to which my italics point, cuts deeper and is in the fullest sense a problem of interpretation. Is it enough to call Meleager a bold phrasemaker? More generally, is the received reading of the better poets of the *Anthology* adequate?

Page's detailed commentary on the 132 surviving poems of Meleager is unusually appreciative and free from the malice and deliberate obtuseness that disfigure his work on the major Greek poets. He finds in him "uncommon fertility of invention, and an ingenuity in expression unsurpassed in the *Anthology*" (*Hellenistic Epigrams,* 2:591), and singles out many individual poems for praise. Notice, though, the terms he uses: "An elaborate version of a common motif. The compression of so much matter into about fifty words, vivid, precise, and clear, makes it a masterpiece of its kind. The internal structure is complex and neat" (p. 612, on *AP* 5.180); "a highly sophisticated epigram, exquisitely expressed in a dozen words" (p. 617, on *AP* 5.57); "a highly original variation on the common motif, 'Bittersweet Love'" (p. 634, on *AP* 5.163); "the last couplet is wonderfully compact" (p. 651, on *AP* 12.127). Meleager, then, is to be approached as a brilliant technician; "it may even be admitted that a glimmer of true emotion can be discerned here and there, but it is quite certain that most of the light is artificial" (p. 592). The criterion is the old Romantic one of sincerity, and we find Page writing of the poem on Heliodora's death admired by Sainte-Beuve (*AP* 7.476): "the imagery, or at least the expression, seems to be original; but . . . true sorrow is not expressed in such terms" (p. 638). The proposed antithesis is clear: on the one hand there is genuine poetry inspired by true emotion which the poet really felt; on the other, the kind written by Meleager which consists of brilliant literary artifice.

I quote Page at some length because he expresses a standard opinion forcefully,[8] and because his commentary on Meleager and on the poets of the Roman period[9] provides the basis on which criticism has to build. The literary person is usually unable to perform the close, and indispensable, philological scrutiny which Page provides. Criticism will start here, but it will hardly be content with his disarmingly simple contrast between sincerity and artifice. For poets living inside a long tradition, as these poets did, the poetry they have inherited is itself *materia poetica* from which new poetry can be created. Not the greatest kind of poetry, but still perfectly genuine. The poet's own experience will have played its part in ways we cannot hope to detect. It is quite vain to do what Page sometimes does and declare that a particular poem springs from "a real occasion" (e.g., *AP* 12.53, commentary on 642–43) rather than from previous literature. There are many poems in the *Anthology* where, though no direct personal emotion is discernable, the critic might find more than clever artifice if he kept in mind some words of Yeats on a lyric by Bridges: "Every metaphor, every thought a commonplace, emptiness everywhere, the whole magnificent."[10]

What one would expect to find, in genuine poets working within an encasing tradition, is that fresh experience will sometimes be stirring within the old form but incapable of finding full expression, or finding it only fitfully. Occasionally Page allows this, and he rightly singles out for praise the superb poem by Philodemus, Ξανθὼ κηρόπλαστε (*AP* 9.570: "This memorable epigram strikes a romantic note of plaintive melancholy seldom if ever heard in earlier poetry. The vocabulary is exquisite, the phrasing most carefully moulded. The tone of true feeling is unmistakeable" (*The Garland of Philip*, vol. 2, 383). One has the sense of a brilliant surface stretched precariously over a void, a theme that Philodemus's student Horace was to make a permanent part of European poetry, as in the second half of *Festo quid potius die* (Ode 3.28) where the girl and the poet sing of Neptune and the green hair of the Nereids and the shining Cyclades until the poem dies down to its quiet close,

dicetur merita Nox quoque nenia

with *nox* pointing exquisitely to bed and beyond bed to death.

In Meleager too, I would claim, new life is stirring, if less boldly. Take the famous adjective οὐρεσίφοιτα, "mountain-wandering," which he applies to lilies (*AP* 5.144; Page's commentary, *Hellenistic Epigrams*,

vol. 2, 625). This did not trouble a late-Victorian scholar like Headlam who, no doubt with Wordsworth's daffodils somewhere in mind
("fluttering and dancing in the breeze"), let the lilies "ramble o'er
the hills."[11] Page will not stand for this: "it is not at all in the manner
of Meleager" to permit flowers to behave in this way, since "lilies do
not wander and are not especially associated with hills," and he ap-
provingly quotes a previous editor's verdict: "non ita parum sobrie
loqui solet, ut lilia in montibus vagari dicat . . . non enim unquam a
poeta sanae mentis flos οὐρεσίφοιτος dici potuit." If one protests that
the adjective is visually perfect—stirred by the breeze the hillside
seems alive with moving flowers—the scholar's answer is that Greek
poets did not see nature in this romantic way. If one of them objects
that Meleager did nonetheless use this word, the reply is that it makes
no sense. But this is preposterous. All the learning in the world cannot prove that Meleager did not one day look at a hill covered with
flowers (he can't have spent his whole time studying the *Anthology*)
and, in a flash of vision, found not a "picturesque epithet" (Page) but
a new way of seeing.

The possibility should at least be kept open—for the better poets
of the *Anthology*. To retrieve good writers from disparagement and
neglect is the piety of humanism.

13

Ekphrasis: Lights in Santa Sophia
from Paul the Silentiary

1.

Your stunned eyes will remark
   all caved with light.
   No words reflect
this radiance and this dark.
   Has a sun of night risen
in the holy architecture?

With slow science Caesars come
   knotting the supple bronze
   chains sired by fire
fast to that stony circuit on
   whose back Sophia
strides up the round root of her dome

training her head into the middle air.
   Chains sparkling down
   so fast they die, mere blur
   of metal to the circle
wheel, not grazing the ground
and reeling up dance in star order.

On such long side the disks'
   high silvers climb
   the dome's dis-
   solving height
over heads in ritual time;
a tall journey and coil light.

"Ekphrasis: Lights in Santa Sophia from Paul the Silentiary," *Arion* 4, no. 4 (Winter 1965): 563–81.

Craftsman's delicate scruple
  bruised their iron
  to grip a glassy horn
  poised there, pupil
of light that ruffles the wan
light-maddened dark till the dark is torn,

but not in disks only but under
  the dome's wide
  O light-mad darkness runs,
blundering into the flare of a winged
  cross jetty with eyes
searing the circle groping with fire fingers.

A chorus of pure lights, an arc
  of lights winds round:
near the Dragon's Jaw you have found
  near demon-red Arcturus
a sky built with stars? This
  is the flame by dark

that swirls through Sophia acute
  with consolation
and circling to its root
  one disk still
of white smiling conflagration.
Darkness gutters out, an exile.

—Ian Fletcher

2.

Πάντα μὲν ἀγλαΐῃ καταειμένα, πάντα νοήσεις
ὄμμασι θάμβος ἄγοντα· φαεσφορίην δὲ λιγαίνειν
ἑσπερίην οὐ μῦθος ἐπάρκιος. ἢ τάχα φαίης
ἐννύχιον Φαέθοντα καταυγάζειν σέβας οἴκου.
καὶ γὰρ ἐμῶν πολύμητις ἐπιφροσύνη βασιλήων				[810]
ἀντιπόροις ἑλίκεσσι πολυγνάμπτοισι δεθείσας
πλεκτὰς χαλκελάτους δολιχὰς ἐτανύσσατο σειρὰς
λαϊνέης προβλῆτος ἀπ᾽ ἄντυγος, ἧς ἐπὶ νώτῳ
νηὸς ἀερσικάρηνος ἐρείσατο ταρσὰ καλύπτρης.
αἱ δὲ κατειβόμεναι περιμήκεος ἔκποθεν οἴμου
ἀθρόαι ἀΐσσουσι κατὰ χθόνα· πρὶν δ᾽ ἀφικέσθαι
ἐς πέδον, ὑψικέλευθον ἀνεκρούσαντο πορείην.
καὶ χορὸν ἐκτελέουσιν ὁμόγνιον. ἐκ δέ νυ σειρῆς

ἀργυρέους στεφανηδὸν ἀπ᾿ ἠέρος ἥψατο δίσκους
ἐκκρεμέας περὶ τέλσα μέσου τροχάοντα μελάθρου. [820]
οἱ δὲ καθερπύζοντες ἀφ᾿ ὑψιπόροιο κελεύθου
ἀνδρομέων κυκληδὸν ὑπερτέλλουσι καρήνων.
τοὺς μὲν ἀνὴρ πολύϊδρις ὅλους ἐτόρησε σιδήρῳ
ὄφρα κεν ἐξ ὑάλοιο πυρικμήτοιο ταθέντας
οὐριάχους δέξαιντο καὶ ἐκκρεμὲς ἀνδράσιν εἴη
φέγγεος ἐννυχίοιο δοχήϊον. οὐδ᾿ ἐνὶ δίσκοις
μούνοις φέγγος ἔλαμπε φιλέννυχον· ἀλλ᾿ ἐνὶ κύκλῳ
καὶ μεγάλου σταυροῖο τύπον πολύωπα νοήσεις,
γείτονα μὲν δίσκοιο, πολυτρήτοισι δὲ νώτοις
ἄγγος ἐλαφρίζοντα σελασφόρον. εὐσελάων δὲ [830]
κύκλιος ἐκ φαέων χορὸς ἵσταται. ἦ τάχα φαίης
ἐγγύθεν ἀρκτούροιο δρακοντείων τε γενείων
οὐρανίου στεφάνοιο λελαμπότα τείρεα λεύσσειν.
οὕτω μὲν κατὰ νηὸν ἑλίσσεται ἑσπερίη φλόξ,
φαιδρὸν ἀπαστράπτουσα· μέσῳ δ᾿ ἐνὶ μείονι κύκλῳ
δευτατίου στεφάνοιο σελασφόρον ἄντυγα δήεις.
μεσσοπαγὲς δ᾿ ἐπὶ κέντρον ἀπ᾿ ἠέρος ἄλλος ὀρούσας
δίσκος ἐὺς σελάνιζε· φυγὰς δ᾿ ἀπελαύνεται ὄρφνη.[1]

(You will mark how everything is clothed in splendor, everything astounds
the eye; words cannot clarify this evening brightness. A nocturnal Phaethon, you might say, shines on the holy house. For the supple wisdom of
my lords has stretched long, twisted chains of brass from curved hooks on
the jutting stone cornice on whose back the soaring temple rests the base
of its dome. These chains flow shimmering down one beside the other
from their high circle to the ground, but before they reach it they thrust
their tall way up again and dance the same road back. To these chains is
attached a diadem of silver disks hanging around the broad central floor.
The disks creep down from their high orbit, a circle of them poised above
men's heads. A skilled artificer has pierced them, so that they hold long
candlesticks of wrought glass, that men might have bearers of light hanging for them in the evening. Nor in the disks alone shines the light that
loves the darkness, for beside them you may also mark a circle of great
eyed crosses, bearing vessels of light on their pierced sides. A circling chorus of flashing lights is set there [that is, around the cornice, or more exactly, on the chains hanging from it]. Truly you might say that near Arcturus
and the Dragon's jaws you see the shining marvel of a heavenly crown.
   In this fashion evening fires circle through the temple and sparkle with
joyful lightning. And in an inner, smaller circle you will find the glittering round of a second garland [that is, a smaller, concentric circle of
lights]. By the fixed center [of the dome—i.e., around the lantern], on
high, other disks thrust up their flashing light. Darkness is driven away
in exile.)

3.

One obstacle to reading the ekphrastic poetry of antiquity is that it depends on what to us is a confusion of genres. Everyone who cares for more than one art values those moments when, in reading, he has the sense of *déjà vu* or, in looking, of *déjà ouï*; when his response to the cadence of words or the disposition of stone resembles feelings previously aroused in him by color and line or by music. One's pleasure in Milton's "Knit with the Graces and the Hours in dance" tangles with memories of Botticelli. Moving through a church by Brunelleschi one can suddenly be aware that in listening to Bach one has experienced the sense of awe and happiness at so massive an intellectual power assuming the form of such clarity. What we do not now greatly value is the mere imitation by one art of the special effects of another; and this is what ancient ekphrastic poetry often amounts to. Were it all as good as Homer's description of Achilles' shield, it would be foolish to complain, but far more often it is like this—one of a group of thirty epigrams celebrating the verisimilitude of Myron's statue of a heifer:

> It is the base it is fastened to that keeps the heifer back; if it were freed from that, it would run away and join the herd. Look how alive the artist has made it; if you yoke another heifer to it, perhaps it will plough.
> (*AP* 9.740)[2]

Critical insistence on the importance of *enargeia*, the ability to set an object vividly before the eyes, was responsible for a lot of writing which antiquity admired but which we find boring. How much more interesting, we think, if an ancient writer had taken a work of art—the Parthenon, say—and not merely described it but tried to re-create in words the architectural (or sculptural?) excitements it aroused in him. One would give a great deal for an Athenian version of Valéry's *Cantique des colonnes*:

> Vois quels hymnes candides!
> Quelle sonorité
> Nos éléments limpides
> Tirent de la clarté! . . .

Nos antiques jeunesses,
Chair mate et belles ombres,
Sont fières des finesses
Qui naissent par les nombres!

Filles des nombres d'or,
Fortes des lois du ciel,
Sur nous tombe et s'endort
Un dieu couleur de miel.

Pindar, whose straddling sense of the unity of being made synesthesia his inevitable mode of expression, would be the most likely author of such a poem, and there are in fact a number of passages in the *Odes* where, as he moves in the border area between different arts, not mimicking their special effects but re-creating verbally the emotions they stir in us, he hints at the kind of thing he might have written. There is a passing example of what I mean in a phrase like μελιγαρύων τέκτονες / κώμων νεανίαι, "young craftsmen of the honey-tongued victory songs," at the start of the third Nemean, which may be felt as playing off the sensuous richness of the young men's voices as they move through musical time against the spatial, architectural quality of the structure they cut out in the air. A clearer example occurs in the tenth Nemean where Pindar is speaking of a vase which a young Argive athlete has won at the Panathenaic festival:

γαία δὲ καυθείσα πυρὶ καρπὸς ἐλαίας
ἔμολεν Ἥρας τὸν εὐάνορα λαὸν ἐν ἀγγέων ἔρκεσιν παμποικίλοις.

Lattimore catches the note very well:[3]

and in earth burnt by fire and the keeping of figured vessels
the olive's yield has come to Hera's land of brave men.

Like an object seen under mescalin or by the eye of the analytical Cubist, the vase is broken down into its constituent elements—the earth out of which it was made, the fire that shaped it, the "yield" (literally, the fruit) it holds, the painted round of its circumference—and then built up again in a new sensuous fullness. Pindar does here what Santayana (in "The Elements of Poetry") says the poet must always do; he "disintegrates the fictions of common perception into their sensuous elements" and re-creates in poetry's special terms the visual experience of the physical object.

This is not, certainly, what antiquity meant by ekphrastic poetry; it is in fact remarkably close to what one may call the modern ekphrastic tradition, the tradition to which Valéry's *Cantique*, Yeats's *Sailing to Byzantium*, and a good deal of Stevens belong. This is not the place to comment on that tradition, but a word may be said about the reasons why we admire Pindar's vase and smile at the verisimilitude of My-ron's cow.

The negative part, at least, of our modern distaste for what seems mere confusion between the arts is classically expressed in the *Laokoon*. Lessing, it will be remembered, made a comparison between Ariosto's description of Alcina and Homer's Helen in chapter 20. The passage in Ariosto, stanzas 11 through 15 of Canto VII, is a static, deliberately pictorial catalogue of Alcina's charms which sets out, stroke by de-scriptive stroke, to rival the painters at their own game. (Her beauty is "quanto me' finger san pittori industri.") Homer, on the other hand, Lessing notes, "refrains from all piecemeal delineation of physical beauties" and presents Helen's attractions in action by showing their power on the old men of Troy. Poetry almost as pictorial as the of-fending lines in Ariosto did of course continue to be written in con-siderable bulk long after Lessing (by Gautier, for instance, or the French Parnassians), but in our eyes, at least, it is overshadowed by a quite different ambition, articulated a little before Lessing wrote by Rousseau and Diderot, the attempt to blend and fuse the various arts, not their formal means but rather the emotions they arouse in us, which points forward to the Symbolist total art construct. But the Sym-bolist work is very complex and very unlike anything that preceded it. (To be fair, one should rather compare antique ekphrasis with Ren-aissance or Baroque ekphrasis, with Spenser's Temple of Venus in *Faerie Queene* 4.10, for example, or Milton's Pandaemonium, that false triumph of demonic illusionism.) We had best at this point reverse our course and head back to antiquity and the ekphrastic tradition proper.

As one leafs through a late, characteristic product of this school like the *Imagines* of Philostratus (third century AD), one cannot help regretting that no Irving Babbit came up with an *Ur-Laokoon* casti-gating this dreary "debauch of descriptive writing" in which literary men laboriously pretended to be painters while painters, real or fic-tive, met them more than halfway by behaving as though they were writers.[4] It was the new orientation of Christianity that pointed a way out of this impasse. When nature became not a world of appearances to be enjoyed by the eye but a great hieroglyph of God's intentions to be understood by the mind, the prestige of mere pictorialism de-clined and the ekphrastic writer was no longer called on to render the external aspect of things but rather to re-create their internal sig-nificance in his own proper verbal medium.[5] Among the more am-bitious examples of Christian ekphrasis, the *Descriptio ecclesiae Sanctae Sophiae* by the sixth-century Byzantine aristocrat and court functionary Paul the Silentiary occupies a distinguished position.[6]

Since Paul is for many of us a somewhat shadowy presence, it may be interesting, before turning to his major poem, to try to form some impression of his secular verse. Of the eighty or so pieces preserved in the *Palatine Anthology,* a number may be dismissed without ceremony: Zeus's visit to Danae illustrating the seductive power of money (*AP* 5.217) at one blank extreme, "Lines to a Mosquito-Net" (*AP* 9.764) at another. The doubtful attempt to find for Paul a characteristic note, a thematic area, must be undertaken mainly in the latter part of the fifth (amatory) book, to which he contributes some fifty poems. I call the attempt to read these poems as *poems,* not as learned exercises, "doubtful"; others might prefer to call it impossible. For the fact that these late writers are Christians working in pagan modes, describing a life very unlike their own in a language artificially preserved in the schools—this is frequently taken to mean that they cannot be treated seriously as poets. Thus Hermann Beckby, in his introduction to the Tusculum-Bücherei edition of the *Anthology,* makes fun of the *dolce vita bizantina* which Paul and other figures of the Justinian renaissance seem to conjure up. The girls they sang were mere literary fantasies, he says, while they themselves, "these supposed epicures and hedonists, were probably for the most part worthy husbands and fiancés, solid imperial bureaucrats, good Christians and assiduous church-goers" (vol. 1, p. 59). No doubt they may have been. And no doubt most of this verse was simply a cultural game, something that belonged to the margins of men's emotional and professional life.[7] Nonetheless, the concept of "sincerity," as it is here invoked, is critically naive. A genuine poet (which the *Descriptio* shows Paul to be, whatever the judgment on his secular verse) can work through conventions that seem to bear little relation to his personal life. The poetry of a very literary period like the Italian Cinquecento provides a number of examples. The sonnets of Giovanni della Casa are highly "artificial," and no doubt they draw more nourishment from his study of Petrarch than from his presumed experience of women. But this does not mean that they are mere literary exercises. His sensibility genuinely expressed itself through the motifs and diction and rhythms of the older poet. The possibility (I claim at the moment no more) is that Paul's poetry is of this sort. At least he should be given the benefit of the kind of reading such poetry requires.

If his love poems are set together, what appears to be a fairly coherent poetic personality does in fact emerge. There is (to start somewhere) some brisk erotica, to be read or left unread as taste suggests. "Galatea's kisses are long, and smacking; Demo's are soft; Doris bites. Which is the most stimulating—?" And the interesting question is pursued through several couplets (*AP* 5.244). Poems of this sort (one can imagine the manly relish with which Dryden might have handled them) are not, however, typical of the Silentiary who, at his best, proposes himself as the poet of an age of anxiety. Even where he deals with the achievement or the happiness of love, the mood is charged with uncertainty and the premonitions of loss, there is a sense of the necessary fragility of human relations. A girl lies in his arms all night, weeping at the thought of the approach of dawn (*AP* 5.283). A girl cries suddenly, because "Men were deceivers ever," but the tone of these graceful, poignant lines ("worthy of a Heine," Romagnoli declared)[8] is far sadder than Shakespeare's song:

Ἡδύ, φίλοι, μείδημα τὸ Λαΐδος, ἡδὺ καὶ αὐτῶν
    ἠπιοδινήτων δάκρυ χέει βλεφάρων.
χθιζά μοι ἀπροφάσιστον ἐπέστενεν, ἐγκλιδὸν ὤμῳ
    ἡμετέρῳ κεφαλὴν δηρὸν ἐρεισαμένη.
μυρομένην δὲ φίλησα· τὰ δ᾽ ὡς δροσερῆς ἀπὸ πηγῆς
    δάκρυα μιγνυμένων πῖπτε κατὰ στομάτων.
εἶπε δ᾽ ἀνειρομένῳ· "Τίνος εἵνεκα δάκρυα λείβεις;"—
    "Δείδια, μή με λίπῃς· ἐστὲ γὰρ ὁρκαπάται."

[She is lovely when she smiles; or when a tear falls from her gently quivering eyelids. Yesterday she had been resting her head against my shoulder; suddenly, for no reason, she sighed. I kissed her as she started to cry, and the tears that fell on our mouths were cool as spring water. When I asked her why she was crying—"I am afraid you will leave me," she said. "Men are always unfaithful."]

(*AP* 5.250)

The theme of lovers' parting lends itself readily to this threatened vision and inspires some no less affecting lines:

"Σώζεό" σοι μέλλων ἐνέπειν, παλίνορσον ἰωὴν
    ἂψ ἀνασειράζω, καὶ πάλιν ἄγχι μένω·
σὴν γὰρ ἐγὼ δασπλῆτα διάστασιν οἷά τε πικρὴν
    νύκτα καταπτήσσω τὴν Ἀχεροντιάδα.
ἤματι γὰρ σέο φέγγος ὁμοίιον· ἀλλὰ τὸ μέν που
    ἄφθογγον· σὺ δέ μοι καὶ τὸ λάλημα φέρεις
κεῖνο τὸ Σειρήνων γλυκερώτερον, ᾧ ἔπι πᾶσαι
    εἰσὶν ἐμῆς ψυχῆς ἐλπίδες ἐκκρεμέες.

[*Goodbye* is what I have to say, but I bite the word back and stay where I am. I shrink from this fearful parting as though it were the bitter night of hell. You shine on me like the sun, but the sun can say nothing and you

speak to me, and the little words you speak (they sound sweeter than the
sound of the Sirens singing) hold all the hope of my heart.]

(*AP* 5.241)

The language of the second couplet is considerably more powerful
than my prose sketch is able to suggest. δασπλῆτα διάστασιν . . .
καταπτήσσω (literally, "I cower from this fearful parting"): since any
parting is a type of man's final parting, it must be the sense of mortality that gives the words their power, but one may wonder how far
it is a Christian, and how far a pagan, sense; and whether one can, in
fact, or should, distinguish between them. Could one give these lines
a "Horatian" reading and take this "fearful parting" as a foretaste of
the moment when the soul must set out on its journey to "eternal exile," leaving sun and earth and wife behind (*linquenda tellus et domus
et placens uxor*, Ode 2.14)? Though if I am in any real sense reading
the words that Paul wrote there is, rather than the broad Horatian
melancholy, something more like terror here (οἷά τε πικρὴν νύκτα
καταπτήσσω τὴν Ἀχεροντιάδα). It may help to look at the words more
closely. The adjective δασπλῆτις, or δασπλής, is used in classical poetry
of Erinys and the Eumenides; Simonides, we remember, and perhaps
Paul did too, spoke of the "fearful Charybdis (δασπλῆτα Χάρυβδιν)
to which all things must come" in a powerful fragment known to Sto-
baeus.[9] To whatever degree these older meanings may still be active
in Paul's poem, it is difficult not to believe that they are colored, too,
by the darker horrors of Christian eschatology. For the Christian
writer who used classical modes to do anything more than "compose
versus"—and if words mean anything, Paul is doing much more here—
must have been aware that he was playing with fire. The girl's voice is
sweeter than the Sirens' song: a beautiful but dangerous song sounding along a coast white with the bones of incautious mariners. Perilous
indeed the plight of the man who keeps his hopes *there*! And Paul can
hardly not have been aware of the long allegorical tradition which interpreted the Sirens as "symbols both of deadly lust and of deadly
knowledge," symbolizing specially the ever-present seductions of pagan knowledge. "With their lusts and their demonic songs they lead
men's souls astray," said Eusebius.[10] The late poets of the *Anthology* are
not, I know, supposed to need this sort of commentary, but the skep-
tical reader who does not deny the poem some sort of power should
ask himself in what terms, then, he proposes to explain it.

One can point to these and a few other pieces of a quality that any
fine minor poet might be proud to write, distinguishing them sharply
from the bulk of Paul's amatory verse, mere exercises in the fleshly

school. Paul is very conscious, certainly, of the power of the senses, but what interests him at his best is the *frustration* of the senses. It is in the fate of Tantalus—Τάνταλος ἀκριτόδακρυς, as he calls him in some moving lines, "Tantalus of eternal tears" (*AP* 5.236)—that he discovers the pattern of the βίος ἐρωτικός. And the role he requires of his mistress is that of *allumeuse*, the girl who grants part of her favors but denies the rest. "I wear myself out pursuing a young woman who refuses me her bed: half of herself she has given to Aphrodite, the other half to Pallas. And I waste away between the two" (*AP* 5.272). Or again, "Her love does not go beyond her lips, the rest is virginal" (*AP* 5.246). She gives him a pair of apples, and the appropriate sexual torment follows:

> I am fastened in flame, but instead of breasts my hands clutch uselessly at apples.
>
> (*AP* 5.290)

"If, my dear," the next poem continues, "you have given me these apples as tokens of your breasts (σύμβολα μαζῶν), I bless you for your kindness. But if you stop there and refuse to put out the cruel fire you lit, you do wrong." The Tantalus theme emerges again, at a cheap, graceless level, in a poem from the ninth book about the pleasures of segregated bathing:

> The prospect of sex is there, but you can't get at the women. A little gate shuts out the great Cyprian. However, this situation has its attractions, for in sexual affairs the prospect is nicer than the reality.
>
> (*AP* 9.620)

Sometimes, predictably, this theme edges toward perversion. "I saw the lovers," *AP* 5.255 begins, "driven by the fury of their desire, they fastened their lips together "—and so on. This may sound rather specialized, but it begins to look less like an exercise in voyeurism when one realizes that the opening may be a means of distancing what is perhaps a highly personal poem (whatever—to make the point just once more—*la vie amoureuse* of a Byzantine silentiary may in fact have been). The structure and to some extent the tone recall some of Cavafy's poems of erotic memory, like "Days of 1896" or, more closely, "Young Writer, Aged 24," which begins (in Marguerite Yourcenar's prose):

> Et maintenant, mon esprit, oeuvre si tu peux . . .

The memory-image arises (cf. "Corps, souviens-toi . . ."), pared down to its essentials and yet in all its disturbing power. This is a subtler device than Paul's "I saw the lovers," but it serves much the same purpose, and there is the same movement from the first to the third person.

Une jouissance incomplète l'épuise . . .

Cavafy's next line starts.[11] "Longing, were it possible," Paul continues (there is a compressed intensity in the language), "to enter into each other's hearts, *they* tried to ease just a little the torments of confusion by exchanging clothes":

ἱέμενοι δέ,
εἰ θέμις, ἀλλήλων δύμεναι ἐς κραδίην,
ἀμφασίης ὅσον ὅσσον ὑπεπρήυνον ἀνάγκην
ἀλλήλων μαλακοῖς φάρεσιν ἑσσάμενοι.

Again their lips fastened. Raging sexual hunger preyed on their flesh and gave them no peace:

καὶ πάλιν ἠρήρειστο τὰ χείλεα· γυιοβόρον γὰρ
εἶχον ἀλωφήτου λιμὸν ἐρωμανίης.

How much finer, certainly, is Cavafy:

Une jouissance incomplète l'épuise, lui retire toute force. Il baise chaque jour le visage aimé, ses mains effleurent sans cesse le corps exquise. Il n'a jamais éprouvé passion si brûlante. Mais la parfaite réalisation de l'amour lui manque, et l'accomplissement qui doit être désiré de part et d'autre avec une égale ardeur.
   (Ils ne sont pas semblablement adonnés à ces anormales voluptés. Lui seul est complètement asservi.)
   Et cet état l'épuise, lui enlève toute force.

For his theme—the inevitable human distance, whatever the physical closeness—is embodied in the scene itself, whereas Paul, to show that he too is concerned with distance, with separation, must return at the end to his first-person stance: *They* are together—"but *we* burn far away from each other."
   The big question with Paul—and I leave it as a question: to attempt an answer would require an inwardness with this fragile, stylized verse that few possess—is how far, at his best, he *uses* this frustration of the

senses to create an artificial world in which the impulses that cannot
be fulfilled (cannot, because there is no place in his society for the
sexual freedoms of his poetry; and because his Christian conscience
forbids them in real life) deliberately elect nonfulfillment? Could
one, the question is, say of Paul, or could he, had he been as good a
poet as Mallarmé, have said of himself:

> Ma faim qui d'aucuns fruits ici ne se régale
> Trouve en leur docte manque une saveur égale . . .
>
> Le pied sur quelque guivre où notre amour tisonne,
> Je pense plus longtemps peut-être éperdûment
> À l'autre, au sein brûlé d'une antique amazone.
>
> ("Mes bouquins refermés")

Is it making absurdly much of Paul to invoke Mallarmé (who admittedly had different ends in view from the ones I am attributing to
Paul), or is he, however hampered by the restrictions of his medium,
a poet of the *docte manque,* inhabiting a contrived middle area between
Aphrodite and Pallas, a Tantalus who prefers symbolic apples to real
breasts? Let another poem speak:

> Πρόκριτός ἐστι, Φίλιννα, τεὴ ῥυτὶς ἢ ὀπὸς ἥβης
> πάσης· ἱμείρω δ' ἀμφὶς ἔχειν παλάμαις
> μᾶλλον ἐγὼ σέο μῆλα καρηβαρέοντα κορύμβοις
> ἢ μαζὸν νεαρῆς ὄρθιον ἡλικίης.
> σὸν γὰρ ἔτι φθινόπωρον ὑπέρτερον εἴαρος ἄλλης,
> χεῖμα σὸν ἀλλοτρίου θερμότερον θέρεος.

[I prefer your wrinkles, Philinna, to the fresh glaze of youth. I had rather
cup your apples with their nodding clusters than the firm breasts of a girl.
Your autumn is better than another's spring; your winter is warmer than
her summer.]

(*AP* 5.258)

This raises a recurrent problem of interpretation. One is about to
strike out the trite antitheses of the final couplet which insist unnec-
essarily on the "plot," when one pauses to wonder if it doesn't contain the point of the poem—or at least Paul's point, which may be
a different matter. For it recalls—and reverses—the theme of a
well-known poem by Asclepiades, which itself uses (or establishes?)
a recognized erotic topos, praise of the *viridis senectus* of an aging
courtesan:

Here lies Archeanassa, the playgirl from Colophon, on whose very wrinkles sweet Love sat. O you lovers who plucked the flowers of her first youth, through what a blaze you passed!

(*AP* 7.27)[12]

Whereas Philinna burns brightlier towards her setting day. How are we to take Paul's lines? Are they simply the neat reversal of a topos; or would they, if we could read Greek as we read a modern language, sound something like these lines of Baudelaire?

> Je ne trouve pas monotone
> La verdeur de tes quarante ans;
> Je préfère tes fruits, Automne,
> Aux fleurs banales du Printemps!
> Non! tu n'es jamais monotone!
>
> ("Tu n'es plus fraîche, ma très chère")

There is a sardonic savagery in Baudelaire's poem which Paul lacks and which he perhaps needs (Palladas had it), but like the great Frenchman and unlike his antique predecessors he rejects the merely "natural," preferring the fruits of autumn with their message of dissolution and decay to the brazen tokens of youth. This may, as I said, be no more than a formal trick. But there is another possibility. It has often been asked why antiquity produced no industrial revolution. One may equally wonder why it produced no poetic revolution. It may be argued that the new Christian poetry constitutes such a revolution, but I have in mind not a decisive new start of this kind but something comparable to the poetic revolution which Baudelaire initiated and which has perhaps now run its course. A genuine revolution of this sort can only be understood in its place in history, and since history does not repeat itself we should not expect to find in antiquity the particular features of the nineteenth- and earlier twentieth-century movement. We might however expect to find some of the raw materials, so to say, the impulses which could have led to a modern movement sui generis—the sense of alienation, from nature, from society, from one's instinctual being, a self-conscious, eclectic attitude towards the past, an interest in areas of experience and in objects previously thought unpoetic—and which may have failed to do so because there was no poet great enough to work out the new forms required by the shift in sensibility. The English nineteenth century to some extent provides a parallel situation. Arnold had glimpses of Baudelaire's vision, but he was too tied to the English poetic tradition to be able to do anything interesting with them. His friend Clough was far more successful, and the hero of *Amours de Voyage*, hovering self-consciously around the point of commitment, is very much a figure *de nos jours*. But the *Amours*, for all its intelligence and suggestiveness, is a slight work beside *Les Fleurs du mal*, and neither Clough nor anyone else in England was able to do what Baudelaire did: to make his life the tragic exemplification of the new role of the artist.

To find the impulses towards a comparable poetry in antiquity one would most naturally turn not to Justinian's Byzantium but to "open cities" like Alexandria. There is a sense in which Callimachus is the first "modern poet," the first poet who showed himself conscious of a cultural split and deliberately set out to create a minority art. And we find a profounder sense of alienation—that has turned, despairingly, against life itself—in a much later poet of the same city, Palladas, in whose verse we sometimes seem to catch the accent of a lesser Baudelaire or Eliot:

> We are the men of ashes
> Our hopes the hopes of buried men
>
> (*AP* 10.90)

or

> Are we the dead, do we only seem to live,
> We Greeks, fallen on evil days?
> Life is a dream, we say,
> Or are we alive, and is life dead?
>
> (*AP* 10.82)

In Paul, too, as I have tried to show, one comes across attitudes and images that suggest the poetry of nineteenth-century France. Historically, this may seem surprising, but there is perhaps a sense in which the Byzantine poet who works in classical modes becomes "Alexandrian" again, reliving older perplexities by reviving the old forms. I do not know if it is perverse, for example, to find something "modern" in the way Paul seems to have been conscious of the different poetic, and human, roles he could assume, sacred ekphrastist (and "fleißiger Kirchgänger") one day, pagan, erotic elegist the next.[13]

This attempt to present Paul as a decadent *ante litteram* may still sound unconvincing, and if pressed very hard I might confess that my interest is less in establishing *kulturgeschichtlich* parallels than in "hanging" his poems in the most favorable light and so drawing attention to his undoubted merits as a writer. Let the poems once speak for themselves and I do not mind if my props fall away. The whole question is very complex, and one can only make tentative suggestions until such time as someone is moved to undertake a systematic study of late antique literature, both Greek and Latin, looking for the impulses that might have led to the creation of a genuinely new poetic and explaining their failure to do so. Only then could a poet like Paul receive his rights. One would need to work closer to his text than I have dared to do, trying to determine what elements are new, what are purely traditional and "literary," what elements are, although traditional, appropriated for original purposes. Only then could one establish the distance, and the superiority—surely Paul's contemporary Agathias was right in thinking: in diction and imagery and sheer creative confidence—of his *Descriptio* to all but the best of his secular work.[14]

I am concerned not with the *Descriptio* as a whole, but with a single, celebrated passage: the description of the illumination of the dome of Santa Sophia. And not even directly with that passage, but with those aspects of it which have been caught in the contrived distortions of Ian Fletcher's poem. This is, in one sense, a translation; it makes a page of half-forgotten poetry actual again. It is also a highly personal performance, and a word on the author will not be out of place.

Fletcher's *Ekphrasis: Lights in Santa Sophia* is the work of a man who, both as poet and critic, has always been attentive to the late, fugitive accents of a great tradition, to those ambiguous periods when the shadows confuse the pure structures of a classical inheritance into strange new forms, poignantly evocative of the past and yet pregnant with the future. Periods, we may note, which confront the poet, and the cultivated amateur, with problems of response. We can neither re-create the past nor write it off; it is there, always, watching us improvise our awkward, ingenious gestures of recognition and respect. We admire the wrong things, of course; or the right things for wrong reasons. That is our fate. It is also our pleasure. Few aesthetic experiences pose these problems more acutely than that of a great building, and Fletcher has rehearsed a variety of responses through several notable ekphrastic poems, including a couple on the great Nicholas Hawksmoor, one on the Bom Jesus pilgrimage church at Braga, and a virtuoso treatment of Ovid's Palace of the Sun which launches the Roman poet into deeper ekphrastic waters than he really had the bottom for.[15]

The interest of the present poem seems to me to consist in the way Fletcher has used the resources of a modern sensibility and poetic to help Paul move further along the road he had set out on. The extreme case (which I don't quite want to make) is that he has allowed Paul to write the kind of poetry that was not possible within the literary traditions of late antiquity. Paul, that is, unlike the earlier ekphrastic writers, is genuinely trying to re-create in words the special experience of architecture. His *Descriptio*, as Friedländer says, is "a translation of architectural ideas into the language of poetry" (p. 124). But, although he would have understood what Mallarmé meant when he advised the poet to "peindre non la chose, mais l'effet qu'elle produit" (letter to Henri Cazalis, October 1864), he still feels some obligation to describe what his eye sees. What gives this poem its high place in ekphrastic literature is the way he is able to make his description a continual, implicit metaphor. The point should emerge from a confrontation of the two texts.

It is an easy guess that "caved," in line 2 of Fletcher's poem, started life as "clothed," the dictionary meaning of Paul's καταειμένα. Given the intensely metaphorical nature of English poetry, the English translator usually feels the need to metaphorize more boldly than his original. And anyway "clothed," apart from being dull (in English), is visually not very accurate: light, as Paul experiences it, is not something laid round the structure of the building but rather the element which creates that structure. I have not been to Santa Sophia, nor has Fletcher, but anyone who has visited San Vitale in the evening has marked how light and shadow hollow out spatial concavities between the great pilasters of the inner octagon. "No words reflect": the prose of the matter, in Greek or English, is *express*, but both Paul and Fletcher wanted a word that kept their central metaphor working. Paul's λιγαίνειν, which, cheating just a little, I translated as "clarify," uses synesthesia to stress the central problem of ekphrastic writing. ("No speech could be clear enough to render the clarity of this interior.") Fletcher's "reflect" adopts a more direct strategy: speech is the (inevitably inadequate) mirror held up to these polarities of light and darkness. "Sun of night" is a naive but pleasing device, using pun and rhyme to bring the Greek conceit (ἐννύχιος Φαέθων) to hand. Phaethon is the son of Apollo, god of *light*; so Phaethon ἐννύχιος, nocturnal Phaethon, must plainly be the son/sun of *night*. Fletcher's phrase does more (for us) than Paul's mythological conceit to render the drama of conquering, despotic light (yet still needing the darkness for its conquest to be made manifest) which underlies the whole passage.

The second stanza, notable for its slow, exactly controlled tempo giving the key words their due emphasis and position, perhaps suggests why Fletcher transposed Paul's hexameters into stanzas. The business of finding formal equivalents is always interesting, and always problematic, the only rule being that there is no rule of thumb (e.g., twelve syllables in Greek: twelve syllables in English). One would probably want to discourage a new Shadwell from doing the *Iliad* in

Marvellian quatrains,[16] but there is no Atlantic surge in Paul's hexameters, and in fact I doubt if his meter contributes actively to the
shape of the poem. (He doesn't seem to have had great confidence
in his choice, since he went on to treat of the pulpit of the church—
ἔκφρασις τοῦ ἄμβωνος—in iambics.) As I read his lines, I am more
conscious of individual words and phrases than of their hexametric
encasement, and Fletcher's stanza lets these verbal and rhythmical
units stand out in the same way.

Stanza 4. "On such long side": the disks "creep down" in Paul,
"climb" in Fletcher. The direction is immaterial, and Paul's "high
orbit" (ὑψίπορος κέλευθος) and Fletcher's "dissolving height" alike
carry the memorable experience of looking up into a great cupola.
Perhaps Fletcher's de bas en haut perspective helps to give his poem
what Paul doesn't quite have, a consistent "point of view," that of the
grounded spectator. (Incidentally, the disks do not "climb the dome,"
if I interpret Paul correctly. The chains to which they are attached
hang from the cornice on which the dome rests. However, they might
appear to do so when seen from the ground.)

Stanza 5. The first line gets the Greek delight in craftsmanship very
well. "Bruised their iron" one might call, laughingly, a mistranslation,
but no doubt there is some more interesting explanation. The stanza
as a whole raises a more important point. Paul was along one line, the
heir of a tradition in which the writer acted as admiring midwife to
the artist's literary pictorialism. (Birds tried to peck the grapes off
Zeuxis's canvas etc.) His more spiritual interest is in the inner dimension, the inscape, of things, but he still to some extent feels obligated
to name objects. Doubling for a contemporary guide bleu, he directs
your attention to all those candlesticks. The modern poet, writing
from a tradition that has decisively sorted out verse from prose, proceeds more indirectly, via a kenning ("glassy horn") and a pun: pupil
(of the eye, anticipating the eyed cross of the next stanza) and pupil
(student) of light, taught by the light to shine.

The last two lines of stanza 5 dramatize the cosmic war between
light and dark more strongly than Paul, who merely says that the candlesticks are there "that men might have bearers of light hanging for
them in the evening." Fletcher has read the sense (or rather his, more
dramatic, sense) of φέγγος φιλέννυχον (light that loves the night) in
line 22 into the more neutral φέγγος ἐννύχιον (light in the evening)
in the line above; and, translating "light-mad[dened]," has transposed
the perspective. You may respond to the illuminated interior of Santa
Sophia by saying, as Paul does, that the light shines in the dark, loves
the dark, lovingly seeks out the dark and by implication subdues it.
Or you may look at it through the enemy's eyes and say, with Fletcher,

that the darkness is maddened by the light; is also mad "for" the light, is drawn irresistibly to its cosmic antagonist.

Stanza 6. "The dome's wide O": wide circle; and the O of *O altitudo!* as you stare up in awe. The spectator's point of view is again stressed. The last three lines of the stanza respond very energetically to Paul's powerful phrase, "the form of a great many-eyed cross bearing a vessel of light" (line 23). Fletcher's darkness, "blundering into the flare of a winged cross," becomes a kind of bomber caught in the divine searchlights. But the cross itself, menacingly, is airborne too. There is a dramatic sense of movement that one can hardly not call baroque. "What are baroque effects doing in a Byzantine interior?" one may wonder. But this is a poem, not a building, the arts are not always synchronous, and whatever the immaterial purity of Santa Sophia's architecture, Paul's poetry is far from "pure." It is lavishly ornamental, dramatic often, loaded in a way that recalls his master, Nonnus.[17] And, as Friedländer notes, Paul is remarkably successful in translating the still architectural structure into physical, motor images (p. 126). We find the dome resting its *foot* on the *back* of the cornice, the chains *shimmering* to the ground and then *dancing* up again, and the lights taking the form of a *circling* chorus. Fletcher, once again, has merely intensified something that is emphatically present in the original.

The cross is "jetty [jet-black] with eyes" in the sense that Milton's God is "dark with excessive bright." It sends out *jets* of light, like a searchlight. The cross is also a *jetty*, a solid object projecting into an alien element; and a means of connecting land and sea (human and divine, etc). The primary senses, once established, set up a series of secondary meanings.

This tumult is stilled to tranquil, triumphant peace in the last two stanzas, which follow the Greek relatively closely, though Fletcher has not tried for a Baedeker's precision in presenting the relation of the two circles of illumination. But then Paul himself is decidedly impressionistic, and the interpretation of his final lines is by no means self-evident. The "chorus of pure lights," at the start of the seventh stanza, carries the image underlying the whole passage. "Santa Sophia is," Fletcher writes, "like all cathedrals an emblem, an earthly image of the new Jerusalem and for the service is dressed like the Bride of God." It is the triumph of Paul's ekphrastic art that he has largely subordinated mere description to the sensuous presentation of this complex image.

It would not have been worth spending so much time on Fletcher's *Ekphrasis*, in a book about classics and translation, were it simply a twentieth-century poem prompted by Paul's lines. The critically interesting point, I believe, is the way he has shown that rendering the passage in the terms of a later, more subtle ekphrastic tradition does not denature it but rather liberates it and reveals its deeper intentions. For Paul does not merely word-paint, as classical writers were generally content to do. Nor does he attach a "meaning" to his word-painting, as nineteenth-century poets often do. The word-painting carries the meaning, it *is* that meaning. His *Descriptio* may seem to describe; it is really (but would we have seen this without Fletcher's intervention?) a prolonged metaphor: an emblem.

14

Horace in English

WHEN AT THE END OF HIS MOST SUBSTANTIAL VOLUME OF LYRIC PO-
etry, the first three books of *Odes,* Horace claimed that he had achieved
a monument more durable than bronze that would last as long as
Rome itself, he could hardly have imagined that it would last a great
deal longer. The immediate future he could foresee: classic status,
read by the literati and used to teach children the rudiments. But
beyond that? Barbarism moving in, the fall of eternal Rome . . . What
hope had he of surviving through the shadowy interregnum stretch-
ing out on the far side of calamity? Yet survive he did; his book, unlike that of Catullus, never vanished, but it suffered a partial eclipse.
The Christian world could accept the *Satires* and *Epistles,* for they were
moral poetry, even though the morality was pagan. The *Ars poetica* was
useful, full of good tips for aspiring writers. The *Odes* were another
kettle of fish, too sophisticated and too unlike any medieval lyric to
be understood, let alone enjoyed. With the revival of classical studies
in the eleventh and twelfth centuries Horace emerged a little further;
his complete work was available, for those qualified to read it, in the
better libraries, but some amiable lines of rhyming Latin (they can be
Englished with no loss whatever) show that full acceptance was some
way ahead:

> Horace is the next who comes, a wise discerning mind,
> Enemy of every vice, resolute and kind.
> Three in number are the main works this author wrote,
> And composed a couple more, though of less note,
> Epodes and a book of Odes. These, so people say,
> Are not highly valued by readers of today.

(The *Ars poetica* was counted as the third of the main works.) It is in
this diminished guise that Horace makes his brief but memorable

"Introduction," *Horace in English,* ed. D. S. Carne-Ross and Kenneth Haynes (London: Penguin, 1996): 1–58.

appearance among the famous authors of antiquity in Dante's limbo. First comes Homer, "sovran poet," sword in hand, and stepping out bravely behind him, *Orazio satiro*. Could our friend Quintus Horatius have seen himself in the pages of the great Christian epic, one may imagine him murmuring, "What the devil am I doing in this *galère?*"

It is in the next literary generation, in the more congenial environment afforded him by Petrarch, that the lineaments of the Horace we know come together. In the *Rime* for the first time we find a poet doing what poets were to do until yesterday, working a Horatian phrase or line into the texture of their verse. Just as Milton will write "fit audience find though few," confident that everyone will have in mind *contentus paucis lectoribus*, or Tennyson write "our dark Queen-city, all her realm / Of sound and smoke," recalling words that Horace used of Rome in the great ode to Maecenas,[1] so Petrarch in his introductory sonnet says with feigned dismay that his love poetry has made him a byword among people everywhere: "al popol tutto / favola fui gran tempo," flattering instructed readers on their ability to supply from Epode 11 *heu me per Vrbem . . . fabula quanta fui*. In Petrarch's prose, allusions to Horace are frequent and drawn from the whole range of his work. They are less so in the poems, often merely glancing though sometimes taking a more substantial form. Horace ends a playful ode (1.22) by announcing that wherever he may be, he will always love sweetly laughing, sweetly speaking Lalage: *dulce ridentem Lalagen amabo, / dulce loquentem*. Turning Horace to very different purposes, Petrarch ends a sonnet to Laura on a note of rapt adoration: "He does not know how Love heals and how Love kills, who knows not how sweetly she sighs, how sweetly speaks and sweetly laughs":

> non sa come Amor sana e come ancide,
>   chi non sa come dolce ella sospira,
> e come dolce parla e dolce ride.

Behind Petrarch's echo of Horace in his soft new Latin we can hear, though he could not, the voice of Sappho:

> καὶ πλάσιον ἆδυ φωνεί-
> σας ὑπακούει
> καὶ γελαίσας ἰμέροεν.[2]

The early notes of the full concert of European poetry are beginning to sound as the great dead speak again through living lips.

As usual Petrarch was ahead of the field, for it was over a century before the next important step in the recovery of Horace took place, again in his native Italy.[3] In the second and third decades of the sixteenth century Ariosto composed his seven satires. Not predominantly satirical, though the tone is sometimes more acerbic than Horace's, they are rather epistles, verse letters written in a terza rima as flexible and colloquial as the Horatian hexameter, with the easy confidential manner of friend speaking to friend about matters of mutual interest and giving us between the lines vivid pictures of the life of the time. Ariosto does not imitate, let alone translate, Horace; he uses him to write original poems of his own. His *Satires* marks a notable moment in the history of European poetry, putting back into circulation a sturdy, all-purpose genre, the *sermo* or *causerie*: what Reuben Brower calls the poetry of talk.

The *Odes* proved more difficult to domesticate, though here too efforts were under way in Italy. The sonnet in the Latinized form introduced by Pietro Bembo in the early sixteenth century was seen as the vernacular equivalent of the ode or epistle, and although not much was done that we can confidently call Horatian, Milton took over the Italian experiments a century later and wrote sonnets to great public figures like Cromwell or Sir Henry Vane as Horace had written odes to the eminent men of his day, and issued an invitation to dinner in the sonnet to Lawrence with its beautiful sestet, Horace's plainer manner transposed to fastidious Miltonic. The first translation or rather imitation of any quality seems to be the version of the love duet, Ode 3.9, of 1519 or thereabouts by Giangiorgio Trissino. Writing an elegant Petrarchan, Trissino captures the light, graceful movement of the original more successfully than Jonson or Herrick were to do a century later, and to find anything as accomplished we must move forward to the version by John Oldham in the Restoration period.

Spain and France were quick to follow the Italian lead. The Augustinian friar Luis de León translated twenty-three or twenty-four odes, using the five- or six-line stanza of seven and eleven syllables which Spaniards call the *lira*, the first of the many forms devised for Horace's strophes. This is early work, not of great interest in itself, and Spanish critics judge his versions to be more truly Horatian when he imitates Horace, as he does very freely in his celebrated poem "Vida retirada" inspired by the second epode, *Beatus ille*. The contribution of France is more notable as Ronsard turns to Horace and makes the *Odes* part of French literature as English poets were soon to do for their own literature. Native students of Ronsard distinguish an initial Pindaric phase followed by an Anacreontic phase where the influence of Horace makes itself felt, but in reality Horace was there from the start and was far closer to him and left a profounder mark on his lyric poetry. There are virtual translations like "A la fontaine Bellerie," modeled closely on Horace's ode to the Bandusian fountain where Ronsard risks the introduction of Latin syntax into French: "moi çelebrant le conduit / Du rocher persé" (*me dicente cavis impositam ilicem / saxis*). There are imitations like "A sa Muse" beginning "Plus dur que fer, j'ai fini mon ouvrage" (*Exegi monumentum aere perennius*), or festive poems like "Du retour de Maclou de la Haye" with its charming recall of Ode 2.11 where a servant is told to summon Lyde, *in comptum Lacaenae / more comas religata nodum* ("her hair bound back neatly in the manner of a Spartan girl"):

> Et di à Cassandre qu'el' vienne
> Les cheveus tors à la façon
> D'une follatre Italienne.

There is nothing pedantic in these classical allusions; they are all for our delight, bidding us drink our fill from this fresh poetic source that has just opened up, yielding verse more delicious than France was to know again. Yet graver purposes were at work here too, for Ronsard and his colleagues of the Pléiade were seeking to fulfill the ambitions set out by du Bellay in his *Deffence et illustration de la langue françoyse* and raise French poetry to the level of Greek and Latin, introducing new forms like the ode and the epistle (elegy, to use his term).

England was slower off the mark. Surrey at some point during his brief life translated Ode 2.10, aiming no doubt at an English equivalent of the compression of the Latin, but the ease he sometimes achieved in his handling of Virgil escaped him. Diction, syntax, and meter are clumsy, and the sentence beginning "Once Phoebus to lowre" is scarcely comprehensible without reference to the original. Compared, however, with the first of the two anonymous translations in Tottel's *Miscellany* (first edition 1557), Surrey's must be counted an accomplished rendering. Tottel's author is like someone doggedly hacking his way through a thicket of brambles, not seeing where he is going nor why he is going, except that somewhere in this tangle of words which he seems hardly to understand he believes that Horace is to be found. It was left to Sidney two decades or so later to find him with a translation of the same ode that can claim the honor of being the first that can stand in its own right as a fine English poem. Where Horace's fluid movement runs the sense on from line to line and in one case beyond the stanza, Sidney's less flexible syntax and rhythmically end-stopped lines make the poem seem to consist of a series of gnomic statements ("The golden meane who loves, lives safely free," "The wynde most oft the hugest Pine-tree greeves"). In itself un-Horatian and too overtly didactic, this gives the writing a sturdy moral note too often missed or misrepresented by later translators. Despite Sidney's breakthrough, the Horatian ode was still well out of reach, and if a poet of Surrey's caliber had difficulty with it, routine versifiers were completely at a loss, not so much failing to capture the sophistication of the style as failing even to recognize it. What they did recognize or thought they recognized was the moral note, but they got the moralism wrong. Tottel included an anonymous version of Ode 4.7 which reveals by its very title, "All worldly pleasures fade," the homiletic Christian tone that the author felt bound to impose on Horace's somber pagan melancholy. It begins:

> The winter with his griesly stormes no lenger dare abyde.

Horace does it in two words, *Diffugere nives*. The rapid succession of the seasons in lines 9–12 (*frigora mitescunt Zephyris . . .*) is admittedly hard to manage with anything like the Latin concision. Centuries later Housman was to do it superbly; Tottel's man wambles through eight lumbering fourteeners ("For Zepharus doth mollifye . . .").

An age which judged this to be the right measure for a Horatian ode was inevitably going to use it for his hexameter poems. Thomas Drant did so in his 1566 version of the *Satires* (*A Medicinable Morall*, he called his book) and, in the following year, of the *Epistles* and *Ars poetica*. He too was a Christian moralist and found that his theological preoccupations got in the way (should a reformed Christian spend time on a heathen poet?) no less than his dray-horse meter. He begins the *Ars poetica* like this:

> A Paynter if he shoulde adjoyne
>   unto a womans heade
> A longe maires necke, and overspred
>   the corps in every steade
> With sondry feathers of straunge huie,
>   the whole proportioned so
> Without all good congruitye:
>   the nether partes do goe
> Into a fishe, on hye a freshe
>   welfavored womans face:
> My frinds let in to see this sighte
>   could you but laugh a pace?

Apparently this was felt to be the right way about it, for no less a personage than Queen Elizabeth began her partial translation of the poem in the same meter two decades later.

But if the English were slow to make themselves at home with Horace, they soon caught up with him in the new century. The decisive figure is Ben Jonson, the decisive event *The Poetaster* (1601), in which, he tells us, he chose

> Augustus Caesars times,
> When wit, and artes were at their height in Rome,
> To shew that Virgil, Horace, and the rest
> Of those great master-spirits did not want
> Detractors, then, or practisers against them.

In similar fashion Jonson saw himself subject to the envious slanders of rival poets, Marston and Dekker. Even if a cast composed of so many glittering figures, some of them, like Maecenas, having little more to do than pass an occasional remark, may sometimes remind us of Beerbohm's "*Savonarola*" *Brown*, the effect of putting Horace and the other leading Roman poets of the day on the stage was to make them more accessible. Naturalizing Horace was the necessary prelude to translating him. Jonson himself made only one translation that can be called successful, of Ode 4.1, but he prepared the way for other translators. And he taught the members of his tribe to strengthen their own original poetry by drawing on Horace at need, sometimes using the *Odes* as so much *materia poetica*. Herrick adopted this procedure in "His age, dedicated to his peculiar friend, M. John Wickes, under the name of Posthumus," studded so thickly with Horatian allusions that the poem is almost a cento, though the voice remains his own. He begins with a direct translation of the Postumus Ode (2.14), "Ah, Posthumus! Our yeares hence flye," introduces a detail of his own, then turns back to Horace: "The pleasing wife, the house, the ground, / Must all be left" (2.14 again), but by the end of the stanza cheerfulness breaks in: "Let's live, my Wickes, then, while we may, / And here enjoy our holiday." The third stanza distantly recalls Ode 4.7, the fourth returns to the Postumus Ode: "But on we must, and thither tend, / Where Anchus and rich Tullus blend." And so forth. "Crown we our Heads with Roses then, / And 'noint with Tirian Balme" is generalized Horace, "no roofs of Cedar" is from 2.18, the "shining Salt-seller" from 2.16. Other poets of Jonson's school used Horace more subtly by taking a single ode and assimilating it into the substance of a poem of their own, as Carew did in "The Spring" or Lovelace in "Advice to my Best Brother." In so doing, as Joanna Martindale writes in her paper "The Horace of Ben Jonson and His Heirs," they achieve "a translation of Horace into contemporary idiom and style."[4]

Translation proper was by this time well under way, if with less success. By midcentury three complete translations of the *Odes* had appeared and several volumes of selections.[5] With one exception, these attempts show how hard it was to capture anything of Horace's style. Prudently concealing his identity, "Unknown Muse," translating the little poem (2.4) in which a man who has fallen in love with his servant is told not be ashamed since the heroes of old suffered the same fate, writes "servant Briseis mov'd / Achilles, though in Venus rude, / With pulchritude," trying for the snap of a neat rhyme with reckless disregard for diction. More pleasingly, some translators sought to feel Horace into contemporary English by introducing touches of local color as John Ashmore did in his rendering of 1.13, giving us a fine tang of Jacobean London with "jarre-breeding war / Caus'd roaring Boyes to wrong thy shoulders faire." The dialogue between "Horace" and Lydia, 3.9, the most popular ode of the century with some twenty or more versions known to have been written between 1608 and 1684, lent itself readily to this treatment. Francis Davison, in his collection called *A Poetical Rhapsody* (1602–21), has the lady telling her former lover of the talents of the present incumbent:

> Though Crispus cannot sing my praise in verse,
> I love him so for skill in Tilting showne,
> And graceful managing of Coursiers fierce:
> That his deare life to save, ile lose mine owne.

With less metrical address Ashmore in the first and best of his three translations of the poem shows the gentleman returning the ball:

> Now Thracian Chlo' has my heart sure,
> That Sweetly bears a part in prick-song, and can play:
> For whom I would deaths paine indure,
> If so the Dest'nies would put off her dying day.

Taking a loftier line, the author of an anonymous version found among the papers of Sir Henry Wotton transmogrifies the ode into a dialogue between God and the soul.

The one exception is Sir Richard Fanshawe, a translator of real accomplishment. Metrically enterprising, instead of sticking to rhyming couplets as many of his predecessors had done, he tries to suggest Horace's metrical variety by using different English stanza forms— the 8:6 syllable quatrain, for instance, which Marvell was to use in his "Horatian Ode":

Shut to thy gate before it darken,
Nor to his whining Musick hearken:
And though he still complain
Tho'rt hard, still hard remain.

(3.7)

His version of 4.7 is the best we have of this great poem before
Housman:

But the decays of time, Time doth repair:
     When once we plunged are
Where good Aeneas, with rich Ancus wades,
     Ashes we are, and shades.

"Wades" is unhappy since Charon provided dry conveyance across
the infernal rivers, but the verb allows Fanshawe to find a better equivalent for the slow thunder of *pulvis et umbra sumus* than Housman's
"we are dust and dreams." He gives a vigorous account of 3.1, the first
of the Roman Odes, which translators have found difficult to bring
across. And he at least makes something of 1.27, a story-poem of a
kind we seem hardly to have in English, where the story has to be read
between the lines. One may perhaps prefer the very free rendering
by Dr. P. which follows Fanshawe's translation in Brome's collection,
an imitation that, if it quite fails to reflect the subtlety and different
stylistic levels of the original, does, while bringing it down, bring it
to life—*The Marriage of Figaro*, as it were, transposed into rousing Jacobean ragtime. Fanshawe has a shot at the Ode to Pyrrha (1.5), far
from the worst attempt at this famously untranslatable poem, even if
it is disconcerting to find the inexperienced and soon-to-be-jilted
lover turned into "the poor cuckold," an example of the hearty gross-
ness that often marks or mars translation of this period (as when Fairfax in his *Jerusalem Delivered* writes "He sided with a lusty lovely lass, /
And with some courtly terms the wench he boards," light years distant from Tasso's high, nervous manner). Standing utterly aloof from
this juicy, coarse-fibered work is Milton's version of the Pyrrha Ode.
Something more will be said later of this poem, sometimes highly
praised, often severely censured.

Not of the school of Jonson and too original a poet to fit neatly into
any category, Andrew Marvell contributes centrally to the process of
domestication which makes it possible to describe Horace's poetry as
an integral part of English literary experience. To speak of adaptation
here would be inadequate, still more so to speak of imitation unless
in the Renaissance sense of *superare imitando*, for "To his Coy Mistress"

may well be superior to any of Horace's love poems, and "An Horatian Ode" is more searching in its implications and engages the mind more deeply than the only work of Horace to which it can be directly compared, the Cleopatra Ode (1.37). The greatness of Marvell's ode, most readers have believed, is the way it holds in balance two seemingly or truly irreconcilable claims: the claim for Cromwell, "Much to the Man is due . . . ," and the King's claim not only for our sympathy but also to our allegiance: "He nothing common did or mean," and the incomparable lines that follow. The two opponents in Horace's briefer work (32 lines against 120) are set against each other more by the poetic structure than by any complex issue. Horace first presents Cleopatra in the terms of Roman propaganda as a half-crazed Oriental who dared to try to bring down Rome in ruin and is effortlessly repulsed by the heroic Octavian. To see through this vulgar stuff required no great breadth of mind, and in the second half of the poem Horace turns, very skillfully, on a relative pronoun and presents the queen in a light we cannot but see as noble, scorning flight, bravely contemplating her fallen palace, and dying by her own hand rather than allowing herself to be led in triumph through the streets of Rome. The poem ends with Cleopatra as "no common woman," the phrase set between two words officially applied to Octavius's victory, *superbo* non humilis mulier *triumpho*, which in effect hands over the triumph to Cleopatra. For Horace's great achievement in the poetry we call public or political we need to look elsewhere, to the Roman Odes at the start of book 3, above all to the fourth which sees the order of the Roman state as an analogue to the order of the heavens, both always potentially threatened, one by cosmic, the other by political disorder. No translation that rises to the height of this great poem exists, because we have nothing comparable in English. Translation aiming at more than an efficient transfer of content requires that there be something in the soul of the translator and in his cultural tradition akin to the original. English poets have often taken pride in their country and sometimes criticized its failings, but we have nothing resembling what Gordon Williams calls the Roman "poetry of institutions." Nothing in our poetry and perhaps in any poetry can stand beside the lines with which Virgil concludes the story of Nisus and Euryalus in book 9 of the *Aeneid* (446–49):

> fortunati ambo! si quid mea carmina possunt,
> nulla dies umquam memori vos eximet aevo,
> dum domus Aeneae Capitoli immobile saxum
> accolet imperiumque pater Romanus habebit.

Dryden's translation is mere chaff beside them:

> O happy Friends! For if my Verse can give
> Immortal Life, your Fame shall ever live:
> Fix'd as the Capitol's Foundation lies;
> And spread, where e're the Roman Eagle flies!

Horace cannot rise to these Virgilian heights, but he too has the sense of Rome as not simply a state or empire but a necessary, eternal idea in a labile world.

Meanwhile the ground was being prepared for the reception of the *Satires* and *Epistles*, poems that in a familiar style touch on some feature of contemporary life, tell a story, address a friend, and so forth. Horace is not the only model here, but he is the most important one. The third epistle of his first book begins:

> Julius, I long to know in what part of the world
> Augustus's stepson Claudius is now serving.

Ariosto, opening up the field, begins his first satire:

> I want the pair of you to tell me, please,
> Alex my brother and you too, friend Bagno,
> If people still remember me in court.

Wyatt, the first in the English field, drawing not on Ariosto but on the less rewarding Luigi Alamanni, begins an epistolary satire:

> Myne owne John Poyntz, sins ye delight to know
> The Cawse why that homeward I me draw.

And the explanation follows. Although Wyatt's diction is still Chaucerian, nevertheless, as K. W. Gransden writes, his three satires "offer a new *idea*, based on classical models, of what a verse-satire ought to be like in spirit and structure. He successfully sustains . . . the Horatian convention of a man talking in private to a friend, rather than shouting indignantly in public."[6] During the sixteenth century poets minor and sometimes major (Spenser, Donne) worked in the new form, but it was left to the magisterial hand of Jonson to establish the Horatian *sermo* as a *useful* genre, a verse conversation pitched at the appropriate stylistic level, grand and ceremonious in the superb lines to Camden ("Camden, most reverend head"), courtly ("To Mary, Lady

Wroth"), more colloquial in "An Epistle answering to One that Asked to be Sealed in the Tribe of Ben" where he speaks out bluntly on the behavior of the literati, "those that merely talk, and never think, / That live in the wild anarchy of drink." The verse invitation belongs here too ("Inviting a Friend to Supper") and at a slight remove the country-house poem where Jonson scores again with "To Penshurst."

The *Odes*, repeatedly Englished though they have been, are often so complete in their perfection as to be intimidating. The *Satires* and, in their more formal but still conversational manner, the *Epistles*, left poets a more tractable bequest, providing them with a medium in which to move at their ease within the accommodating constraints of metrical form without which ease can become sloven, and keeping poetry close to the ordinary ways of life, checking its tendency to put on airs and become too big for its boots. Yet these poems were to prove resistant to translation in the strict sense. The larger freedom of imitation was often a better medium, allowing poets to come nearer to Horace's manner and, at some removes, his matter, and nearer still in original poems in the Horatian mode. These pleasantly relaxed verses of Drayton, for instance, to Henry Reynolds:

> My dearely loved friend how oft have we,
> In winter evenings (meaning to be free,)
> To some well chosen place us'd to retire;
> And there with moderate meate, and wine, and fire,
> Have past the howres contentedly with chat,
> Now talk'd of this, and then discours'd of that.

A century and a half later Cowper, again in an original poem, his "Epistle to Joseph Hill, Esq.," writes what one may think the most perfect Horatian verse letter in the language:

> Dear Joseph—five and twenty years ago—
> Alas, how time escapes!—'tis even so—
> With frequent intercourse, and always sweet,
> And always friendly, we were wont to cheat
> A tedious hour—and now we never meet!

If translators found it difficult to pitch the tone right for the hexameter poems, the explanation may be that the form that was increasingly to be adopted, the end-stopped couplet, is not really appropriate, despite the marvelous uses it was put to, above all, by Pope. It is too neatly shaped, too balanced, inclining too readily to epigrammatic point, too resounding often (think of Dryden's epistle to his cousin John Driden), to represent the satiric or epistolary hexameter which is an agile, flexible medium, rhythmically inconstant and allowing much variation of pause. The couplet, as Cowper uses it here, can serve, but an apter medium, if one could forget the tone of voice and think only of the meter and sentence structure, might well be the blank verse of Browning's "Bishop Blougram's Apology."

With the second half of the seventeenth century a new Horace comes on the scene, shorn of moral weight while gaining in wit and urbanity. It was moral Horace who had most impressed previous translators; they were not much drawn to the love poems. A witty Horace interested in affairs of the heart now appears and calls for a new treatment. Fanshawe's handling of Ode 2.8, a poem about a young woman whose deplorable conduct does nothing to diminish her attractions, is decent enough:

> If any punishment did follow
> Thy perjuries, if but a hollow
> Tooth, or a speckled nail, thy vow
>   Should pass. But though—

and an account of her iniquities follows. But how much better is Sir Charles Sedley some fifty years later:

> Did any Punishment attend
>   Thy former Perjuries,
> I should believe a second time,
>   Thy charming Flatteries:
> Did but one Wrinkle mark this face,
> Or hadst thou lost one single Grace.

Sedley's lines have a dash, an easy well-bred polish that marks a new stage in the Englishing of Horace. "The best master of wisdom and virtue," as Jonson had seen him, is now a thoroughly likeable fellow, one of the wits of Restoration London. "The most distinguishing part of all his Character," Dryden said in the preface to *Sylvae*, "seems to me, to be his Briskness, his Jollity, and his Good humour." The Stoic sage has become an Epicurean, a bon vivant, sometimes even a libertine; a Horace grossly reduced by Otway to the poet of "A generous bottle and a lovesome she," reduced very amiably by Prior to a companion on a gallant occasion: "In a little Dutch Chaise on a Saturday night, / On my left hand my Horace, a Nymph on my right." In a free and easy version of the Soracte Ode (1.9) that has been attributed both to Tom Brown and to Elijah Fenton, *permitte divis cetera* becomes "We'll have no more of Business; but, Friend, as you love us, / Leave it all to the Care of the good Folks above us," a nonchalance about divinity which Horace, hardly *pratiquant* yet always conscious (in the words of a great latter-day Horatian) "of what the unaltering gods require," would surely have found unseemly.[7]

With Pope Horace becomes a moralist again, but a moralist of a different, more amenable kind:

> *Horace* still charms with graceful Negligence,
> And without Method *talks* us into Sense,
> Will like a *Friend* familiarly convey
> The *truest Notions* in the *easiest way.*
>
> (*An Essay on Criticism*, lines 653–56)

Though we may feel some reduction of stature here, this hits off essential qualities of the *Epistles* very nicely (the *Epistles* rather than the *Satires*), the conversational tone of a friend speaking to friend about everyday matters, passing every so often to serious moral issues but without presuming to lecture. This is a new Horace reflecting a change in English poetry and in English civilization. The Rome of the Renaissance—Mantegna's monumental figures inhabiting a distant, nobler world, the world which provided Shakespeare's heroes with the pattern for great actions performed in "the high Roman fashion"— has given way to a more approachable Rome, one that, as we move into the world we still call Augustan, was felt to be very like contemporary England. "For the eighteenth-century gentleman," Reuben Brower writes, "the world of Horace's *Satires* and *Epistles* offered striking parallels to his own . . . Whatever may have been the actualities of English life in the reign of Anne, it was quite easy for a citizen of that world to see himself and his fellows through Horace's eyes."[8] And this new relation called for a new way of translating Roman poetry, the way of imitation.

It is in Pope's imitations of Horace that the genre comes to full flower, but both the theory and the practice of this form of translation were well established in the previous century. In the 1680 preface to *Ovid's Epistles Translated*, Dryden wrote that the growing distaste for literal, word-for-word renderings led "two of our famous Wits, Sir John Denham and Mr Cowley, to contrive another way of turning Authors into our Tongue, called by the latter of them, *Imitation*." He was referring to Denham's imitation of Virgil in *The Destruction of Troy* (a version of the *Aeneid*, book 2) and Cowley's of Pindar, both published in 1656. With his usual clarity Dryden provided the classic definition: "I take Imitation of an Author in their sense to be an Endeavour of a later Poet to write like one who has written before him, on the same subject: that is, not to Translate his words, or be confined to his Sense, but only to set him as a Patern, and to write, as he supposes, that author would have done, had he lived in our Age, and in our Country." Rochester ten or eleven years later led the field of Horatian imitation with his version of the tenth satire of the first book, a swingeing attack on Dryden, and handled the new genre with great brio in his "Timon," an imitation not of Horace but of his French disciple, Boileau. Oldham followed with his 1681 imitation of the *Ars poetica* and in the "Advertisement" to it described his intentions much as Dryden had done: putting Horace "into a more modern dress . . . which I conceiv'd would give a kind of new Air to the Poem, and render it more agreeable to the present Age."

With this we can pass directly to Pope's imitations, which bring two great poets together in a relation that is perhaps without parallel. Of Pope's version of Satire 2.1 Frank Stack writes in a fine study: "It is impossible to describe this adaptation of Horace in simple terms, that it is either 'like' or 'unlike' Horace. Every point in Pope has been inspired by Horace, and yet every point is different. And it is this lively, endlessly open, play between the texts which makes reading the poem as an Imitation so invigorating. Each poem seems to open up the other and give it new vitality. What we are aware of is the endless play of similarity and disparity, re-creation and transgression."[9] Still more impossible in a broad survey of this kind is to give an adequate account of the various stratagems of re-creation which Pope employs, and all that can be done is to prepare readers unfamiliar with this eighteenth-century genre for what to expect. Take these lines from Epistle 1.1 where Horace is talking about human inconstancy. To make his point he tells a little story:

> "There's not a beach in the world to outshine Baiae,"
> says the rich man, and his waters feel the lust
> of the impatient magnate; but if some morbid whim
> has lent its sanction, it's "Off with your tools tomorrow
> to Teanum, workmen!"

Though the harmony of the numbers has gone, Colin Macleod's straight rendering gives a fair account of the sense of the original. Turn now to Pope's imitation:

> Sir Job sail'd forth, the evening bright and still,
> "No place on earth (he cry'd) like Greenwich hill!"
> Up starts a Palace, lo! th'obedient base
> Slopes at its foot, the woods its sides embrace,
> The silver Thames reflects its marble face.

> Now let some whimzy, or that the Dev'l within
> Which guides all those who know not what they mean
> But give the Knight (or give his Lady) spleen;
> "Away, away! take all your scaffolds down,
> For Snug's the word: My Dear! we'll live in Town."

Put case the original had been lost, we could scarcely use Pope to reconstruct it. Horace's anonymous rich man has acquired a name, his projected mansion that in due course will push its foundations into a lake or the sea has provided Pope with the water of the Thames reflecting the marble face of the completed building which, lo! rises miraculously before us like an exhalation, and prompts Sir Job, now with his own style of speech and a wife to boot, to reveal his weathercock propensities. A superb performance, for which Horace has done little more than provide Pope with his cue. More often, though, he reaches deep into Horace and writes something that is neither simply Pope nor simply Horace but something new, an amalgam created by what Gadamer calls the fusing of horizons. We find this amalgam at its richest in the imitation of the epistle to Augustus (2.1) where Horace writes of the way Rome's cultural inferiority to Greece is counterpoised by the native energies of the Roman spirit: *Graecia capta ferum victorem cepit*—but let Macleod again stand in modestly for Horace:

> The capture of Greece took her brutish victor captive
> and civilized rustic Latium. Thus the crude
> Saturnian verse ran out, good taste expelled
> the smell of muck; and yet for years the traces
> of rusticity remained, and still remain.
> For it was late when they trained their minds on Greek:
> at peace after the Punic wars, they started
> to see what the tragedians could teach them.
> They tried their hand at composing too, and well,
> in their own eyes; to soar came naturally,
> they had inspiration and a happy boldness—
> but also a foolish horror of crossing out.

Pope:

> We conquer'd France, but felt our captive's charms;
> Her Arts victorious triumph'd o'er our Arms:
> Britain to soft refinements less a foe,
> Wit grew polite, and Numbers learn'd to flow.
> Waller was smooth; but Dryden taught to join
> The varying verse, the full resounding line,

> The long majestic march, and energy divine.
> Tho' still some traces of our rustic vein
> And splay-foot verse, remain'd, and will remain.
> Late, very late, correctness grew our care,
> When the tir'd nation breath'd from civil war.
> Exact Racine, and Corneille's noble fire
> Sho'd us that France had something to admire.
> Not but the Tragic spirit was our own,
> And full in Shakespear, fair in Otway shone:
> But Otway fail'd to polish or refine,
> And fluent Shakespear scarce effac'd a line.
> Ev'n copious Dryden, wanted, or forgot,
> The last and greatest Art, the Art to blot.

With appropriate additions and not too much forcing, Horace's account of Roman literary culture becomes England's. English poetry has much to offer, and yet:

> Late, very late, correctness grew our care.

The gravity of the cadence tells us that correctness, to our loose ears a limited, cramping thing, means a great deal more to Pope than observing the rules, means at full stretch as much as he meant when he told Bolingbroke: "To write well, lastingly well, Immortally well, must one not leave Father and Mother and cleave unto the Muse?" In these high words Pope is asserting the concept which lies at the heart of humanism and the art of letters first articulated by Isocrates in the fourth century BC. Correctness, yes, and all that it implies, and yet there is something else, the "energy divine" of Dryden, the "noble fire" of French Corneille that shone even more fully in English Shakespeare. And yet, again, as Pope doubles back on himself, there is something else, "The last and greatest Art, the Art to blot," that English poets forget too easily.

Is Pope's passage richer than Horace's? A bad question: there is no comparison here but rather an enriching collaboration. If, after Pope, we find more in Horace's lines than we did before, this may be because he read Horace better than we do and was closer to him, bound by the dream that for a generation or so seemed possible of building on England's green and pleasant land not Jerusalem but Rome.

Imitation at this level was not to be written again except by Johnson with his grand version of Juvenal's tenth satire, "The Vanity of Human Wishes," but the Horatian *furor imitandi* was at its height; Stack counted thirty-eight imitations in a single decade, the 1730s. Horace was felt to be endlessly adaptable and could always be made to speak to the interests of the day. He has, for instance, by now read Newton and become something of a scientist. "The eighteenth-century translator," Maren-Sofie Røstvig writes, "often felt compelled to enrich Horace's Sabine farm with telescopes, microscopes, and similar incongruous equipment. This Newtonian invasion of the quiet precincts of cows and buttercups seemed logical enough to the age."[10] In Christopher Pitt's epistle, "Invitation to a Friend at Court," an original poem as Horatian in tone as his imitations of Horace, we find the *beatus vir* of the second epode busy with his telescope:

> Thro' the long levell'd tube our strengthen'd sight
> Shall mark distinct the spangles of the night;
> From world to world shall dart the boundless eye,
> And stretch from star to star, from sky to sky.

"In the summer [Røstvig again] the telescope will be exchanged for the microscope":

> Thro' whose small convex a new world we spy,
> Ne'er seen before, but by a Seraph's eye!
> So long in darkness shut from human kind
> Lay half God's wonders to a point confin'd.

Like his Roman persona this eighteenth-century English Horace also keeps a close eye on the political scene, but unlike his Roman persona he sometimes supports and sometimes opposes constituted authority. During the two Jacobite rebellions he can be found on either side of the fence. A few decades later, now decidedly subversive, we see him in the unappetizing company of John Hall-Stevenson, who introduces a group of Horatian imitations (*Lyric Consolations*, 1769), beginning with one of Ode 3.3 dedicated to the radical John Wilkes, by protesting against the way "the nobility and opulent gentry of this land . . . have enjoyed, time out of mind, an exclusive right to all imitations of the odes of Horace . . . no one, say they, that is not saturated with claret and champaigne should presume to imitate his odes." Some truth in this, no doubt, but truth and Hall-Stevenson have little to say to each other. With the next big political excitement, the turmoil across the Channel, Horace is back on the other side of the ideological fence. Lord Morpeth, Eton and Christ Church, uncovers in the Ode to Fortune, 1.35, an "Ode to Anarchy" put in the mouth of a fervent spokesman for the French Revolution:

Goddess, whose dire terrific power
Spreads, from thy much-loved Gallia's plains,
Where'er her blood-stain'd ensigns lower
Where'er fell Rapine stalks, or barb'rous Discord reigns!

Whatever is happening, Horace with a little help can always be trusted to provide the timely words.

Although imitation was all the vogue, translations continued to be called for. Then as now, it was interesting to see how far Horace could go directly into English verse, and even in a Latinate age there were the unfortunate souls who did not read Latin. (George Ogle quotes some lines from Juvenal and then gives them, "English'd for the Benefit of the Ladies," in translation.) As we have seen, several complete Horaces were published in the course of the seventeenth century, but none showed any staying power until the appearance in 1684 of *The Odes, Satyrs, and Epistles of Horace. Done into English by Thomas Creech.* His rendering of Lucretius had been published two years before, a work good enough for Dryden to steal from, but his Horace seems never to have enjoyed the same favor. No doubt an age that was demanding polish found Creech too homespun. So far as posterity is concerned, if his name survives at all it is because Pope began his imitation of the sixth epistle of the first book by quoting or rather misquoting him:

> "Not to Admire, is all the Art I know,
> To make men happy, and to keep them so."
> (Plain Truth, dear Murray, needs no flow'rs of speech,
> So take it in the very words of Creech.)

But these are not Creech's very words and Pope is not playing fair. Creech wrote, "It is the only method that I know"—"all the Art I know" is Pope's gift, and he makes Creech sound slightly ridiculous by changing "To make Men happy, and to keep 'em so" to "keep them so," insisting with a fussy precision on the pronoun as though there could be some doubt of its antecedent. Pope's malice goes astray here, for he apparently did not see that Creech's line is modeled on *Paradise Regained* 4.362, "What makes a Nation happy and keeps it so." Quite legitimately Creech is drawing on the plain style of Milton's poem to render the didactic manner of Horace's epistle.

By Pope's standards Creech's versification may be splayfoot, but his Horace has its sturdy virtues and held its ground from the time of the first edition to that of the last in 1743 or thereabouts. He did not, it must be granted, have a reliable ear, and in the *Odes* and *Epodes* often simply jogs along, content if he has supplied the required number of iambs ("Yet, faith, if vext, my Rage will rise, / And when these hated Chains are broke, / I'll leave these dull Complaints, be wise, / And scorn to take another Yoke," from Epode 11). Yet he can sometimes write with lyrical ease:

> Thee, Thee for *Troy* the Gods design
>   Where *Simois* Streams do play,
> *Scamander*'s thro' the Vallies twine
> And softly eat their easie way.

(Epode 13)

He can rise a little when the occasion calls for it and bring off a Dry-denesque swagger ("Than all the Spices of the Eastern King," Ode 3.23), and achieve a sufficiently dignified level in some of the graver odes, but it is in the homely style—what Pope superciliously calls "our rustic vein"—that he is at his best, as in the happy little poem about a rural *festa*: "The Ditcher, with his Country Jugg / Then smiles to Dance where once he dug" (Ode 3.18). He performs well enough with the hexameter poems, particularly the *Satires*, for there, although Horace's satirical hexameter is a more finely tempered instrument than Creech commands, the impression Horace wants to convey is of everyday speech, a casual, seemingly offhand manner. Horace created this style through conscious artistry; to Creech it came naturally. If he avoided the flowers of speech which Pope bestowed on Horace, he did not do so because he judged them to be out of place; they did not grow in his garden. Students of translation looking for a forgotten master of the art will not find one in Creech's Horace. He is not a great translator but he is a good one, an honest one, better certainly than those who know of him only through Pope's maltreatment have been led to suppose.

The final edition of Creech's Horace appeared at about the same time as the first edition of the translation by Philip Francis which was to replace it. Francis ranks as the Horatian translator-general of the second half of the eighteenth century and the first half of the nineteenth, with new editions constantly called for. Though now hardly more than a name even to connoisseurs of English poetry, he has good claims to be considered the best translator of Horace, certainly of the *Odes*, to date, and Johnson's praise is just: "Francis has done it best; I'll take his, five out of six, against them all" (*Life*, May 17, 1778). He had the luck to be born just at the right moment. Horace had by now been thoroughly domesticated and Pope's description of Ciceronian prose, "So Latin, yet so English all the while" (*Epilogue to the Satires*), was felt to apply no less to Horatian verse. Moreover, Francis was writing at a time when the art of versification had reached a very high standard. As eighteenth-century memorial poems in English parish churches show, many educated people could do some very decent versing when the occasion called for it, and the more professional poets, whose names have sunk to the footnotes of literary history, handled the style of the period with a more practiced skill. "Who now reads Cowley?" Pope asked. Cowley some people still do read, but who now reads Richard Duke, George Stepney, William Walsh, William Somerville, Christopher Pitt, Samuel Boyse? Yet these men wrote well, and are still worth reading. Not perhaps having a great deal to say, they translated or for preference imitated, turning repeatedly to Horace, the presiding poet of the day. It is in this good company that Francis belongs, translating, not imitating, Horace, and tackling the whole oeuvre rather than picking on a handful of continually Englished odes. Open his book almost anywhere (if you can find a copy—it is practically unobtainable) and you are likely to come across something as sound as this (from Ode 2.12):

> You in historic Prose shall tell
>   The mighty Power of Caesar's War;
> How Kings beneath his Battle fell,
>   Or dragg'd indignant his triumphal Car.
>
> Licymnia's Voice, Licymnia's Eye,
>   Bright-darting its resplendent Ray,
> Her Breast, where Love and Friendship lie,
>   The Muse commands me sing in softer Lay;
>
> In Raillery the sportive Jest,
>   Graceful her Step in dancing charms,
> When playful at Diana's Feast
>   To the bright Virgin Choir she winds her Arms.
>
> Say, shall the Wealth by Kings possest,
>   Or the rich Diadems They wear,
> Or all the Treasure of the East,
>   Purchase one Lock of my Licymnia's Hair?

Francis can write like a poet but, not being a poet himself, does not have to clear the ground of his own poetry to make way for Horace's. His achievement is to have made himself at home in the *Odes* more completely than any other translator had done. He does not give us everything. He is less witty than Horace can sometimes be, the weight of mortality does not press so hard upon him, he lacks Horace's quiet, unsentimental feeling for nature, for the still heat of Mediterranean noon and the movement of water in rivers. He does not give us everything, but he gives us as much as a translator can be expected to do. What he gives us, it is true, is an eighteenth-century Horace, but if we feel the need to add, "Not *merely* an eighteenth-century Horace," it is because so much in the culture of the age could then be seen, and in a measure still can, as genuinely Horatian. Johnson's judgment stands: Francis has done it best.

On one occasion he wrote something that leaves us perplexed. He begins his translation of the Ode to Maecenas, 3.29, in this way:

> Descended from an antient Line,
>   That once the Tuscan Sceptre sway'd,
> Haste thee to meet the generous Wine,
>   Whose piercing is for Thee delay'd.

But, this is Dryden, not Francis? No, not exactly. Dryden has "*of* an ancient Line," not "from," "that *long*" not "once," not "Haste thee" but "Make haste." The fourth line is left unchanged. From this point on, apart from a few echoes, Francis leaves Dryden and turns directly to Horace, translating where Dryden paraphrases and replacing his "Pindarique" stanza, irregular in line- and syllable-length, with a regular six-line stanza. Whatever his intentions, by beginning as he does (a note by a later hand tells us "the first four lines of his translation are taken from Dryden's translation of this ode"), Francis implicitly invites us to compare the two approaches, translation and paraphrase. There are probably readers today, particularly those of the academic persuasion, who would vote for Francis. Dryden (a great translator who did not feel the need to clear the ground of his own poetry before he translated another man's) is splendid, but does he not often lose sight of the original and strike out on his own whereas Francis keeps faith with the original? It is true that where Dryden is great, as in the lines beginning "Happy the Man, and happy he alone," Francis is no more than good. Further than that he cannot go. But is this far enough? The ode is after all agreed to be one of the finest things Horace ever wrote. Is Francis's good good enough? His performance raises troubling theoretical questions that cannot be pursued here but cannot simply be passed over. It is often said that only a poet can translate poetry. If we mean that only a poet of Dryden's stature can do what he did here, write a great English poem inspired by a great Latin poem, then plainly the assertion is correct. But if we mean that no poetry can be translated except by someone who has written fine original poetry of his own, then very little poetry has ever been or ever will be translated, and Horace has hardly been translated at all. The world, however, continues to demand translation—without it, George Steiner powerfully observes, "we would live in arrogant parishes bordered by silence"[11]—and in all sanity we must lower our sights sufficiently to grant the name of translation to good verse that stands in a responsible relation (vague enough term, heaven knows) to its original, and also recognize that a good verse-man can sometimes, lifted above his normal level by what he is translating, write what we need not hesitate to call poetry. (Is Francis's limpid version of 4.10 not a poem?)

Still, it is the poet-translators who matter most, for although they may not rise to Dryden's heights, they can do something that the ordinary good translator cannot. They may break fresh ground and (like Milton's Death) snuff the smell of change on earth. Of the two poet-translators who next claim attention, Christopher Smart and William Cowper, this is true primarily of Cowper, in whose translations we sense new forces stirring, the initial tremors of the vast movement that was to dislodge Horace from the preeminent position he had enjoyed since the Renaissance and bring him into a world he never made. Put it that he is now keeping strange company. He would have been surprised had he been able to read some of the poems these two men wrote when they were not translating him. "A Song to David," for example. Longinus found something to admire in Moses ("no common man," 9.9); Horace would surely have been perplexed to learn that as "the Heathen Psalmist" he shared with the Judaic the place he occupied in Smart's esteem, and more than perplexed by Cowper's "The Cast-away" or the poem beginning "Hatred and vengeance, my eternal portion." That the gods could be cruel he knew; deity of this insane malignity would have been beyond his comprehension.

Smart, in his translation of Horace, belongs to the eighteenth (the earlier eighteenth) century in a way that Cowper does not. He is, however, at his more rewarding, or anyway more pleasing to modern taste, when he writes not in the resounding manner we think characteristic of the period, affecting its mannerisms (the "finny race" and so forth), but comes down several pegs and adopts a colloquial style. Writing in the conventional neoclassical way he can be dull (Ode 2.4):

> The slave Tecmessa at her feet
> Saw her lord Ajax—Atreus' son
> Lov'd his fair captive in the heat
> Of conquest, that he won.

(The last three words tacked on for the rhyme.) But in his earlier imitation of this sprightly poem he writes with the neat point and wit of
Prior:

> The thund'ring Ajax Venus lays
> In love's inextricable maze.
> His slave Tecmessa makes him yield,
> Now mistress of the seven-fold shield.
> Atrides with his captive play'd,
> Who always shar'd the bed she made.

Cutting through the classical cackle he can see a Roman soldier, object or victim of a lady's affection, as "the dear enamour'd boy . . .
dress'd in his regimentals" (1.8), a lively young fellow from the pages
of Fielding. He can bring into sharp focus the famous Pyrrha of Ode
1.5 "whose plainness is the pink of taste." This may not have worn
well, but it is good eighteenth-century usage, in its day pleasantly *à
la page*, and at least makes something of the untranslatable *simplex
munditiis*.[12] Sometimes he is waggish. In his version of 4.13, an old
woman who still aspires to the honors of youth is told "You would
be beauteous with a beard," that is, you want to look beautiful even
though you now have a beard, but in vain, for you are no longer of
interest to Cupid, "a sauce-box" who "scorns dry chips." Now and
then we meet Smart the Latinist, as when he risks an internal accusative for the benefit of the fugitive Chloe of 1.23 who "trembles knees
and heart." He can be charming, finding agreeable young persons he
calls "Damsels of condition" in *honestae clientae* of 2.18 (well-born female dependants?). We hear Smart the poet in his version of the Ode
to Leuconoe (1.11), turning Horace's beautiful choriambics into a
graceful English lyric, or when in 1.3 he speaks of "the sweet star-light
smile" of Helen's enskied brothers the Dioscuri, giving the Latin *lu-
cida sidera* more poetry than it deserves. His treatment of the *Odes* is
uneven but very often rewarding, sometimes a good deal more, and
quite unlike anyone else's. It deserves far better than the neglect into
which it has fallen, with no new edition after its first appearance in
1767 until the academic publication of 1979.[13]

John Conington, speaking of Cowper's translation of a couple of
Satires, remarked, as others have done, that "in his original poems [he
is] perhaps the greatest master of the Horatian style."[14] An interesting judgment, especially if we apply it to his all-too-few translations of
the *Odes* which uncover something in the famous style which previous
translators had missed, something plainer, more heartfelt, the neo-
classical patina scraped off to reach through to the human reality
beneath the cunning words. In the first chapter of *Biographia Liter-*

aria, Coleridge praised him for the way he "combines natural thoughts with natural diction," and in a letter to William Unwin of January 17, 1782, Cowper wrote of the art of making verse "speak the language of prose, without being prosaic." We can measure his success in bringing this new more natural diction to Horace by comparing his version of 2.16 with that of Francis. It is a poem about the human longing for *otium*, peace of mind and heart, "A Blessing never to be sold," Francis wrote,

> For Gems, for Purple, or for Gold.
> For neither Wealth, nor Power controul
> The sickly Tumults of the Soul,
> Or bid the Cares to stand aloof,
> That hover round the vaulted Roof.
>
> Happy the Man, whose frugal Board
> His Father's Plenty can afford.

The verse is external to the feelings it purports to present, the even beat of the iambics does nothing to bring them home to us. Cowper writes:

> For Neither Gold can Lull to Rest,
>   Nor all a Consul's Guard beat off,
> The Tumults of a troubled Breast,
>   The Cares that Haunt a Gilded Roof.

Specifying where Francis generalized, he continues:

> Happy the Man whose Table shews
> A few clean Ounces of Old Plate.

This is a direction that the translator of the *Odes* can profitably take. Many have tried in different ways to reproduce the manner, the *curiosa felicitas*, and failed. They might have done better to follow Cowper and try for the matter, the broad middle range of human experience, the good sense and yes, the wisdom that have made Horace dear to so many readers.

New in a different way is the religious "Reflection" which Cowper appends to his translation of 2.10, an ethical poem previously translated by Surrey and Sidney and many others:

> Sweet moralist! afloat on life's rough sea
> The christian has an art unknown to thee.

Or, if not new, Cowper's addition raises an issue that seems not to have been troubling since the earlier seventeenth century. Christians had always been aware that on the gravest questions facing human-kind the classical authors they revered were either quite simply wrong or possessed of only a partial truth, but the hard-won, uneasy con-cordat between Rome (and Athens) and Jerusalem allowed them to inhabit both realms. Samuel Johnson, a profoundly devout man, in the month before his death translated Horace's great poem of pagan melancholy, 4.7. The seasons follow their eternal round:

> But wretched man, when once he lies
> Where Priam and his sons are laid,
> Is naught but ashes and a shade.

As a Christian Johnson knew that after death man is very much more than ashes and a shade, and yet, with the great assize only just ahead of him, he could still turn to Horace with no apparent sense of con-flict. Yet conflict there always potentially was, and various attempts to solve it had been made. Although the ancients could not themselves be converted, nothing prevented the translator from converting their works. Thomas Randolph in the early seventeenth century translated the second epode, which unexpectedly ends by revealing that the wise and happy countryman is really a usurer who, having chosen a life on the land, "calls his Money in, / But ere the Moon was in her Wane, / The Wretch had put it out to Use again" (Francis). Randolph pro-vides a more charitable ending: "Lord, grant me but enough; I ask no more / Than will serve mine, and helpe the poore." This is no more than a local improvement. Wholesale baptism was undertaken by the Polish Latinist Casimire Sarbiewski, who in the 1620s brought out four books of odes, and a fifth of epodes in which Horace—*Horatius redivivus*, a title often given to Casimire himself—writes as a Christian. Concentrating on the Stoic elements in Horace, Casimire combined "Horatian elegance and Horatian motifs with a partly mystic Chris-tian piety [which] gained instant popularity with the public"[15] and influenced a number of English poets of the period. William Habing-ton, in an epistle on the Horatian theme of country versus town, ad-vocated retirement "To the pure innocence oth' Country ayre":

> There might not we
> Arme against passion with Philosophie?

A sound Stoic procedure that Horace too commends. Habington con-tinues, however:

> And by the aide of leisure, so controule
> What-ere is earth in us, to grow all soule.

An aspiration that would have graveled the Roman moralist.

Cowper did not feel able, as Johnson did, to inhabit both realms, nor did he adopt the extreme measures taken by Casimire. Instead he faithfully translated the heathen poet while adding his gentle "Reflection" telling him that "The christian has an art unknown to thee." In its small way this eight-line postscriptum signals a momentous change in Horace's fortunes, a distancing that was also a diminution, coming from several quarters. Those affected by the persuasions of the Evangelical movement could not find the solace they craved in the *Odes.* They looked to very different sources:

> There is a fountain fill'd with blood
>   Drawn from EMMANUEL's veins;
> And sinners, plung'd beneath that flood,
>   Lose all their guilty stains.

Horace's fountains were not of this kind. Cowper himself, the author of the Olney Hymns, remained, and we may wonder at the fact, a lover of Horace, but even for him Horace could no longer be what he had once been, the best master of virtue and wisdom. Diminution on another front he faced from the growing professionalism of classical scholarship, leading in the nineteenth century to German "science" of antiquity, *Altertumswissenschaft*, which discouraged that easy, slippered commerce with Greek and Latin writers which Goethe agreeably called *Hausgebrauch.* Tully's *Offices* shrank into Cicero's *De officiis*, Horace was left not much more than a stylist, a master of the Latin language, the truth of what he had to say and its bearing on human life all but irrelevant. And if this were not enough he was confronted by the great changes in poetic taste and sensibility which made the qualities for which he had always been admired look more like limitations.

Before we follow Horace into the Romantic world, however, he must first be transported to the New World across the Atlantic. His earlier experiences there are reassuring; he seems to survive the passage very well:

> And now the Fields, in native Beauty drest,
> Are by the Arms of Frost no more carest;
> The Cytherean Goddess graceful moves,
> Encircl'd with a Crowd of blooming Loves;

Whose nimble Steps fly o'er the verdant Meads;
While the gay Morn her Silver Lustre sheds.   [*Moon?*]
The Graces, who with heavenly Features glow,
And comely Nymphs, whose Eyes Destruction throw
O'er the soft Grass lead up a bright and solemn Show.

(from 1.4)

Charming verses, that give no indication of their provenance. The author is the Reverend John Adams, the place of publication Boston, the date 1745. No less English is the volume by Phillis Wheatley (1773), described on the title page as "Negro Servant of Mr John Wheatley of Boston, in New England." A drawing shows the young author in her mob-cap, quill in hand, waiting for the muse to descend. She writes accomplished eighteenth-century verse, but unfortunately does not fall within our purview, for although her first poem is addressed "To Maecenas," she was drawn not to Horace but to Terence, "an *African* by birth," she reminds us. No less English in tone though published several decades later, in Boston in 1804, are some translations by Susanna Rowson, the daughter of an English naval officer, the best a version of an ode to Maecenas (2.17) which plain persons may persist in being moved by, even though authority warns us not to take it too seriously—an instance of translation's power to save a poem's life from the academy's underreading.

By this time, however, the country is making its voice heard and a new Horace is emerging, not always, it must be said, a very happy one. A decidedly American note is sounded by Philip Freneau, "Poet of the American Revolution," in a spirited adaptation of the tenth epode launched against the turncoat General Arnold on his departure for England after the capitulation at Yorktown in 1781:

With evil omens from the harbour sails
    The ill-fated barque that worthless Arnold bears,—
God of the southern winds, call up the gales,
    And whistle in rude fury round his ears.

In the same decade, from the Coffee-House at Philadelphia, comes *The Lyric Works of Horace translated into English verse . . . by a Native of America.* The first poem, an imitation of 1.12, composed by this native, whose name was John Parke, is addressed to "The Illustrious Order of the Cincinnati":

What deity employs the Muse's lore?
    What man or hero fills this ample round?
What name shall sportive echo's voice resound

Along the Delaware's loud-sounding shore?
    Or to the banks of Mississippi's shore?   [*flood?*]
Or desart Allegany's hostile wave;
Or, where St Lawrence's lake-swoln torrents lave,
    The earth yet crimson'd with Columbia's blood.
'Twas there, trepan'd by British arts,
Montgom'ry drew his latest breath;
    'Twas there, transfix'd, —a thousand hearts,
The sons of freedom bow'd to naught, but death.

This is Horace writing as he would (perhaps) have done "had he lived in our Age, and in our Country," only now the country is America. Horace's lighter manner proved still more difficult of capture. From Virginia in 1806, in sapphics, comes this distant recall of 1.22 by Royall Tyler. The faithful lover has now ceded his place at the center of the action to the lady, a Southern belle:

Such a smart tippy fashionable England
Ne'er could produce through all her realms of Bond-Street,
Nor dressy France, that nursery of fashion,
Land of petit-maîtres.
Place her where never lemonade or silk fan

(*pone me pigris ubi nulla campis* . . .) and so forth. On a very different level is the unexpectedly witty treatment of the same ode by America's sixth president, John Quincy Adams, in whom the light of the eighteenth century still shone. Scoring a first for his country, Adams urbanely leads the lover into regions where he had not previously ventured, Zara's burning desert, Popacatapetl, and Chimborazo. But the light soon guttered and had gone out completely by the time another servant of the state, John D. Long, governor of Massachusetts in 1880 and later secretary of the navy, had a go at *Persicos odi* (Ode 1.38), as graceful an odelette as Horace ever made:

I hate this Persian gingerbread,
These fixin's round a feller's head;
The lingering roses from their bed
    Cut not asunder.

One should, however, put in a word for poor James Garfield, assassinated a few months after becoming president. Though he came of unlettered stock, he was an eager student of antiquity and, as his correspondence shows, a devoted Horatian. He made a translation of Ode 1.3 in blank verse, but unfortunately this seems not to have survived.

To follow Horace in nineteenth-century America is unrewarding. It was not his country nor was it his century, there or elsewhere, and what leads could be discovered were frustrated. Longfellow, during his senior year at Bowdoin College in Maine, translated an ode so successfully, it was judged, that he was subsequently appointed to the chair of Romance Languages, an adventurous choice since he scarcely knew even French at that time. Regrettably, this translation too seems to have vanished without trace. The report that "the greatest Latin scholar of Louisiana" translated Horace sounded worth following up, but this gifted person, by the name Constant Lepouzé, turned out to be a Frenchman. Having lived in Louisiana for over twenty years, he felt that he had the right to consider himself a native, hence, he claimed, "the volume that I offer to the public belongs to the literature of Louisiana." Perhaps so, but although it was published in New Orleans (in 1838), France has a strong claim on it, and Pyrrha's young man preserves a distinctly Gallic air:

> Pyrrha, dis-moi, quel est ce tendre adolescent,
> Aux cheveux parfumés, à la taille élégante.

So Horace had best be returned to Europe, until such time as America is ready for him, to make his reluctant entry into the Romantic age. In most great classical poets there is something that if we wish we may term Romantic. It is not common in Horace, but it is there. It is there very strongly in 3.25, an ode that readers have found difficult because of the way it combines a theme of the kind we call political with a vision at the furthest remove from the public realm of politics. Horace describes himself as inspired by the god Bacchus (it may help to call him Greek Dionysus), driven by a power greater than himself to undertake a subject never treated before, "nothing trivial or of humble scale, nothing of mortal utterance": he is to praise Augustus and set his immortal glory among the stars. As an analogue to the exalted emotion that has taken possession of him, he tells how a ministrant of the god, a bacchanal, standing on a mountain ridge at night, gazes in wonder at a strange remote world, trodden only by wild, barbarian feet. Critics disagree about his success in blending elements seemingly so discordant. Novalis, that most Romantic of German poets of the period, responding to the visionary quality of the writing, took hold of the ode with both hands and translated it as Horace had never been translated before:

> Wohin ziehst du mich,
> Fülle meines Herzens,
> Gott des Rausches,

Welche Wälder, welche Klüfte
Durchstreif ich mit fremdem Mut.
Welche Höhlen
Hören in den Sternenkranz
Caesars ewigen Glanz mich flechten
Und den Göttern ihn zugesellen.
Unerhörte, gewaltige
Keinen sterblichen Lippen entfallene
Dinge will ich sagen.
Wie die glühende Nachtwandlerin,
Die bacchische Jungfrau
Am Hebrus staunt
Und im thrazischen Schnee
Und in Rhodope, im Lande der Wilden,
So dünkt mir seltsam und fremd
Der Flüsse Gewässer,
Der einsame Wald.

[Where are you drawing me, fullness of my heart, god of drunken ecstasy, what woods, what chasms am I roaming through with strange courage. What caves hear me weave Caesar's eternal splendor into the garland of stars and rank him with the gods. Enormous, mighty words fallen from no mortal lips I want to say. As she the passionate night-wanderer, the Bacchic maid, marvels at the Hebrus and in the Thracian snow and in Rhodope, land of savages, so to me seem strange and alien the waters of the river, the lonely wood.]

Intensified to some extent by Novalis yet undeniably present in the Latin is something quite outside Horace's normal range, a vision of nature seen not *sub specie humanitatis*, a spectacle affording urban man a serenity of spirit denied him by the city, but existing in its own strange nonhuman being.

There is nothing else like this in the *Odes*, but some lines in 4.3 may also suggest an "unclassical" response to the natural world, not a sense of "unknown modes of being," but rather a more than usually intimate relation between human and natural. Ode 4.3 is a song of thanksgiving to the muse who has given the poet (will give him, by the poem's fiction) his gift. It will not be athletic or military achievements that bring fame to the man she has once looked on—

> sed quae Tibur aquae fertile praefluunt
> et spissae nemorum comae
> fingent Aeolio carmine nobilem

[but rather the waters that flow past fertile Tibur and the thickly leaved groves will make him famous for Aeolian song].

The last line is regularly translated in this way, but the verb *fingere* properly means to fashion or form, not make, and it may be that what Horace means is that the beauty of the natural scene will form him, pass into him, and make him what he is—a poet famous for Aeolian song. The young Hölderlin translated the poem in 1798 and his rendering of the last line, with *fingere* given its full meaning, suggests that he understood the Latin in this way: "Werden ihn trefflich bilden zum äolischen Liede," "will form him wonderfully for Aeolian song." It looks as though he found in Horace, that pillar of the classical establishment, something akin to "And beauty born of murmuring sound / Shall pass into her face."[16]

In the same decade Wordsworth translated the famous ode for the fountain of Bandusia (3.13). Still largely neoclassical in style, it is not a notable performance. It matters because the ode left its mark on his work, overtly in the first of the sonnets for the river Duddon ("that crystal Spring, / Bandusia, prattling as when long ago / The Sabine Bard was moved her praise to sing") and again in "Liberty" ("Or when the prattle of Bandusia's spring / Haunted his ear"). More interesting than these clear allusions is the fifth of the *Poems on the Naming of Places*, "To M. H." Although there is nothing here that directly recalls Horace's ode, we sense its informing presence in the description of "the small bed of water in the woods" round which cattle can drink sheltered from the sun and wind, a veiled classical echo that also describes a known place near where Wordsworth and his sister chose a home. "The scene comes from Horace, and also from life," David Ferry writes. Ronsard in "A la fontaine Bellerie" had imitated Horace's ode and at the same time celebrated a spring near his own birthplace, but with Wordsworth the relation between poem and place is more intimate, the imprint of the ode more lasting.

Wordsworth's feeling for Horace—"my great favourite," he called him; "I love him dearly"—is by this time somewhat unusual. The great tidal changes in taste and sensibility did not leave Horace high and dry, but they left him a diminished figure. Like other Latin poets he suffered from nineteenth-century *Gräkomanie*—"we are all Greeks," Shelley said enthusiastically. And within the Latin field he faced stiff competition from Catullus, who was passionate and sincere whereas he withdrew defensively into irony to distance himself from his tepid emotions. "No passion here," Landor complained of an ode for the death of a friend, a charge that was to continue to be leveled against him in the present century. "Against the granite acridity of Catullus's passion," Pound wrote, "Horace has but the clubman's poise." Eliot, quoting some lines from Marvell's "Coy Mistress," observed the presence of Horace there, adding, "And not only Horace but Catullus himself." *Himself*—we move on to a higher plane.[17]

Virtues for which he had always been admired—Horace the great artificer, the cunningest maker we have ever had—begin to look more like defects. He is seen as a technician, skillfully manipulating Latin words into complicated Greek metrical forms. His verbal artistry and *curiosa felicitas*? Why yes, a gift for the well-turned phrase, for the well-rubbed tags that come pat to their occasion. A clever, entertaining poet certainly, but perhaps not a sufficiently serious one? Arnold, sounding more like Beerbohm's earnest little girl in pigtails than his own distinguished self, addressed the question frontally, not to say ponderously, in his 1857 inaugural address as Professor of Poetry at Oxford:[18]

> Horace wants seriousness . . . the men of taste, the men of cultivation, the men of the world, are enchanted with him; he has not a prejudice, not an illusion, not a blunder. True! yet the best men in the best ages have never been thoroughly satisfied with Horace. If human life were complete without faith, without enthusiasm, without energy, Horace . . . would be the perfect interpreter of human life: but it is not . . . Horace warms himself before the transient fire of human animation and human pleasure while he can, and is only serious when he reflects that the fire must soon go out:—
>
> "Damna tamen celeres reparant coelestia lunae:
>   Nos, ubi decidimus—"
>
> "For nature there is renovation, but for man there is none"—it is exquisite, but not interpretative and fortifying.

Others were less polite. For Meredith, Horace was "the versifier of the enthroned enemy . . . poet of the conforming unbeliever," for "old men who have given over thinking, and young men who never had feeling." Victorian reservations about Horace's poetry do not mean that he was less read or less well known. He was all too well known, that was part of the trouble. Everyone with a formal education had read him at school, and they often disliked what they read. "Then farewell, Horace, whom I hated so," Byron sang in *Childe Harold*, recalling "The drill'd dull lesson, forc'd down word for word." Swinburne wrote to a friend expressing his regret that "you are spending any part of your valuable time on Horace . . . My dislike of him—dating from my schooldays—is one of the very few points on which I find myself in sympathy with Byron." Kipling wrote in his autobiography that his classics master "taught me to loathe Horace for two years; to forget him for twenty, and then to love him for the rest of my days and through many sleepless nights."[19] In his story "Regulus" he gives a vivid picture of the classroom grind, the boys struggling to

come up with a construe accurate enough to pass muster, the poem
itself meaning nothing to them. Tennyson suffered in the same way
in his youth, but his mature work shows that he too came to love Horace and did him splendid service with his invitation poem "To the
Rev. F. D. Maurice," bringing the genre back to life at a level that can
stand beside the best seventeenth-century work.

If translation of Horace does not show to advantage in the Victorian age, this is hardly surprising; it was not a period when the art
flourished. Early in the century there is Shelley, still insufficiently recognized as one of our major poet-translators, but in the years that follow little is worth reading apart from FitzGerald's *Rubáiyát*, Rossetti's
delicate versions from early Italian lyric, and Swinburne's Villon and
the superb chorus from Aristophanes' *Birds*. The best Horace is the
not quite complete translation of the first of the Roman Odes which
Hopkins wrote in his twenties, ballasting his lines—with an English,
not a Latin, weight—in a way that may distantly remind us of Jonson:

> One better backed comes crowding by:—
> That level power whose word is Must
> Dances the balls for low or high:
> Her urn takes all, her deal is just.

But the Horace who went so well into Jacobean or Augustan dress does
not readily pass disguised as a Victorian. One of the very few translators who managed to make him do so is Sir Stephen De Vere in his
version of Ode 2.16:

> When the pale moon is wrapt in cloud,
> And mists the guiding stars enshroud;
> When on the dark Aegean shore
> The bursting surges flash and roar;
> The mariner with toil opprest
> Sighs for his home, and prays for rest.

The blurred, evocative effect (evoking what? Perhaps, though hardly
to the purpose, Shelley's waning moon, "like a dying lady, lean and
pale / Who totters forth, wrapt in a gauzy veil") is attractive in its way,
but how anemic it feels beside Horace's Latin or beside Cowper's
sturdy verse:

> Ease, is the weary Merchant's Pray'r,
>   Who Ploughs by Night th'Aegean Flood,
> When neither Moon nor Stars appear,
>   Or Glimmer faintly thro' the Cloud.

"Why hope that foreign suns can dry our tears?" De Vere writes, but Horace (who wrote *quid terras alio calentis / sole mutamus?*) does not break up his lines to weep. There is iron in the *Odes* as in all the best poetry and it must not be softened.

John Conington, the Horatian translator-general of the nineteenth century as Francis had been of the eighteenth, cannot be accused of writing in the style of the day, and indeed laid it down that "the chief danger which a translator has to avoid is that of subjection to the influences of his own period."[20] In avoiding this danger, however, the translator runs into another, that of writing in the style of no period, writing of actions and emotions that take place nowhere:

> What, fight with cups that should give joy?
>   'Tis barbarous; leave such savage ways
> To Thracians. Bacchus, shamefaced boy,
> Is blushing at your bloody frays.
>   The Median sabre! lights and wine!
> Was stranger contrast ever seen?
>   Cease, cease this brawling, comrades mine,
> And still upon your elbows lean.
>
>   (from 1.27)

But no one is brawling here and the scene takes place nowhere except in a limbo marked Classical Roman. It is refreshing to turn back to Dr. P.'s hearty Jacobean rumpus. Vigorous but, a reader may object, the good doctor doesn't give you Horace. Nor does Conington, even though his words match Horace's as closely as a rhyming version can, for he was a distinguished classical scholar, Corpus Professor of Latin at Oxford. It is a curious performance, this long labor of—what? Hardly of love, for of the *Odes* at least he seemed to have thought rather poorly, finding them full of "lyrical commonplace" made tolerable only by the attractive Latin.

It is easy to be unjust to Conington. His accomplishment is of a kind that now gives the least pleasure, and if he leaves us with no sense of intimacy with Horace, that sense was no part of his purpose. The Horace whom Francis could describe as a poet "who was by no means an Enemy to a Glass of good Wine" (note on Ode 1.20) has become a classic; one doesn't have to like him, merely know all about him. If Conington's verse is chilly and unloving—so that one is pulled up short by the sudden adventitious warmth of an ode beginning "The rain, it rains not every day" (Ode 2.9)—it is very efficient and metrically dexterous. Here the *Odes* all are, Latin on the left page, English on the right, except when a minatory note informs us that "this ode is not included in Professor Conington's translation." His handling of the *Satires* and *Epistles* is no less competent and on the whole more satisfying. Writing in heroic couplets, he aimed at a generally eighteenth-century style in the manner of Cowper, but if you use eighteenth-century couplets you risk coming fatally close to the master of the couplet. ("With sword and shield the commonwealth protect, / With morals grace it and with laws correct," Conington at the start of Epistle 2.1.) Conington was praised in his day because readers with good Latin admired his skill in packing so much of the literal sense of the original into neat rhyming lines; but until such time as living poets are moved to try their hand at the hexameter poems, those wishing to enjoy this substantial part of Horace's oeuvre had best remount the stream and turn to plain, honest Creech, to the accomplished Francis and the many eighteenth-century gentlemen who wrote with ease, or—the best course—to their final successor, the now quite forgotten Francis Howes. Although not published until 1848, his translation of the *Satires* and *Epistles* (he did not tackle the *Odes*) seems to have been written early in the century and still has the old confidence and style.

It is a relief to pass from Conington to C. S. Calverley, whose translation of fifteen odes and of Epode 2 appeared in the same period, the 1860s. He too keeps close to the Latin and uses a standard poetic koine bearing no special mark of the time, but he is a writer in a sense that Conington isn't. He has a finer ear, his diction is superior, and at his best he leaves one wondering whether to speak of a genuine poetic gift or of a knack so clever that it looks like the real thing. The product of a cultivated Victorian amateur, Calverley's poems were popular and reprinted a number of times, the last in 1913. They include translation of Greek and Latin poems into English and of English poems into Latin, with Horace's alcaics done in the *In Memoriam* quatrain, Tennyson's quatrains in Horatian alcaics. There are original poems sometimes in English—an "Ode to Tobacco," for instance, where Horace's Black Care seated behind the rider finds a place in the first of the deft little stanzas—and sometimes in Latin, like *Carmen saeculare*, full of august Virgilian phrases introduced for light purposes, and contemporary references duly explained in Latin footnotes ("*bacciferas tabernas*: id quod nostri vocant 'tobacco shops'"). All hopelessly dated? No doubt, yet those who find themselves ill at ease in the cultural climate of our own happy day (Sisson's phrase) can still read Calverley with pleasure, pleasure that hindsight turns to melancholy at the thought that these are late autumnal graces hanging at the edge of winter: 1913, Armageddon one year away. The sense of an ending, of *tout ce qui se resumait en ce mot: chute*, is still stronger if we turn from Calverley to the Horatian versions by Austin Dobson, the strong Roman stanzas miniatured into dainty late-medieval French forms, rondeaux, rondelles, villanelles. Armageddon just round the corner, the loss of a whole generation of the best-educated in the trenches in France, virtues slowly built up over the centuries blown to nothing in four terrible years, the Russian Revolution, new styles in the arts challenging and threatening to destroy everything that had gone before, the profound social and educational changes that were to dislodge classical culture from its place at the center and leave most literary people less handy with Latin than their forerunners had been in the Dark Ages. We might imagine Horace saying to himself as he looked down from Olympus, "So this is the end of me, and the end of a lot more too. Well, I've had a pretty good run for my money!" As indeed he had, outlasting eternal Rome by fifteen hundred years.

History had a different turn of events in mind. Much was to be lost irreparably, but in all forms of artistic and intellectual life there was also renewal, not least in literature, a recovery of forgotten resources in which two Americans led the way. Eliot, after establishing relations with recent French work, reached back to the metaphysicals and to Jacobean drama, and further still to the great strength of Dante and to antiquity. The lines in *The Waste Land* beginning "Phlebas the Phoenician" are more *classical* than anything written in the nineteenth century. Pound sought for nothing less than the renewal of the whole tradition of Western literature while making a profitable long arm to ancient China, and regained for translation a position it had not enjoyed since Dryden.

These recoveries did not immediately benefit Horace, but they prepared the way for his recovery later in the century, and here too Eliot and Pound played important roles, even though Eliot seems never to have cared for Horace, and Pound turned to him seriously only towards the end of his creative life. Yet he always knew that Horace was there. In a letter of 1917 to Joyce he included a rather poor version of part of Ode 4.10 in "mellifluous archaism" ("I am reduced to translating Horace"), and in the curmudgeonly article on Horace published in the *Criterion* of 1930 he quoted the first line of 1.4 (*Solvitur acris hiems grata vice veris et Favoni*), remarking that it "has a week's work in it for any self-respecting translator." Eliot, in his essay on Marvell, seeking to define the kind of wit found in the seventeenth-century lyric, spoke of "a tough reasonableness beneath the slight lyric grace." Omit the word "slight" and from the same essay add "this alliance of levity and seriousness (by which the seriousness is intensified)," and you might think that Eliot was speaking of the *Odes*. The importance of this essay for our present purposes is that it established a critical climate, critical expectations and standards, more hospitable to Horace than those of the previous century. Eliot's essay dates from 1921. Four years earlier Pound had completed *Homage to Sextus Propertius*, a "regrounding of the original in a contemporary sensibility"[21] which discovered in another Augustan poet the alliance which Eliot spoke of.

Horace was nonetheless to remain on the sidelines for some years yet. Poets seldom worked Horatian allusions into their verse; the New Critics, so concerned with irony and wit, could have found a good deal in the *Odes* that was grist for their mill, had they thought of looking into them. I. A. Richards ignored him; Empson too, who might have pointed to much that in our dullness we have missed, passed him by. Among the poets, however, there were those who did not forget Horace. In Portugal we have the strange phenomenon of Pessoa's Horatian heteronym Ricardo Reis writing the brief lyrics that in translation may seem no more than clever echoes of antiquity but rather are "subtle and original modulations on the Horatian stance" (Alberto de Lacerda). In England there is Kipling, who saw in Horace a virtuoso close to his heart and made creative use of him as few have done. His story "Regulus" (1917) ends with a poem called "A Translation. Horace, Book V, Ode 3," a part of the oeuvre that is of course not easy to lay one's hands on. Nor is this a translation; it is on the face of it a parody of a schoolboy's construe that, as Charles Martindale remarks, reveals "an alert understanding of the nuts and bolts of Horace's style" (*Horace Made New*, 4) and ends with the memorable picture of the poet "sunk in thought profound / Of what the unaltering Gods require," a more serious Horace than had been glimpsed for a long time. Kipling was to go on to write several more odes from "Book V," the finest placed at the end of "The Eye of Allah" (1926), Kipling at his gravest speaking with the grave voice of Horace reincarnate. But the literati were ignoring Kipling just as they were ignoring Horace, and few paid any attention to these masterly poems.

It was not until the middle of the century that Horace began to make himself felt again. He had to contend with the general lack of Latin, but this was less of a disaster than one might have expected, for it meant that he was no longer dogged by memories of classroom drudgery, no longer was he all-too-familiar boring old Horace, greatuncle's favorite bard. Having lain idle for fifty years, the soil was ready to be turned again, his poetry once again virgin territory that it might be fun to inspect. The title of Lawrence Durrell's poem "On First Looking into Loeb's Horace" probably reflects the experience of a certain number of people, poets on a day when the fish were not biting and literary types here and there who, stumbling on a promising phrase in the stilted Loeb translation, might try to elicit it from the facing original, acquiring a smidgen of Latin in the process and picking up a bit more later.

The first important indication of a real return comes with Auden, who in "Thanksgiving," written in the last months of his life, named Horace, "adroitest of makers," as one of the poets without whom "I couldn't have managed / even my weakest of lines." There may be some suggestion of Horace in the formal, rather stiff stanzas of his 1939 "In Memory of Sigmund Freud," but the Horatian presence only comes clear in a poem like "Ischia" (1948), where for once an English poem in syllabic form offers pleasures for the ear, in lines that not only move to the natural rhythms of speech but also yield English approximations to classical metrical units, choriambs, bacchiacs, iambs, trochees, cretics, like cut Roman bricks strengthening the walls of a laxer age:

> Deàrèst tŏ eách hĭs bírthpláce; bùt tŏ rĕcáll ă greén
> vállĕy whĕre múshroòms fáttèn ĭn thĕ súmmĕr níghts
> ănd sílvèred wíllŏws cópy̆
>   thĕ círcŭmfléctiòns ŏf thĕ streám.

(An acute in this rough and ready notation marks a stressed syllable, a grave a syllable carrying a lighter stress [nònplússed], ˘ a syllable with no or minimal stress.) The single lines in this poem have their place in sentences that overrun the stanzas (indented in a manner resembling the Horatian Alcaic stanza), sometimes in ways as syntactically complex as this:

> Always with some cool space or shaded surface, too,
> you offer a reason to sit down; tasting what bees
>   offer from the blossoming chestnut
>   or short but shapely dark-haired men
>
> from the aragonian grape distil, your amber wine,
> your coffee-coloured honey.

The construction is chiastic:

tasting what bees from the chestnut   or men from the grape distil

your amber wine   your coffee-coloured honey

This is more Latin than English, certainly than modern English, and it seems likely that Auden, feeling his way into the role of a latter-day

Horatian, was led to try his hand at complicated constructions of this sort because he had found similar things in the *Odes*—the intricate architecture of the final stanzas of the Cleopatra Ode (1.37), for example, to which Fraenkel drew attention:[22]

> quae generosius
> perire quaerens nec muliebriter
>   expavit ensem nec latentis
>   classe cita reparavit oras;
>
> ausa et iacentem visere regiam
> vultu sereno, fortis et asperas
>   tractare serpentis, ut atrum
>   corpore combiberet venenum,
>
> deliberata morte ferocior,
> saevis Liburnis scilicet invidens
>   privata deduci superbo
>   non humilis mulier triumpho.

[But she, seeking to die more nobly, neither in woman's fashion feared the sword, nor tried to reach some secret shore with her swift fleet. She brought herself to look with serene face on her fallen capitol, brace enough to handle the poisonous asps, that she might draw the black venom into her body, fiercer now that she had resolved on death; grudging the cruel Liburnian galleys her passage to Rome, a queen no longer, for a haughty triumph—no common woman this!]

Enclosed within the two participial clauses (*quaerens, invidens*) are two *nec* clauses followed by two *et* clauses, the second opening out with *ut* into a final clause. A diagram may show the pattern more clearly:

> quaerens   nec muliebriter
>   nec latentis
>
>   ausa et iacentem
>   fortis et aspera . . . ut . . .
> invidens . . .

Auden knew Latin and read Horace in the original. We may however find qualities that seem genuinely Horatian—the tough reasonableness beneath the lyric grace, the alliance of levity and seriousness by which the seriousness is intensified—in the poets who show no interest in Horace and may not even have had any Latin. These qualities we can expect to find in poets at home in English poetry and hence influenced, consciously or not, by the pervasive presence of

Horace. Poets in full command of their medium, capable of moving up and down the tonal scale and unaffected by "the rumour that verse has been liberated" (Eliot's impeccable words).[23] Philip Larkin suggests himself as a poet who meets these conditions, "Lines on a Young Lady's Photograph Album" as a poem that might be worth looking at in the light of an ode like 1.19. Let admirers of Larkin who prize his stern insularity not be affronted by the relation to Horace proposed here. Let them, if they wish, insist that no such relation ever entered Larkin's mind, and attend rather to what his poem, one written in our own day in our own idiom, may have to tell us about Horace's poem, written in Latin two thousand years ago.

Both poems start from a particular occasion, Larkin's from the album which the girl has let him look at, Horace's (after a flourish of mythology which can be left to look after itself) from a party he has just left, very excited by someone he met there.[24] Larkin's snapshots show different aspects of the girl, Horace provides several descriptions. The first is quite conventional: her beauty shines like Parian marble (famous for its dazzling whiteness). He is not so deeply involved after all. Larkin's way of misdirecting us is by his tone or pose of amused detachment: "Too much confectionery, too rich: / I choke on such nutritious images." Horace now becomes more specific, recalling the girl's *grata protervitas*—she is attractive in a provocative way; so perhaps he is a little involved. Larkin looks at a shot of the girl wearing a trilby hat: "faintly disturbing, that, in several ways," putting the line in brackets—only *faintly* disturbing, you understand. Then abruptly, no longer detached, his carefully maintained balance shaken, he speaks out: "From every side you strike at my control." Horace too is jolted and uses a word that in this context is startling: her face is *lubricus*, "slippery" ("slippery looks that balk the lover's gaze," Smart translated). Then he too speaks not out but up, very far up: *in me tota ruens Venus*, "Venus rushing on me in full force." Editors speak of "the high tragic tone." Roman readers would recall a powerful line from Greek tragedy, we are likely to recall Racine's version of the Greek line, "C'est Vénus tout entière à sa proie attachée" (*Phèdre*, act 1, scene 3). Both poets then go their different ways.

The English and the Roman poets interact, helping each other and helping us to read them better, or could do so if we let them. By negotiating Larkin's shifts of tone and perspective we respond more sensitively to similar maneuvers in Horace. And responding to Horace's ability suddenly to rise to a higher stylistic level (or to similar effects in a great English Horatian like Pope) allows us, since this is a resource less readily available to modern poets, to bring an extra edge of admiration to the way that Larkin, after the beautifully modulated banter of "Not quite your class, I'd say, dear, on the whole," invokes photography of all things, in the formal eighteenth-century manner: "But o, photography!" Not "O," that would be too period, and not of course "oh."

The time had come to start translating Horace again, and three poets set to: C. H. Sisson, Basil Bunting, and Pound. Sisson and Bunting both translated the same poem, 2.14, the Postumus Ode, and their versions reveal a range of options open to the translator today. Sisson, trusting to the traditional resources of English poetry, has given us the gravest account of this great poem that we have:

> The years go by, the years go by you, nameless,
> I cannot help it nor does virtue help.
>   Wrinkles are there, old age is at your elbow,
>   Death on the way, it is indomitable.

This does everything that translators in the past have been expected to do; taking the permissible liberties, it matches Horace's powerful Latin with hardly less powerful English. What it does not do and does not try to do is directly convey the "feel" of the original, the weight, the slow implacable thud, of the Latin syllables:

> Eheu fugaces, Postume, Postume,   — — ◡ — —   — ◡ ◡ — ◡
> labuntur anni, nec pietas moram   — — ◡ — —   — ◡ ◡ — ◡
>   rugis et instanti senectae   — — ◡ — — — ◡ — —
>   adferet indomitaeque morti.   — ◡ ◡ — ◡ ◡ — ◡ — —
>
> [Alas, rapid, Postumus, Postumus,
> glide by, years, nor will piety a barrier
> against wrinkles and forward-pressing age
> bring and, unconquerable, death.]

The first naked encounter with Horace's words lies in some way behind Sisson's version; they have been absorbed, transmuted, and an English poem has taken the place of the Latin poem. Bunting, by contrast, has tried to make his English words enact the physical impact of Horace's Latin:

> You can't grip years, Postume,
> that ripple away nor hold back
> wrinkles and, soon now, age,
> nor can you tame death.

Allowing for the fact that English words are usually shorter than Latin, this moves at about the same slow pace of the original, some fifteen seconds to Horace's twenty, and has some of the Latin weight. Bunting believed, like Pound, that quantity plays an important role in English verse, not quite Latin syllabic length but weight enforcing our native stress accent, and his lines must be scanned in something of the way that we scan the Latin lines. "You cán't gríp yeárs, Póstŭmĕ," three weighted syllables (a molossus, if one wants classical terms) followed by a dactyl, followed in the next line by a choriamb, "that rípplĕ ăwáy," followed by another molossus, "nór hóld báck," still another in the next line, "soón nów, áge," with the stanza coming to an end with a spondee and with "death" the final word, as in Horace though not in Sisson.

Where Sisson's allegiances are to the English tradition, Bunting tries to move on English ground as though it were Roman. Readers will have their own views about the method and merits of the two translations. What can be said against Bunting's verse form is that it requires the translator to keep at it all the time; he can never relax and let his form work for him. Bunting picks the wrong place to relax when he comes to *linquenda tellus et domus et placens / uxor*. This calls for poetry at the level of "Men must endure / Their going hence, even as their comming hither" (*Lear*, act 5, scene 2). Beyond any translator's reach; but something better is needed than Bunting's casual "We must let earth go and home, / wives too." Sisson scores here, using words as simple as Horace's set within our traditional metric, which has carried some of the greatest poetry ever written: "Your house, your wife, and the familiar earth, / All will recede." This has something of what is required, what Christopher Ricks, speaking of another poet, calls "a flat fidelity" with "no sense of grievance or of being victimized."[25]

Remarkable too is Sisson's treatment of the *Carmen saeculare* or Centennial Hymn, an imitation in the full eighteenth-century manner (as Lowell's for the most part are not, being very free paraphrases), with Rome and Roman circumstance replaced by England and English circumstance. Not often translated and not much admired, the hymn is a religious, patriotic ode commissioned by Augustus, a prayer for the prosperity of Rome designed to support the moral reforms which the *princeps* was calling for, and in particular to endorse his proposed marriage laws. A difficult assignment, since Horace felt himself called on to assert that the traditional Roman virtues were now truly returning, a claim that many must have treated with skepticism. A far more difficult poem, one would imagine, for Sisson to English in the decade after the swinging, miniskirted sixties. What he does is pick his way through the original, abandoning whatever is beyond his reach, imitating when he can (where Horace speaks of Aeneas bringing the survivors of ruined Troy to Italy, Sisson describes the legendary founding of England by Brutus), and replacing affirmation by questions about the all but impossible possibility of recovering the old English virtues. When Horace affirms (lines 57–59, in Michie's close translation)

> Now Faith and Peace and Honour and old-fashioned
> Conscience and unremembered Virtue venture
> To walk again,

Sisson asks

> Might you not even remember the old worship?
> Can you remember the expression "Honour"?
> There was, at one time, even Modesty.
> Nothing is so dead it does not come back.

Having gone, questioning, as far as he can, Sisson, a man of the old covenant, a Christian, a patriot, a monarchist, finally comes down plump on affirmation:

> There is God. There are no Muses without him . . .

> It is he who holds London from Wapping to Richmond . . .
> Have you heard the phrase: "the only ruler of princes"?
> Along the Thames, in the Tower, there is the crown.
> I only wish God may hear my children's prayers.

> He bends now over Trafalgar Square.
> If there should be a whisper he would hear it.
> Are not these drifting figures the chorus?

If these drifting figures are closer to Eliot's hapless crowd flowing over London Bridge than to the comely Roman children who sang Horace's hymn on a June day in 17 BC, so be it. Sisson will not, as Horace felt himself compelled to do, affirm more than he himself can believe. His imitation is a finer, truer poem than the stately original.

Pound, recognizing virtues he had missed before, eventually, inevitably, turned to Horace, perhaps in the 1950s. The three translations he made may be taken as the final testament of *le grant translateur*. Ode 1.31, notable if only, though not only, for two lines as beautiful as those of Horace, with the gentle felicity of cadence he achieved in his final phase:

Land where Liris crumbles her bank in silence
Though the water seems not to move.

[Non rura quae Liris quieta / mordet aqua taciturnus amnis.]

Ode 3.30, *Exegi monumentum*, which makes for Horace the proud claim
for work done and achieved that in his sad old age Pound felt unable
to make for his own. And 1.11, probably the most closely thought-
through translation of Horace that we have. The burden of long familiarity lifted, the *Odes* are now open at every point to fresh reading;
they must be reexplored, reimagined, all over again with nothing taken
for granted. Fully to read this uncommonly dense piece of writing is
not possible here, so a couple of passages must suffice. Horace writes:

> ut melius, quidquid erit, pati,
> seu pluris hiemes seu tribuit Iuppiter ultimam,
> quae nunc oppositis debilitat pumicibus mare
> Tyrrhenum.

[How much better to take what comes, whether Jupiter has granted many
hiemes, or whether this is the last which now wears down the Tuscan sea
against the opposing rocks.]

Hiemes are winters or winter storms, also by convention years, the
years of our life. Horace calls the rocks *pumices*, pumice, volcanic rock
eaten into holes by the sea (the sea that is worn down, Horace says, by
the rocks against which it is driven; like most translators, Pound turns
the sea from patient to agent). The sea's action against the rocks yields
Pound's "gnawing," a more aggressive verb than *debilitat*, which gives
him "tooth" which in turn uncovers the ancient figure of the tooth of
time, Ovid's *tempus edax rerum*, Shakespeare's "devouring time." For
Pound's poem, as Horace's is not, is a poem of old age, still resilient,
facing and fighting against the winter of our days: "winter is winter."
Pound opens up a new stanza for his counterattack, unlike Horace,
who continues without a break:

> spatio brevi
> spem longam reseces. dum loquimur, fugerit invida
> aetas: carpe diem, quam minimum credula postero.

[In the brief space {allotted us}, cut back long hope. While we are speaking, envious time will have run on. Pluck {the flower of} today, believing
as little as possible in tomorrow.]

Reseco means cut back, a metaphor from pruning vines. (*Vina liques*, Horace has just written.) Pound takes the verb in another way which the Latin permits: cut back so as to loosen or remove. Hope is like a trailer that impedes our movements, preventing us from living fully in the moment, our only true possession. Hence, since life is short, we should cut off long hope for a time that is denied us, that we can't count on. While we talk, time will have run on, so: carpe diem. This famous injunction has become hardly more than a cracker-motto; it must be rethought and worked back into the poem by another route. Horace bids us take hold of the brief essence of our day and relish it. Pound provides a stronger defense by turning the tables on time and making it serve us. Time is itself to hold our day, holding it and so making us hold it—in unbelief, the wise unbelief that saves us from the folly of thinking that we have a long span ahead of us. "Trusting as little as possible in tomorrow," Horace ends. Pound's final line has a braver ring, for the old poet has a more urgent enemy to fight against: "Holding our day more firm in unbelief."

There is always something missing in the poetry of an age when Horace is missing, and if there is any charge that can be leveled against even the best nineteenth-century poetry it is that—for the first time since the later days of Elizabeth—his steadying hand is felt so seldom there. It was heartening that in 1997 a true Horatian, the American poet David Ferry, published his translation of all the *Odes*. The versions of the past, however much we may cherish them, cannot keep a poet alive; he must be reembodied in the speech of each new day.

The translations of Pound and still more of Bunting reveal the difficulty of this reembodiment. They acknowledge a rift that has opened up between Horace and ourselves even while seeking with much virtuosity to overcome it. Ferry by contrast has found an English into which Horace's lyrics will pass with no apparent strain; the gravely beautiful language he made for his own poetry will, he has discovered, accommodate Horace's with very little waste. Odes of which one could say that the best translation was made at such and such a date—Bishop Atterbury's late seventeenth-century version of 4.3, for instance, the poet's homage to the muse who gave him his gift—have now a fresh, no less satisfying incarnation. Odes hitherto imperfectly rendered are coming alive for the first time. The opening ode of the first book we can now see as more than a rather trite comparison of men's various pursuits to the poet's calling; Ferry has uncovered a real poem there. The high Roman stance of a patriotic poem like 3.6, too high for our humbler day, has been chastened and given at least a chance of addressing us. Ode 4.13, on the face of it one of Horace's unpleasantly Gilbertian pieces about amorous old women, turns out to be a moving poem. If time has brought once-beautiful Lyce down, it has dealt no more kindly with her former lover who has seemed to be mocking her. There is no mockery in Ferry's final line, "Old crow, old torch burned out, fallen away to ashes," rather a deeply pathetic, even tragic, sense of loss.

More than thirty years before, in England, James Michie had brought off this feat at a consistently readable level. If we may not often feel required to speak here of poetry, we can count ourselves lucky in getting that very honorable and now very rare thing, good verse with no pretensions to be anything more than that. Horace has been the recipient of too much failed poetry from people known as "poets in their own right," for the most part poor poets and even poorer translators. Michie is an accomplished verse-man who can shape a stanza, catch the tone, especially of the lighter poems, very happily, and is skillful at devising English equivalents for Horace's Greek meters. And he has given us credible versions of some of the public, political poems (notably of the Centennial Hymn or *Carmen saeculare*) which poet-translators shy away from, finding them to be outside our present cultural range. Perhaps they are, but we still want to have them in English if we can get them.

The *Satires* and *Epistles* have fared less well than the *Odes* and still await their modern reembodiment. A poem like Frost's "The Lesson for Today" shows, however, that what Reuben Brower calls the Horatian poetry of talk can still be written, and more recently there is Thom Gunn's superb "An Invitation" (*The Man with Night Sweats*, 1992), modeled on Jonson's "Inviting a Friend to Supper," strong Jonsonian coin that rings as true as when the master coined it. We must hope that poet-translators will take the *sermones*, the hexameter poems, in hand too, for this is a useful, all-purpose form generically impure enough to welcome the small change of life, open also to graver issues approached in a seemingly offhand manner, yet written in a formal verse submissive to the proper metrical discipline.

Looking back over the long venture of Horatian translation, one may ask how successfully has Horace been Englished. One answer is: rather more so than one might have expected. Another is: all too successfully, for if there is any charge that can be leveled against even the best translations of Horace over the last four centuries it is that they have made him sound far too English. The fact is that the *Odes* are very unlike any English poems, and unlike other Latin poems. When they first appeared, Charles Martindale remarks, Roman readers may have found them "weirdly experimental. In them we meet a style which combines the arty and the prosaic, along with a highly artificial, man-nered word order and a structural willfulness which can require a reader to strain in the attempt, taxing or vain, to apprehend" (*Horace Made New*, 3). The contortions of Kipling's parody ("There are whose study is of smells") are closer to the way that Horace actually writes than any translation. To bring Horace over into English and make an English poet of him is certainly a great achievement, but for which he would not have left so lasting a mark on our poetry and our na-tional culture, yet it is open to the accusation which George Steiner makes when he claims that the translator who takes this course "only appropriates what is concordant with his own sensibility and the pre-vailing climate. He does not enforce new, perhaps recalcitrant sources of experience on our consciousness. And he does not preserve the autonomous genius of the original, its powers of 'strangeness.'"[26] We may regret that translators did not on occasion go this way about it and force English into Horace's Latin mold. This, Goethe held, is the highest form of translation, the third and chronologically last in the tripartite scheme he proposed. Here the translator more or less aban-dons the genius of his own language and seeks to create something new, an amalgam of the foreign or alien and the native. Translations of this kind are very rare in English and indeed there is only one ex-ample that can be considered successful, Milton's version of the Ode to Pyrrha. One must speak cautiously here, since much depends on when it was written. If early, perhaps in his later teens, then it may be that he was doing simply what he described himself as doing with no theoretical purpose in mind, rendering the original "almost word for word without Rhyme according to the Latin Measure, as near as the Language will permit." If, however, this translation was written in his full maturity after he had studied the linguistic innovations carried out in early sixteenth-century Italy—which aimed at what amounts al-most to a new language, Italian with Latin diction and syntax imposed on the native stock—then the Pyrrha Ode may be more ambitious than either its admirers or detractors have seen. We find Milton in-venting a new form, a stanza that was to have great influence on orig-inal poetry (between 1700 and 1837, it has been reckoned, at least eighty-three poems were written in Milton's stanza, most notably Col-lins's "Ode to Evening"),[27] but not, curiously enough, on Horatian translation. The only instances seem to be the two renderings "after the Manner of Milton" by Thomas Warton. Like Horace, Milton runs the sense on from stanza to stanza, and he does not rhyme. For all *les bienfaits de la rime* (it gave Milton the lovely Bellini blue at the end of "Lycidas"), there is a good case to be made against turning Horace into a rhymer. Quiller-Couch made it, rather too strongly, when he argued that "the nuisance of rhyme [is that] it can hardly help suggesting the epigram, the clinch, the verse 'brought off' with a little note of triumph."[28] Milton's avoidance of rhyme has not caused displeasure, but his Latinisms have. Seen, however, in this experimental light they no longer look like pedantry. It is beside the point to complain that a line like "Who now enjoyes thee credulous, all Gold" is more Latin than English. It is meant to be. To say that it is not comprehensible without the Latin is simply not true; it is perfectly clear in the context that "credulous" applies to the observer, "all Gold" to the person observed. More important, this is convincing poetic speech —of a new kind.[29] A kind that, we must hope, translators in the days to come will learn to write, in the process giving us, sometimes (the word should be stressed), not English Horace but difficult, foreign, *Latin* Horace through whose intricate stanzas we make our careful way as we do with the originals.

Notes

INTRODUCTION

1. Other critics have been as astute—Reuben Brower, Guy Davenport, George Steiner, and Charles Tomlinson, to name four I find most significant—but Carne-Ross is unique in his sustained and detailed attention to classical translation.

2. D. S. Carne-Ross, "The Two Voices of Translation," in *Robert Lowell: A Collection of Critical Essays*, ed. Thomas F. Parkinson (Englewood Cliffs, NJ: Prentice Hall, 1968), 155.

3. Adrian Poole and Jeremy Maule, eds., *The Oxford Book of Classical Verse in Translation* (Oxford: Oxford University Press, 1995), xlii–xliii.

4. John Gibson Lockhart, "Wright's *Inferno of Dante*," *Quarterly Review* 49 (July 1833): 451.

5. D. S. Carne-Ross, "Shall We Dante?" *New York Review of Books*. 32, no. 2 (February 14, 1985): 41.

6. The translation forms part of the mosaic of the story "Wo es war, soll ich werden" in *The Drummer of the Eleventh North Devonshire Fusiliers,* by Guy Davenport (San Francisco: North Point Press, 1990).

7. D. S. Carne-Ross, "The Strange Case of Leopardi," *New York Review of Books* 34, no. 1 (January 28, 1987): 44.

8. D. S. Carne-Ross, "Stendhal: *Le Rouge et le Noir*," *Delos: A Journal on & of Translation,* no. 3 (1969): 80–119.

9. In other respects—his commitments to the high literacy of the Renaissance, to Horace and Virgil, to the novels of Scott, Stendhal, Dickens, and Eliot—Carne-Ross was neither especially modernist nor apocalyptic.

10. Bernard Knox, "Caviar to the General," *New York Review of Books* 32, no. 16 (October 24, 1985): 42.

1. JOCASTA'S DIVINE HEAD

1. Charles Tomlinson finds a larger achievement in Dryden's translations: "An Anglican Christian and later a Catholic, [he] is entering into a serious dialogue with paganism via his translation of Lucretius and Ovid." "A View of English Poetry," in *The Art of Translation: Voices from the Field*, ed. Rosanna Warren (Boston: Northeastern University Press, 1989), 269. This may well be right. I am referring primarily to *diction.*

2. Walter Benjamin's famous essay "The Task of the Translator," which ends with the claim that "the interlinear version of the Scriptures is the archetype and ideal of all translations," has won for the radically literal rendering a new theoretical status. I have in mind here the humble trot.

3. From Dryden's preface to Ovid's *Epistles* (1680).

334

4. See Reuben A. Brower, *Hero and Saint: Shakespeare and the Graeco-Roman Heroic Tradition* (New York: Oxford University Press, 1971), 279.

5. See *L'Énéide*, trans. Pierre Klossowski (Paris: Gallimard, 1964), 97, 234. I have drawn here on Antoine Berman's paper, "*L'Énéide* de Klossowski," in *Les Tours de Babel: Essais sur la traduction* (Mauvezin: Trans-Europ-Repress, 1985), 127–50.

6. Compare the famous letter where Machiavelli, out of office and favor and rusticating in his small property a few miles from Florence, describes how he passes the time dicing and gossiping at the local tavern until evening comes. Then, returning home, he takes off his sluttish everyday clothes: "et mi metto panni reali et curiali, et rivestito condecentemente entro nelle antique corti degli antiqui huomini" (December 10, 1513).

7. George Steiner, *Antigones* (New York: Oxford University Press, 1984), 208ff.

8. R. C. Jebb, *Sophocles: The Plays and Fragments*, 2nd ed., vol. 3: *The Antigone* (Cambridge: Cambridge University Press, 1981), 8.

9. Did Hölderlin's Lutheran upbringing play a part too? John Hollander draws my attention to these verses from Bach's *St. Matthew Passion*: "O Haupt voll Blut und Wunden / voll schmerz und voller Hohn! / O Haupt, zu Spott gebunden / mit einer Dornenkron! / O Haupt, sonst schön gezieret / mich Hochster Ehr' und Zier / jetzt aber hoch schimpfiret: / gegrüsset seist du mir!"

10. I borrow this no doubt too excited sentence from an early attempt to grapple with Sophocles' words: "Scenario for a New Year," *Arion* 8, no. 2 (1969): 215.

11. E. R. Dodds, *The Greeks and the Irrational* (Berkeley: University of California Press, 1951), 5.

12. A thank-you here to friend Christopher Middleton, one of our most resourceful poet-translators. He writes: "I see no reason (except a whole labyrinth of 'proprieties') why one couldn't recompose English to reach out and touch Sophocles—but where would the aura go?"

13. Milman Parry, *The Making of Homeric Verse: The Collected Papers of Milman Parry*, ed. Adam Parry (Oxford: Clarendon Press, 1971), 305.

14. Samuel Johnson, *The Lives of the Poets*, ed. Roger Lonsdale, 4 vols. (Oxford: Clarendon Press, 2006), 1:293.

15. F. T. Prince, *The Italian Element in Milton's Verse* (Oxford: Clarendon Press, 1954), 103.

16. The note of Roman gravity is consummately sounded in the sestet of Bembo's sonnet to the humanist Francesco Molza: "Che detta il mio collega, il qual n'ha mostro / col suo dir grave e pien d'antica usanza / sì come a quel d'Arpin si pò gir presso? / Che scrivi tu, del cui purgato inchiostro / già l'uno e l'altro stil molto s'avanza? / Star neghittoso a te non è concesso" ("Molza, che fa la donna tua . . .").

17. See chapter 3 ("Greece") of James William Johnson, *The Formation of English Neo-Classical Thought* (Princeton, NJ: Princeton University Press, 1967).

18. Matthew Arnold, *On the Classical Tradition*. ed. R. H. Super (Ann Arbor: The University of Michigan Press, 1960), 191 ("On Translating Homer: Last Words").

19. Christopher Ricks, *Milton's Grand Style* (Oxford: Clarendon Press, 1963), 49ff.

20. F. J. H. Letters, *The Life and Work of Sophocles* (London: Sheed and Ward, 1953), 70.

21. Jebb, *Sophocles*, 1:15; J. C. Kamerbeek, *The Plays of Sophocles*, vol. 4: *The Oedipus Tyrannus* (Leiden: Brill, 1967), 37.

22. Johnson, *Lives of the Poets*, 1:293.

23. I take these quotations from Richard Jenkyns, *The Victorians and Ancient Greece* (Cambridge, MA: Harvard University Press, 1980), 15.

24. "There are instances . . . when Hölderlin's words only take on their full texture when read in the light of Greek. His frequent usage of the adverb *nämlich* ('namely') and the conjunction *aber* ('but') throughout the late hymns reflects the elusive nuances of the Greek particles *gar, men,* and *de.*" Richard Sieburth, *Hymns and Fragments by Friedrich Hölderlin* (Princeton, NJ: Princeton University Press, 1984), 29.

25. Robert Browning, *The Agamemnon of Aeschylus* (London, 1877), v.

26. George Steiner, *After Babel* (New York: Oxford University Press, 1975), 312–15. Richard Stoneman, in his anthology of verse translations of classical poetry *Daphne into Laurel* (London: Duckworth, 1982), 284, makes the dubious claim that Browning's work "represents a serious attempt to come to terms with the strangeness of Aeschylus, and sometimes conveys more of a sense of Aeschylean power than any other version."

27. W. H. Auden, "Reply to an *Arion* Questionnaire," *Arion* 3, no. 4 (1964): 9.

28. C. S. Lewis, *English Literature in the Sixteenth Century Excluding Drama* (Oxford: Oxford University Press, 1954), 365.

29. The meter is discussed by John von B. Rodenbeck in the opening pages of his article "The Classicism of Meredith's 'Love in the Valley,'" *Victorian Poetry* 11, no. 1 (1973): 27–37.

30. I understand that Derek Walcott carried out this exercise in one of his poetry classes at Boston University.

31. Lewis, *English Literature in the Sixteenth Century,* 551ff.

32. *The Letters of Gerard Manley Hopkins to Robert Bridges,* ed. Claude Colleer Abbott (London: Oxford University Press, 1955), 157.

33. Herbert Read, *Phases of English Poetry* (New York: Harcourt, Brace, 1929), 14.

34. John Hollander, *Vision and Resonance: Two Senses of Poetic Form,* 2nd ed. (New Haven, CT: Yale University Press, 1985), 198.

35. *The Poems of Algernon Charles Swinburne,* 6 vols. (London: Chatto and Windus, 1904), 5:42 (*Studies in Song,* 1880).

36. The line is corrupt. I print the emendation that best illustrates the point.

37. The curious may find the latter composition, by Giovanni Fantoni, in *I lirici del seicento e dell'Arcadia,* ed. Carlo Calcaterra (Milan-Rome: Rizzoli, 1936), 853ff.

38. George Saintsbury, in his *Historical Manual of English Prosody* (London: Macmillan, 1910), 123, informs us that "the proper run of the Sapphic line is—tumti-tumtum-tumtity-tumti-tum-[ti/]tum." Up to a point, Lord Copper.

39. Professor Hollander, who knows a great deal more about these matters than I do, warns me against using the term *quantity.* He writes: "Quantitative really only means a metrical system in which vowel quantity is phonemic, and upon whose phonology a system of long and short syllables can be used to generate rhythmical patterns. The absolute duration of syllables—in articulatory phonetics—is *not* a phonological matter, and is often tricky. An apparent 'long-vowelled' syllable like 'high' will show up on a sound spectrogram as taking less time to enunciate than one with a short vowel like 'twitch.' The duration periods of consonantal white noise is crucial in these matters."

40. Campion "bases quantity on accent . . . , so that his quantitative verse follows, in the main, the normal auditory patterns of English speech." Walter R. Davis, ed., *The Works of Thomas Campion* (New York: Norton, 1970), 289.

41. Ezra Pound, *ABC of Reading* (1934; New York: New Directions, 1960), 201.

42. I rest my case for Swinburne's use of quantity on this one poem, an act of formal homage to "the supreme head of song," although it could, I believe, be found elsewhere in his work. Further investigation is needed.

43. David Jones, *The Anathémata* (1952; London: Faber and Faber, 1979), 91.

44. David Blamires, *David Jones: Artist and Writer* (Manchester: Manchester University Press, 1971), 137.

45. David Jones, *The Sleeping Lord and Other Fragments* (London: Faber and Faber, 1974), 71.

46. D. S. Carne-Ross, "Pound in Texas: 2. New Tunes for Old," *Arion* 6, no. 2 (1967): 207–32.

47. Charles Tomlinson, in *The Oxford Book of Verse in English Translation* (Oxford: Oxford University Press, 1980), xiii.

48. Ezra Pound, *The Confucian Odes* (Cambridge, MA: Harvard University Press, 1954), 149 (translating ode 235).

49. Tomlinson, "View of English Poetry" (see n. 1), 263.

50. "There is an artificial elongation of long syllables, which often makes his verse sound quantitative," George Fraser, *Ezra Pound* (Edinburgh: Oliver and Boyd, 1960), 31. The elongation is *deliberate*, rather than "artificial." Pound nowhere does what Sidney does when he treats the last syllable on "violence" as long. The three passages from Pound occur in *Literary Essays* (London: Faber and Faber, 1954), 92, 12, and *The Letters of Ezra Pound, 1907-1941*, ed. D. D. Paige (New York: Harcourt, Brace, 1950), 142.

51. T. S. Eliot, "Ezra Pound: His Metric and His Poetry" (1917), reprinted in *To Criticize the Critic* (New York: Farrar, Straus and Giroux, 1965), 174.

52. Donald Davie, *Ezra Pound: Poet as Sculptor* (New York: Oxford University Press, 1964), 34.

2. THE POEM OF GILGAMESH

1. In *Ancient Near Eastern Texts*, ed. James B. Pritchard (Princeton, NJ: Princeton University Press, 1955). The standard text is now *The Babylonian Gilgamesh Epic*, ed. A. R. George (Oxford: Oxford University Press, 2003).

2. John Gardner and John R. Maier, *Gilgamesh* (New York: Vintage, 1985); Maureen Gallery Kovacs, *The Epic of Gilgamesh* (Stanford, CA: Stanford University Press, 1989); Stephanie Dalley, *Myths from Mesopotamia* (Oxford: Oxford University Press, 1989); Robert Temple, *He Who Saw Everything* (London: Rider, 1991); Andrew George, *The Epic of Gilgamesh* (London: Penguin, 1999); Gary Beckman, *The Epic of Gilgamesh* (New York: Norton, 2001); Stephen Mitchell, *Gilgamesh: A New English Version* (New York: Free Press, 2004). A little earlier we have the sympathetic retelling in free verse by Herbert Mason, *Gilgamesh: A Verse Narrative* (Boston: Houghton Mifflin, 1971), and the prose version by N. K. Sandars, *The Epic of Gilgamesh* (Harmondsworth, England: Penguin, 1972).

3. *Gilgamesh: A New Rendering in English Verse*, by David Ferry (New York: Farrar, Straus and Giroux, 1992).

4. Ezra Pound, *The Confucian Odes* (Cambridge, MA: Harvard University Press, 1954), 149 (translating ode 235).

5. E. R. Dodds, *The Greeks and the Irrational* (Berkeley, CA: University of California Press, 1951), 29.

6. Dalley, *Myths from Mesopotamia*, 141.

7. Herbert Weir Smyth, *Aeschylus*, 2 vols. (London: Heinemann, 1922–26), 1:xii.

3. The Poem of Odysseus

1. Samuel Butler, *The Authoress of the Odyssey*, 2nd ed. (1897; London: Cape, 1922), 8.

2. Ezra Pound, *Guide to Kulchur* (1938; New York: New Directions, 1970), 31.

3. Alexander William Kinglake, *Eothen* (1844), chap. 4 ("The Troad"). For the allusion, see Wordsworth, "Elegiac Stanzas," line 15.

4. W. P. Ker, *Epic and Romance: Essays on Medieval Literature* (London: Macmillan, 1897), 13.

5. Douglas Young, "Never Blotted a Line? Formula and Premeditation in Homer and Hesiod," *Arion* 6, no. 3 (1967): 279–324.

6. Those who wish to acquaint themselves with the multiple ramifications of the Homeric Question, as it is called, may consult Alfred Heubeck's authoritative general introduction in volume 1 of *A Commentary on Homer's Odyssey*, ed. Heubeck et al., 3 vols. (New York: Oxford University Press, 1988–92), and E. R. Dodds's balanced contribution to *Fifty Years (and Twelve) of Classical Scholarship* (New York: Barnes and Noble, 1968): "Homer and the Analysts," "Homer and the Unitarians," "Homer as Oral Poetry."

7. William S. Anderson, "Calypso and Elysium," in *Essays on the Odyssey: Selected Modern Criticism*, ed. Charles H. Taylor, Jr. (Bloomington: Indiana University Press, 1963), 81.

8. Cesare Pavese, *Dialogues with Leucò*, trans. William Arrowsmith and D. S. Carne-Ross (Ann Arbor: University of Michigan Press, 1965), 97–100.

9. The account of this feature of Odysseus's travels is indebted to the article by Stephen Scully, "Doubling in the Tale of Odysseus," *Classical World* 80 (1987): 401–17.

10. This is the ninth of thirty-six versions found in appendix 13 to James Frazer's Loeb edition of Apollodorus's *Library* (1921).

11. Fitzgerald spells "Nohbdy" like this to represent the Greek word (Οὖτις) accented in a way that would have made it sound different.

12. It may seem sufficient simply to say, as some scholars do (e.g., Alfred Heubeck in his notes on this book in his *Commentary*, 2:26) that the narrator is looking back on events. This amounts to the same thing but does not explain why Homer makes this obvious mistake.

13. Denys Page, *The Homeric "Odyssey"* (Oxford: Clarendon Press, 1955), 9. Page neatly points to inconsistencies in the story, not without some donnish wit at the expense of the poet, poor old buffer.

14. This fits the story, but ancient memories have worked their way into the episode and there may be another explanation, indicated by a detail in the description of the animals missed by Fitzgerald and other translators. Fawning on the men, lions and wolves stood on their hind legs (ἀνέσταν). This suggests the depiction of the goddess flanked by two rampant animals on Mycenean seals.

15. Denys Page, *Folktales in Homer's Odyssey* (Cambridge, MA: Harvard University Press, 1973), 60.

16. *Gilgamesh*, trans. David Ferry (New York: Farrar, Straus and Giroux, 1992), 30–32.

17. Charles H. Taylor, Jr., in "The Obstacles to Odysseus' Return," in *Essays on the Odyssey*, 88 suggests that what he faces are "temptations to the surrender of his individuality." This is another—perhaps too modern?—way to put it.

18. W. B. Stanford, *The Odyssey of Homer*, 2nd ed., 2 vols. (London: Macmillan, 1961): comment on 11.225ff.

19. Chapman translates: "She deathlesse is and that immortal ill / Grave, harsh, outrageous, not to be subdu'd"; Pope is content to rant: "Tremendous pest! abhorr'd by man and Gods!" Cowper follows Pope with "that enormous pest / Defies all force; retreats not; cannot die." Leconte de Lisle in the nineteenth century writes: "Skyllè n'est point mortelle, et c'est un monstre cruel." Butcher and Lang have "she is no mortal, but an immortal plague."

20. Martin P. Nilsson, *Greek Folk Religion* (New York: Harper, 1961), 74. The poet is Archilochus, fragment 173 in West's edition.

21. In the dedication to Somerset, preceding his translation of the *Odyssey* (1614).

22. It is reported that elders of the Church of England, uneasy about attributing to the deity so malign a purpose, have voted to replace the offending words with "Save us from the time of trial."

23. Norman Austin, *Archery at the Dark of the Moon: Poetic Problems in Homer's Odyssey* (Berkeley, CA: University of California Press, 1975), 118, 207.

24. Readers who wish to consider this book in further detail will find much that is profitable in two remarkable studies, criticism of a kind that classical literature rarely receives: Anne Amory, "The Reunion of Odysseus and Penelope," in *Essays on the Odyssey*, pp. 100–21, and Norman Austin, "Penelope and Odysseus," *Archery at the Dark of the Moon*, 200–38.

25. "Rusé personnage": Amadis Jamyn's translation (1584) of "polytropos" Odysseus, which Ezra Pound took up.

26. Heubeck et al., *Commentary*, 3:102.

27. Why false dreams come through the ivory gates, true ones through the horn, has never been satisfactorily explained.

28. Gilbert Murray, *The Rise of the Greek Epic* (Oxford: Clarendon Press, 1907), 119.

29. Heubeck et al., *Commentary*, 3:506.

30. A different interpretation of Odysseus's name is given in ibid., *Commentary*, 3:97 (on 19.407).

31. From the refrain of Eustache Deschamp's ballade addressed to Chaucer. (For "calm of mind all passion spent," see the end of *Samson Agonistes*.)

4. Robert Fitzgerald

1. Robert Fitzgerald, trans., *The Antigone of Sophocles* (New York: Harcourt, Brace, 1939); *Oedipus at Colonus* (New York: Harcourt, Brace 1941); *Oedipus Rex* (New York: Harcourt, Brace 1949); *The Odyssey* (Garden City, NY: Anchor Press / Doubleday, 1961); *The Iliad* (Garden City, NY: Anchor Press, 1974); *The Aeneid* (New York: Random House, 1983).

2. It is buried in that somber compilation *The Oxford Book of Greek Verse in Translation* (Oxford: Clarendon Press, 1938), 34–35.

3. C. Day-Lewis, *The Georgics of Vergil* (London: J. Cape, 1940), xii.

4. Guy Davenport, "Another Odyssey," in *The Geography of the Imagination* (San Francisco, CA: North Point Press, 1981), 35.

5. C. S. Lewis (attributing the line from Schiller's "Dilettant" to Goethe) applies the phrase to the epic diction of Homer; see *A Preface to Paradise Lost* (London: Oxford University Press, 1942), 25.

6. Robert Fitzgerald, *The Third Kind of Knowledge*, ed. Penelope Laurens Fitzgerald (New York: New Directions, 1993), 270.

7. *Inferno* 5.30. Robert Lowell once remarked that even a quite minor poet can probably make a few small improvements on almost any page of Shakespeare.

8. Denys Page, *History and the Homeric Iliad* (Berkeley: University of California Press, 1959), 222.

9. By, for example, Norman Austin, *Archery at the Dark of the Moon* (Berkeley: University of California Press, 1975), chap. 1, "The Homeric Formula," and Paolo Vivante, *The Epithets in Homer: A Study in Poetic Values* (New Haven, CT: Yale University Press, 1982).

10. Lattimore translates sedately: "Athena of the ordered hair, a dread goddess."

11. *Paradise Lost* 2.1; Pope's *Iliad* 16.204 and 19.438.

12. It seems likely that Fitzgerald was influenced by W. B. Stanford's remarks on the word φρίξ = "cats-paw" in *Greek Metaphor* (Oxford: B. Blackwell, 1936), 140–42. Probably they are also behind Day-Lewis's perhaps a shade too energetic rendering of the similar Virgilian phrase, *inhorruit unda tenebris*, as "the sea's face darkened with shuddering catspaws" (*Aeneid* 3.195).

13. E. R. Dodds, *The Ancient Concept of Progress* (Oxford: Clarendon Press, 1973), [i].

14. Samuel Johnson, *The Lives of the Poets*, ed. Roger Lonsdale, 4 vols. (Oxford: Oxford University Press, 2006), 4:72–73. On Bentley's *mot*, see Lonsdale's note on p. 314.

15. Hugh Kenner, *The Pound Era* (Berkeley: University of California Press, 1973), 554.

16. Oliver St. John Gogarty: "The sound comes to me / of the lapsing, unsoilable, / Whispering sea" ("Ringsend").

17. Brilliantly guyed by Christopher Logue in his version of book 16. Immediately after a solemn and beautiful passage we read: "While this was done Achilles' overreaching vicar killed"—then, in very small type: "Eckelus, of whom nothing is known; Perimas, the son of Meges; Sistor, an Egyptian horse dealer; Keth and San, slaves to the former; Krates, a silversmith from Cyme; Doron, a regular; Pilarty, a cook; Fanes, Geyan, & Mastor, farriers; Toris, a merchant slaver." See Christopher Logue, *Patrocleia* (Lowestoft, England: Scorpion Press, 1962), 29.

18. *The Poems of Alexander Pope*, ed. John Butt, 10 vols. (New Haven, CT: Yale University Press, 1961–67), 7:cxciii.

19. *Francis Bacon*, ed. Brian Vickers (Oxford: Oxford University Press, 1996), 47 ("Of Tribute").

20. R. A. Brooks, "*Discolor Aura*: Reflections on the Golden Bough," *American Journal of Philology* 74, no. 3 (1953): 260–80.

21. Ralph Johnson, *Darkness Visible: A Study of the Aeneid* (Berkeley: University of California Press, 1976).

22. Friedrich Nietzsche, *Basic Writings*, trans. and ed. Walter Kaufmann (New York: Modern Library, 1966), 274 (*Beyond Good and Evil*).

23. Ezra Pound, *The ABC of Reading* (1934; New York: New Directions, 1960), 44.

24. Brooks, "*Discolor Aura*," 280.

25. In his dedication to the *Aeneis*, Dryden writes that he cannot translate *mollis amaracus* (1.693) as "sweet marjoram," since such "village words" give the reader "a mean idea of the thing."

26. Tennyson, "To Virgil."

5. RICHMOND LATTIMORE

1. *The Odyssey of Homer*, trans. Richmond Lattimore (New York: Harper and Row, 1967).

2. [Peter Green], "On Translating Homer," *Times Literary Supplement*, no. 3446 (March 14, 1968): 241–43.

3. Richmond Lattimore, *Greek Lyrics* (Chicago: University of Chicago Press, 1955), 66, translating Bacchylides 17.14–18.

4. "The live man among duds": Ezra Pound, *Literary Essays*, ed. T. S. Eliot (New York: New Directions, 1968), 212 ("Hell," 1934). "Ce rusé personnage": from Amadis Jamyn's translation of the beginning of the *Odyssey*, published in 1584. Pound quotes the phrase in Canto LXXVIII and mentions it in the *ABC of Reading* (1934); in *Polite Essays* (1937), he misattributes it to Hugues Salel. "Naked Ulysses, clad in eternall Fiction": from Chapman's dedication to Somerset, preceding his translation of the *Odyssey* (1614).

5. Matthew Arnold, *On the Classical Tradition.* ed. R. H. Super (Ann Arbor: University of Michigan Press, 1960), 167 ("On Translating Homer").

6. *Odissea*, trans. Rosa Calzecchi Onesti (Turin: Einaudi, 1963). Onesti also translated the *Iliad* (Turin, 1963), on which see the comments by her editor, Cesare Pavese, in *Cesare Pavese: Lettere, 1945–50* (Turin: Einaudi, 1966), 319, 331ff., 440, 442.

7. In the "Translator's Note" to his *Odyssey* (1932), Lawrence wrote that "the *Odyssey* by its ease and interest remains the oldest book worth reading for its story and the first novel of Europe."

8. As in this sentence from *Madame Bovary*: "Le drap de sa robe s'accrochait au velours de l'habit, elle renversa son cou blanc, qui se gonflait d'un soupir; et, défaillante, tout en pleurs, avec un long frémissement et se cachant la figure, elle s'abandonna." The way Flaubert leads up to the decisive final verb with a carefully articulated tricolon is masterly. This is prose at full stretch. It is also the sort of effect that a poet like Virgil brings off on every other page. In his essay "Is Verse a Dying Technique?" Edmund Wilson compared passages of Flaubert and Virgil and argued that Flaubert "is no less intense and precise in his use of words and rhythms than Virgil." This may be true, but what Wilson does not say is that this kind of prose seems to be much harder to write than correspondingly subtle verse—certainly far fewer men have managed to write it—and is always in danger of falling into preciosity, as Flaubert and his pupil Joyce demonstrate. All the same, it is a great pity that we have no translation of classical poetry that uses the full resources of nineteenth- or earlier twentieth-century prose. (A Virgilian eclogue by Flaubert, for instance.) Probably it is too late now. Nobody believes in prose in the way Flaubert and Joyce did.

9. With two variants: at 4.580, "we dashed," and at 9.564, "their oars."

10. The twelve-syllable line which Lattimore uses to translate the tragic iambic tends in a similar way to turn into blank verse plus two unmetrical syllables: "they sat upon their thrones and kept their pride *of state*, / and they are lovers still. So may you judge *by what* / befell them, for as they were pledged their oath *abides*" (*Choephoroe* 975–77).

11. Pound, *Literary Essays*, 250 ("Early Translators of Homer," 1920).

12. J. S. Morrison, *Greek Oared Ships, 900–322 B.C.* (London: Cambridge University Press, 1968), 48. For ἐπίκριον and σπεῖρον, see 56.

13. C. M. Bowra, *Heroic Poetry* (London: Macmillan, 1961), 155.

14. The perfect translator, Gogol said, is one who becomes a pane of glass so transparent that the reader doesn't notice there is any glass.

15. Alexander William Kinglake, *Eothen* (1844), chapter 4 ("The Troad").

16. Walter Pater, *The Renaissance*, ed. Donald L. Hill (Berkeley: University of California Press, 1980), 79.

17. The passage also provides one more illustration of Lattimore's fondness for unidiomatic English and awkward construction. In the second line, one supposes that the handmaidens went off, or away, from wherever they were to attend upon Penelope. But no, the Greek says simply that they followed her, or went with her. In

the fourth line the sense is not, as one might think, that the pillar, by means of its joinery, somehow contrived to support the roof. One must understand "the roof-with-its-joinery" or, as Homer says, "the solidly built roof." (The last three lines occur on three other occasions in exactly this form.)

18. With two interesting variants: "Then in turn resourceful Odysseus spoke to him/her in answer" at 13.311 and 22.105; and "Then in turn resourceful Odysseus said to him/her in answer" at 23.263 and 24.406.

19. Cf. Dryden on Juvenal in the *Discourse of Satire.*

20. See the damaging comments by H. A. Mason in "Some Versions of *The Iliad,*" *Cambridge Quarterly* 1, no. 1 (1965) and the same author's critique of Lattimore's *Odyssey* in the *New York Review of Books* 10, no. 9 (May 9, 1968). See also Guy Davenport, "Another *Odyssey,*" *Arion* 7, no. 1 (1968): 135–53 (later reprinted in Guy Davenport, *The Geography of the Imagination,* 1981).

21. Samuel Johnson, *The Lives of the Poets,* ed. Roger Lonsdale, 4 vols. (Oxford: Clarendon Press, 2006), 1:239.

6. CHRISTOPHER LOGUE

1. Logue's version of the *Patrocleia* has gone through several published versions. It appeared as "The *Iliad*: Book XVI: An English Version," *Arion* 1, no. 2 (Summer 1962): 3–26. It was published in book form, with relatively minor alterations, as *Patrocleia* (Lowestoff, England: Scorpion Press, 1962) and as *The Patrocleia of Homer* (Ann Arbor: University of Michigan Press, 1963). The Scorpion Press reprinted the 1962 version in 1969. A heavily revised version was published in *War Music: An Account of Books 16 to 19 of Homer's Iliad* (London: J. Cape, 1981), a volume which was published in America under the same title in 1987. This translation was further revised for *War Music: An Account of Books 1–4 and 16–19* (New York: Farrar, Straus and Giroux, 1997).

Other fragments include "From Book XXI of Homer's Iliad" (the battle with the river) in *Songs* (London: Hutchinson, 1959): 92–100; *Pax: Book XIX of the Iliad* (London: Rapp and Carroll, 1967); and "The Fight for Patroclus . . . from *Iliad* 18," *Arion* 8, no. 4 (Winter 1969): 465–76. The latter two were also heavily revised when they appeared in *War Music* (1981) and further revised for *War Music* (1997).

Kings: An Account of Books One and Two of Homer's Iliad (1991) and *Husbands: An Account of Books Three and Four of Homer's Iliad* (1995) were reprinted in revised form in *War Music* (1997). Subsequent fragments include *All Day Permanent Red* (2003) and *Cold Calls* (2005).

2. E. M. W. Tillyard, *The English Epic and Its Background* (London: Chatto and Windus, 1954), 502.

3. *Patrocleia* (1962), 5; cut from *War Music* (1981).

4. See Tillyard, *English Epic,* 502–3.

5. *Patrocleia* (1962), 9; *War Music* (1981), 11.

6. Marguerite Yourcenar, *Présentation critique de Constantin Cavafy* (Paris: Gallimard, 1978), 146.

7. *Patrocleia* (1962), 9–10; *War Music* (1981), 12, preserves the wolf simile but omits the muster.

8. *Patrocleia* (1962), 10; cut from *War Music* (1981).

9. "Pyraechmes" in "The *Iliad*: Book XVI" (1962), 11; "Pyraykemese" in *Patrocleia* (1969), 13; and "Akafact" in *War Music* (1981), 15.

10. *Patrocleia* (1962), 15; cf. *War Music* (1981), 23: "Of several incidents, consider two."

11. *Patrocleia* (1962), 16; cut from *War Music* (1981).

12. *Patrocleia* (1962), 22; cut from *War Music* (1981).

13. This simile, however, also occurs at *Iliad* 13.389–91.

14. The tiger hunt simile in *Patrocleia* (1962), 31 (cut from *War Music*, 1981, 35) also draws on our moviegoing habits. This, I think, is part of Logue's deliberate "exposure" of the poem to our everyday experience.

15. *Patrocleia* (1962), 19; cut from *War Music* (1981).

16. Simone Weil, *Intimations of Christianity among the Ancient Greeks*, trans. Elizabeth C. Geissbuhler (London: Routledge, 1957), 50 ("The *Iliad*, Poem of Might").

17. Douglas Knight, *Pope and the Heroic Tradition* (New Haven, CT: Yale University Press, 1951), 66ff.

18. *Patrocleia* (1962), 26; *War Music* (1981), 31.

19. *Pax* (1967), 8; *War Music* (1981), 68. Cf. *Iliad* 19.11–18.

7. Bacchylides

1. T. S. Eliot, *Selected Essays* (New York: Harcourt, Brace, and World, 1964), 50 ("Euripides and Professor Murray," 1920).

2. Denys Page, *Sappho and Alcaeus* (Oxford: Clarendon Press, 1955), 18, v.

3. I take the expression from Frank Kermode's excellent short study, *Wallace Stevens* (Edinburgh: Oliver and Boyd, 1960), 25; Stevens is a poet who could, I think, help to open an approach to Pindar. For an example of Pindaric "destruction," see *Nemean* 10.35–36.

4. It is sad that the excitement caused by this discovery has been allowed to die down so completely. There is a quite "unscholarly" enthusiasm in the way his second editor, Friedrich Blass, refers to the event: "Resurgunt litterae vetustae, ζῶσιν οἱ γᾶς ὑπαὶ κείμενοι, atque utinam etiam alii, qui nunc nondum videntur!" (Sophocles *Electra* 1418). There is striking evidence of the (lost) unity of European culture, a unity centered in Greece and Rome, in the fact that a couple of Bacchylides' odes should have been translated into Croatian within two years of the discovery of the papyrus.

5. *Bacchylides: Complete Poems*, trans. Robert Fagles (1961; New Haven, CT: Yale University Press, 1998). Fagles follows the Teubner edition of Snell. Other editions referred to in the essay are those by Frederick G. Kenyon (London, 1897), Friedrich Blass (Leipzig, 1898, and subsequent revised editions), Hugo Jurenka (Vienna, 1898), Richard C. Jebb (Cambridge, 1905), and J. M. Edmonds (London, 1927 [Loeb Classical Library, vol. 3 of *Lyra Graeca*]).

6. "Who or what is Gongula?" they inquire. "Is it a name of a person? of a town? of a musical instrument . . . ? Or is it perhaps a mistake for Gongora . . . ?", Laura Riding and Robert Graves, *A Survey of Modernist Poetry* (1929), 218. "Papyrus" is exactly what it claims to be, a poem suggested by an actual Sapphic fragment (95 in Lobel-Page and in Voigt), first published in 1902. Pound's *Lustra*, in which "Papyrus" appears, was published in 1916; the poem seems to be based on the text by J. M. Edmonds in *New Fragments of Alcaeus, Sappho and Corinna* (1909).

7. Cf. Pindar *Olympian* 6.3–4.

8. E.g. "deep-girdled" for βαθύζωνος. So Lattimore when he meets the word at *Iliad* 9.594, καὶ ἄλλοι ἄλλοθι. I cannot understand this sort of translation. What *is* a deep-girdled woman? What does she look like? Where has Lattimore seen one?

9. See Roger Shattuck in "Artificial Horizon: Translator as Navigator": "In its truest role translation does not consist solely in reducing all foreign works to the limitations of, say, English, but equally in reshaping and enlarging English to reach

meanings which it has not yet had to grapple with." Shattuck, *The Craft and Context of Translation*, ed. William Arrowsmith and Roger Shattuck (Austin: University of Texas Press, 1961), 152.

10. W. H. Gardner, *Gerard Manley Hopkins*, 2 vols. (London: Oxford University Press, 1948), 1:126ff. The examples from Keats occur in "Ode to Psyche" and *Hyperion*, book 2.

11. *Odyssey* 20.87 [56–57]. Chapman here fuses a phrase—λύων μελεδήματα θυμοῦ—and a compound epithet—λυσιμελής. For some comments on this feature of his style, see George D. Long, *Homeric Renaissance: The Odyssey of George Chapman* (London: Chatto and Windus, 1956), 139–41. Yeats may have had this remarkable formation in mind when he produced his magnificent "haystack- and roof-levelling wind" in "A Prayer for My Daughter."

12. I fancy he may have had somewhere in his mind the line about the grove of Colonus, φυλλάδα μυριόκαρπον ἀνήλιον, at Sophocles *Oedipus at Colonus* 676, supplemented by the description of the "sacred place," βρύων / δάφνης, ἐλαίας, ἀμπέλου, at 16–17.

13. For example, the "forehead" of "Away in the loveable west, / On a pastoral forehead of Wales" (*The Wreck of the Deutschland*, stanza 24, lines 1-2) strikes one as a strong piece of English metaphor. It is also very Greek. Compare the "shining breast" (i.e., hill) on which Battus is told to build a city at Pindar *Pythian* 4.8; or the (strictly pleonastic) description of the Isthmus as the "festal neck [or perhaps, "throat"] of Corinth" in Pindar *Olympian* 8.52 (similarly Bacchylides 2.7). Alcman, in a vivid fragment (90 PMG), writes of "Mount Rhipe, aflower with forest, breast [or "chest"] of dark night."

14. Gardner, *Gerard Manley Hopkins*, 2:123, cites Aeschylus *Agamemnon* 201–4, which he translates: "The seer proclaimed, urging Artemis (as cause), so that the earth-with-their-staves-smiting-sons-of-Atreus [χθόνα βάκτροις / ἐπικρούσαντας Ἀτρείδας] stifled not their tears." This sort of compression, or fusion, is common in Greek poetry. See Dodds on Euripides *Bacchae* 866–70: the expression "χλοεραῖς λείμακος ἡδοναῖς has perhaps the effect of a compound, 'green-meadow-joy.'" For further examples, see Wilamowitz on Euripides *Heracles* 468 ("we must think of the substantives as coalescing into a single compound"), Jebb on Sophocles *Antigone* 794, and Fraenkel on Aeschylus *Agamemnon* 504.

15. See Joyce Green, "Tennyson's Development during the 'Ten Years' Silence,'" *PMLA* 66, no. 5 (1951): 691.

16. Richmond Lattimore, *Greek Lyrics* (Chicago: University of Chicago Press, 1955), 42.

17. "Hurrahing in Harvest," "The Caged Skylark," *The Wreck of the Deutschland* (stanza 13, line 5), and "The Loss of the Eurydice."

18. William Arrowsmith, "The Criticism of Greek Tragedy," *Tulane Drama Review* 3, no. 3 (1959): 34.

19. Wallace Stevens, "A Primitive Like an Orb."

20. Wallace Stevens, "Esthétique du Mal."

21. H. J. Rose, *A Handbook of Greek Literature from Homer to the Age of Lucian* (London: Methuen, 1964), 124.

22. See C. M. Bowra, *Greek Lyric Poetry* (Oxford: Clarendon Press, 1961), 314.

23. Bruno Lavagnini, *Aglaia: Nuova antologia della lirica greca da Callino a Bacchilide* (Turin: Paravia, 1947), 295.

24. There may be an explanation of the way Bacchylides handles the scene in a piece of information preserved by the scholiast at *Iliad* 21.194: Pindar also wrote a poem about Heracles' encounter with Meleager in the underworld, in which it was

Meleager who asked Heracles to marry Deianiera. This makes much better sense: Meleager knows that his sister is being pestered by the local river god and does what he can to help her by sending Heracles to the rescue. One guesses that Pindar's poem came first, and that Bacchylides had to be odd in order to be original (see Jebb's edition of Bacchylides, 472).

25. E.g. at *Odyssey* 8.267 and 18.193; *Homeric Hymns* 5.6, 175, and 287 and 6.18; Solon 19.4 (West). See Allen-Halliday-Sikes on *Homeric Hymns* 5.175.

26. A. E. Harvey, "Homeric Epithets in Greek Lyric Poetry," *CQ*, n.s., 7:3-4 (1957): 214.

27. ἱμερόφωνος, for example, in Sappho (fr. 136 Lobel-Page and Voigt), if no longer in Alcman (fr. 26 PMG); or such sensuous compounds as ἐρασιπλόκαμος or ἀγανοβλέφαρος in Ibycus (frs. 303 and 288 PMG).

28. Eliot, *Selected Essays*, 268 ("John Dryden," 1921).

29. Quintilian 10.1.62 ("Stesichorum . . . epici carminis onera lyra sustinentem").

8. Pindar's Pythian 12

1. Ettore Romagnoli, *Pindaro: Le odi e i frammenti* (Florence: Olschki, 1921).

2. Richmond Lattimore, *The Odes of Pindar* (Chicago: The University of Chicago Press, 1947); 2nd ed., 1976.

3. Matthew Arnold, *On the Classical Tradition*, ed. R. H. Super (Ann Arbor: University of Michigan Press, 1960), 191 ("On Translating Homer: Last Words," 1862).

4. H. T. Wade-Gery and C. M. Bowra, *Pindar: The Pythian Odes* (London: Nonesuch Press, 1928).

5. Friedrich Hölderlin, *Sämtliche Werke*, ed. D. E. Sattler, vol. 15 (Frankfurt: Verlag Roter Stern, 1987).

6. *Selections from the Brief Mention of Basil Lanneau Gildersleeve* (Baltimore: Johns Hopkins University Press, 1930), 310.

7. "I cannot but deem it . . . an advantage in the Italian tongue, in many other respects inferior to our own, that the language of poetry is more distinct from that of prose than with us. From the earlier appearance and established primacy of the Tuscan poets, concurring with the number of independent states, and the diversity of written dialects, the Italians have gained a poetic idiom, as the Greeks before them had obtained from the same causes, with greater and more various discriminations." Samuel Taylor Coleridge, *Biographia Literaria*, ed. James Engell and W. Jackson Bate (Princeton, NJ: Princeton University Press, 1983), pt. 2, p. 35 (chap. 16).

8. C. J. Billson, *Pindar's Odes of Victory: The Olympian and Pythian Odes* (Oxford: B. Blackwell, 1928) and *Pindar's Odes of Victory: The Nemean and Isthmian Odes* (Oxford: B. Blackwell, 1930).

9. *Pythian* 1.18, *Olympian* 7.50, *Olympian* 6.42, *Pythian* 3.25

10. Abraham Cowley, *Poems*, ed. A. R. Waller (Cambridge: University Press, 1905), 155 ("Preface" to *Pindarique Odes*, 1668).

11. August Boeckh, ed., *Pindari opera quae supersunt*, vol. 2, pt. 2 (Leipzig, 1821), 54.

12. J. E. Sandys, *The Odes of Pindar* (London: Heinemann, 1915), 421. William H. Race, in the Loeb version of 1997, has "from Sikyon they departed laden with silver wine bowls."

13. Following the manuscript reading, ἀπέβαν.

14. Coleridge, *Biographia Literaria*, 86–87 (chap. 18).

15. Pindar, *The Olympian and Pythian Odes*, ed. Basil L. Gildersleeve (New York: Harper, 1885), 273.

16. Except for occasional, virtuoso performances, like Herbert's "Easter Wings," written in imitation of the Greek *technopaegnion,* or the repeated initial letters in Dante's terrace of the proud (*Purgatorio* 12) spelling out the word "VOM" and reminding MAN that his primal sin is pride.

17. Paul Valéry, *Œuvres,* vol. 1, ed. Jean Hytier (Paris: Gallimard, 1957), 624.

9. THE BEASTLY HOUSE OF ATREUS

1. "Burst into flame" in the third sentence renders βλαστοῦσι, literally "grow, come into being," found in our single manuscript of this play but not in either Denys Page's Oxford text or Martin L. West's Teubner text (which both read βλάπτουσι, "cause harm"). In the previous sentence, however, "teem" derives not from the manuscript but from an emendation. My translations, which attempt to be close (usually) and interpretative, are based on no one text and keep to the tradition where it seems possible to do so.

2. Eduard Fraenkel, ed., *Aeschylus: Agamemnon,* 3 vols. (Oxford: Clarendon Press, 1950). References to Fraenkel henceforth indicate a quotation from the commentary, in volumes 2 and 3 of this edition, on the passage of Aeschylus under discussion.

3. Compare John Jones, *On Aristotle and Greek Tragedy* (New York: Oxford University Press, 1968), 124, on this passage: "The human offence and the straining of nature are dramatically one." For my debt to this important book see my later discussion of the psychic unity of the house of Atreus.

4. I write "she brought" since English requires the subject to be stated. Greek does not, hence there can emerge from the dulcet sequence of images a figure we may take to be Helen, who can without warning modulate into the fury of the final line. For which, having no idea how it should be translated, I borrow words from Weir Smyth's Loeb. Even less possible to convey is the mocking effect of the sweet Ionic rhythm to which the first four lines of the dreadful second sentence move (⌣⌣‒‒ ⌣⌣‒‒, combined with ⌣⌣‒⌣‒⌣‒‒).

5. Hugh Lloyd-Jones, note on the passage in his translation of the *Agamemnon* (Englewood Cliffs, NJ: Prentice Hall, 1970). His careful translation of the *Oresteia* is most serviceable and the best basis for anyone with insecure (or no) Greek wishing to read the trilogy closely.

6. Joseph Fontenrose, *Python: A Study of Delphic Myth and Its Origins* (Berkeley, CA: University of California Press, 1959), 219.

7. "The city will fall." I refer not to the various allusions to the fall of Troy in the *Iliad* but to the vision at the start of book 12, apocalyptic and yet utterly serene, of the gods' destruction of the Greek wall, built to defend the ships, which Homer somehow makes emblematic of the fall of very city and the eventual ruin of every work of human hands. Contrast Virgil's far more darkly apocalyptic visions in the *Aeneid*—of Aeolus in book 1 standing constant guard over the winds which would otherwise overwhelm heaven and earth, or the simile of the citizen bees in their ruined home in book 12, discussed by W. R. Johnson in his very fine *Darkness Visible* (Berkeley, CA: University of California Press, 1976), 93–94.

8. C. J. Herington, "Aeschylus: The Last Phase," *Arion* 4, no. 3 (1965): 398, 396, 397.

9. See G. S. Kirk, *Myth: Its Meaning and Functions in Ancient and Other Cultures* (Berkeley, CA: University of California Press, 1970), particularly chap. 4.

10. Claude Lévi-Strauss, *Mythologiques: Le Cru et le cuit* (Paris: Plon, 1964), 74–81. I take only the myth itself from Lévi-Strauss. The reading I attempt is quite different.

11. Their role was of course always more comprehensive. It reached into the realm of the divine. "Helios will not overstep his measures," Heraclitus says, "otherwise the Erinyes, ministers of Δίκη [not simply Justice but everything from "the way things are done" to a cosmic principle of order] will find him out" (fr. 94 D-K). In exceptional circumstances the Erinyes may also intervene in the natural world. When in *Iliad* 19 one of Achilles' horses speaks and warns him of his coming death, the Erinyes "check its voice" because, a scholiast explains, "they are the overseers of things done against nature."

12. J. D. Denniston and Denys Page, eds., *Aeschylus: Agamemnon* (Oxford: Clarendon Press, 1957). References to Denniston and Page henceforth indicate a quotation from their commentary on the passage of Aeschylus under discussion.

13. I am indebted to M. S. Silk's comments on this passage in his remarkable book *Interaction in Poetic Imagery* (Cambridge: University Press, 1974), vii–viii, 24, 140–1. His use of the word "interaction" is technical and quite different from mine.

14. Martin P. Nilsson, *Homer and Mycenae* (Philadelphia: University of Pennsylvania Press, 1972), 220.

15. Norman Austin, *Archery at the Dark of the Moon* (Berkeley, CA: University of California Press, 1975), 127. What I go on to say about omens is influenced by Austin's thoughtful discussion, 118ff.

16. For the first school, see E. R. Dodds, *The Ancient Concept of Progress and Other Essays* (Oxford: Clarendon Press, 1973), 57. For the second, Denniston and Page, *Agamemnon*, xxvii.

17. "Now" needs some stress or we are involved in the sort of simplification Lloyd-Jones seems to me guilty of when, asking why Zeus allows Agamemnon, the minister of his just revenge against Troy, to be faced with such a choice, he answers bluntly: "Because Agamemnon is the son of the guilty Atreus." Hugh Lloyd-Jones, *The Justice of Zeus* (Berkeley, CA: University of California Press, 1971), 91. If the matter were as plain as this, there would have been no argument. Lloyd-Jones presents his case more fully in "The Guilt of Agamemnon," *Classical Quarterly*, n.s., 12, no. 2 (1962): 187–99.

18. Martin P. Nilsson, *Greek Folk Religion* (New York: Harper and Brothers, 1961), 74. The poet is Archilochus, fragment 166 in the Budé edition by Lasserre and Bonnard, and fragment 173 in M. L. West's *Iambi et Elegi Graeci*.

19. See, for example, Hugh Lloyd-Jones, "Zeus in Aeschylus," *Journal of Hellenic Studies* 76 (1956): 55–67 and the introduction and commentary in the Denniston and Page *Agamemnon*. Lloyd-Jones offers a somewhat modified view in *Justice of Zeus*.

20. Dodds, *Ancient Concept of Progress*, 61–62.

21. See Oliver Taplin, *The Stagecraft of Aeschylus* (Oxford: Clarendon Press, 1977), 362. I draw on this useful book for several details of dramatic presentation.

22. The lexicon allows only the rendering "come down to one's aid" for the verb here (συγκαταβαίνειν), but it can mean "agree" in later Greek and must surely have that sense in this passage (like the single compound συμβαίνειν, which can mean "come to an agreement, come to terms" in fifth-century Greek).

23. "It still remains to complete the work of reconciliation where the gods are concerned. The goddesses of revenge rage and threaten in defeat; but Athene . . . is able to win them over." Albin Lesky, *A History of Greek Literature*, trans. James Willis and Cornelis de Heer (New York: Crowell, 1966), 263. "No longer is it [the conception of Δίκη] blind retribution; it is now Justice." H. D. F. Kitto, *Form and Meaning in Drama* (London: Methuen, 1969), 86.

24. The translation is given in the first edition of Thomson's *Oresteia* (Cambridge: University Press, 1938); it was reprinted by W. H. Auden in *The Portable Greek Reader*.

25. I don't at all wish to suggest that this reading of the central ode in the *Eumenides* has occurred only to me, though I think it is still a minority view. Kitto, for instance, can write: "The climax of the trilogy is not the institution of the Court of the Areopagus, but [the conversion of the Erinyes] from blind and bloodthirsty persecutors (*Eumenides* 186ff.) into awful defenders of that true Justice " and so forth. Kitto, *Form and Meaning*, 85 n. 23. Against this, Lloyd-Jones says of them: "Far from being primitive relics of a vanished order . . . they are the pillars of every government, including that of Apollo's own father, Zeus." Lloyd-Jones introduction to *Eumenides* (Englewood Cliffs, NJ: Prentice Hall, 1970), 5. When, however, he goes on to claim that "the trilogy ends with their triumph," he flies in the face of the text, as I try to show.

26. In another play of Aeschylus it is said of someone leading an army against his native city: "What claim to right could justify a man in quenching the fountain-head, the mother?" (*Seven against Thebes* 585). This is hardly metaphor.

10. GREEK TRAGEDY

1. T. S. Eliot, *Selected Essays* (New York: Harcourt, Brace and World, 1964), 50 ("Euripides and Professor Murray," 1920).

2. Ezra Pound, *Literary Essays of Ezra Pound* (New York: New Directions, 1954), 92–93 ("The Tradition," 1913).

3. W. B. Yeats, *The Oxford Book of Modern Verse, 1892–1935* (Oxford: Clarendon Press, 1936), xxvi.

4. H. D., *Choruses from the Iphigeneia in Aulis and the Hippolytus of Euripides* (London: Egoist, 1919); H. D., *Ion* (London: Chatto and Windus, 1937).

5. H. D., *Collected Poems, 1912–1944*, ed. Louis L. Martz (New York: New Directions, 1986), 71; cf. Euripides, *Iphigenia in Aulis* 164–70.

6. Louis MacNeice, *The Agamemnon of Aeschylus* (London: Faber and Faber, 1936).

7. Richmond Lattimore's translation of the *Agamemnon* appeared in Dudley Fitts, ed., *Greek Plays in Modern Translation* (New York: Dial Press, 1947). His version of the trilogy was published in Aeschylus, *Oresteia* (Chicago: University of Chicago Press, 1953).

8. *Eumenides* 368–76 is an even more striking example. Three long, basically dactylic lines, seemingly calm but full of profound menace; then, as the Furies speak of the "avenging rhythm" of their feet, there is a jolting change of movement and a single trochaic line introduces a series of convulsive cretic metra. It is easy to believe that Aeschylus was a great choreographer. (Persuading many people that Greek meter is a dull subject has been one of the more striking achievements of classical scholarship.)

9. Robert Lowell, *Interviews and Memoirs*, ed. Jeffrey Meyers (Ann Arbor: University of Michigan Press, 1988), 62.

10. Ibid.

11. Robert Lowell, *The Oresteia of Aeschylus* (New York: Farrar, Straus and Giroux, 1978).

12. Aeschylus, *The Oresteia*, trans. Robert Fagles (New York: Viking, 1975), 160.

13. T. S. Eliot, *Selected Prose*, ed. Frank Kermode (New York: Harcourt Brace Jovanovich, 1975), 145 ("Poetry and Drama," 1951).

14. Antonin Artaud, *The Theater and Its Double*, trans. Mary Caroline Richards (New York: Grove Press, 1958), 89–90.

11. Introduction to *Antigone*

1. Bernard M. W. Knox, *The Heroic Temper: Studies in Sophoclean Tragedy* (Berkeley, CA: University of California Press, 1966), one of the most important studies of this poet in English.

2. The translation here, and in subsequent quotations, is by Elizabeth Wyckoff, in *Sophocles I* (Chicago: University of Chicago Press, 1954).

3. Almost her last words (lines 927–28) are: "But if it is the others [i.e., Creon] who are wrong / I wish them no greater punishment than mine." She means *no less*. Let them—*him*—suffer as I suffer!

4. E. R. Dodds, *The Greeks and the Irrational* (Berkeley, CA: University of California Press, 1951), 50.

5. Compare Knox, *Heroic Temper*, 161–62: "The last of the Sophoclean heroes, the most fiercely angry of all those intractable figures who defied the limits set to human power and assumed the attributes of divinity, is here recognized by the gods as their peer and welcomed to their presence."

12. The *Anthology* Transplanted

1. Peter Jay, ed., *The Greek Anthology and Other Ancient Greek Epigrams* (New York: Oxford University Press, 1973). Revised edition published by Penguin in 1981.

2. A. C. Graham, *Poems of the Late T'ang* (Harmondsworth, England: Penguin, 1965), 14.

3. Dudley Fitts, *Poems from the Greek Anthology* (New York: New Directions, 1956), 16.

4. Salvatore Quasimodo, *Dall' Antologia Palatina* (Milan: Mondadori, 1968), 31.

5. J. W. Mackail, *Select Epigrams from the Greek Anthology*, 3rd ed. (London: Longmans, Green, 1911), 34.

6. *AP* 9.651. More literally: "From three sides I gaze on the joyous back of the sea as the day's light falls on me from every side. For when Dawn saffron-robed spreads itself about me, in its joy it is reluctant to set." The Greek:

Τρισσόθεν εἰσορόω πολυτερπέα νῶτα θαλάσσης
πάντοθεν ἡματίῳ φέγγεϊ βαλλόμενος·
εἰς ἐμὲ γὰρ κροκόπεπλος ὅταν περικίδναται Ἠώς,
τερπομένη στείχειν πρὸς δύσιν οὐκ ἐθέλει.

7. A. S. F. Gow and D. L. Page, eds., *The Greek Anthology: Hellenistic Epigrams*, 2 vols. (Cambridge: University Press, 1965), 2:635. Only the commentary on Meleager is by Page; the other poets fall to Gow.

8. Standard, I mean, on the *Anthology* as a whole. Not all share his relatively high estimate of Meleager. Lesky, for instance, is content to write: "Meleager of Gadara entirely follows the tradition of the Alexandrian epigram with his poems of wine and love." *A History of Greek Literature*, trans. James Willis and Cornelis de Heer, 2nd ed. (New York: Crowell, 1963), 740f.

9. A. S. F. Gow and D. L. Page, *The Greek Anthology: The Garland of Philip*, 2 vols. (Cambridge: University Press, 1968). Here Page is "primarily responsible" for all the poets included except for Antipater.

10. William Butler Yeats, Introduction to *The Oxford Book of Modern Verse* (Oxford: Clarendon Press, 1936), xviii.

11. Walter Headlam, *Fifty Poems of Meleager* (London: Macmillan, 1890), 9.

13. Ekphrasis

1. The text is that of Paul Friedländer, *Johannes von Gaza und Paulus Silentiarius* (Leipzig: Teubner, 1912).

2. Cf. *AP* 6.56; 9.761; 16.54, 57, 58, 97; Martial 3.54, 41; 4.47; and *Satyricon* 83.1 (Encolpius admires "sketches of Protogenes, so lifelike that they were a challenge to nature herself").

3. Richmond Lattimore, *The Odes of Pindar*, 2nd ed. (Chicago: University of Chicago Press, 1976), 130.

4. Irving Babbitt, *The New Laokoon* (Boston: Houghton Mifflin, 1910), viii. Philostratus writes like this: "The painting has such regard for realism that it even shows drops of dew dripping from the flowers and a bee settling on the flowers—whether a real bee has been deceived by the painted flowers or whether we are to be deceived into thinking that a painted bee is real, I do not know. But let that pass" (1.23, trans. Arthur Fairbanks, Loeb ed..)

5. See Jean H. Hagstrum, *The Sister Arts* (Chicago: University of Chicago Press, 1958), chap. 2. For some minor examples of Christian ekphrasis, set beside Philostratus these two poems on an icon of an archangel: "How bold to give form to the incorporeal. Yet the image leads us to spiritual recollection of the heavenly ones." Or, "Ah, greatly daring was the wax that fashioned the invisible archangel, incorporeal in the essence of his form . . . The eye stirs up the depth of the mind, and art by its colors can guide the prayers of the soul" (*AP* 1.33, 34).

6. See Friedländer, *Johannes von Gaza und Paulus Silentiarius,* 41ff. To understand the tradition to which Paul's *Descriptio* belongs, we need to go to the later historians rather than to the poets or literary men. See for example the description of the temple in Jerusalem in Josephus *Bellum Judaicum* 5.184ff., especially 212–14, the veil before the doors of the sanctuary: "Nor was this mixture of materials without its mystic meaning: it typified the universe. For the scarlet seemed emblematical of fire, the fine linen of the earth, the blue of the air, and the purple of the sea" (H. St. J. Thackeray, Loeb ed.). For a prose description of Santa Sophia, see the elaborately rhetorical account in Procopius *De aedificiis* 1.1.22ff. Descriptions of temples are of course common in the romances—see for example Philostratus *Vita Apollonii* 2.20 or Apuleius *Metamorphoses* 5.1ff.—but there the temple is interesting primarily because of the pleasance in which it is set or the sculptures and reliefs which it contains, an approach also found in the historians, cf. Diodorus Siculus 5.43ff.

7. Cavafy catches this situation very well in his poem, "A Byzantine Aristocrat, in Exile, Composes Verses."

8. Ettore Romagnoli, *I poeti della Antologia Palatina*, 4 vols. (Bologna: Zanichelli, 1940–43), 4:119.

9. The adjective (*LSJ* notes) is frequent in Nonnus, whom Paul studied very carefully. This is probably the immediate source.

10. See Hugo Rahner, *Greek Myths and Christian Mystery* (London: Burns and Oates, 1963), 353–70, esp. 354 and 360. One may however recall (at whatever cost to my argument) that Petronius's Circe inspires the same allusion: "haec ipsa cum diceret . . . tam dulcis sonus pertemptatum mulcebat aëra, ut putares inter auras canere Sirenum concordiam" (*Sat.* 127.1–5).

11. Marguerite Yourcenar, *Présentation critique de Constantin Cavafy* (Paris: Gallimard, 1978), 212 (cf. 147).

12. Cf. *AP* 5.13, 48, 62, and 282.

13. There is one very odd piece—*AP* 5.286—in which Paul boldly juxtaposes his two roles. It starts as a fleshly love poem ("Only let me fold you in my arms, my

sweet, and browse on your limbs"), but it ends: "And then I don't mind if a stranger sees me . . . or a priest, or even my wife." I confess I am not sure how this should be taken.

14. καὶ τοίνυν πεποίηταί οἱ καὶ ἄλλα ὡς πλεῖστα ποιήματα μνήμης τε ἄξια καὶ ἐπαίνου, δοκεῖ δέ μοι τὰ ἐπὶ τῷ νεῷ εἰρημένα μείζονός τε πόνου καὶ ἐπιστήμης ἀνάπλεα καθεστάναι, ὅσῳ καὶ ἡ ὑπόθεσις θαυμασιωτέρα (Agathias Historia 5.9).

15. Ian Fletcher, Motets (Reading: University of Reading, 1962).

16. Charles Shadwell, that is, Pater's friend, and translator of Dante in the stanza of Marvell's Horatian ode to Cromwell.

17. Whose style is often described as baroque. Friedländer finds in Paul "denselben dithyrambischen Schwung, dieselbe Üppigkeit in Ornament" as in Nonnus (Johannes von Gaza und Paulus Silentiarius, 124). "Strepitus verborum," Scaliger responded sourly, "compositio dithyrambis audacior."

14. Horace in English

1. Milton, Paradise Lost bk. 7, line 31 and Horace Satire 1.10.74; Tennyson, "To Mary Boyle," lines 25–26 and Horace Odes 3.29.12.

2. Petrarch, Rime, 159 ("In quel parte del Ciel"), lines 12–14. Sappho fr. 31 (L-P and Voigt): "And close by hears your sweet speech and lovely laughter."

3. There is no good reason, certainly no necessity, to believe that Chaucer's "Envoi a Scogan" shows the influence of the Horatian epistle. The Ars poetica he may well have seen, for it was common property; other allusions that have been detected or suspected are likely to derive from florilegia, collections of classical sayings.

4. Charles Martindale and David Hopkins, eds., Horace Made New (Cambridge: Cambridge University Press, 1993), 72.

5. Henry Ryder (1638), John Smith (1649), and "Unknown Muse" (formerly confused with Barton Holyday, 1653) all translated the complete Horace, and John Ashmore (1621), Thomas Hawkins (1625), and Sir Richard Fanshawe (1652) translated selected works. In 1666 Alexander Brome edited an anthology of translations by different hands.

6. K. W. Gransden, ed., Tudor Verse Satire (London: Athlone Press, 1970), 16.

7. Thomas Otway, "Epistle to Mr. Duke"; Matthew Prior, "While with Labour Assiduous due pleasure I mix"; Thomas Brown, "Ode ix. Lib. 1 in Horace imitated," Works (1715); Elijah Fenton, "An Imitation of the Ninth Ode of the First Book of Horace," in Oxford and Cambridge Miscellany Poems (1708); Rudyard Kipling, "A Translation: Horace, Ode 3, Bk. V" (see "Regulus" in A Diversity of Creatures).

8. Reuben Brower, Alexander Pope: The Poetry of Allusion (Oxford: Clarendon Press, 1959), 164.

9. Frank Stack, Pope and Horace: Studies in Imitation (Cambridge: Cambridge University Press, 1985), 33.

10. Maren-Sofie Røstvig, The Happy Man, 2 vols. (Oslo: Oslo University Press, 1954–58), 2:127.

11. George Steiner, The Penguin Book of Modern Verse Translation (Harmondsworth, England: Penguin, 1966), 25.

12. Compare the rendering by Anthony Hecht: "For whom do you / Slip into something simple by, say, Gucci?" from "An Old Malediction," in The Venetian Vespers (New York: Atheneum, 1979).

13. Christopher Smart's Verse Translation of Horace's Odes (Victoria: English Literary Studies, 1979), edited by Arthur Sherbo, who contributes a useful introduction. It

also appears as volume 5 in *The Poetical Works of Christopher Smart*, ed. Karina Williamson, 6 vols. (Oxford: Clarendon Press, 1980–96).

14. John Conington, *The Satires, Epistles, and Art of Poetry of Horace* (1870; London: Bell, 1902), xi.

15. Maren-Sofie Røstvig, "Casimire Sarbiewski and the English Ode," *Studies in Philology*, 51, no. 3 (1954): 443–44.

16. L. P. Wilkinson, *Horace and His Lyric Poetry* (Cambridge: University Press, 1945), 57, caught the Wordsworthian note.

17. Christopher Wordsworth, *Memoirs of William Wordsworth*, ed. Henry Reed, 2 vols. (Boston: Ticknor, Reed, and Fields, 1851), 2:479; Shelley, preface to *Hellas* (1821); *Landor as Critic*, ed. Charles Louis Proudfit (Lincoln: University of Nebraska Press, 1979), 197 ("The Pentameron," 1837); Pound, "Horace," *Criterion* 9 (January 1930): 217; T. S. Eliot, *Selected Essays* (New York: Harcourt, Brace, and World, 1964), 254 ("Andrew Marvell," 1921).

18. Matthew Arnold, *On the Classical Tradition*, ed. R. H. Super (Ann Arbor: University of Michigan Press, 1960), 36.

19. George Meredith, *The Tragic Comedians* (1880; 1892), chap. 14; Byron, *Childe Harold's Pilgrimage*, canto 4, stanzas 77 and 75; Swinburne, letter of May 16, 1888, to A. H. Bullen; Kipling, *Something of Myself* (London: Macmillan, 1937), 37.

20. John Conington, *The Odes and Carmen Saeculare of Horace*, 3rd ed. (1863; London: Ball and Daldy, 1865), xxviii.

21. J. P. Sullivan, *Ezra Pound and Sextus Propertius* (Austin: University of Texas Press, 1964), 20.

22. Eduard Fraenkel, *Horace* (Oxford: Clarendon Press, 1957), 160.

23. T. S. Eliot, "Ezra Pound," in *An Examination of Ezra Pound*, ed. Peter Russell (New Directions: New York, 1950), 32.

24. To speak in this way is to disregard the warning in the standard commentary that "Needless to say the ode has no bearing on real life." Classical scholars have a touching faith in their ability to decide what constitutes the real life of a poem.

25. Christopher Ricks, *The Force of Poetry* (Oxford: Clarendon Press, 1987), 279.

26. George Steiner, *After Babel* (London: Oxford University Press, 1975), 259.

27. Raymond Dexter Havens, *The Influence of Milton on English Poetry* (Cambridge, MA: Harvard University Press, 1922), 560.

28. Arthur Quiller-Couch, *Studies in Literature* (Cambridge: University Press, 1919), 66 ("The Horatian Model in English Verse").

29. Clough tried his hand at translation of this sort, juggling *qui fragilem truci / commisit pelago ratem* (Ode 1.3) into "who, frail to fierce, / committed bark to billow," but he lacked the strength effectively to force English into the Latin mold.

A Bibliography of the
Works of D. S. Carne-Ross

1949

"A Commentary on Yeats' 'Coole and Ballylee, 1931.'" *Nine: A Magazine of Poetry and Criticism,* no. 1 [also 1, no. 1] (October 1949): 21–24.

1950

"The Cantos as Epic." In *Ezra Pound: A Collection of Essays Edited by Peter Russell to Be Presented to Ezra Pound on His Sixty-fifth Birthday,* 134–53. London: Peter Nevill, 1950.

Reprinted: New York: Haskell House Publishers, 1968. The volume was also printed as *An Examination of Ezra Pound: A Collection of Essays,* ed. Peter Russell (Norfolk, CT: New Directions, 1950). Revised and enlarged: New York: Gordian Press, 1973.

"Translation and Anthology." *Nine: A Magazine of Poetry and Criticism,* no. 2 [also 2, no. 1] (January 1950): 58–60.

Review of François Villon, *Ballades: French and English* (1946), ed. Andre Deutsch and Mervyn Savill; Pierre de Ronsard, *Lyrics* (1946), trans. William Stirling, ed. Mervyn Savill; *Anthology of European Poetry: From Machault to Malherbe* (1947), trans. William Stirling, ed. Mervyn Savill; *Fifty Romance Lyric Poems* (1948), trans. Richard Aldington; Heinrich Heine, *The North Sea and Other Poems* (1947), trans. William Stirling.

"Ransom's 'Judith of Bethulia.'" *Nine: A Magazine of Poetry and Criticism,* no. 3 [also 2, no. 2] (May 1950): 91–95.

Untitled Review. *Nine: A Magazine of Poetry and Criticism,* no. 3 [also 2, no. 2] (May 1950): 146–47.

Review of John Crowe Ransom, *Selected Poems* (1947).

"'Our' Catullus?" *Nine: A Magazine of Poetry and Criticism,* no. 3 [also 2, no. 2] (May 1950): 157–58.

Review of Catullus, *The Complete Poems,* trans. Jack Lindsay (1948).

"Giovanni Meli: 'Summer': Translations and Commentary." *Nine: A Magazine of Poetry and Criticism,* no. 4 [also 2, no. 3] (August 1950): 227–31.

Carne-Ross served as editor or coeditor of several journals, but unsigned editorial contributions have not been included in this bibliography.

"Ruunt in Servitutem." *Nine: A Magazine of Poetry and Criticism,* no. 4 [also 2, no. 3] (August 1950): 240–42.

Review of Bertrand de Jouvenel, *Power: The Natural History of Its Growth* (1948).

"Organic Architecture." *Nine: A Magazine of Poetry and Criticism,* no. 4 [also 2, no. 3] (August 1950): 242–43.

Review of Bruno Zevi, *Towards an Organic Architecture* (1950).

"Euhemerus Astrophysicus." *Nine: A Magazine of Poetry and Criticism,* no. 4 [also 2, no. 3] (August 1950): 246–47.

Review of H. S. Bellamy, *Moons, Myths and Man* (first publ. 1936, repr. 1949).

"Current Periodicals." *Nine: A Magazine of Poetry and Criticism,* no. 4 [also 2, no. 3] (August 1950): 261.

Review of *The Catacomb* and *Pagine nuove.*

"The Position of *The Family Reunion* in the Work of T. S. Eliot." *Rivista di letterature moderne* 1 (October 1950): 125–39.

"Editorial Statement." *Nine: A Magazine of Poetry and criticism,* no. 5 [also 2, no. 4] (November 1950): 269–79.

"Mr. Read's Phases." *Nine: A Magazine of Poetry and criticism,* no. 5 [also 2, no. 4] (November 1950): 336–37.

Review of Herbert Read, *Phases of English Poetry* (first publ. 1928, repr. 1950).

"Mr. Spender Again." *Nine: A Magazine of Poetry and criticism,* no. 5 [also 2, no. 4] (November 1950): 351–52.

Review of Stephen Spender, "Task of an Autobiographer" (BBC talk broadcast on October 14, 1950).

"Bread and *The New Statesman.*" *Nine: A Magazine of Poetry and criticism,* no. 5 [also 2, no. 4] (November 1950): 352–53.

Response to a column in *The New Statesman.*

"Current Periodicals." *Nine: A Magazine of Poetry and criticism,* no. 5 [also 2, no. 4] (November 1950): 354–56.

Review of *Reunión: Publicación trimestral de artes y letras; Ausonia;* and *Adam.*

"Death who takes what man would keep . . ." *Nine: A Magazine of Literature and the Arts,* no. 6 [also 3, no. 1] (December 1950): 67–69.

Review of William Bell, *Mountains Beneath the Horizon* (1950).

"Benevolent Humanism." *Nine: A Magazine of Literature and the Arts,* no. 6 [also 3, no. 1] (December 1950): 84–85.

Review of Charles Baudouin, *The Myth of Modernity*, trans. Bernard Miall (1950).

"Current Periodicals." *Nine: A Magazine of Literature and the Arts*, no. 6 [also 3, no. 1] (December 1950): 92.

Review of *Il ponte: Rivista mensile di politica e letteratura*.

"Correspondence." *Nine: A Magazine of Literature and the Arts*, no. 6 [also 3, no. 1] (December 1950): 94.

Response to Rob Lyle's letter regarding "Editorial Statement," *Nine*, no. 5 [also 2, no. 4] (November 1950): 269–79.

1951

"Introduction to Ariosto." *Nine: A Magazine of Literature and the Arts*, no. 7 [also 3, no. 2] (Autumn 1951): 113–25.

"A Note on Gongora's *Polifemo*." With Iain Fletcher. *Nine: A Magazine of Literature and the Arts*, no. 7 [also 3, no. 2] (Autumn 1951): 188–90.

1952

"The Case of Dr Leavis." *Colonnade* 1, no. 1 (Spring 1952): 54–60.

Review of F. R. Leavis, *The Common Pursuit* (1952).

"Terrible Sacrament." *Nine: A Magazine of Literature and the Arts*, no. 8 [also 3, no. 3] (April 1952): 277–78.

Review of *Sophocles: Oedipus Rex*, trans. Dudley Fitts and Robert Fitzgerald (1951), and *The Helen of Euripides*, trans. Rex Warner (1951).

1953

"The *Hippolytus* of Euripides: A New Version by Iain Fletcher and D. S. Carne-Ross." *Colonnade* 2, no. 4 (Autumn 1953). Also in *Adam International Review* 21, nos. 235–37 (1953): 15–48.

Reprinted in *Joseph and Potiphar's Wife in World Literature: An Anthology of the Story of the Chaste Youth and the Lustful Stepmother*, ed. John D. Yohannan (New York: New Directions, 1968): 28–77.

1954

Unsigned article[s]. *People: A Volume of the Good, Bad, Great & Eccentric Who Illustrate the Admirable Diversity of Man*, ed. Geoffrey Grigson and Charles Harvard Gibbs-Smith. London: Grosvenor Press, 1954.

Individual entries are not signed.

Reprinted: New York: Hawthorn Books, 1957.

"The Heroic Tradition." *Times Literary Supplement,* March 5, 1954, 152.

Review of F. T. Prince, *The Italian Element in Milton's Verse* (1954).

"The Line of Epic." *Times Literary Supplement,* April 30, 1954, 280.

Review of E. M. W. Tillyard, *The English Epic and Its Background* (1954).

"Italy's Greatest Novelist." *Spectator,* June 25, 1954, 790.

Review of Archibald Colquhoun, *Manzoni and His Times* (1954).

"Period Translation." *Times Literary Supplement,* July 16, 1954, 455.

Review of Euripides, *Ion,* trans. Gilbert Murray (1954).

"Euripides in England." *Times Literary Supplement,* August 20, 1954, 530.

Review of Euripides, *The Bacchae and Other Plays,* trans. Philip Vellacott (1954).

"The Tuscan Muse." *Times Literary Supplement,* September 24, 1954, 608.

Review of *Lyric Poetry of the Italian Renaissance,* ed. L.R. Lind (1954).

"Word for Word." *Times Literary Supplement,* October 1, 1954, 625.

Response to several letters critical of Ezra Pound.

"Why Read Italian?" *Spectator,* December 10, 1954, 762.

Review of Ernest Hatch Wilkins, *A History of Italian Literature* (1954).

"Greek Drama in America." *Times Literary Supplement,* December 10, 1954, 796.

Review of Aeschylus, *Oresteia,* trans. Richmond Lattimore (1953); *Sophocles I* (1954), comprising *Oedipus Rex,* trans. David Grene, *Oedipus at Colonus,* trans. Robert Fitzgerald, and *Antigone,* trans. Elizabeth Wyckoff.

1955

"Guide to Italian Literature." *Times Literary Supplement,* February 11, 1955, 84.

Review of Ernest Hatch Wilkins, *A History of Italian Literature* (1954).

"Ariosto and the Renaissance." *Times Literary Supplement,* March 18, 1955, 164.

Review of Ariosto, *Orlando furioso,* ed. Lanfranco Caretti (1954) and *Opere minori,* by Ariosto, ed. Cesare Segre (1954).

"Dithyramb." By Pindar. Trans. Robert Garioch, with the help of D. S. Carne-Ross. *Times Literary Supplement,* April 29, 1955, 204.

"Field for Experiment." *Times Literary Supplement,* May 27, 1955, 289.

Review of *Botteghe oscure,* vols. xiii–xv, ed. Marguerite Caetani.

1956

"Life and Letters in the Trecento." *Times Literary Supplement,* June 22, 1956, 376.

Review of *Poeti minori del trecento,* ed. Natalino Sapegno (1952).

"Echoes from the Italian." *Times Literary Supplement,* July 6, 1956, 410.

Review of A. Lytton Sells, *The Italian Influence in English Poetry from Chaucer to Southwell* (1955).

"Dante and Petrarch." *Times Literary Supplement,* August 17, 1956, 488.

Review of Michele Barbi, *Life of Dante,* trans. Paul G. Ruggiers (1954); *The Divine Comedy of Dante Alighieri,* trans. George Bickersteth (1955); and *The Rhymes of Francesco Petrarca: A Selection of Translations,* ed. Thomas G. Bergin (1954).

"Gesture without Notion." *Spectator,* August 31, 1956, 296–98.

Review of Maria Bellonci, *A Prince of Mantua: The Life & Times of Vincenzo Gonzaga,* trans. Stuart Hood (1956).

"Seventy-Four Poets." *Times Literary Supplement,* October 26, 1956, 635.

Review of *Poetry Now,* ed. G. S. Fraser (1956).

"Italy Then and Now." *Spectator,* November 2, 1956, 616.

Review of Daniele Varè, *Ghosts of the Rialto* (1956) and James Reynolds, *Pageant of Italy* (first publ. 1954; repr. 1956).

"Poetry Now." *Times Literary Supplement,* November 9, 1956, 665.

Reply to G. S. Fraser's letter in response to Carne-Ross's review of *Poetry Now* in the *Times Literary Supplement,* October 26, 1956, 635.

"Italophiles and Italomaniacs." *Spectator,* December 28, 1956, 939.

Review of Bernard Wall, *Italian Art, Life and Landscape* and Giuliana Artom Treves, *The Golden Ring: The Anglo-Florentines, 1847–62,* trans. Sylvia Sprigge.

1957

"Baroque Monarchy." *Spectator,* March 29, 1957, 416.

Review of Harold Acton, *The Bourbons of Naples (1734–1825)* and John Rosselli, *Lord William Bentinck and the British Occupation of Sicily, 1811–1914*

"Patterns of the Past." *Times Literary Supplement,* May 31, 1957, 329–30.

Review of *The Italian Journal of Samuel Rogers,* ed. J. R. Hale (1956).

1958

"Introducing Italian Poetry." *Times Literary Supplement,* June 20, 1958, 346.

Review of *The Penguin Book of Italian Verse,* ed. George R. Kay (1958).

"A Reading of Boccaccio." *Times Literary Supplement,* August 15, 1958, 458

Review of Herbert G. Wright, *Boccaccio in England* (1957).

1959

"Wandering Jew of Love." *Times Literary Supplement,* July 3, 1959, 398.

Review of *The Memoirs of Jacques Casanova de Seingalt,* trans. Arthur Machen (1959).

1961

"Translation and Transposition." In *The Craft and Context of Translation,* ed. William Arrowsmith and Roger Shattuck, 3–21. Austin: University of Texas Press for the Humanities Research Center, 1961.

Reprinted Garden City, NY: Anchor Books, 1964.

1962

"Guslar with Rose-Tipped Fingers." *Arion: A Quarterly Journal of Classical Culture* 1, no. 1 (Spring 1962): 118–25.

Review of *The Odyssey of Homer,* trans. Robert Fitzgerald (1961).

"Structural Translation: Notes on Logue's *Patrokleia.*" *Arion: A Quarterly Journal of Classical Culture* 1, no. 2 (Summer 1962): 27–38.

Also published as the postscript to *Patrocleia of Homer,* trans. Christopher Logue (1963).

"The Gaiety of Language." *Arion: A Quarterly Journal of Classical Culture* 1, no. 3 (Autumn 1962): 65–88.

Review of *Bacchylides: Complete Poems,* trans. Robert Fagles (1961).

Reprinted in *Essays on Classical Literature,* ed. Niall Rudd (Cambridge: W. Heffer & Sons, 1972): 221–44.

"The Latin Penguin." With J. P. Sullivan. *Arion: A Quarterly Journal of Classical Culture* 1, no. 4 (Winter 1962): 96–108.

Review of *The Penguin Book of Latin Verse,* ed. Frederick Brittain (1962).

"How Good Is Tasso?" *Times Literary Supplement,* December 14, 1962, 965–66.

Review of Tasso, *Gerusalemme liberata*, ed. Anna Maria Carini (1961); Tasso, *Jerusalem Delivered*, trans. Edward Fairfax, ed. Roberto Weiss (1962); Tasso, *Prose*, ed. Ettore Mazzali (1959).

1963

"Contemporary Greek." *Poetry* 101 (January 1963): 283.

Review of *George Seferis: Poems*, trans. Rex Warner (1960); *The Complete Poems of Cavafy*, trans. Rae Dalven (1961); and *Six Poets of Modern Greece*, trans. Edmund Keeley and Philip Sherrard (1960).

Foreword and "Postscript: Structural Translation." In *Patrocleia of Homer*, trans. Christopher Logue, 6–7, 51–63. Ann Arbor: The University of Michigan Press, 1963.

"Six Dialogues with Leucò: The Lady of Beasts through the Muses." By Cesare Pavese. Trans. William Arrowsmith and D. S. Carne-Ross. *Arion: A Quarterly Journal of Classical Culture* 2, no. 2 (Summer 1963): 80–104.

"Sophocles in the Veneto." *Arion: A Quarterly Journal of Classical Culture* 2, no. 2 (Summer 1963): 123–27.

"Structure A to Z." *Times Literary Supplement*, September 27, 1963, 764.

Review of Umberto Eco, *Opera aperta* (1962) and *Diario minimo* (1963).

1964

Federigo Tozzi. "Journal of a Clerk." Trans. D. S. Carne-Ross. In *Six Modern Italian Novellas*, ed. William Arrowsmith, 3–44. New York: Pocket Books, 1964.

"A Plunge into Real Estate." By Italo Calvino. Trans. D. S. Carne-Ross. In *Six Modern Italian Novellas*, ed. William Arrowsmith, 313–98. New York: Pocket Books, 1964.

Reprinted in Italo Calvino, *Difficult Loves* (London: Secker and Warburg), 1983, 161–250.

"Six Dialogues with Leucò: 'The Flower' through 'The Gods (Epilogue).'" By Cesare Pavese. Trans. William Arrowsmith and D. S. Carne-Ross. *Arion: A Quarterly Journal of Classical Culture* 3, no. 2 (Summer 1964): 67–85.

1965

Dialogues with Leucò. By Cesare Pavese. Trans. William Arrowsmith and D. S. Carne-Ross Ann Arbor: University of Michigan Press, 1965.

"T. S. Eliot: Tropheia." *Arion: A Quarterly Journal of Classical Culture* 4, no. 1 (Spring 1965): 5–20.

"How Good Is Marino?" *Times Literary Supplement*, August 19, 1965, 705–6.

Review of James V. Mirollo, *The Poet of the Marvelous: Giambattista Marino* (1963).

"A Modest Proposal: To Whom It May Concern." *Arion: A Quarterly Journal of Classical Culture* 4, no. 3 (Autumn 1965): 358–60.

"Ekphrasis: Lights in the Santa Sophia, from Paul the Silentiary." With Ian Fletcher. *Arion: A Quarterly Journal of Classical Culture* 4, no. 4 (Winter 1965): 563–81.

1966

"Aeschylus in Translation." *Arion: A Quarterly Journal of Classical Culture* 5, no. 1 (Spring 1966): 73–88.

Review of Aeschylus, *The Oresteia Trilogy; Prometheus Bound*, ed. Robert W. Corrigan, trans. George Thomson (1965) and *Aeschylus: The Oresteia*, trans. and ed. Peter D. Arnott (1964).

"Prima Donna." *New York Review of Books* 6, no. 3 (March 3, 1966): 5–6.

Review of Sappho, *Lyrics in the Original Greek with Translations*, trans. Willis Barnstone (1965) and Sappho, *Poems and Fragments*, trans. Guy Davenport (1965).

"Sappho Herself." *New York Review of Books* 6, no. 9 (May 26, 1966): 34.

Response to Willis Barnstone's letter on "Prima Donna," *New York Review of Books* 6, no. 3 (March 3, 1966): 5–6.

"The One and the Many: A Reading of *Orlando Furioso*, Cantos 1 and 8." *Arion: A Quarterly Journal of Classical Culture* 5, no. 2 (Summer 1966): 195–234.

"A Master." *New York Review of Books* 7, no. 6 (October 20, 1966): 5–8.

Review of *Eugenio Montale: Selected Poems* (1966).

1967

"Getting Close to Catullus." *New York Review of Books* 8, no. 5 (March 23, 1967): 3–4.

Review of *The Poems of Catullus*, trans. Peter Whigham (1966).

"Pound in Texas: New Tunes for Old." *Arion: A Journal of Humanities and the Classics* 6, no. 2 (Summer 1967): 216–32.

1968

"The Two Voices of Translation." In *Robert Lowell: A Collection of Critical Essays,* ed. Thomas F. Parkinson, 152–70. Englewood Cliffs, NJ: Prentice Hall, 1968.

"Conversation with Robert Lowell." *Delos: A Journal on & of Translation* 1 (1968): 165–75.

"Translation: Some Myths for Its Making." *Delos: A Journal on & of Translation* 1 (1968): 205–15.

Review of *The Penguin Book of Modern Verse Translation*, ed. George Steiner (1966).

"A Mistaken Ambition of Exactness." *Delos: A Journal on & of Translation* 2 (1968): 171–97.

Review of *The Odyssey of Homer*, trans. Richmond Lattimore (1967).

"For the Rare Birds." *New York Review of Books* 10, no. 4 (February 29, 1968): 34.

Letter in response to D. J. Enright, "Speak Up!" *New York Review of Books*, October 12, 1967 (review of George Steiner, *Language and Silence*, 1967).

"Notes toward a Department of Literature." *Arion: A Journal of Humanities and the Classics* 7, no. 1 (Spring 1968): 69–101.

"Polygram / 1: Pindar's Twelfth Pythian." *Arion: A Journal of Humanities and the Classics* 7, no. 2 (Summer 1968): 249–63.

"Omnipresence." *Times Literary Supplement*, August 15, 1968, 873.

Letter in response to W. W. Robson, "The Future of English Studies," *Times Literary Supplement*, July 25, 1968.

"Delian Voices." *Times Literary Supplement*, August 29, 1968, 928.

Letter in response to a review of *Delos*.

"Penguin Classics: A Report on Two Decades: Homer." *Arion: A Journal of Humanities and the Classics* 7, no. 3 (Autumn 1968): 400–408.

Untitled Reply. *Arion: A Journal of Humanities and the Classics* 7, no. 3 (Autumn 1968): 520–21.

Response to Wayne A. Rebhorn, "Notes towards a Department of Literature: A Reply to D. S. Carne-Ross" *Arion: A Journal of Humanities and the Classics* 7, no. 3 (Autumn 1968): 515–20.

"The Means and the Moment." *Arion: A Journal of Humanities and the Classics* 7, no. 4 (Winter 1968): 549–56.

1969

"Stendhal: *Le Rouge et le Noir*." *Delos: A Journal on & of Translation* 3 (1969): 80–119.

"Writing between the Lines." *Delos: A Journal on & of Translation* 3 (1969): 198–207.

Review of Italo Calvino, *Cosmicomics*, trans. William Weaver (1968).

"Scenario for a New Year." *Arion: A Journal of Humanities and the Classics* 8, no. 2 (Summer 1969): 171–287.

1970

"Dark with Excessive Bright: Four Ways of Looking at Góngora." *Delos: A Journal on & of Translation* 4 (1970): 45–81.

Reprinted as "Una oscuridad con excesiva claridad (Cuatro modos de mirar a Gongora)," trans. Carlos R. de Dampierre, *Cuadernos Hispanoamericanos* 259 (January 1972): 5–43.

Cf. chapter 5 of *Instaurations* (1979).

"Reverent Songs." *Arion: A Journal of Humanities and the Classics* 9, no. 4 (Winter 1970): 421–31.

Review of *The Homeric Hymns*, trans. Charles Boer (1970).

1972

"The Arts of Resistance." In *Toothing Stones: Rethinking the Political*, ed. Robert E. Meagher, 223–54. Chicago: The Swallow Press, 1972.

"Ariosto Approached." *Times Literary Supplement*, October 6, 1972, 1195–96.

Review of Ariosto, *Orlando furioso*, trans. Sir John Harington, ed. Robert McNulty (1972).

1973

"Classics and the Intellectual Community." *Arion: A Journal of Humanities and the Classics*, n.s., 1, no. 1 (Spring 1973): 7–66.

"Ezra Pound." *Times Literary Supplement*, April 13, 1973, 420–21.

Letter in response to reviews in the *Times Literary Supplement* of Mary de Rachewiltz, *Discretions* (April 21, 1972); Hugh Kenner, *The Pound Era* (September 15, 1972); and *Ezra Pound: The Critical Heritage*, ed. Eric Homberger (March 16, 1973).

"Second Strings: 2: The Poetry of Michelangelo." *Times Literary Supplement*, June 8, 1973, 639–40.

"Sophocles Our Contemporary?" *New York Review of Books* 20, no. 12 (July 19, 1973): 8–10.

Review of Jan Kott, *The Eating of the Gods: An Interpretation of Greek Tragedy* (1973).

"Epic Overreach." *New York Review of Books* 20, no. 15 (October 4, 1973): 35–36.

Review of John Gardner, *Jason and Medeia* (1973).

"The Music of a Lost Dynasty: Pound in the Classroom." *Boston University Journal* 21, no. 1 (Winter 1973): 25–41.

Translated as "La música de una dinastia perdida: Pound en el salón de clases," *Plural: Critica, arte, literatura* 28 (1974): 47–54.

Cf. chapter 7 of *Instaurations* (1979).

"Warrior's Rest." *Times Literary Supplement,* December 28, 1973, 1589.

Letter with William Arrowsmith in response to "Warrior's Rest," *Times Literary Supplement,* November 30, 1973, 1471 (review of Peter Green, *A Concise History of Ancient Greece,* [1973]).

1974

Mario Luzi. "A Toast." Trans. D. S. Carne-Ross. In *Twentieth-century Italian Poetry: A Bilingual Anthology,* ed. L. R. Lind, 320–27. Indianapolis, IN: Bobbs-Merrill, 1974.

"Dionysus in Cambridge." *Arion: A Journal of Humanities and the Classics,* n.s., 1, no. 3 (1973/1974): 538–49.

Review of Euripides, *The Bacchae,* trans. Geoffrey S. Kirk (1970).

"David Jones (1895–1974)." *Arion: A Journal of Humanities and the Classics,* n.s., 1, no. 4 (1973/1974): 693–706.

"On Looking into Fitzgerald's Homer." *New York Review of Books* 21, no. 20 (December 12, 1974): 3–8.

Review of *The Iliad,* trans. Robert Fitzgerald (1974).

1975

Introduction to *Antigone,* by Sophocles, 7–17. Trans. Elizabeth Wyckoff. [Haarlem]: Limited Editions Club, 1975.

"Three Preludes for Pindar." *Arion: A Journal of Humanities and the Classics,* n.s., 2, no. 2 (1975): 160–93.

"Dante Agonistes." *New York Review of Books* 22, no. 7 (May 1, 1975): 3–8.

Review of *The Divine Comedy,* 3 vols. in 6 parts, trans. with a commentary by Charles S. Singleton (1970–75).

Cf. chapter 4 of *Instaurations* (1979).

"Cracking the Code." *New York Review of Books* 22, no. 17 (October 30, 1975): 38–40.

Review of George Steiner, *After Babel: Aspects of Language and Translation* (1975).

"In Quest of Mutability." *Times Literary Supplement,* October 31, 1975, 1303–4.

Review of Ariosto, *Orlando Furioso: A Romantic Epic, Part 1,* trans. Barbara Reynolds (1975).

"The Nipping of Our Cultural December." *Boston University Journal* 23, no. 1 (Winter 1975): 12–24.

Cf. chapter 1 of *Instaurations* (1979).

1976

"Weaving with Points of Gold: Pindar's Sixth Olympian." *Arion: A Journal of Humanities and the Classics*, n.s., 3, no. 1 (1976): 5–44.

Cf. chapter 2 of *Instaurations* (1979).

"The One and the Many: A Reading of the *Orlando Furioso*." *Arion: A Journal of Humanities and the Classics*, n.s., 3, no. 2 (1976): 146–219.

"The Anthology Transplanted." *Arion: A Journal of Humanities and the Classics*, n.s., 3, no. 4 (1976): 507–17.

Review of *The Greek Anthology, and Other Ancient Greek Epigrams*, ed. Peter Jay (1973).

1979

Instaurations: Essays In and Out of Literature: Pindar to Pound. Berkeley: University of California Press, 1979.

"Lowell and the Furies." *New York Review of Books* 26, no. 3 (March 8, 1979): 23–27.

Review of *The Oresteia of Aeschylus*, trans. Robert Lowell (1978).

1980

"The Last of the Modernists." *New York Review of Books* 27, no.15 (October 9, 1980): 41–3.

Review of David Jones, *The Dying Gaul and Other Writings*, ed. Harman Grisewood (1978) and *Introducing David Jones*, ed. John Matthias (1980).

1981

"The Beastly House of Atreus." *Kenyon Review* 3, no. 2 (Spring 1981): 20–40.

"Questions of Equivalence." *American Scholar* 51, no. 1 (Winter 1981–82): 132–36.

Review of John Frederick Nims, "Sappho to Valéry: Poems in Translation" (1971).

1983

"The Return of Virgil." *New York Review of Books* 30, no.16 (October 27, 1983): 3–4.

Review of Virgil, *The Aeneid*, trans. Robert Fitzgerald (1983).

1984

"Messages from Elsewhere." *Partisan Review* 51, no. 1 (1984): 151–54.

Review of *The Oxford Book of Verse in English Translation*, ed. Charles Tomlinson.

"Horacescope." *New York Review of Books* 31, no. 8 (May 10, 1984): 7–8.

Review of *The Complete Works of Horace*, trans. Charles E. Passage (1983) and *The Essential Horace: Odes, Epodes, Satires, and Epistles*, trans. Burton Raffel (1983).

"Giants in Dwarfs' Jackets." *New York Review of Books* 31, no. 20 (December 20, 1984): 9–12.

Review of *Paradiso: The Divine Comedy of Dante Alighieri*, trans. Allen Mandelbaum (1984).

1985

Pindar. New Haven, CT: Yale University Press, 1985.

"Shall We Dante?" *New York Review of Books* 32, no. 2 (February 14, 1985): 41.

Response to a letter by Irma Brandeis on "Giants in Dwarfs' Jackets," *New York Review of Books* 31, no. 20 (December 20, 1984).

"Fitzgerald and the Modernist Movement." *Translation* 15 (Fall 1985): 170–77.

1987

"The Strange Case of Leopardi." *New York Review of Books* 34, no. 1 (January 28, 1987): 42–44.

Review of Leopardi, *The Moral Essays*, trans. Patrick Creagh (1983); Leopardi, *Operette Morali: Essays and Dialogues*, trans. Giovanni Cecchetti (1982); Leopardi, *Pensieri*, trans. W. S. Di Piero (first publ. 1981; repr. 1984); *A Leopardi Reader*, ed. and trans. Ottavio Casale (1981).

1988

Foreword to *Callimachus: Hymns, Epigrams, Select Fragments*, ix–xi. Trans. Stanley Lombardo and Diane J. Rayor. Baltimore, MD: Johns Hopkins University Press, 1988.

"Greek Tragedy and the Shakespearian Example." *Essays in Criticism* 38, no. 3 (1988): 237–45.

Review of Adrian Poole, *Tragedy: Shakespeare and the Greek Example* (1987).

1989

"Montale: Translated, or Translator?" In *Art of Translation: Voices from the Field*, ed. Rosanna Warren, 217–21. Boston: Northeastern University Press, 1989.

1990

"Jocasta's Divine Head: English with a Foreign Accent." *Arion: A Journal of Humanities and the Classics,* 3rd ser., 1, no. 1 (Winter 1990): 106–41.

1991

"Is Your Translation Really Necessary?" *New Criterion* 9, no. 5 (January 1991): 31–36.

Review of Homer, *The Iliad,* trans. Robert Fagles (1990); *The Odyssey of Homer,* trans. Allen Mandelbaum (1990).

1992

"Pantagruelism for Our Time." *New Criterion* 10, no. 9 (May 1992): 33–39.

Review of *The Complete Works of François Rabelais,* trans. Donald M. Frame (1991).

"From the Baked Bricks: The Poem of Gilgamesh." *New Criterion* 11, no. 1 (September 1992): 68–74.

Review of *Gilgamesh: A New Rendering in English Verse,* trans. David Ferry (1992).

"For a friend who was chased by a shark, and later lay for three minutes on the bed of a lake." *Arion: A Journal of Humanities and the Classics,* 3rd ser., 2, no. 1 (Winter 1992): 221.

Greek epigram.

1993

"The Bravery of Life." *Arion: A Journal of Humanities and the Classics,* 3rd ser., 2, nos. 2–3 (Spring and Fall 1992/1993): 249–50.

"Scott and the Matter of Scotland." In *The Worth of Nations,* ed. Claudio Véliz, 19–29. Boston: Boston University, The University Professors, 1993.

1994

"Wording the Pulse Afresh." *New Criterion* 13, no. 2 (October 1994): 70–75.

Review of *Sappho: A Garland,* trans. Jim Powell (1993) and *Andalusian Poems,* trans. Christopher Middleton and Leticia Garza-Falcón (1993).

1995

Untitled Review. *International Journal of the Classical Tradition* 1, no. 3 (Winter 95): 153–56.

Review of *The Penguin Book of Renaissance Verse*, ed. H. R. Woudhuysen, selected and with an introduction by David Norbrook (1992).

1996

Horace in English. Edited with Kenneth Haynes. London: Penguin Books, 1996.

"Walter Scott Travesti." *Essays in Criticism* 46, no. 4 (1996): 359–66.

Review of John Sutherland, *The Life of Walter Scott: A Critical Biography* (1995).

"No Greek & Very Little Latin: Classical Verse in Translation." *New Criterion* 14, no. 7 (March 1996): 18–27.

Review of *The Oxford Book of Classical Verse in Translation*, ed. Adrian Poole and Jeremy Maule (1995).

Untitled Review. *International Journal of the Classical Tradition* 3, no. 2 (Fall 1996): 251–53.

Review of Sir Philip Sidney, *Selected Poems*, ed. Catherine Bates (1994).

1997

"John Herington, 1924–1997." *Arion: A Journal of Humanities and the Classics*, 3rd ser., 5, no. 1 (Spring–Summer 1997): 1–6.

1998

Introduction to *The Odyssey*, ix–lxx. Trans. Robert Fitzgerald. New York: Farrar, Straus and Giroux, 1998.

"Horace Transplanted." *New Criterion* 16, no. 5 (January 1998): 56–59.

Review of *The Odes of Horace*, trans. David Ferry (1997).

1999

"Two Greek Epigrams." *Arion: A Journal of Humanities and the Classics*, 3rd ser., 7, no. 2 (Fall 1999): 92.

2001

"Three Pieces from Ariosto." *Arion: A Journal of Humanities and the Classics*, 3rd ser., 8, no. 3 (Winter 2001): 1–31.

2003

"Horace for Our Time?" *New Criterion* 21, no. 6 (February 2003): 68–71.

Review of Horace, *The Odes: New Translations by Contemporary Poets*, ed. J. D. McClatchy (2002).

2004

"Angelica's Flight through the Forest." *Literary Imagination: Review of the Association of Literary Scholars and Critics* 6, no. 2 (Spring 2004): 175–92.

Index of Classical Passages

369

Index of Translators